Guitar Makers

Guitar Makers

The ENDURANCE of ARTISANAL VALUES

in NORTH AMERICA

KATHRYN MARIE DUDLEY

THE UNIVERSITY OF CHICAGO PRESS Chicago and London

The University of Chicago Press, Chicago 60637

The University of Chicago Press, Ltd., London

© 2014 by The University of Chicago

All rights reserved. Published 2014.

Paperback edition 2017

Printed in the United States of America

23 22 21 20 19 18 17   3 4 5 6 7

ISBN-13: 978-0-226-09538-7 (cloth)

ISBN-13: 978-0-226-47867-8 (paper)

ISBN-13: 978-0-226-09541-7 (e-book)

DOI: 10.7208/chicago/9780226095417.001.0001

Library of Congress Cataloging-in-Publication Data

Dudley, Kathryn Marie, author.

Guitar makers : the endurance of artisanal values in

North America / Kathryn Marie Dudley.

pages ; cm

Includes bibliographical references and index.

ISBN 978-0-226-09538-7 (cloth : alk. paper) —

ISBN 978-0-226-09541-7 (e-book)

1. Guitar makers—United States. 2. Guitar makers—

Canada. 3. Artisans—United States. 4. Artisans—Canada.

I. Title.

ML1015.G9D93 2014

787.87′197—dc23

2014008020

♾ This paper meets the requirements of

ANSI/NISO Z39.48–1992 (Permanence of Paper).

Once upon a time there was . . .

"A king!" my little readers will say right away.

No, children, you are wrong.

Once upon a time there was a piece of wood.

—Carlo Collodi, *The Adventures of Pinocchio* (1883)

Oh the logs are sliced
And split down their middle
Then sawn into billets and sent
    to me
I cut and glue them
And listen to them
For I bring the music out of the
    tree

Chorus
I'm a guitar maker
A tone extricator
Give me wood and I'll make it
    sing for you
One soundhole and six strings
    later

Now it remains a myst'ry
From the fog of hist'ry
Exactly when somebody thought
    to say
I've got drums to pound
And pipes to sound
But I wish I had something with
    strings to play

Though the very first of them
Was the worst of them
Listen to this one I'm strumming
    here
It's been demanding
Fine-tuning the sanding
That made 'em more musical year
    by year

They're central in Spain
They're on the coast of Maine
They're the tools of buskers and
    rock stars
Forgive the boast
But it's clear the most
Predominant instrument is guitar

Not to prevaricate
Let me speculate
A world where nobody made
    guitars
Bobby Zimmerman
Would still be Zimmerman
Segovia would've played accor-
    dion

Grit Laskin,
"Guitar Maker" (1994)
© Grit Laskin, Strutting Day
    Music

Contents

Prologue

Politics revolves around what is seen and what can be said about it, around who has the ability to see and the talent to speak, around the properties of spaces and the possibilities of time. —Jacques Rancière, "The Distribution of the Sensible" (2000)

The guitar lies face up on the workbench, warmed in the glow of a halogen lamp. George Youngblood bends over it in concentration, his wire-rimmed glasses pushed up on his forehead. He rests a three-corner file against the edge of the fret to be crowned and pauses for a brief moment; then the dancing motion begins. The file slides forward, twists up, and lifts away, each stroke sprinkling the ebony fretboard with glistening bits of nickel silver. I stand to his side, closely watching the complicated movement, as the quick, scratching sound of metal against metal fills the room. Soon he will hand the file to me, and say, "Don't mess up!"

A soft midwinter light falls through two large windows, creating silhouettes of the bar clamps hanging from the top of their frames. A large guitar mold rests on the cabinet in front of one window, and neck blanks are stacked behind a drill press on the sill of the other. An antique bow saw holds pride of place on the wall above a rack of chisels, and on the bench below, the serpentine ribs and braced top of a guitar-in-progress wait for Youngblood's attention—a luxury that has been in short supply for over a decade, as he works through an endless backlog of stringed instrument repairs and restorations. Against the far wall sits a band saw hunched forward like a gargoyle, its pensive head seeming to contemplate the full-bodied lute on the tool chest nearby. In a few short weeks, I have come to love the stillness of this morning tableau in the hour before the shop officially opens.

On this particular day, I am a month into my "apprenticeship" at Youngblood Music Workshop in Guilford, Connecticut. In exchange for hourly compensation, Youngblood has agreed to teach me the basic elements of guitar repair and let me observe his work and interactions with clients. His reputation as one of the premier restoration special-

FIGURE 0.1. *George Youngblood reattaching a separated fretboard,*
Youngblood Music Workshop, 2007. Photograph by the author.

ists on the East Coast results in a high volume of foot traffic, as instruments in need of care are brought to him from near and far. Aware that I am writing a book about acoustic guitar makers, he has taken it upon himself to answer my many questions about guitar history and share the knowledge he has gained as a pioneer in the North American lutherie movement.

Shortly after ten o'clock a car turns off the main road and drives down the rutted driveway past the shop window. Moments later the door opens, jingling a tiny bell. Youngblood greets our middle-aged visitor with a warm handshake and, glancing in my direction, explains, "Kate's learning a few things about lutherie."[1]

Ed Putnam's face lights up with approval. "It's a privileged life to be able to do what you're doing," he says. I grin in agreement and return to dressing frets, aware of how hard I have to concentrate to perform this routine task. Putnam sits on a tall stool and thanks Youngblood for working on his sister-in-law's guitar. "For a little nothing guitar," he muses, "it sounded so sweet after you were through!"

"It's just fairy dust from my apron pocket," Youngblood replies modestly, flicking his fingertips in the air.

"Whatever works," Putnam chuckles, "that's good!"

"What Kate has learned so far is that it's amazing what you can do with just a few minor adjustments, just the right adjustments, here and there on the guitar to make it play its best. We've gone through frets and nuts and saddles. I said this morning, you can have a wonderful instrument, but unless it's set up right, you've got nothing."

Like many of the shop's customers, Putnam has come to shoot the breeze, not drop off or pick up an instrument. Taking time out of their day, a shifting assortment of regulars—mostly men but a few women as well—stop by to engage in freewheeling conversation about guitars. Youngblood's shop is located on the first floor of his home, a two-story colonial saltbox that once housed the town's barber. Since 2001, he has rented the two adjoining rooms to Leonard Wyeth and Brian Wolfe, proprietors of Acoustic Music, a retail store that sells high-end guitars and mandolins. Whether customers have come to try out instruments, buy a pack of strings, or jam with Wolfe, most eventually gravitate to the workshop where Youngblood holds forth, serving up stories as nimbly as a bartender does drinks.

Putnam has just returned from a vintage guitar show in California. "God strike me dead," he exclaims, "there was a series of tables and this guy literally had a 1950-something Gibson for $115,000! He had Rickenbackers for $28,000! And people were buying the stuff!"

Youngblood is unfazed by these prices. "A lot of people have realized that wealth in this nation, when it's on paper or in theory, isn't necessarily always going to be there for you. So they're investing in tangible goods, like instruments, oriental rugs, paintings, and fine furniture. Like my coin collection, these things could collapse in value, but the silver and gold will still be good, no matter what the dollar does!"

"I think a lot of it is male menopause," Putnam jokes, producing laughter all around. "First it was Hatteras powerboats, then Harley-Davidsons, and now . . ."

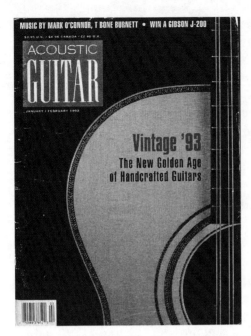

FIGURE 0.2. *The 1990s onward were formally dubbed "the New Golden Age" by Acoustic Guitar magazine, January/February 1993. Founded in 1990, the periodical was itself a product of the market phenomena it commemorated and encouraged.*

Youngblood finishes his sentence: "They're putting their purchasing power toward home goods."

The satisfaction of owning material goods that involve connoisseurship—knowing how they are made and by what criteria their quality is judged—is a central theme of "guitar talk" in the shop. When customers inquire about the investment value of restoring or purchasing an instrument, Youngblood and Wolfe are adept at reframing their question. What matters, they advise, is not so much what an instrument might be worth in the future but whether it will enrich the lives of those who enjoy "homemade music" today. In contrast to speculative financial vehicles, they argue, well-crafted acoustic guitars have an intrinsic worth that remains unaffected by whatever their market value happens to be.

It is an ongoing challenge, however, to get customers to look beyond the eye-popping prices fetched by "holy grail" instruments. Since 2001, the international market for vintage and custom guitars has soared to new heights, fueled by the spending habits of baby boomers entering their prime earning years. Trade magazines such as *Vintage Guitar* and

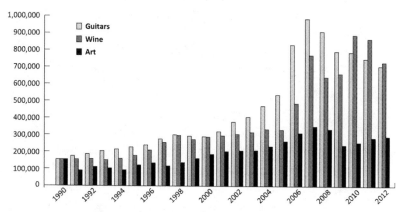

Vintage Guitars, Wine, and Art Cash Value

FIGURE 0.3. *Vintage guitars, wine, and art cash value, 1990–2012. Over the past twenty years vintage guitars have outperformed other collectible asset classes such as wine and art. Data sourced from the Liv-Ex Index/Decantor.com, the Mei/Moses All Art Index, and Vintage Guitar magazine's 2012 Price Guide by Tommy Byrne of Anchor Capital Investment Management for the Guitar Fund, a $100 million, ten-year closed end fund listed on the Channel Island Stock Exchange (CISX).*

Acoustic Guitar have added to the frenzy with tantalizing photo spreads and product reviews. Not only are "golden era" instruments—those made during the two decades before World War II—deemed to be excellent investments; guitars built more recently by individual artisans and small shops are heralded as products of a "second golden era," which has finally reached, if not surpassed, the quality of the first. In 2007 the global financial crisis put a damper on rampant speculation, but the notion still persists that you can actually *make* money buying the right stringed instrument.

Thus when Putnam launches into a tale about a flea market "picker" named Charlie, it is sure to end with a hit-the-jackpot find. One day, he tells us, Charlie got a call from an old Yankee with "bad grammar and bad teeth" who wanted to sell him "the biggest damn *sello*" he had ever seen. The instrument turned out to be pieces of a German upright bass delivered in grocery bags. Charlie reassembled it with Elmer's glue and proudly showed it to Rick, a professional luthier. Rick gave Charlie an

F-5 mandolin in exchange for the bass and told Putnam that when he took it apart, scraped off the glue, and restored it properly, he could retire on the proceeds of its sale. "That'll end up with a concert player many years from now," Putnam concludes with a smile.

Without missing a beat, Youngblood counters with a story of his own:

I once had a woman walk in with two big shopping bags with guitar parts. She had found the guitar on the gravel floor in the basement. It was a 1942 Epiphone Emperor that the old guy used to sit in the basement and play jazz tunes on, had actually leaned it up against the wall in this damp basement and proceeded to die or something, and it just stayed there decade after decade. All the glue joints came apart, and it disintegrated into a pile and then the mold crept over that. There was this pile of moldy guitar parts that they knew was down there. Finally, she cleaned off the dirt, stuck them in the bags, walked through the door here—and I was thrilled. It's an Epiphone Emperor! So I made a deal. I didn't realize that I'd gotten in over my head; it was decades ago. But the short story is, it's now being used in a big band orchestra down in Florida by a guy who was really pleased with how it sounds and looks. It was a blond, top-of-the-line Emperor that lives on, that was once a pile of mold on a dirt floor. I love those stories!

Putnam and I nod in agreement, and I feel a surge of joy. The Emperor lives on!

In that moment, I recall what Youngblood told me on my first day in the shop. "I work for the instrument," he said, "not the owner." And I realize that his tale differs from Putnam's. His story of obsolescence and rebirth is told from the instrument's point of view. Dwelling on the guitar's sensuous materiality, Youngblood emphasizes the style of music it gave voice to and how it fell to ruin when the popularity of that music waned. Rather than focusing on the profit made with every transaction, he highlights changes in the instrument's body over time and how that transformation compelled human action. Were it not for the claim that the dismembered bass and archtop guitar made on a toothless Yankee, a glue-happy picker, a woman drawn to a "pile of mold," and luthiers willing to "get in over their heads," the remains of these instruments could easily have been taken for trash and consigned to landfill oblivion.

By calling attention to the *life* of stringed instruments, Young-blood renders sensible the complex nature of human interactions with things—a realm of experience that has value, he suggests, apart from that which is measured by commodity exchange. If Putnam's story depicts the luthier as an agent of commodification—someone who turns raw or damaged goods into objects with market value—Youngblood interrupts that narrative, not by disavowing it but by refusing to reduce the practice of lutherie solely to calculations of economic value. Together with artisans in other craft industries, guitar makers complicate taken-for-granted assumptions about the rewards of manual labor and the passivity of physical matter. But their intimate engagement with the lively materiality of wood poses a direct challenge to the cultural logic of capitalism. The living on of lutherie as a craft tradition is by no means guaranteed.

Introduction Geppetto's Dream

I thought of making myself a fine wooden puppet; but a wonderful puppet who can dance, and fence, and make daredevil leaps. I intend to travel around the world with this puppet so as to earn my crust of bread and a glass of wine. —Geppetto in Carlo Collodi, *The Adventures of Pinocchio* (1883)

In 1968 an unusual item appeared in *New York* magazine. Listed among the happenings around town was a guitar-making course at the Craft Students League in Manhattan. A frizzy-haired young man who could often be found playing his guitar at the Brooklyn Botanical Gardens sat up and took notice. Recently graduated from Pratt Institute's School of Art and Design and now working for a furniture design firm, William Cumpiano looked at his factory-made instrument and marveled at the thought that something like this could be made by hand:

> I was very enamored of the aesthetic of the guitar—the idea of this little singing cabinet that makes beautiful sounds. It was inconceivable to me that somebody could build something that scientists built in factories. Somebody just make a guitar? The whole concept was just intriguing to me. And that it was an art. It's not like making an automobile or a rocket ship—that you have to be an expert in acoustics to make this device. No, there was something artistic about it. I had just graduated from art school, so it appealed to me at that level.[1]

The course was taught by Michael Gurian, a builder of lutes and classical guitars since 1965. With the long hair of a hippie and the supercilious air of a prince, Gurian exuded brilliance, ambition, and impatience in equal measure. Not one to coddle the clueless, he had no tolerance for persistent questions and frequently left the room after a demonstration, leaving students to figure out how to do things on their own. Being largely self-taught, he may have felt that this pedagogical approach was justified, perhaps even inspired. But for the half-dozen or so students who gathered to receive his instruction, it led to a comedy of errors as they endeavored to teach one another. As Cumpiano describes it, "There we were, all these little elves pushing these chisels and—*oops!*" At course's end, with no more than a guitar-shaped object to show for his efforts, he felt none the wiser. But the experience proved to be a turning point in his life. The desire to make guitars had grown from idle curiosity to a quixotic quest:

> So I set out to learn. I tried to meet people and look for books, and there was *nothing*. It was an absolute void. And the people who knew didn't want me in their shops. They'd let me in if I wasn't inquiring, but if I was inquiring, they'd shut me out. Because there was this European—they were all immigrants—guild [system] holdover, the fact that you never told anybody your business was very strong. The phrase was 'You don't put your business out on the street.' You never tell anybody how you do your thing; that can only hurt you. It will create competition. That's what I ran up against. Nobody wanted to tell me how to make good guitars.

For aspiring guitar makers of Cumpiano's generation, Old World secrecy was the flipside of proprietary information zealously guarded by American guitar factories. Short of landing a job on the assembly line or an apprenticeship with a classical builder, opportunities to learn acoustic guitar making were limited and controlled by ethnic patronage systems. Determined builders like Gurian acquired their knowledge by hanging out with luthiers who tolerated prying eyes, gleaning what insight they could, and returning to their own shops to experiment and improvise. Some, like cabinetmaker John Gallagher in Wartrace, Tennessee, sacrificed factory guitars on their band saws to see what made them tick.[2]

Others were drawn to the trade when they modified factory instruments to suit their playing style or evolving taste in acoustic sound. Nowhere was this do-it-yourself ethos more evident than in the folklore centers, used guitar stores, and repair shops that sprang up around college campuses in the 1960s to support the folk music revival. With a readymade clientele clamoring for their services, enterprising enthusiasts began to realize that they did not need to be bona fide luthiers to build or tinker with a variety of stringed instruments.

An empowering sense of self-sufficiency was of a piece with a generational zeitgeist that questioned authority and resisted bureaucracy.

Cumpiano had grown up in a middle-class family in Puerto Rico, believing in the value of education. Yet following the standard path—excelling in grade school, high school, and four years of college—had landed him in a cubicle with a tie around his neck and a supervisor who monitored his every move. Headstrong and yearning to chart his own course in life, he soon left the white-collar world behind:

> I had a boss and I had clients, and I was in this room being told what to do, having to suck up to people above me. It was something that I didn't fit into very well—office culture, working in a hierarchy, having crucial events in my life being determined out of my control. I was working to make somebody else's dream come true. And I'm thinking already, at the age of twenty-five at that time, I got this intimation of mortality. Is this it? From now on? Is this what my journey is going to be? I said, "No way! I'm going to work to make my personal dream happen, not somebody else's." I wanted to be the captain of my own ship, not the guy down there shoveling coal on somebody else's ocean liner!

Newly unemployed and with his first guitar in hand, Cumpiano headed to Greenwich Village, where he summoned the courage to ask Gurian for the help needed to make it playable. To his surprise, Gurian took one look at the guitar, saw his potential, and offered him an apprenticeship on the spot. The thrill of a once-in-a-lifetime opportunity trumped the fact that this position would pay considerably less than his office job. Such tradeoffs may seem inconsequential to the young, but as every guitar maker discovers, entrepreneurial risk-taking is an integral aspect of being an artisan in North America today. Then as now, "being the captain of your own ship" is a cultural ideal more glamorous in fantasy than in reality. At a time when the occupation of guitar maker was virtually nonexistent and demand for handmade steel-string guitars but a gleam in the maker's eye, devoting one's life to lutherie was as fanciful as it was visionary. When Cumpiano reflects on what motivated him to pursue his dream, he sighs:

> I must have fallen prey to the romance of the guitar and to the Geppetto story. If you think about the Geppetto story, what is it but bringing the wood to life? It's almost godlike to think that somebody

could do that—you know, that the work jumps off the worktable and becomes something more than what the builder intended. The guitar is like Pinocchio, I guess you could say. Because it's *strong medicine*, so to speak, in the Native American sense. People who master the guitar—and any musical instrument really—have great power. So you can go behind the curtain, and somehow I'm providing the tool that makes that possible. That's very appealing.

Although Cumpiano would be the first to admit that he had to get beyond the "romance" of lutherie in order to make a living at it, the desire to "go behind the curtain" to make the "tool" that enables a musician's wizardry has not diminished with time for him or any of the builders I interviewed for this book. The "Geppetto story," and its enchanted scene of making, captures for many the allure of guitar making as well as its uncertain status in today's market culture. As a "godlike" figure who "brings wood to life," the kindly old woodcarver in *Pinocchio* dramatizes the satisfactions of artisanal labor and its dangers. Geppetto may be his own boss, but he lives in poverty. He is out of step with the Industrial Revolution, but he has the skill to turn a willful piece of wood into an object that possesses special powers. Like Native shamen, guitar makers also communicate with nonhuman matter to produce a ritual object that—as "strong medicine" or an "instrument of magic"—makes audible, to those who wish to hear it, the transformative effects of acoustic music.[3]

Yet to say that one "falls prey" to Geppetto's dream is to express ambivalence about its real world implications. Getting by on "a crust of bread and glass of wine" may be a price worth paying at the start of one's career, but it can undermine self-respect and a sense of social belonging if extended beyond young adulthood. Those who take up lutherie hail largely from the white middle class, and most are men. They enter the craft believing they have the right to work in an occupation of their own choosing.[4] But securing this "right" is no easy matter, and the economic insecurity endemic to self-employment tests the mettle of every maker. Under pressure to establish a viable business, luthiers confront a stark choice between two different ways of organizing their labor and finding meaning in the work they do. Making guitars for a living in contemporary North America requires adopting either an "industrial" or an "artisanal" mode of production and finessing the culturally contested boundary between the two.

This book explores the ways in which luthiers articulate and enact differences between mass production and handcraft, and how their attitude toward capitalism shapes the choices they make. I argue that all builders, regardless of the business model they pursue, negotiate their professional identity in relationship to the Geppetto story. Whether its romantic plot is embraced or disavowed, it offers middle-class men and women a cultural script for what it *feels* like to privilege individual creativity and artisanal labor in an unconventional career choice. Tapping into a sentimental imaginary popularized in nineteenth-century Europe and North America, this narrative establishes craftwork—and the sensory knowledge it demands—as a source of kinship with a broader public and the craft object itself. Although cognizant of being underdogs in an epic struggle against mechanization, hand builders drawn to lutherie's scenes of making have elected to persist against the odds, fortified by the optimism that consumers will recognize the value of their endeavor. Geppetto's dream may be a siren's song in a postindustrial society, but to those who listen, it holds out the promise that the dignity of manual labor will be redeemed.

THE TONE OF THINGS

At first glance, the romance of guitar making may seem to be a love story about the guitar itself. A thing of "beauty and tone," the acoustic guitar is usually figured as an object of desire that bears an uncanny resemblance to the female body and voice. Indeed, many guitar makers describe their initial encounter with violin-family instruments or fretted instruments like the guitar, mandolin, banjo, ukulele, and dulcimer as the experience of falling in love with some thing. The intensity of this attraction, they often report, is what drove them to learn how to make stringed instruments with their own hands. Yet the coherence of this account becomes vexed when luthiers are asked to explain why they make guitars and what distinguishes extraordinary instruments from merely good ones. As their reflection on these issues attests, the desire to be involved in lutherie is more unruly and capacious than an exclusive focus on the guitar's sexiness allows.

Guitar Makers tracks the intimacies and intensities of a romance, but

FIGURE 0.4. *The Beauty and Tone Healdsburg Guitar Festival poster offered a bold visualization of the artisanal guitar as a field of human and nonhuman encounter, 2003. Image by Gale Mettey, guitar by Rick Davis.*

it is the story of being committed to an economically marginalized form of work, not just to its product. In contrast to dominant accounts of masculine job satisfaction, which emphasize the prestige of intellectual labor or the value of work as a means to monetary ends, luthiers' stories of making dwell on the rewards of an emotionally absorbing and aesthetically challenging trade. The romantic plot of Geppetto's dream sets the stage for dramatizing conflicting ideas about what kind of work makes life worth living in the United States and Canada today, and who or what can be said to "have a life" under conditions of capitalist commodification.[5] This drama plays out, I suggest, in how guitar makers perform their craft repertoire and evaluate the quality of the craft object. What matters to them—and to those of us who appreciate their work—are ultimately the sentiments contained and expressed in the tone of things.

In this rarefied domain of guitar connoisseurship, talk of desirable instruments quickly gravitates from erotic curves to the ineffability of acoustic sound and individual taste. Good guitars, most agree, must have visual and aural charm. But truly spectacular guitars—those that makers dream of, players long for, and collectors covet—are said to have a special, elusive, but instantly recognizable difference in "tone." In the lutherie community, tone generally refers to the sound of a specific note or to the diffuse palette of sonic attributes that characterize a given instrument. As commonly used, it designates a property inherent in the instrument itself. Thus a guitar's tonal qualities—such as the length of time it sustains notes, the complexity of its "overtones," and the overall impression of its "voice"—are held to be a physical expression of the materials and skill with which it was made. Guitar makers use the term tone wood to identify species of wood that have especially prized sonic capabilities.

At the same time, however, a guitar's tone is thought to elicit idiosyncratic feelings and judgments in its listeners, such that what sounds delightfully "chocolaty" to one person may be unpleasantly "muddy" to another. Luthiers tend to dismiss the subjective aspect of tone as a linguistic problem. The vocabulary we use for sound, they point out, is largely metaphorical and drawn from other realms of sensory experience. What people actually hear are "vibrations in the air," not material phenomena that are literally "rich" or "dry."[6] In the absence of a trained ear, makers say, people tend to respond to the tonal properties of stringed instruments in capricious ways. Like consumers of any art, they may "know" what they like but have difficulty identifying the aesthetic qualities they prefer.

The subjective problem of tone is compounded by guitar makers' own struggle to articulate how they actually make an exceptional instrument. Beyond testifying to a heightened threshold of competence—marked by years in the craft, study of vintage instruments, apprenticeship with a renowned builder, or endorsement by famous musicians—they invoke the idea of "intuition." Much of the mystique that surrounds lutherie's scenes of making stems from the fact that artisanal know-how is largely embodied not just as habitual practices but as intuitive ways of responding to the characteristics of particular pieces of wood.[7] This is especially true of the critical process known as "voicing" the guitar, which involves selectively reducing the thickness of the soundboard and its braces to produce a desired tone. Working from memory and in sensuous interaction with the tools and materials of their trade, guitar makers "know" what they are doing but often find it difficult to explain to someone else.[8]

To account for these puzzling aspects of tone, I find it useful to think of a guitar's tonal presence—its effect on us and our response to it—as the product of an aesthetic encounter much like that which we have with works of art such as paintings or novels. Tone, in this sense, is "the dialectic of objective and subjective feeling" that occurs when we apprehend things aesthetically—that is, as things capable of making a sensory impression on us and *moving* us to experience the world in particular ways.[9] A stringed instrument's tone is not simply "built into" it by the luthier or "heard" in more or less sophisticated ways by the listener; it is also the "structure of feeling" that organizes the encounter and invests it with a force and intensity that is hard to put into words.[10] Reducible to neither the properties of artifacts nor the sensibilities of individuals, tone demarcates an affective field of inter-action between people and things that materializes the general mood or feeling of that relationship. As a kind of *affect*, tone is characterized by its "in-betweenness" as it is "found in those intensities that pass body to body (human, nonhuman, part-body, and otherwise), [and] in those resonances that circulate about, between, and sometimes stick to bodies and worlds."[11] An acoustic guitar's tone, in short, tells us about the care with which the instrument was made.

The implications of conceptualizing tone as a field of encounter, rather than as the property of things, are profound. Rather than asking why a particular guitar is desirable, or why a particular person de-sires a guitar, we can ask, what is happening in this interaction to pro-duce the feeling of desire? Likewise, instead of assuming that what we desire is the object in whose presence we feel desire, we can entertain the possibility that what we long for is to be in a particular kind of re-lationship *with* things. What is desired, we could say, is not the thing itself but the tonal experience of being "oriented" toward things—and having things "oriented" toward us—in such a way that the interaction produces desire.[12]

The desire to make guitars, as I trace its permutations here, is pre-cisely such a yearning. What guitar makers are attracted to, and what their customers value, is the tonality of a relationship with things that involves a fully embodied aesthetic experience. In lutherie's scenes of making, tone is the manifestation of artisans' "ability to affect and be affected" by the vitality of the tone woods with which they work.[13] Routinely transgressing dominant cultural perceptions of what constitutes "animate" and "inanimate" matter, luthiers approach their craft primed to recognize the aliveness or "animacy" of material entities that are neither human nor animal. *Animacy*, defined as our conceptual hierarchy of living and dead matter, is both a "craft of the senses" that "endows our surroundings with life, death, and things in between" and a form of politics that is "shaped by what or who counts as human, and what or who does not."[14] Guitar makers' refusal to treat wood as the "dead" remainder of once-living trees infuses their work with the political potential of an "alternative social project" that harbors forms of life and labor at variance with market values.[15]

Central to luthiers' project is a conception of animacy that predisposes them to interact with physical phenomena beyond the limits of human rationality, not through domination and control but through playful inquiry and experiential knowledge. In this orientation to wood, the unpredictable acoustics of vibrating soundboards become not a bane to be suppressed but a host of nonhuman agents to be coaxed into harmonious and spirited collaboration. Even the notorious "wolf tone," the howling sound or "dead spot" produced by errant overtones and the oscillation of uneven frequencies, has a place in lutherie's scenes of making.[16] A lone wolf dancing on the horizon of Geppetto's dream, mocking illusions of mastery, it is but one of the many constituents of wood's vocality.

Like the obstreperous log that arrests the carpenter's blow in the opening pages of *Pinocchio*, the wood that luthiers use is understood to have a "voice" before it is fashioned into a guitar. But orchestrating the chorus of nonhuman agents that make up an instrument's tone is not a simple matter of commodity fetishism or anthropomorphic thinking. It requires a sure hand guided by an awareness of the "dissonant possibilities" of consumer goods in a market society: not everything we buy hides the labor that produced it, and recognizing the "capacity of nonhuman things to *act upon us*" can lead us to value material objects in terms other than their market price.[17] Indeed, we can read *Pinocchio* as a parable of

GEPPETTO'S DREAM

9

FIGURE O.5. "W is for Wolf-Tone," from Fred Carlson, A Luthier's Alphabet of Imaginary Instruments: Woodcuts and Poems (Guild of American Luthiers, 2011).

Geppetto's efforts to "socialize" a wayward piece of wood, orienting it toward the possibility of becoming something more than a commodity.[18]

Consider William Eaton's memory of his first encounter with lutherie. In 1971, he answered a knock on his dorm room door and met a young man selling a handmade guitar. At the time, Eaton was a business major on a pole-vaulting scholarship at Arizona State University. He was also a guitar player who enjoyed improvising soothing melodies late at night, composing the ethereal, meditative music that would become his trademark. Impressed by the instrument he saw, he decided to visit the workshop where it was made to see what else might be available:

> When I arrived there, this big Quonset hut was sitting there in the desert, kind of a desolate thing, but some unseen life was happening that I sensed. You start to walk up close and you smell this rosewood. I still remember that first experience, because it's a very sensual experience to breathe in that quality [of wood]. Because where are you going to find rosewood dust in Arizona, or anywhere, unless you're in Central America at a sawmill? Breathing that in, and walking in

that Quonset and seeing these guitar parts hanging everywhere, and watching these people work on these guitars in this mystical place—Juan Roberto Guitar Works! Then the gentleman, John Roberts, who was the proprietor there, said, "Oh, are you here to make a guitar?" That's the first time I even thought of it. My first thought was that I'd never worked with my hands; I wouldn't be capable of doing that.[19]

Central to artisans' stories of making is the evocation of a scene in which the line between objective and subjective sensory perception is blurred. In Eaton's account, the aroma of Brazilian rosewood is not merely in the air outside of his body; it is inhaled into his lungs as a "sensual experience." Although the workshop appears to be "a desolate hut" outside of civilization, he intuits "unseen life" happening inside. What makes this site of production "mystical" is the way it is apprehended: through an embodied awareness of alterity or "otherness" that sparks a longing to become someone with special powers.[20] Eaton may never have "worked with his hands," but this barrier is only a "first thought," soon to be swept aside. Ironically, part of the scene's mystique—"Juan Roberto Guitar Works!"—was the fabrication of John Roberts, who reinvented himself with Spanish panache.[21] As a pilot for a lumber company in the jungles of Nicaragua, Roberts had speculated on a large shipment of rosewood and mahogany. When three boxcars full of wood rolled into Phoenix in 1968, he scrapped his plan to start a hardwood import business and began making guitars instead.

Eaton fit time at Roberts's shop in between his academic and athletic activities. After four months, he finished a guitar and, with ecstatic triumph, drove back to school at two in the morning "yelling at the top of [his] lungs." Upon graduating, Eaton went on to earn a master's degree in business at Stanford, with the goal of becoming an international banker. Not far into his studies, however, he saw a documentary about the maverick composer Harry Partch, who wrote music with microtonal scales for instruments that he created himself. Shortly thereafter, Eaton awoke from a dream in which he built a twelve-string guitar with unique features. He sketched out his idea and spent his winter break with Roberts building this instrument. He also had another motive for being there. Assigned to develop a business plan for his management course, he thought it would be fun to write one for a guitar-making school, using Juan Roberto as his case study. He pitched the idea to Roberts and his new business partner, electric guitar maker Robert Venn, and they endorsed his proposal. Upon completion of this project, Eaton recalls, "The wheels were turning. I thought, 'This is a possibility, I could actually *do* this.'"

Meanwhile, his life was "taking a bigger turn." He was reading deeply in physics, philosophy, and religion, pondering such questions as "What does it mean to be human?" He began "toying with the idea of living in the natural world" and assumed that he would do this later in life, after he made enough money to live comfortably. But at that point, he realized, he might lack the courage of his convictions. "I had the idea of living in the desert and having a part-time role in the guitar-making school that I could start," he says, "and that's what I did." Roberto-Venn was founded in 1975, and for several years Eaton lived in the Sonoran Desert. Parking his car at the school and "traipsing down the riverbed" to sleep under the stars or driving greater distances to spend one or two weeks alone, he had life-changing revelations:

> You simply find yourself not doing or being, but paying attention to the world around you. All of sudden you see the world differently. From my experience, which has informed how I see the world now, it is different to sleep out every night on the ground, feel the ground, and learn things like the feet and the hands have all the nerve endings in them, so when you walk barefoot on the earth you get these small amperage charges. That's part of being human that I would never have known had I not done something like that. To physically know where the moon cycles are on a daily basis, and be able to point at "Well, the moon's right down there." Now of course we say the earth has turned—which is an interesting paradigm, in that our ancestors wouldn't have interpreted it that way. The sun goes down into the earth; the moon goes into the earth. Those mythologies have just as much validity, even physically, in terms of what occurs—even though now we have a solar centrality to the way we think about things. But that experience changed everything about what I do.

Learning to "see the world differently," Eaton suggests, meant coming to appreciate a way of understanding the physical universe that is not necessarily legitimated by mainstream science. Exposed to the primordial pedagogy of the desert, he underwent an epistemological shift that is emblematic of how hand builders distinguish themselves from guitar factories. Rather than adopting a "solar centric" view of guitar making—as a system analyzable from afar—they remain embedded in the production process, trusting that intuition gained from corporeal experience has "just as much validity" as a disembodied, technologically mediated perspective.

Eaton's epiphany has been incorporated into how instrument building is taught at Roberto-Venn. There, as in other lutherie schools and apprenticeships, the knowledge that students develop is as much about themselves as their guitars. Although the challenge of building an instrument may not be as physically demanding as a desert sojourn, it too is an encounter with nonhuman nature that confers a sense of masculine efficacy.[22] Like Eaton, students often emerge from lutherie's scenes of instruction empowered to forge meaningful alternatives to the normative career expectations that stalk young men and women of their race and class. And like Geppetto's, their journey often begins with a dream—in their case, a dream of making a wondrous guitar.

Yet a dream is never simply about the fulfillment of a wish. It is also a window onto aspects of self and society that we may not want to know, and it can reveal emotional truths at odds with our stated intent.[23] The yearning to participate in a craft economy as a free agent has its origins in the history of capitalism and the European guild system, which operated to secure economic independence for privileged men. Craft unions worked to preserve this hierarchy in North America, but industrialization eventually replaced or marginalized most forms of artisanal production—guitar making included—by the mid-nineteenth century.[24] Efforts to revive traditional handcrafts—such as the Arts and Crafts movement in the 1860s and Renaissance fairs in the 1960s— are united by antimodernist longings for authentic lifestyles. But these movements also expressed a racially inflected desire to reclaim the economic autonomy and privileged status once associated with European craft traditions.[25]

Long after the collapse of craft economies, a heady brew of popular culture has continued to identify the "master craftsman" with a type of white masculinity that can be enacted only through the skilled labor involved in making and fixing things. Such work is often portrayed as expressing an innately human—and thus "authentic"—capacity for tool use.[26] In the 1960s and 1970s, hippies, back-to-the-landers, and high-tech entrepreneurs all came to share the idea that personal empowerment, if not the fate of civilization, depended, as the *Whole Earth Catalog* put it, on "access to tools" and embracing the cosmic possibilities they engender: "We *are* as gods and we may as well get good at it."[27] Yet as iconic cover images of the Earth viewed from space implied, the *Catalog*'s apotheosis of "tool users" glossed over differences between machines and hand tools. The new "godlike" ability to see the "whole Earth"—realized by satellite imaging in 1967 and Apollo spacecraft in 1972—was taken to be the aspiration of all tool users.

Pioneering luthiers were avid readers of the *Whole Earth Catalog*, and most would agree that the creative use of tools is what makes us human. But there was a tension inherent in the anthropocentric vision of the Blue Marble that came to signify their generation's global and environmental consciousness: the celebration of power wielded by those who used technology on their own or humanity's behalf took for granted the history of North American imperialism that underwrote the postwar economic expansion and the ongoing extraction of resources from vulnerable ecosystems and weak nation-states. How technology is used, and toward what ends, does not occur in a political vacuum. The notion that only humans and gods possess creative agency is foundational to a political ecology that authorizes the domination, whether destructive or benevolent, of forms of life that are not considered "human."[28] This conception of animacy has aided and abetted the technologies of governance that have, since the 1970s, significantly transformed the global political economy.

Guitar makers have not been immune to the seismic shift in governmental policy away from the Keynesian liberalism that protected workers toward a free-market ideology that favors the financial sector and entrepreneurial risk-taking on the part of individuals and corporations.[29] Seeking to increase their incomes, a number of early builders began hiring apprentices and investing in machinery in order to increase production, reduce the price of their instruments, and compete with leading guitar factories. While a core group remained committed to an artisanal repertoire, another sizable contingent sought a middle

Super Guitars

Up till about two months ago it would have been impossible to even consider listing ourselves in your catalog due to the fact that our instruments were very highly priced; with a long backlog of orders. We felt at that point that we had an obligation and committment to people other than the large money-making groups and single entertainers (i.e. Bob Dylan, The Band, Richie Havens, John Sebastian, Jake Holmes, Judy Collins, etc.); so we reorganized the shop and started training people in building fine quality, handmade guitars.

We are now in the process of having our catalog printed. For the time being we have enclosed a description and price list of all our instruments; we will try to forward some pictures to you, so that you can see and judge for yourselves our high quality standard.

> Yours faithfully,
> Michael Gurian
> Gurian Guitars, Limited
> 100 Grand Street,
> N.Y., N.Y. 10013

STEEL STRINGS

Size 1	Mahogany sides and back; spruce top; black ebony fingerboard; Schaller machine heads; 12 frets to the body; plays best with light or extra light guage strings; price, $250.00
Size 3	Mahogany sides and back; spruce top; black ebony fingerboard; Schaller machine heads; 14 frets to the body; plays best with light or medium guage strings; price, $325.00
Size 3	same as above, but, with rosewood sides & back; price, $425.00
Jumbo	Mahogany sides & back; spruce top; black ebony fingerboard; Schaller machine heads; 14 frets to the body; plays best with medium or heavy guage strings; price, $300.00
Jumbo	same as above, but, with rosewood sides & back; price, $400.00

Classical Guitars

Cl. 1	Mahogany sides & back; European spruce top; black ebony fingerboard; Landstorfer machine heads, when available; price, $325.00
Cl. 2	Indian rosewood sides and black; European spruce top; black ebony fingerboard; Landstorfer machine heads, when available; price, $425.00
Cl. 3	Concert model; Brazilian rosewood sides & back; best quality European spruce top; black ebony fingerboard; Landstorfer machine heads, when available; price, $525.00

Flamenco

In keeping with the tradition of the flamenco guitar, I have developed a guitar that possesses the brightness and clarity of sound sought after by flamenco guitarists. In addition, my guitars have the sound projection of a classical guitar. For this result, I use specially selected woods for the top, back, and sides. If preferred, the traditional Spanish cypress would be used. As in the classical models, Peruvian mahogany and black ebony are used for the neck and fingerboard. The head may be fitted with friction pegs or Landstorfer machines. This model also has a handmade rosette. The price of the flamenco guitar is $750.00.

Lutes

1) Elizabethan: This model is constructed with either 7 or 8 courses, depending on personal preferences. Woods employed are Peruvian mahogany for the neck with black ebony for the the fingerboard, curly maple for the boat and spruce for the top. Rosettes are designed and handcarved in the traditional manner.
The price for this model is $850.00.

FIGURE 0.6. *The pressures and rationales that prompted luthiers to expand their operations in the 1970s varied. Michael Gurian cites the goal of bringing down prices in his advertisement for Gurian Guitars in* The Last Whole Earth Catalog *in 1971.*

ground between hand building and assembly-line manufacturing. These competing visions of authenticity and technological progress eventually led to a schism within the lutherie movement. In the pages that follow, I present testimony from a variety of stakeholders in the community's ongoing debate about how high-quality instruments are made. The question of how to evaluate an acoustic guitar ultimately pivots, I argue, on the tone of things: on the meaning of commodification and what it portends for the craft object and artisanal labor.

————

Consider Judy Threet's presentation at the 2007 symposium of the Association of Stringed Instrument Artisans. Threet began building guitars in Calgary, Alberta, after leaving her job as a professor of philosophy at the University of Calgary in 1990. A regular presence at professional meetings and guitar shows for two decades, she is known for her disarming bonhomie and beautiful inlay art, which often features wild animals. Her work achieved acclaim in 2003 when Tracy Chapman appeared on the cover of *Acoustic Guitar* playing a Threet guitar. But in her talk, "The End of Our Golden Era?" Threet's take on the state of lutherie was decidedly *not* upbeat:

> There is a magazine article that came out, and I think these things recur, where they talk about "Oh, there's just so much for the customer to choose from! The prices are so great, and look at all these styles!" And that's what the general public tends to think the "golden era" means. Notice: it's *real* good for them! It's not surprising that this gets pointed out to them as "Hey, this is this great golden era!" But what I want us builders to notice is, oh yeah, it's really nice for the customer, but these sorts of things that are so jolly for the customer are absolutely *horrific* for us.[30]

Threet identified several trends that threaten the future of guitar making. High on her list was the surfeit of guitars currently in the market. Not only do hand builders with various levels of experience now vie with one another for market share, but they compete with manufacturers and boutique shops whose brands extend to a wide range of price points and instrument styles. The result, Threet argued, is that it has become ever harder for consumers to correlate price with quality and recognize the "value" that skilled artisanship adds to an instrument.

This problem is compounded, she observed, by the ready availability of prefabricated kits and instructional DVDs, which permit hobbyists to claim that they too build guitars — reinforcing the impression that guitar makers, like factory workers, simply assemble machine-made parts.

Moreover, Threet pointed out, what passes for shoptalk in lutherie circles is largely procedural information about how to make instruments quickly and more efficiently. Vanished, she argued, is the spirit of collective inquiry and innovative theory building that originally galvanized the lutherie movement and pushed the envelope of what the guitar can be. Without a shared commitment to advancing knowledge of what makes some guitars better than others, she concluded, luthiers can have no "golden era":

> And so we come to what I've started calling our "inconvenient truth." In an age awash in information about guitars — about building them, selling them, buying them — the guitar itself is in danger. It's becoming frozen in time — a mere commodity, whose only "improvement" will be the speed at which it — a merely adequate it — can be produced. Worse yet, if that commodity then falls out of favor — as stagnant things often do — no one will even care about the myriad choices, about their prices, or about how many can be churned out per week. The whole lot of them will land, like the bowl-back mandolin of yore, on the trash heap of time.

Threet's lament gave voice to sentiments that hand builders rarely air in public. Talk of commodification — what it is and who is guilty of it — reveals fault lines that now divide the lutherie world. The ever-present danger that guitars will be valued in terms of their comparative cost, not their unique characteristics, poses a greater threat to artisans than it does to industrial manufacturers. Were their guitars "mere commodities," priced competitively in relation to other makers' instruments, the value of their labor would be reduced to its productivity — to "how many they could churn out per week" — and it, too, would be commodified. Were luthiers to conceive of themselves primarily as small businesses in competition with one another, the only information exchanged within the community would be nonproprietary technical advice, not the substantive knowledge necessary to sustain a living craft tradition.

Commodification, however, does not begin with the guitar itself. The natural resources out of which it is made are commodified by imperial and corporate powers long before they reach the luthier's bench. Threet acknowledges this "inconvenient truth" only indirectly in her allusion to the consequences of global warming and the unfolding environmental disaster it portends.[31] Yet traces of lutherie's occulted history and its legacy appear in her invocation of the Neapolitan mandolin. This lutelike instrument, which originated in Naples, Italy, was an unapologetic showpiece of mercantile trade and colonial expansion. At its most elaborate, it featured rosewood ribs and intricately carved inlay of ebony, ivory, and tortoiseshell. It came to America with Italian immigrants and remained popular until 1910, when musicians flocked to the new violin-style mandolin designed by Orville Gibson. Seen as a harbinger of the fate that could befall the acoustic guitar, it is a sign not only of the obsolescence inherent to market culture but of the ecological imperialism that still haunts lutherie and imperils rainforests around the world.

––––––––

The tone of acoustic guitars is a sonic expression of how they are made, what they are made with, and how they make us feel. What we "hear" when we attend to the sound of particular instruments is more than just vibrations in the air; we are also listening to how the materials that compose them were treated in the production process—from the felling of trees to the builder's finishing touch. The more we know about that process, the more nuanced our appreciation of tone becomes. In a market economy, tone is diagnostic of the commodity chains and the social relations of production that bring guitars into being as objects intended for sale. The tone that instruments convey reflects social differences in how industrial labor and artisanal labor are performed and organized in a postindustrial society—a society that is dominated by the logic of the market and a modernist social imaginary.[32]

What we hear in the tonal characteristics of guitars, I argue, is a cultural debate about how commodities come to have value in a consumer culture. Are products made by hand worth more than those made in factories? Can cutting-edge technology enhance a craft tradition? And why have artisanal values endured in the twenty-first century? Are they merely anachronisms in a digital age? Our answer to these questions depends how we understand the relationship between human labor, material reproduction, and commodification. The lutherie movement, along with other contemporary crafts, represents an alternative approach to commodification, not an escape from it altogether.[33] Guitar makers and their relevant public—musicians, collectors, instrument dealers, lutherie schools, guitar show promoters, and trade media—are magnetized by the desire for a relationship with things in which the vitality of human and nonhuman making can be directly or vicariously experienced. In this imaginary, premodern and industrial craft practices offer a model of commodification in which artisans and artifacts come to have "a life" in and through the marketplace.

Geppetto's dream expresses a longing for entrepreneurial independence in an era of growing economic precarity. It registers the hope that the artisan's encounter with the liveliness of wood will endow the craft object and the maker's labor with an absolute value that enables both to interrupt and revitalize the deadening effects of commodification. At the turn of the new millennium, however, the global market within which luthiers operate has changed substantially. Now, more than ever before, hand builders confront the technological reality that much of what they do can be done by robots. Whether this matters—to whom and how—is the question posed by the tone of things.

Crossroads of Knowledge

Standing at the crossroad, I tried to flag a ride
Didn't nobody seem to know me, everybody pass me by
The sun going down, boy, dark going to catch me here
Boy, dark going to catch me here
— Robert Johnson, "Cross Road Blues" (1936)

1

At ever-larger and glitzier guitar shows across the United States and Canada, a common refrain can be heard: none of this was imaginable forty years ago. Asked to reflect on the history of the lutherie movement, "old timers" will shake their head in amazement and recall a past when customers refused to give "homemade" instruments a second look. Why that changed, and how a vibrant market for the artisanal guitar emerged, is the subject of much speculation and mythmaking. In these "origin narratives," luthiers offer a selective recall of history that renders market exchange and their place in it sensible in moral terms.[1] What they seek to account for is less a matter of historical record than the miraculous emergence of a social movement committed to the value of manual labor in postindustrial society.

Unlike origin stories that attribute the founding of a new field of knowledge or creative endeavor to an influential ancestor or school of thought, builders rarely lay credit for the current renaissance of guitar making at the feet of particular individuals. To be sure, key figures are lionized for giving others their start in the business. Michael Gurian and Jean-Claude Larrivée stand out in this regard, and their "patrimonies" are often identified as a guide to who's who in the lutherie world. But this pathway into the profession was not the norm. Far more common, as Portland-based luthier Charles Fox observes, was an experience of social isolation and independent invention:

> Because we had no instruction, there was no *way* that we could follow; there was no tradition that we could consult. We all had to

figure it out for ourselves, and because we didn't know each other, we were literally on our own. I was figuring out some methods to make this happen, and someone else I didn't know yet was doing the same thing. So already there were many ways coming down, you know? There were all these parallel approaches to the same problem developing, and developing rather quickly. Quickly enough and completely enough to produce a first instrument, however misguided our approaches were. That's influential in many ways. One way is that today we have thousands of people practicing this craft here in North America. That would never be the case if we had a "tradition" of guitar making. With a tradition, there would be one way to make a guitar, and if that didn't suit you, you wouldn't enter the craft. But in our country, there was a way for everybody. You could practice this in any way that suited you, so long as the product was a valid instrument. And that is unheard of in craft, certainly in any previous European culture.[2]

In this popular account of the movement's origins, democracy and free enterprise allowed North American luthiers to break decisively with their European forebears. The opportunities available to them in the 1960s and 1970s were a recapitulation, in this view, of the continent's colonial history, a period when craft apprentices were able to slip free of the shackles on entrepreneurship imposed by the old guild system.[3] Unfettered by "tradition," builders felt at liberty to explore uncharted territory in whatever "way" they wished, with only the discipline of the market to constrain them. Much as the ingenuity and independent character of early settlers is popularly imagined to be the result of an unmediated encounter with "wilderness," luthiers attribute the success of their collective enterprise to their pioneering spirit and willingness to take economic risks.[4]

Yet builders' sense of freedom and national exceptionalism glosses over their complicated relationship to history and the political and economic shifts under way at the time they entered lutherie.[5] As a countercultural project, the lutherie movement sought to revive a craft tradition that was both "preindustrial" and "industrial" at the very moment that North America was careening toward a "postindustrial" future.[6] Employment in basic manufacturing was in precipitous decline as corporations took advantage of new technologies and increasingly pro-business policy to outmaneuver organized labor and move production facilities to low-wage zones in Mexico and overseas.[7] Deindustrialization, not unlike the closing of the western frontier at the turn of the twentieth century, marked the pursuit of new forms of corporate profit in foreign markets.[8] By highlighting their departure from the "closed" guild system in Europe's past, guitar makers tacitly "forget" the eclipse of opportunity for manual laborers in the United States and Canada over their lifetime.[9]

If builders' origin story downplays the political economy within which their movement developed, it accentuates the uniqueness and complexity of the craft object around which it coalesced. Not only could practitioners devise their own way of making guitars, Fox observes, but they could approach that challenge from many directions:

> Guitar building is one of the most multidimensional crafts that I'm aware of. There's art, there's science, there's philosophy, there's the spiritual aspect to it; they're right there if you want to go there. It's sociologically significant. It's aesthetic. It's all very balanced. And actually, it's all required to do the work. That richness, both of the fulfillment and of the richness of the challenge, that's very seductive, certainly to a young man still feeling all his powers, you know—wow! This is a craft that you can enter from any angle and be working from your personal strength to get the rest. Even back then, that's perhaps why it could appeal to so many people—because there are many handles, many doors into that building. It was a source of fulfillment on many levels and from many directions. That can't be underestimated. This was not like "I think I'll be a craftsman, I think I'll turn pens," or "I think I'll make leather belts and go to the weekend art fair." Yeah, that's technically craft, but [lutherie] was a *whole* different thing. Perhaps a way of saying it is, it was a challenge worthy of anyone who accepted it. And one that would never run out—you'll never get to the bottom of this thing or hit the wall at the other end. This was always deeper and deeper, if you were up to it.

As a "building with many doors," lutherie is imagined to be a space of self-actualization not unlike the nation itself. Just as citizens are said enter a democratic polity from different walks of life and build on their "personal strengths" to realize their potential as human beings, builders come into guitar making "feeling their powers" and eager to prove themselves worthy of their national birthright as autonomous economic actors. As if drawing a sword from the stone, they "accept the challenge" of lutherie not as an idle hobby but as a test of moral character and their ability to contribute to the greater good. Yet the conditions of national belonging that luthiers embrace reflect deep ambivalence about their participation in a capitalist society. The success they have enjoyed, I was repeatedly told, is a sign of their resistance to market competition. Fox puts it this way:

> All of this [the renaissance of guitar making] is a result of the sharing of information. Again, when we began, no schools or notebooks or anything. But the times were about being supportive, not exclusive. Competitive was what this whole thing was *anti*—or at least that was a strong aspect of the world that this was the antidote to. Of course it was enlightened self-interest: we all needed to know what anyone could tell us, and we were happy to share what we knew. That principle of the '60s, you know, that information is free, was very clear. You would see that written: *information is free*. That is one principle—at least in this craft—that is alive and well. The value of the commitment to those few words is what you see [at guitar shows]. They are proof of what that can be.

Contrasting their ethical stance to the tight-lipped practices associated with Europe's guild system, guitar makers cleave to the mantra of "information sharing" in order to affirm their countercultural origins as well as explain their present economic success. The tension inherent in this position—that a noncompetitive exchange of technical knowledge is what enables a vibrant consumer market to flourish—has dogged the notion that "information is free" since the 1960s. Even Stewart Brand, founder of the *Whole Earth Catalog* and vociferous champion of information sharing, acknowledged that information also "wants to be expensive," given that it has great value to those who access it at an opportune moment.[10]

Information sharing among luthiers also has a double-edged quality. Although it was a source of solidarity during the early years of the movement, it now causes friction when parties to the exchange are not in agreement about what should be *done* with the information and who should profit from it. The idea that everyone benefits from swapping shop secrets as a matter of "enlightened self-interest" may have made good sense to a small group of isolated builders who would otherwise have been left in the dark. But whether this principle continues to operate as an "antidote" to economic competition remains an open question today.

ACCIDENTAL ENTREPRENEURS

Richard "R. E." Bruné "dabbled with guitar" as a teenager growing up in Dayton, Ohio, in the 1960s.[11] Unable to afford the flamenco guitar he wanted, he built one from the dining-room table his parents had when they married in the 1930s. When he was fifteen, the death of his father, a German immigrant, prompted him to take his guitar playing seriously, and he began playing in nightclubs and coffee houses to earn money. In 1967, immersed in flamenco music and culture, he traveled to Spain, where the symbiotic relationship between luthiers and players reignited his interest in guitar making.[12]

Attending college in Mexico City, he began making classical and flamenco guitars while "knocking his head against the wall" trying to make a living as a musician. "Any blond, blue-eyed, northern European-looking fellow who tries to go out and present himself on stage as a flamenco player," he says of this time, "has a big, big marketing problem." Eventually he discovered that guitar making generated more income than guitar playing—relatively speaking. "What was it that Groucho Marx said?" Bruné jokes. "He said, 'I started with nothing and after ten years, I worked myself up to an extreme state of poverty.'"

Having bluegrass banjo as a "sideline endeavor," Bruné accompanied a friend to a muzzle-loading rifle meet near Dayton, where evening sessions of "parking lot picking" lasted late into the night. At this event he met dulcimer and harpsichord maker Jerrold "Jerry" Beall, a Newark, Ohio, native who was selling dulcimers from his truck. "Jerry appealed to me because he had a lot of the old American medicine-man huckster in him," recalls Bruné. "He was a really clever guy. He had the all these production techniques and engineering things that allowed him to crank dulcimers out, as he called it, 'by the bushel-basket full.'" The two men became friends, and in 1972, when Beall decided to create an organization for stringed instrument makers, Bruné was among the first to hear about it:

> Jerry called me up one day and he says, "R. E.! I'm going to make a guild!" "A what?" "A guild. We are going to make a guild of American luthiers." He said, "We'll put out a newsletter and we'll charge them admission, and we'll get them to submit articles, and we'll get all this free information. It will be great!" I said, "Oh man, that sounds like a lot of work." He says, "Oh, I'm going to get some people out in Tacoma to do the newsletter." He says, "We won't have to do anything!"[13]

The idea of harnessing the ingenuity of social networks to produce information for profit was fast becoming a mainstream enterprise by the early 1970s. From World War II through the Cold War, military and industrial research laboratories developed a cybernetic understanding of physical and social systems that encouraged collaboration and the leveling of hierarchical management. In the late 1960s, as historian Fred Turner writes, "the cybernetic notion of the globe as a single, interlinked pattern of information" also took hold among countercultural youth longing for a harmonious, interconnected world. Stewart Brand's *Whole Earth Catalog*, published from 1968 to 1972, demonstrated that pooling information on a wide range of subjects and consumer goods could foster research and education as well as entrepreneurial activity. Turner uses the term *network entrepreneur* to describe Brand's legendary ability to link people through meetings and publications into "network forums" that, in turn, produced their own social networks.[14]

In similar fashion, the North American lutherie movement was catalyzed by the efforts of network entrepreneurs. When Beall announced his intent to start a lutherie organization in a 1972 letter to the editor of *Guitar Player* magazine, he hoped to tap into a growing community of practicing and aspiring guitar builders. In the early 1970s, the idea that stringed instruments could be made by hand was circulating beyond word of mouth through national left-leaning and antiestablishment publications. During this period, Charles Fox advertised his Earthworks guitar-making school in *Mother Earth News*, and Michael Gurian placed an ad for his guitars in the *Last Whole Earth Catalog*. Like Brand, these luthiers recognized that social networks were incipient markets in the making, whether the object of exchange was information, instruction, or material goods. But if Beall's vision of a network forum for lutherie was prescient, his claim that it would require no work was self-interested bluster.

Eighteen-year-old Tim Olsen was among those who responded to Beall's ad. The year before, Olsen had started his own guitar-making business and repair shop in Tacoma. "I soon discovered that I didn't have nearly the knowledge or skills that I thought I did," he admits.[15] Enclosing a small contribution for a newsletter, he urged Beall "not to forget about electric guitar makers." Observing that Olsen "seemed like a go-getter," Beall asked him if *he* would like to make the Guild of American Luthiers a reality by producing the newsletter. Olsen accepted this mission in 1972.[16] Forty years later, he continues to serve as the founding editor of the guild's quarterly journal and other publications.[17]

Today, membership in the world's largest professional lutherie organization far exceeds the list of forty names that Olsen received from Beall. Yet the guild's purpose, Olsen says, remains the same:

> The role of our organization has been to create a framework for information sharing. A wonderful thing was that all these hippies had the idea of sharing information, but it was really the idea of *getting* information because nobody *had* any. So if there was any source of it, you'd run to it and try to get some information. Since everybody was in the same boat, it was sharing because you would gladly tell anything you knew, and not in a cynical way. It was just like "There's another guitar maker! Oh, this is so great!" And you'd just spill your guts. We've institutionalized that and it's still going strong. Other countries and cultures don't have this because they started with established, trained makers with their markets, their customers, their techniques, and it's been a matter of controlling access to the market through apprenticeships and guilds and that sort of thing. But in our case, it was "Everybody join the party, because this is so great! We found out that there is such a thing as hide glue! This is so great!"

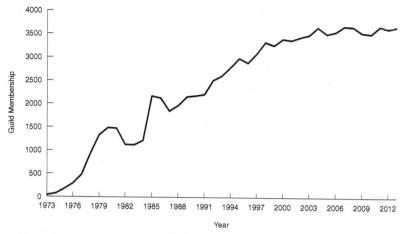

FIGURE 1.1. *Guild of American Luthiers membership, 1974–2012. From humble beginnings in 1972, the guild has grown to become the largest international professional organization for luthiers. Note the drop in the early 1980s during back-to-back recessions in the United States, commonly known as "the dark ages" for acoustic music. Data provided by the Guild of American Luthiers.*

The social dynamics of the early lutherie community bear a striking resemblance to what anthropologist Marshall Sahlins called the "original affluent society." Sahlins was referring to small hunting and gathering bands in which people adapt to conditions of resource scarcity by engaging in "generalized reciprocity"—that is, sharing what little they have without immediately expecting something in return. These societies, he argued, enjoy a greater sense of well-being than ones in which resources are abundant but distributed unequally.[18] Likewise, young builders were all "in the same boat," Olsen says, because everyone was equally ignorant. Sharing what little they knew meant they could learn more collectively than they could on their own. In a situation of "information poverty," everyone could feel rich, exult in new discoveries, and invite others to "join the party."

The historical circumstances that underwrote this situation—a lack of publicly available information and the low economic value of this information and its product—were ideal for the formation of an organization based on interpersonal trust. "We were eager to share any kind of information that we had," Olsen avers, "because nobody felt like they had anything to protect. There was no market for handmade guitars, so there was no market to protect. There was nobody who was established and protecting themselves against people coming in." Unlike trade associations, which create social hierarchies by restricting access to knowledge and markets, the guild could conceive of itself as a "framework for information sharing."

But the effort to institutionalize an urge to "spill your guts" did not go unchallenged. From the guild's inception, a commercial interest in advancing luthiers' economic situation has competed with its educational mandate. The organization that Beall originally envisioned was structured by skill categories in which apprentices, journeymen, and masters were charged different annual fees. But at the first "convention" in 1974—two small gatherings at Beall's farm and Olsen's home—Bruné, not Beall, was elected president. Bruné focused his energies on organizing the 1975 convention, and Olsen opposed a skill hierarchy on principle.[19]

But the question of whether the guild should actively promote the financial interests of its members has been a recurrent issue. In the "information society" that took shape in the early 1970s, pursuing knowledge "for its own sake" became increasingly difficult to separate from economic considerations.[20] By adopting the structure of a nonprofit educational organization, the guild's founding members hoped to promote the "quality" of the artisanal object while placing its market value—and the labor status of its makers—outside their purview.

The character of the guild's activities was largely in place by the May 1975 convention. Held at Northwestern University in Evanston, Illinois, the three-day event was promoted as "Exhibition of Twentieth Century Makers and Their Instruments." To everyone's delight, National Public Radio covered the gathering, giving it a fervently desired stamp of cultural legitimacy. In exchange for the use of its facilities, Northwestern stipulated that the convention would be held during the school year, that it would be open to the public at no charge, and that "no commercial transactions [would] take place."[21] The university provided accommodations that were well suited to the guild's needs. A three-hundred-seat auditorium offered a stage for lectures and seminars given by experienced members, demonstrations of techniques such as bending guitar sides and carving lute rosettes, and concerts by professional musicians on members' instruments.

Access was also granted to an art gallery with "a parquet floor and spotlights" for a display of harpsichords; a nearby student lounge for the exhibition of other instruments, tools, and tone woods; a conference room for business meetings; a cafeteria; and free parking outside the building. The use of student dorms for lodging was not part of this package, but it has since become a regular feature of the convention experience. Thirty members attended this meeting, and twenty brought instruments to exhibit.[22] In all but size, the 1975 meeting was indicative of what future conventions would become, containing all of the elements that are now standard fare, except for notable additions such as a benefit auction and sessions devoted to the evaluation of members' instruments.

The guild's effort to distinguish its educational mission from economic advocacy has been an ongoing flashpoint for controversy. Holding conventions on a university campus—a motion to do so in perpetuity was passed at the 1975 business meeting[23]—has erected a barrier against the encroachment of the market, in symbolic as well as practical terms. Although exhibition areas are open to the public, the primary audience tends to be luthiers themselves—a boon for material supply vendors but a drawback for anyone trying to sell instruments. Moreover, convention organizers must walk a fine line in their promotional efforts, for to advertise the exhibition as commercial affair would jeopardize the guild's favorable tax status as a nonprofit educational corporation.[24] As Olsen explains it:

> The guild itself isn't a source of anything. We don't do research or anything. We are only a format for exchange, and that's all we want to be. People have suggested over time that we do things like facilitate people buying insurance or pooling their money to buy materials, and we've wisely avoided all those pitfalls. We only facilitate the sharing of information. That's all we do. We don't pay people to write [for the quarterly journal]. We don't decide what's right and wrong. We don't commission research. We don't do anything except create a forum for people to share what they've learned.

Yet the stance of noninvolvement in the work lives of its members has been a disappointment to those who have looked to the guild for something more, whether it was group rates on health and life insurance or financial assistance in times of distress. Before the first commercial guitar show was established in 1996, disaffected members saw in the guild's charter evidence of an ivory-tower mentality that was out of touch with the economic realities they faced. At issue was whether, and in what way, information sharing was incompatible with market competition. In a newsletter distributed before the 1975 convention, Richard Bruné outlined the rationale for the guild's first public event:

> It should be realized that this exhibition will be strictly *non-competitive*. We are *not* organizing this to give a golden capo to somebody from some know-nothing panel of near sighted judges. This is strictly an exhibition of twentieth century makers *and* their instruments. Period. Frankly, I hope to see many makers who will show other prospective makers lurking in the public that a large impressive shop and years of experience are not necessary to produce a credible instrument, an instrument, I might add, that in many cases, is infinitely superior to the production instrument encountered in the local retail establishment.[25]

The "noncompetitiveness" of the exhibition, Bruné suggests, is restricted to the instruments and makers featured in the exhibition itself. They will not be judged, at least not officially, against one another. But market competition is earnestly hoped for between handcrafted guitars and the factory alternative hanging in stores. Not only are members of the public expected to recognize the "infinite superiority" of well-made artisanal guitars; they are called upon to question their assumptions about what it takes to "produce a credible instrument." While the hubris of youth may be speaking when Bruné dismisses "years of experience" and state-of-the-art shops, he succeeds in making a case for the triumphant rebirth of a craft tradition in the work of "twentieth century makers."

In this promotional gambit, makers as well as their instruments were on display. Like actors who perform craft skills at cultural heritage museums, luthiers were aware that they offered a glimpse of the past in the present. Unlike those tourist destinations, however, they were staging an economic comeback. Their mode of production is presented as the time-honored way of making the *best* instruments in the present. In this spirit, Bruné cites their media coverage as evidence of a national interest in the future of lutherie. "After all," he writes, "we are the last of a dying breed." Out of place in the modern age, he implies, hand builders are newsworthy because their very persistence, their determination to *live on* against the odds, can alter perceptions of how guitars can and should be made.

But the public is not the only audience for this edifying message. Of equal or greater importance are "prospective makers lurking" in the crowd and members of the guild itself. Maintaining an atmosphere of trust and egalitarian exchange requires cultivating an appreciation for the craft that transcends the bottom line. By raising the profile of the hand builder, the guild spurred other elite institutions to notice luthiers and, not so incidentally, offer them an "ethical alibi" for pursuing an otherwise suspect "career."[26] In 1978–79, the Smithsonian broke new ground with its "Harmonious Craft" exhibit, which displayed instruments made by contemporary hand builders. Luthier John Mello, now located in Kensington, California, recalls how important this form of validation was to him at the time:

> I was the first person in my family to graduate from college. It was only becoming marginally untrue then that a BA in anything would get you a well-paying job, but it was still part of the promise. I went to Oberlin, and I remember looking in at the Oberlin Inn and seeing these Ohio Bell Telephone people in their training sessions. I looked at the pie chart of what they were going over, and I thought, "I'm reasonably affable; if I really just want the 1.67 television sets and the 2.4 kids and the car, I could get this job. I could do a middle management job and it would be just fine." Those jobs have all gone away. They are either in India now or they are boxed on the floor, but at least there *was* that promise there. So my parents were just horrified I was being a guitar maker! I talked to my dad. I said, "Dad, I grew up watching you work with your hands and work with your mind at the same time—what did you expect?" My wife's family was horrified—this was before we got married. But at least when I got in the Smithsonian, to me, being so insecure—I wasn't insecure about

doing it [making guitars] — but it just gave me something to give them, to say, "Hey, I'm okay."[27]

Mollifying anxious parents and in-laws through the "okayness" conferred by prestigious institutions enabled guitar makers to pursue lutherie as form of higher education in its own right, a move that allowed them to avoid run-of-the-mill careers and defer expectations of a middle-class income. In support of this endeavor, the guild normalized a worldview in which nonmarket values took precedence over economic ones. As an account of the second golden age, this origin story casts guitar making as a quest for cultural distinction that comes from specialized knowledge rather than monetary assets.[28] As Tim Olsen puts in, makers were drawn to lutherie by the desire to do something "cool," not by hard-headed business acumen:

> The whole North American lutherie thing — I know I didn't think this [renaissance] would happen. It's like "You mean people want to *buy* these things? Wow!" Who knew that would happen? So the root of the whole thing is *not* selling guitars. It's just sheer love of wanting to try and do something. And that really is still — I mean, people have learned to make instruments that people want to buy, and they've learned how to make them quickly enough that they can make a living doing it, but under it all is still this underlying root of just wanting to do something that's cool. [When guitar makers ask themselves,] Why am I doing this? It's because it's so cool. It's *not* because I can sell it. That comes along as a necessity.

In his role as editor of the guild's publications and president of its board of directors, Olsen has witnessed fellow luthiers come to terms with the challenges and rewards of their work. By placing the "sheer love" of building guitars at the heart of why luthiers do what they do, he portrays luthiers as accidental entrepreneurs surprised by the market spectacle their craft has become. The concept of "cool" — as a marker of status (being cool) and a valued practice (doing something cool) — explains why anyone takes up playing, collecting, or making guitars.[29] As such, it indexes a sense of community in which others value you for your proximity to the guitar and the depth of your interaction with it. "Coolness," as Olsen suggests, is intrinsic to the instrument itself:

FIGURE 1.2. Tim Olsen, in the "Take a Luthier to Lunch" T-shirt,
at an early guild postconvention party, 1977. Photograph by Dale Korsmo,
courtesy of the Guild of American Luthiers.

You look at a thing like a Martin guitar, and you say, "Hey, that's cool." The closer you look at it, the more you realize that the coolness of it just goes down and down. It's like the Mandelbrot set, the infinite geometric figure—the closer you look, the more complex it is. It's the infinity of it that just draws you in. Richard Bruné calls it crawling into the funnel from the little end. It's something that appears to be a little hole, but when you get into it, it just gets bigger, and the farther you go, the bigger it is. I'm talking about people of my generation. These days it's a whole other matter because [now] you can look at [guitar making] as a career and decide how to enter that career. Which is not something we did. The career wasn't part of the question. It was "There's that little hole, what's in there?" And before you know it, you're pulled in, and it's too late.

Nostalgia creeps into the voices of those who recall the 1960s and 1970s as a period of spiritual awakening and self-actualization. The ethos of coolness is a far cry, they insist, from the goal-oriented careerism of today's youth. The image of "crawling into a funnel from the little end" captures the feeling of a generation that searched for fissures in the status quo through which to imagine and experiment with new possibilities for living. As a quintessential point of entry into the counterculture, the acoustic guitar offered a template for the consciousness raising that characterized an antinormative journey.[30] What began as a peek into another world—peering into the sound hole in wonder at the guitar's inner workings—led to the apprehension of a cosmic system that "just gets bigger, and bigger, the farther you go."[31] To those who let curiosity be their guide, turning back, it seems, was never an option.

BREAKING THE MOLD

At the age of ten, Michael Millard got his first job at the Branford, Connecticut, boatyard. Working on his father's sailboat with a block of wood and sandpaper led to other "professional, under-the-table" employment during the summer and school vacations.[32] The early 1960s were "the dawning of the age of fiberglass, of plastic," he recalls, "and all the young guys, college students, thought it was the coolest thing." But Millard hated the new boats and their smell. He was taken under the wing of a few "old timers," men over the age of sixty, who wanted to share their wisdom with "the kid who likes wood." In time, he found a kindred spirit in John Miller, a young man a few years older than himself, whose family also owned a wooden boat. Miller was a guitar player, and he became a mentor and inspiration:

> One day [Miller] came into the boatyard with a turntable and some LPs under his arm. In short order, I was listening to Gary Davis, Robert Johnson, Bill Broonzy, Blind Willie Johnson, and all these players. It was, just about literally, put a clear glass 400-watt light

bulb up there [over his head]. It was like *Oh!* So the woodworking, the guitars, and the music all were happening at once. I was sort of waking up as an adolescent in those ways. So my formative years were all embroiled in this local culture of old men, wooden boats — people who did things with woodworking without a lot of jigs or fixtures. It was all *free-form* stuff: figure out how to do it, and do it really, really, really well.

Millard's adolescent epiphany coincided with a generational politics of authenticity that looked across the color line to identify ways of being that challenged normative prescriptions for white masculinity. Whether it was the percussive rhythms and raw vocals of African American bluesmen or "free-form" arts and crafts that produced high-quality results without "jigs or fixtures," the mode of self-realization that Millard and his peers adopted was often out of sync not just with the status quo but also with the mainstream inclinations of others their own age. The intertwined sensibilities of the folk music revival, the civil rights struggle, and the antiwar effort turned on a "light bulb" in the mind of each individual, one consciousness at a time. For those coming to terms with their identities in raced, classed, and gendered terms, the guitar could be an organizing principle for aspects of self-fashioning that "all were happening at once."

Unlike other students at his prep school, Millard did not go directly to college. He opted instead to work on the political campaign of a local congressman who opposed the war in Vietnam. When he enrolled at Southern Connecticut State University the following year, the academic hiatus caught up with him in the form of an induction notice from the Selective Service. Rather than requesting a college deferment, he applied for exemption as a conscientious objector, but he was given a "rubber-stamp" college deferment nonetheless. He appealed this classification on the grounds that it was "a politically biased system" stacked against racial minorities and the working class.[33] Letters flew back and forth until Millard's application for CO status was denied and he was drafted. More legal wrangling ensued after he refused to take the oath of allegiance at the draft board. In the final correspondence he received, he was reclassified as 4-F based on a history of migraine headaches. While it was not the moral victory he desired, Millard remained

steadfast in refusing the cultural pigeonhole that others of his generation found convenient.

A similar drama unfolded when he got to college and found that his
study of Delta blues guitar—in which he took lessons from Reverend
Gary Davis himself—meant that he "couldn't play with anybody else."
The "broken time, uniquely rhythmic, syncopated" country blues that
he loved was not the "smooth blues" that campus rock and roll musicians wanted to play.[34] Millard resigned himself to cultivating a solo
rather than group performance style. Reflecting on "the whole notion
of things done without a mold," he observes that developing an individual repertoire is, for some, a function of necessity:

> You had somebody like a Willie McTell, or a Willie Johnson, or a
> Gary Davis, blind street singers, playing on the street with a cup or
> a hat. If there was another guy playing the same thing on the next
> street corner, the best you could say is they were going to have half
> as much in their hat at the end of the day. It just didn't work that way
> [for them to play the same way]. Those were people who were very
> guarded, for the most part, with what they showed other people in
> terms of what they played. You can probably count on one hand the
> number of people who are—well, maybe two hands—the number of
> people who can play Gary Davis like Gary Davis really, really well. In
> those days [the 1960s], virtually no one could.

Developing a style that cannot be imitated, Millard suggests, is a
sign of authenticity as well as business savvy. Identifying with the out-
sider persona of Delta bluesmen, Millard performed as a working musician through the 1970s and early 1980s. One night in a Massachusetts bar, confronted with a table of drunken patrons who demanded
that he play the Grateful Dead incessantly, he decided to quit the road
and build guitars full time. His roots in country blues are reflected in
the frog on the headstock of every Froggy Bottom guitar—a name that
evokes the Mississippi lowlands, farmed by black sharecroppers, which
frequently flooded and became amphibious mating grounds. Although
Millard does not mention lutherie explicitly in his reference to duel-
ing musicians, I hear him commenting on market competition among
guitar makers as well. Knowing how to build guitars, he suggests, can

be developed through study and practice. But ultimately, knowledge in lutherie, as in music, expresses individual taste and talent, neither of which necessarily benefits from information sharing.

Not surprisingly, Millard has had limited involvement with the lutherie community. Dismissing conventions and guitar shows as an "awful lot of schmoozing," he says he would rather be "out in the hills of Vermont" by himself or with close friends. "I don't like wasting my time and just talking about, oh, whatever, with great enthusiasm, this, that, and the other thing, and just going around and around about that." Feeling no need to promote himself—his guitars should "speak for themselves," he believes—he keeps a low profile and periodically appears in his own magazine ads. In this regard, Millard articulates an undercurrent of misanthropy felt by a sizable contingent of makers who are not active in the social rituals of the lutherie world. Gesturing obliquely toward a need to remain "guarded," these builders offer a counternarrative to the community's dominant origin story.

———————

On a crisp autumn day, I sit with William Cumpiano in his Northampton, Massachusetts, shop, which is located on the ground floor of an old industrial building. As we talk, I am intrigued by the unusual stringed instruments I see among the guitars populating his workspace. My eyes alight on an armadillo shell on a shelf near the ceiling, and later I learn that it is used to make a traditional South American *charango*. Bicultural and bilingual, Cumpiano is an authority on Caribbean stringed instruments and cofounder of the Puerto Rican Cuatro Project, a research team that collects the music and oral history of the *cuatro*, a rustic folk instrument that has ten strings in five courses. Charmed by his warm and engaging manner, I can see why his guitar-making courses are so popular. We are talking about why he abandoned his career in industrial design in 1972:

> What happened was the folk movement, the new generation, the whole do-it-yourself, do-your-own-thing type of thing—when people began to buy out of the standard way. I went through a similar thing when I was leaving the field of industrial design. It's when I went back to [Michael] Gurian's shop with this amorphous, tormented, rumpled, wrinkled object that kind of looked like a guitar.

This was the guitar that I made in his course that he never saw because he was never there. It was rattling and buzzing; it was unplayable. I never knew anything about setup. He never taught us anything about setup. He just said, "Put the strings on." Turns out that the setup is a vital, painstaking process that turns this wooden cabinet into a musical instrument. I brought it to him to fix it so I could play it. He saw the instrument, and I guess he was flabbergasted that I had accomplished so much with so little, that I must be incredibly motivated, and he offered me a job. "All I can give you is minimum wage," he said.

In the moment he considered Gurian's offer, Cumpiano knew that "buying out of the standard way" was no guarantee of success. If the counterculture gave him permission to "do his own thing," it also left him on his own to figure out what that thing was and how to make it happen. At that point, Gurian was preparing to move from his Grand Street location at the edge of New York's garment district to Hinsdale, New Hampshire, where a state development grant offered him incentives. Not everyone in the shop was willing to leave the city, however, and Cumpiano understood that accepting this job would mean relocating to a "rural ghetto." Reflecting on his decision over thirty years later, he says that it brought his "identity crisis" to an end:

My experience is that I literally was *excluded* out of traditional ways of work. I found my poem in guitar making. I blew out of—it was quite traumatic—this disillusionment I had. My identity crisis was resolved; it was healed through guitar making. I knew who I was; my identity became that: a guitar maker. Of course, at times in my life I wondered if that wasn't kind of a childish thing. But no, that was it. I've had relatives tell me that I'd never left the sandbox, you know? That "you should be thinking of your family," and I went through that. Then there's the cultural thing. The fact that I've grown to this [economic] level and not another level is cultural. My cultural values, above anything else, are humility and moderation. It's not the North American expansive kind of thing. To me it was, you don't call attention to yourself; your value is seen through your works. Those are the values I was inculcated with.

A powerful sense of being "excluded" from mainstream employment ripples through the recollections of guitar makers who made choices like Cumpiano's. Describing an experience of not fitting in—of being misfits—they make it clear that they did not openly rebel against "traditional ways of work." Rather, their alienation involved a "traumatic" process of realizing that their values were not the norm. The admonishment to grow up and "leave the sandbox" rang in the ears of many when they hit milestone birthdays with few accoutrements of adulthood.

"It took me thirty years to finally have some semblance of [financial] security," Cumpiano attests. "The fact that I can now buy a car or have my own home, all these middle-class things, it took me about twenty or thirty years to get to that point, because lutherie is not a money-making proposition. It is a way of losing money, and having a good time while you're doing it." When he thinks about a model for his lifestyle, Cumpiano "takes his hat off" to Manuel Velázquez, a classical guitar maker who came to New York City from Puerto Rico in 1946. In Velázquez he sees "a landsman who didn't put on airs," someone who loved "the search for knowledge" and a "workingman who never acknowledged his greatness." The "poem" that Cumpiano found in guitar making is a Whitmanesque "song of the self" in which the "expansive" values of capitalist enterprise are rejected in favor of "humility and moderation."[35]

Moderation, it would appear, was not a word in the young Michael Gurian's vocabulary. Reaching for the stars was literally emblazoned on the maker's labels in all of his instruments, which read: "Gurian Workshops, Earth, Third Planet from the Sun." When demand for his steel-string guitars rose rapidly in the early 1970s, he stepped up production by hiring shop assistants who accepted low wages in exchange for on-the-job instruction. Many of these employees went on to become independent luthiers themselves—among them shop foreman Michael Millard, who was hired in 1971.[36] As a small shop, Grand Street hummed with the camaraderie and mischievous humor of eight to ten workers. But Gurian's decision to relocate and expand his operation in Hinsdale precipitated a sharp decline in morale.

In the new space, a pre–Civil War factory on the Ashuelot River, the workforce more than doubled in size as locals and high school students were hired to meet new production quotas. "It was like a cattle drive and I was the trail boss," Millard recalls; "I was the ramrod on the job." Workstations were arranged "so that no one could even see another human being," he says, and the overriding "message was 'Shut up, go to work.'" Discontent with working conditions came to a head in March 1974. Attempting to quell the unrest, Gurian held an early-morning meeting and laid down the law, retracting rights and privileges that had previously been enjoyed. Millard and Cumpiano took one look at each other and quit on the spot.

Working for Gurian was an invaluable experience, both men agree, and they remain grateful to him for launching their careers. But their departure that day dramatized their refusal to let their work be valued solely in terms of productivity. Aligning themselves with the plight of craftspeople since the dawn of industrialization, they chose artisanal independence over the servitude of waged labor.[37] Although they pursued different business models—Millard establishing a small shop and Cumpiano a solo career—they shared the same elusive goal: to earn a modest living without sacrificing the creative freedom that had drawn them to the craft. The choice they confronted was not simply whether to work for themselves or for someone else. Rather, as every luthier eventually must, they had to decide whether to build guitars as artisans or as industrial manufacturers. Enterprising builders like Gurian took the latter route, gearing up to compete with factories in North America and elsewhere. Others, like Millard and Cumpiano, opted for the former, pinning their hopes on the alternative market that had begun to form around artisanal guitars.

In the mid-1970s the market for handmade instruments was driven by supply, not demand. When guitarists became dissatisfied with factory instruments, they tended to buy vintage guitars. The quality of handcrafted instruments was uneven at best, and most builders found it hard to sell guitars beyond their circle of family and friends. As a hobby, however, guitar making had captured the imagination of a growing band of artists and musicians, hippies and hardhats, propeller heads and college dropouts. Very few of them, as Cumpiano knew all too well, had access to the information they needed. After leaving Gurian Guitars, he began writing the book he is known for, *Guitarmaking: Tradition and Technology*. It was, I learn, a Sisyphean task.

A leading craft-oriented press offered Cumpiano and Jonathan Natelson, another former Gurian employee, a contract to publish a guide to building steel-string and classical guitars. In the days before personal computers, producing a manuscript illustrated with photographs and line drawings was no small feat. After proofreading their galleys, the authors learned that the press had been sold to publishing giant Simon and Schuster, placing the fate of their book in limbo. Fortunately, their rights were contractually protected in such an event, but retrieving the galleys and film was another matter. When the legal scuffle ended in 1987, they scraped together the resources to self-publish their book. In the mid-1990s, a national press bought their rights and put out a paperback version that remains the primary instruction manual in the field.[38]

A success story? Not to hear Cumpiano tell it. "I had no sense what the consequences would be of deciding to do this book," he tells me. "There's a drop of blood on every page." Motivated to help "all the poor souls out there who were drowning under this need for good guitar-making information," he discovered that his financial situation went from bad to worse:

> I had become a well-known luthier that didn't have a lot of work to do because my prominence was among *other* luthiers. The book gave me an undeserved prominence in the field — undeserved in the sense that I wasn't an economically viable luthier. But I had become a viable lutherie information dispenser with a shop and an ongoing business. My business was very shaky at that time — it was *wounded* by the writing of the book. I was out of the craft for the whole year it took to write the book. I wasn't working and making as many guitars as I could be making or wished I could be making. At that time what was keeping me together [financially] was my repair work.

Not only was the publishers' advance a paltry sum compared to the expense of producing the manuscript, but "profit" came in the form of "prominence in the field" rather than royalties. Of the two authors, only Cumpiano continued to build guitars after the book was finished. So it was he who took on the role of "information dispenser" at lutherie conventions and in the public domain. That this distinction was a mixed blessing highlights a basic characteristic of artisanal knowledge: as embodied know-how, its market value is tied to the craft object.

With the exception of pedagogical situations in which guitar makers are paid directly for instruction, it is virtually impossible to put a price tag on knowledge that is separated from the practice and product of their craft. Information may be "free," as network entrepreneurs were fond of saying, but unless its exchange resulted in reciprocal information of equivalent value, those who volunteered it gained only prestige.

Cumpiano's experience with commercial publishing offers a cautionary tale about the risks of "disembodied knowledge" for artisans.[39] Yet demand for precisely this kind of information rose as North America shifted away from basic manufacturing toward service industries and high-tech data processing in the 1980s. A growing number of builders began to adapt artisanal know-how to assembly line production, and major manufacturers looked to the lutherie movement for fresh ideas. As if presaging the conflict to come, the decade's coda came in 1979, when a boiler explosion set fire to Michael Gurian's factory and sawmill. Lost in the conflagration were all of the company's records, its entire inventory of guitars and wood, and much of its machinery. Gurian tried to start over, but debt and a moribund economy forced him out of business in 1980. Hard times were in store for guitar makers of all sizes, and a stance of disinterest in market competition became increasingly difficult to sustain.

CRAFT ETHIC

The pinball machine in the back room at Gryphon Stringed Instruments in Palo Alto, California, saw a lot of action as sales of stringed instruments spiraled downward in the back-to-back recessions of the early 1980s. "There would be days when the phone didn't ring," says co-owner Frank Ford.[40] Along with his business partner Richard Johnston, Ford witnessed the industry-wide depression from the vantage point of a bellwether retail and repair shop. "During that period we saw our cohort [of guitar makers] shrink drastically," Ford says. "And an equal number of stores, wholesalers, and all of the factories that were in corporate hands were sold or changed hands during that bloodletting."

The sales figures at C. F. Martin said it all. In the mid-1960s, the company produced over 10,000 acoustic guitars a year, and that number climbed to a peak of 22,637 in 1971, before sliding to a low of 3,133 in 1982.[41] As bad as things were at Martin, being in nonfamilial "corporate hands" made the situation at the larger Gibson Guitar Company much worse.[42] Norlin Industries—a transnational conglomerate that owned cement, railroad, flower, and beer companies in Ecuador—had acquired Gibson when it bought the Chicago Musical Instrument Company in 1969. A year later, Norlin dodged a restive union at Gibson's flagship plant in Kalamazoo, Michigan, by moving acoustic guitar production to a new factory in Nashville, Tennessee—a "right to work" state.[43] Over the next decade, Norlin systematically hollowed out and sold off the companies that had once constituted Chicago Musical Instrument's empire. Norlin finally closed the Kalamazoo plant in 1984 and offered up Gibson to the highest bidder in 1986.[44] That the future of America's second-oldest guitar maker could hang by so slender a thread dramatized the unthinkable: acoustic music was not immortal.

Ford attributes the "bloodletting" in the guitar industry to demographics and changing consumer tastes. With mordant humor, he describes the forces that conspired to end the folk revival, if not the world, as his generation knew it:

> The folk "scare" was waning. We had the emergence of the four horsemen of the apocalypse, I suppose. We had the emergence of disco—ugh! We had a national recession. We had the demographic bulge, people my age turning to other pursuits like having families. And we had a total gutting of the music programs in all the schools under the Reagan administration. So music just *ate it* during that period. Richard [Johnston] made an observation about ten years ago. He said, "The irony of this business is that we started as kids making and selling guitars to guys our age; now we're geezers and we're still making and selling guitars to guys our age." There's no hope!

Baby boomers who think of acoustic music as a sacrosanct part of their lives can be excused for seeing omens of the "apocalypse" in the 1980s. Whether it was the ascendance of glam metal and shred guitar solos or the theatricality of MTV—Madonna's 1984 music video of "Like a Virgin" in full bridal regalia comes to mind—evidence was mounting that folk music and its particular brand of authenticity were "waning."[45] As it happened, the "geezers" would be back with a vengeance once their children were grown, discretionary income was their own, and MTV unplugged. But the disco era left little doubt that the fate of the acoustic guitar was largely in their hands. Ford and Johnston put their faith in this belief when, in 1985, their accountant told them they were facing bankruptcy. Although both were "absolutely phobic about debt," Ford explains, they had been compelled to take risks in order to keep their business afloat:

> We were starting to use credit to buy our instruments, not paying the bills immediately, not taking CODs but taking the thirty-, sixty-, ninety-day payment plans, going in arrears, borrowing, getting a credit plan from the bank, and those kinds of things. So during the period of decline, we were converting our assets into debt. Our accountant came to us and said, "Here's the deal: you're two-thirds out of business. You got about a third left of what you started with, and it's disappearing. If you don't sell what you have now and get out, you won't have anything." Richard and I—neither of us has been particularly good at proactive planning. So what did we say? "We don't have anyplace to go; we'll just stay; thanks for the advice." He said, "You guys are crazy!" We said, "You know that this is a cyclical business. We know it's going to come back." He says, "Yeah, so what? You'll be out on the street when it comes back." We said, "Well, you're telling us to go out on the street *now!* Why go out without a fight?"

Had Gryphon been founded solely for the purpose of maximizing a financial investment, the accountant's warning might have prompted a different reaction. But the partnership that Johnston and Ford created in 1969 was the idealistic venture of two college graduates who wanted to share their passion for acoustic music with a wider community. Both came of age at the height of the folk boom—Ford graduated from the University of California in Santa Barbara in 1966 and Johnston from the University of California in Berkeley in 1969. Both opposed the war in Vietnam, and both had been exempted from military service—Johnston as a conscientious objector and Ford for medical reasons. Introduced by a mutual friend who met Johnston playing ragtime guitar on the steps of Sproul Hall, they found in each other fellow travelers on the roads leading to the artisanal guitar. Johnston earned money for college by buying and selling vintage guitars, while

Ford built instruments and did inlay and repair work for friends. "We both were so stunned by what the other knew," Ford recalls, "we just couldn't stop talking."

From the outset, Gryphon was structured as a communal endeavor. Deciding that a company called "Ford & Johnston" sounded hopelessly square, they named their enterprise after the mythical bird that appears on banjos made at the turn of the twentieth century. "We wanted a beast that we could do as a pearl inlay that would involve some engraving and look cool," Ford says, "old timey, but timeless." To avoid conflict over money, the two agreed to buy, build, and repair guitars on their own initiative but pool their proceeds in a "common pot." Power tools used individually were purchased out of their own pockets as needed, but the cost of materials and supplies was shared equally. "Neither of us is really motivated by money," Ford explains. "I mean, if you're motivated by money, you're not building guitars for a living, typically."

In lieu of monetary incentive, however, there was intrinsic satisfaction and cultural prestige: "It was just 'This is *fun*! I love making stuff out of wood. Wouldn't it be great? I could be a cool dude that makes guitars!'" In Ford's case, lutherie was a natural extension of the craft ethic he had always lived by:

> I've never lived in the environment of an apartment or a house that didn't have some kind of a workshop. Even when I was a dormie, the first thing I did when I moved into the dorms is I mounted a machinist's vise on my desk, and I had a drawer full of tools. That's just the way I lived. My dad always used to say, "If a man can put it together, I can take it apart and fix it." That was just the mindset I was started with. Simple as that. If somebody could put it together, I could take it apart and fix it. I can get a little more cynical about it. I can say if a factory full of high school dropouts can make these damn things, I can do just as good. So there was never a second in my mind where I felt that [making guitars] wasn't a logical thing that people could do. Could I do it? Well, I don't know. I'd have to try to find out.

Ford built his first guitar in college, taking his Martin D-28 as a model. Figuring out the sizes and positions of the braces was easy enough. All it took was putting a light bulb inside, a piece of tracing paper on top, and darkening the room. Yet the worldview that this can-do spirit instantiates is more than just a "cynical" attitude about the skill required of workers on an assembly line. An ethical proposition informs Ford's intervention in the world of things. Repairing a guitar, or re-creating one by hand, also recuperates the dignity of the labor that made it by honoring the vitality of the instrument itself. This sensibility is especially pronounced in luthiers' veneration of instruments made during the golden era.

Hanging out with Johnston at Jon Lundberg's guitar shop in Berkeley, Ford gained firsthand knowledge of the difference between guitars made before and after World War II. "The climate for vintage guitars was such that Jon had to *beg* people to fix up their prewar Martins," he remembers, "rather than throw them away and buy a new one." Lundberg was renowned for "revoicing" postwar factory guitars by plunging his hand into the sound hole and shaving bulky braces down to size. Along with others of their generation, Ford and Johnston shared the sense that corporate manufacturers had turned their back on the craft tradition that made American guitars, mandolins, and banjos the best in the world.[46] Fired up by a do-it-yourself confidence, they embarked on a mission to restore the steel-string guitar to its former glory. "We thought we could make something that was a little better," Ford explains, "that was more like the old ones that [Martin and Gibson] had forgotten, and we were naive enough to think we could do it more cheaply too."

Only in hindsight would they realize that they had jumped into guitar making just as the market for acoustic instruments became extremely volatile.[47] During their early years, as Ford tells it, they were "struggling as builders; everyone else was struggling as a builder, and many quit." By 1973, Ford and Johnston had orders that would keep them going for the next year and a half. But when they "tried a little experiment" and hypothetically doubled the amount they would charge for their work, their anticipated income still failed to cover expenses. "We were both living, in effect, on the good graces of our spouses, who had regular jobs," Ford admits. Not willing to abandon their dream entirely, they decided to stop building guitars and turned to selling and repairing them instead. "Neither Richard nor I had a message to deliver or an artistic vision," he observes. "We really were just casting about for a good way to make a living that would be rewarding and fun."

Reinventing Gryphon as a store and repair shop allowed Johnston and Ford to focus their energies on locating and resuscitating golden-era instruments, which were in increasingly high demand. Nashville dealer George Gruhn has identified this trend as the "vintage backlash" of the 1970s. He highlights the prominent role that Crosby, Stills, Nash, and Young played in establishing the market for prewar acoustic guitars by appearing with them on stage and album covers and driving up prices with their own acquisitions.[48] Preoccupied with mergers and acquisitions rather than day-to-day quality control, corporate executives running the major guitar companies were seemingly unaware of the competition that their older models posed to the sale of new ones. As a result, Gruhn argues, they allowed the vintage market to flourish and ceded valuable market share to individual builders and start-up companies:

> Martin, Gibson, and Fender dominated the market so thoroughly that they were able, for quite a few years, to produce absolute crap without it noticeably hurting their bottom line. But then it started to create a demand where the little guys got into [lutherie]. These little guys rapidly gained a reputation for being *better* than the big boys, and the Pandora's box was opened, and you could not stifle what had been opened up. Had these companies responded up front to public demand, many of these little guys would never have gotten into business. So they created their own competition by being oblivious to public demand and totally unresponsive.[49]

In a novel twist on the lutherie movement's origin story, Gruhn calls attention to the market conditions that created an opening for artisanal builders. Instead of celebrating information sharing among hippies, he underscores the paralysis of corporate behemoths that could not respond to consumer demand. Although Gruhn does not specify who unleashed the evils in "Pandora's box," he casts the battle for consumers' souls in a mythic register.[50] While hand builders may wish to identify with Pandora's Eve-like quest for knowledge, Gruhn points to the chaotic, world-changing effects of their market intervention. The craft ethic that drove artisan guitar makers to challenge the monopoly power of industrial giants may have sprung from a sentimental orientation toward work, but it is fueled by more than prelapsarian innocence.

Ren Ferguson started playing guitar as a teenager in 1960. Around the same time, his brother got a hankering for a banjo, and the two visited McCabe's Guitar Shop, "a little beatnik store" in Santa Monica, California.[51] Mesmerized by the instruments they saw but discouraged by the poor quality of what they could afford, Ferguson decided to build one.

> FERGUSON: I bought some hardwood for a banjo. My brother wanted a bluegrass banjo, and I thought I could build him a better banjo in wood shop. I attempted to do that, and failed, repeatedly.
>
> DUDLEY: Where did the inspiration to build an instrument come from?
>
> FERGUSON [with surprise at the question]: Haven't you ever held one? Don't you want to do that? I mean, some people have to—it's not like you want to. You can't wait. And then somebody hands you an F-5 [Gibson mandolin], and then you're really ruined for the rest of your life! I always made stuff. I whittled and carved and painted and sculpted. My mom was an artist. And so I just grew up not knowing that there were things people couldn't do. I thought you could do anything. And she was always like "Oh, go ahead, honey, try." And so I did, and I was able to do enough to keep my interest up.

Impelled by a craft ethic that places a desired object imaginatively within reach, Ferguson was undeterred by his shop class "failures." While still in high school, he got a job at Westchester Music, a dealership located near the Los Angeles airport. Not only was he able to study the new instruments the store carried, but he had an opportunity to inspect and buy any traumatized guitar that came through the door:

> Everything [in the store] was current back then; there was nothing vintage. But there were lots of used guitars being damaged by the airport. The airport would send people to us to get a letter saying the guitar was X amount damaged. I think that they cut them a check right then, because many people would come back with money to buy a replacement guitar. We didn't take trade-ins, so I got to buy them. Before the people left, I said, "Well, I'll buy that guitar."

As a licensed dealer and service center for major manufacturers, the store could order replacement parts directly from the factory and other suppliers. Through these industry connections, Ferguson could procure items in company catalogs that were not available to the general public. Between old parts from the guitars he salvaged and the new parts he ordered, he soon realized that he could reconstruct and resell instruments for a tidy profit. "I was just hustling guitars like crazy," he recalls.

After high school, Ferguson joined the Navy Reserves. As luck would have it, he was stationed in Japan aboard a repair ship that had a foundry and pattern shop. In addition to gaining experience forging industrial parts and machinery, he had access to a workspace where he made banjos to sell to other sailors in his spare time. In 1969, fresh from his tour of duty, Ferguson returned to Los Angeles and, together with a friend, started a lutherie shop of his own. In an early business decision, he bought a portion of the newly defunct Kay Musical Instrument Company.[52] For a relatively small sum, he was able to get a treasure trove of guitar-making tools, fixtures, and forms as well as an assortment of unfinished guitars, which he sold as ready-to-make kits.

But the bread and butter of his operation, Ferguson quickly discovered, came from replicating the necks used on Gibson five-string banjos from the 1920s and 1930s. Popularized in the 1960s by bluegrass sensation Earl Scruggs, these golden era Mastertones were as sought after by banjo enthusiasts as vintage guitars were by discerning guitarists. Instead of buying a new Gibson banjo, which was deemed to be of poorer quality, players in the know sought out prewar banjo "conversions." "I would buy [prewar four-string] tenor banjos for $250 or $450," Ferguson explains, "and I'd put a five-string neck on it and I'd get $750 or $2,500. I could make real money refabricating a neck; it was big business."

Doing as many as three or four conversions a week, often at the request of customers who brought in their own tenor pots, he took care to put his name on the banjo block to indicate that the original instrument had been modified. Nonetheless, in 1973, Gibson brought a cease-and-desist order against him, barring him from inlaying the Gibson name on his reproduction necks. To this day, Ferguson believes he did nothing wrong. "I was selling the banjo and claiming that it was a Gibson," he says, "and in fact, it *was* a Gibson. But I was twenty-five years old; I was freaked out." From then on, he put his own name on the headstock and replaced the Mastertone "flying eagle" or "squashed frog" inlay with a design of his own. Almost immediately his business suffered. "That probably knocked sales down by about two-thirds," he estimates, "because people playing in a bluegrass band want it to say *Gibson*. That's part of the branding that is important; it's part of the uniform."

Hoping to regain his footing in a formidable market, Ferguson hired a dozen workers and began making acoustic and electric guitars in a small factory in Venice Beach. After a hunting accident and illness set him back again, he augmented his income by working late into the night building replicas of Pennsylvania muzzle-loading rifles. Admiring these guns as tools that enabled America's "westward expansion," he felt a deep affinity with their makers:

> They are absolutely the epitome of craftsmanship. They're elegant. Not only were they protection and a way of defending our country or providing food for the table, they had been taken in their crudest form to the level of art that could only be appreciated by somebody who did that kind of work. They don't need to be inlaid. They don't need to be engraved. They don't need to have raised carving. They don't need to have all this stuff, and yet they do. And that comes from the need of the craftsman to sign his work, to embellish. The guy that built the gun put every bit of competence in the craft that he had in it, whether it was forging a barrel or fitting the stock, manufacturing the lock parts, tuning the thing so it operated properly, or finishing it, carving, and engraving. I did the same thing with an awful lot of guitars and banjos over my life.

Like the inlay on vintage banjos, the "embellishment" of muzzle-loaders has little to do with their function as utilitarian objects. Rather, as Ferguson sees it, decorative art is the artisan's "signature"—a sign of "competence in the craft" that can be recognized by anyone, not only those who play the instrument or fire the gun. Embedded in this sentiment is a political critique of the idea that a manufacturer's proprietary claim should deter the artisan who restores or replicates a period piece.

At issue is the moral question of who *owns* the knowledge necessary to make the cultural object: the corporation that owns the brand or the artisan who possesses the skill to honor the object's material integrity. For Ferguson, the answer is clear. Identifying with a craft tradition he dates to medieval Europe, he argues that artisans, past and present, share a "spark" or will to mastery:

> In a nutshell, there is the spark that drives not just me, but all of us [artisans]. Had this been a thousand years ago, we would have all worked for the king or a knight or somebody. We would have been in some feudal state. They'd have picked us out and we'd have worked in the castle making armor. We would have been those artisans that had to do it. And we would have been cherry-picked at that point and maybe would have had to do it for them whether we wanted to or not. Now we have the privilege of choice. But still, there's that inner kind of fire in your belly that *you can't wait*. I can't wait to finish an instrument so I can start another one. I mean, I've already decided that I'm going to live with what imperfections are here and go on.

What unites artisans across time, Ferguson asserts, is the inner drive, the "fire in the belly," that motivates them to make things and make them well, regardless of the political economy within which they labor. In his view, artisanship is the desire to do quality work "for its own sake" on the part of individuals who are "cherry-picked" by God or royalty for their innate talent.[53] This vision of artisanal independence is wholly compatible with the entrepreneurial spirit endorsed by free-market capitalism. All that differentiates artisans today from their preindustrial forebears, Ferguson suggests, is the "privilege of choice," which allows them to decide whether to work for themselves or for an employer. From this vantage point, the Guild of American Luthiers seemed like child's play — "I thought, I don't need no stinking badge." But unrelenting work — a year of "working around the clock" and "abusing his body" with "sex, drugs, and alcohol" — finally took its toll. "I went crazy," Ferguson admits; "there was too much external influence in my body." Over Christmas 1975, he closed his shop, left his wife and child, and took up the peripatetic life of a trapper in the Rocky Mountains.

INFORMATION SHARING

On trips through Nazareth, Pennsylvania, in the early 1970s, Dick Boak drove to the C. F. Martin factory to scour the Dumpster for discarded wood. He used the scraps in his own instruments and artwork and in the high school art classes he taught in New Jersey. Brimming with creative talent, Boak embraced the counterculture wholeheartedly, reveling in its emphasis on self-expression, authentic experience, and existential philosophy.[54] For a major art project at Gettysburg College, he staged a tribute to "The Hunger Artist," the bleak short story by Franz Kafka that decries the poverty and alienation of the artist.

Assuming the role of Kafka's circus performer—who starves to death for lack of an audience and palatable food—Boak set up a cage near the entrance to the campus dining hall and occupied it for the better part of three days. Of his time in that "living sculpture," he says, those days "were among the most liberating days of my life."[55] He soon dropped out of college and went to California, where he built geodesic domes and lived in communes. "I was a huge fan of Buckminster Fuller," he explains, "a huge fan of M. C. Escher. Almost everything that I was interested in, in some way, can be traced back to the *Whole Earth Catalog* and the hippie back-to-earth type of experience."[56]

One day in 1976, while diving in Martin's Dumpster, Boak was greeted by the shop foreman, who wondered what he did with the wood he gathered. Boak showed him one of his guitars and was invited into the machine room, where he met C. F. Martin III. Impressed with Boak's work, Martin suggested that he apply for a job. As it happened, the company was looking for someone with his qualifications—drafting skills, woodworking experience, and familiarity with musical instruments—and Boak got the job. His first assignment was to draw the parts of every model of instrument that Martin manufactured, a staggering task involving "tens of thousands of pieces, all different sizes and shapes."

Most of this information appeared as numerical measurements in foremen's notebooks, but uniform technical drawings would allow Martin to expand its line of low-cost Sigma guitars in Japan and offer insurance against fire and the loss of vital information. Boak was fascinated by the project and his access to proprietary information. "I was really interested in what made Martin guitars so good," he recalls. "Every dimension seemed to be critical and secret. You'd be hard pressed to find any guitar maker that would be willing to share any of that information."

Labor relations were unraveling when Boak joined the company, and in 1978 its unionized employees declared a strike. In the run-up to that event, Boak was fired for insubordination after he was ordered to alter one of his drawings and he reported his concerns to his boss's superior. During this period of unemployment, he resumed his career as an artist and drew the "hippie art" rendering of a D-28 that now hangs in the Martin museum. Boak was rehired when his dispute came to the attention of Frank Herbert Martin and his son Chris, who is a few years younger than Boak. The Martins recognized his loyalty and encouraged him to develop an overview of the company's operations, which included a stint on the factory floor when Boak crossed the picket line to work "as a scab during the strike."

While Frank Martin managed his diverse corporate holdings and disgruntled workforce, his son keyed into current trends in the consumer market—namely, the clamor for vintage models and the rise of the lutherie movement. With Chris Martin's blessing, Boak became an active member of the Guild of American Luthiers. "Chris thought it was valuable to Martin to have me be involved with all of the guitar makers," he explains. "The gist of it was to share information."

But information sharing, as luthiers were discovering, was not always a two-way street. Industrial manufacturers and artisans were not in the same boat with regard to what they could share or what they could do with the information they received. Although a number of individual makers and small shops welcomed corporate builders into the guild, others remained wary of their motives. The place of major guitar factories in the movement became a pressing issue in 1980, when the guild prepared to hold its convention at the Palace of the Arts in San Francisco. Confronted with applications from large manufacturers in the United States and Asia that wished to display their instruments as "luthiers" entitled to free tables, the guild decided to limit the exhibition to shops of no more than two makers.

Almost immediately, a line of skirmish formed that resulted in a protracted struggle for leadership of the organization.[57] In 1982 Boak was elected vice president of the guild's board of directors, and in 1986 he

FIGURE 1.3. Dick Boak's pointillist drawing of a Martin D-28, 1997. The print he gave to C. F. Martin III now hangs in the Martin Company museum.

ascended to president when the incumbent resigned, fed up with the infighting. At issue, in practical terms, was who had the authority to make decisions on behalf of the guild—the elected board members or the salaried staff. Tim Olsen, his wife Debra Olsen, and his sister-in-law Bon Henderson had been serving in the capacity of "staff" since the guild's inception. Prior to the 1980s, they had been largely free to run the organization as they saw fit with the advice and consent of the board. But matters came to a head in the fall of 1986, when the Olsens and Henderson were elected to the board along with Boak. The previous board promptly moved to invalidate the election and extend its own term indefinitely.[58] In the ensuing melee, a lawsuit was filed and the two sides met in court.

In the legal settlement reached in 1987, Olsen and his supporters were vindicated in their reading of the law. The principles and personalities at the core of the conflict, however, were irreconcilable. Boak and a dissident band of makers broke with the guild to start a new organization on the East Coast—the Association of Stringed Instrument Artisans, usually referred to, with some irony, as ASIA. Although the parties to the lawsuit refrained from discussing details of the case with me, the controversy's flavor is evident in public statements as well as in ASIA's founding charter. Bruce Ross, then co-owner of the Santa Cruz Guitar Company, captured the essence of the dispute in a 1986 letter to the editor of *Frets* magazine:

> Underlying the current power struggle between the board of directors and the staff is the realization by the board that the GAL must change and grow. Many members feel the Guild could be of more value, not only to its members but to the instrument-buying public as well. . . . For example, the GAL should: (1) align itself with, and encourage input from, the major instrument manufacturing concerns in the country—Martin, Guild, Ovation, and Gibson, to name but a few. These companies have contributed significantly to the body of knowledge concerning the art and craft of lutherie, and they should be encouraged to become involved with the GAL. (2) Provide health insurance at reasonable group rates. (3) Establish a materials-buying collective to lower costs on items purchased in bulk. (4) Create standards and practices guidelines for luthiers.[59]

With the exception of a purchasing collective, the demands Ross enumerated became central to ASIA's mission statement.[60] When the association applied for tax-exempt status in 1988, its board—over which Dick Boak presided as president and editor in chief—rejected the guild's educational model and registered as a nonprofit "trade organization."[61] The promotion of economic interests, not academic or cultural prestige, was ASIA's mandate—a model, as it happened, that served to enshrine the activities of a business league, not a labor union. Despite efforts to create a certification program and coordinate group access to health insurance, initiatives that aimed to improve the economic status of builders through collective action did not pan out.[62]

The Association of Stringed Instrument Artisans has functioned largely as a network forum for business-oriented entrepreneurs interested in technological innovation and enhancing their competitive edge. Thus, it was ASIA, not the guild, that invited guitar maker Bob Taylor to deliver a talk on the uses of computer numerical control (CNC) technology at its second symposium in 1991. As Taylor remembers the event two decades later:

> That talk may have been the first glimpse for many guitar makers into their future. They nearly all use the advantages of CNC now, whether directly or indirectly. Not everyone, mind you, but most. There are still some luthiers who do this totally by hand, have a following, and get the money required to pay for that when they sell their guitars. But most need modern tools to live in a modern world. These tools equalize their ability to produce at a profit in a way that is consistent with how their customers make their money. It's not fair for an attorney to talk on the phone for three hours and earn enough money to buy three weeks of a luthier's time. I feel the guitar maker should take steps to equalize that, and at the same time explode their design opportunities into worlds unknown to them before.[63]

Taylor's full-throated advocacy for the use of industrial production techniques in lutherie was exactly the message that ASIA's founders wanted to hear and disseminate. The presence of manufacturers' representatives as charter members, on the board, and at large, along with a rising contingent of small companies, material suppliers, and instrument dealers, assured a receptive audience for presentations that defended the use of "modern tools in a modern world." Setting themselves apart from builders characterized as needing a cultlike "following" to practice lutherie the old-fashioned way, members of this new organization, more often than not, shared Taylor's umbrage at the wage differential that usually exists between clients and independent makers. His call to venture forth into "worlds unknown"—through robotic technologies and the pursuit of unapologetic profits—was, for many, a seductive rallying cry.

———

At a mountain man reenactment of a fur trade rendezvous, Ren Ferguson got into a heated argument about a feather. His interlocutor, similarly clad in buckskin and a raccoon hat, had underestimated Ferguson's knowledge of western Americana. As the two parsed the finer distinctions of primary and secondary feathers in Native American decorative arts, they grew to admire each other's moxie. Still footloose and searching for direction in life, Ferguson moved to the town in Montana where his new friend lived and met the woman who became his second wife. Marrying again came with a conversion experience. "I got saved," he says matter-of-factly, "and started going to church, and someone in town put two and two together." Recognized by a guitar buff who knew Ferguson's reputation in the bluegrass world, he was soon drawn into playing guitar during worship service and traveling with the church band.

Not long thereafter, Steve Carlson, owner of Flatiron Mandolin in Belgrade, Montana, called him up and offered him a job. Ferguson had given little thought to restarting a career in lutherie. In addition to his church activities, he now had a gun shop business and a full-time job stocking firearms at a local rifle store. But in May 1985, Carlson offered him a salary he couldn't refuse. By June, he was working at Flatiron, doing the rough carving, basic tuning, binding, and finishing of its F-style mandolins. Soon the small factory was producing more instruments than it could sell.

Confident of the quality of Flatiron mandolins, Carlson approached Gibson management at the 1986 National Association of Music Merchants (NAMM) show and proposed making mandolins for Gibson as an original equipment manufacturer. Ever since Norlin had gone into a tailspin, the production and reputation of Gibson's mandolins had declined apace. Unbeknownst to Carlson, Henry Juszkiewicz and two of his classmates from Harvard Business School had just purchased Gibson in January 1986.[64] When Carlson made the mistake of suggesting to Gibson's new owner that his company was making terrible mandolins, Juszkiewicz threatened to sue him for copyright infringement.

Forced to discontinue the production of mandolins, Carlson and Ferguson brought out a line of banjos and explored the possibility of buying Mossman Guitars, a small guitar factory in Winfield, Kansas, that had fallen on a run of bad luck.[65] Meanwhile, Juszkiewicz was having his ear bent by Stan Jay, proprietor of Mandolin Brothers in Staten Island, New York. With the demise of Gibson's acoustic division under Norlin, Flatiron mandolins had become a mainstay at Jay's store, with few alternatives to take their place. Putting Flatiron out of business was in no one's interest, Jay argued. Why not just buy it?[66] A year later, under Juszkiewicz's leadership, Gibson tendered Flatiron an offer that Carlson accepted. Relishing this turn of events, Ferguson exults in the feeling that a historical wrong was set right:

> In the mid-1980s, Gibson wasn't producing mandolins in any volume. The factory in Kalamazoo was closed, and the only facility left was the one in Nashville. Thank God Henry [Juszkiewicz] bought the company! Because as difficult as things have been over the last twenty years—growing pains and everything—somebody *rescued* it, and we got a chance to go back and redo some of the cool stuff that's been done in our heritage. When Steve decided to sell [his business], I was more than happy to stay on as an employee. I was already the Gibson builder. Everything I was doing [at Flatiron] was to bring our mandolins more in line with [Lloyd] Loar's and stuff back then.

Invoking the name of Lloyd Loar—the luthier credited with making Gibson mandolins from 1919 to 1924 among the most prized instruments in the world—Ferguson acknowledges his role in the perpetuation of a craft tradition that narrowly escaped an ignominious end. But the "rescue" he praises is of a decidedly corporate kind. Without the Gibson brand and the legal right to reproduce instruments bearing its name and likeness, the artisanal labor required to "go back and redo" what the company had done in the past was patently illegal. In an ironic twist, however, it was precisely this illegitimate know-how, preserved in an artisanal repertoire, that enabled the company to reissue its coveted golden-era models.

Juszkiewicz's initial strategy for reviving Gibson placed priority on the company's top-selling electric guitar, the Les Paul, and not on its acoustic division, most of which was in storage containers behind the Nashville plant. In 1988, buoyed by the success of the Flatiron operation, Juszkiewicz turned his attention to Gibson's acoustic guitars and broke ground for a new factory dedicated to their production in Bozeman, Montana. Ferguson was charged with getting the plant up and running—a task that was, it turned out, nothing short of Herculean. When the old machinery was shipped to Bozeman, his heart sank.

"We sorted everything out that was left and realized that we had nothing," Ferguson recalls. "There *was no* guitar factory. Gibson didn't have one to begin with. That's why they weren't making acoustic guitars in Nashville." Most of the tooling the factory needed would have to be made from scratch. Undaunted, he bought two truckloads of used machinery for making tennis rackets from the Head company, melted down the aluminum parts, and created side-bending molds for each of Gibson's classic models. Aware that manufacturers were replacing outmoded machinery with computerized cutting and milling technology, he tapped into the network of industrial guitar makers to get up to speed on the use of CNC:

> The first ten years of that period was a very concerted cooperation of all large manufacturers, whether it be Dana Bourgeois or Bill Collings or Santa Cruz or Larrivée or Gibson or Taylor or Martin. We worked in close cooperation to improve the building of guitars. We learned a lot. We don't have secrets. There's nobody I know that—I mean, he may not go out of his way to teach you, but he's not going to keep something from you. For instance, if you need to know how Bob Taylor builds a neck, he'll send you the program off his Fadal [CNC machine]. He knows you're not going to make a Taylor neck. But he doesn't mind sharing his technology and helping you learn how to do a job better.

Like the belief that there are no "secrets" in lutherie, the idea that "cooperation" arises out of a spontaneous desire to "improve the building of guitars" has surprisingly few naysayers—at least not ones who care to proclaim apostasy within earshot of an anthropologist. Yet there is good reason to wonder whether information really can be shared, and shared equally, by everyone in the lutherie community. To the extent that industrial manufacturers and small companies cooperated in the process of adapting CNC technology to guitar making, they shared the goal of reducing the human labor involved in the cutting and shaping of wooden parts. By its nature, however, this information had value for, and reinforced social bonds among, only the subset of makers who had the inclination, need, and resources to put it to use.

Within their lifetime, luthiers have witnessed a shift from a period of information scarcity that placed a premium on collective reciprocity to one of information abundance that supports a crowded field of hobbyists, artisans, boutique shops, and industrial manufacturers. The movement's favorite origin myth—that there could be no second golden age without information sharing—reinforces an ethical practice upon which the community continues to depend. But this narrative obscures the flow of information from the artisan's workshop to the factory floor, glossing over inequalities in what that information is worth when employed by makers operating at profoundly different economies of scale.

During the late 1970s and early 1980s—as corporations broke the back of unionized labor, downsized their operations to focus on products in highest demand, and deployed technology to maximize their productivity—the knowledge required to resurrect the craft object resided largely in the artisanal repertoire, not corporate archives, machinery, or equipment. Had it not been for hand builders' desire and technical ability to recuperate the craft heritage of prewar instruments, major manufacturers would have lacked the know-how needed to recapture a share of the market for high-end acoustic guitars. Information exchange in this context has not been free or egalitarian. The crossroads of knowledge in lutherie is a site where guitar makers confront the ever-present possibility that artisans' embodied skill—and information about it—can be bought and sold to advance interests that are not necessarily their own.

Stories of Making

Any object of optimism promises to guarantee the endurance of
something, the survival of something, the flourishing of something,
and above all the protection of the desire that made this object or
scene powerful enough to have magnetized an attachment to it.
—Lauren Berlant, *Cruel Optimism* (2011)

2

Before Jeff Traugott caught his "lucky break," his career
followed a path similar to that of other artisan makers. In 1981, he built
a dulcimer from scratch while studying music at Evergreen State College
in Olympia, Washington. The experience united his love of woodworking with his passion for guitar playing and convinced him he had found
his calling. After college, he apprenticed with a violinmaker before landing a job at the Santa Cruz Guitar Company, which Richard Hoover was
expanding to an eight-person operation. Traugott also did repair work
for Frank Ford at Gryphon and Dexter Johnson at Carmel Music. When
he set up his own shop in 1991, he continued to take on repairs while his
business took root. Then, in demonstration of the sociological maxim
that good luck is rarely arbitrary, one of these social ties paid off.[1]

In 1995, *Acoustic Guitar* magazine ran an article on how a handcrafted
guitar is made. An earlier piece on guitar repair—which profiled Frank
Ford—had been a hit with readers, and there was popular demand for
another piece on lutherie. Richard Johnston, co-owner of Gryphon and
noted guitar historian, was asked to write the article. When names were
floated for builders to feature, Traugott's was among them. The magazine's decision to focus its photo essay on him had far-reaching consequences. As Ford observes, the piece appeared at a time when a major
change was under way in the market for handmade guitars:

> They did a big article on Traugott, and he got a real big boost in
> his business. He sells his guitars for a lot of money by anybody's
> standards. His base price [in 2007] is $26,500. So if, just to say for

instance, he's the most highly paid individual builder in the world at $26,500 per guitar, he can make a dozen guitars a year. You do the math on that, and it's not a lot of money compared to the most highly paid member of a different field, like athletes or CEOs or whatever you want to pick. But people do wonder, how does he get so much for his guitars? Well, the fact that he does indicates that the market is very, very different from our lives [as guitar makers] forty years ago.[2]

As doldrums of the 1980s gave way to the Internet boom of the 1990s, a market for handmade guitars roared into being, attracting well-heeled customers in North America and around the world. Gone were the days of having to troll indie music scenes and craft shows to find a few intrepid souls willing to buy a guitar from an unknown maker. Artisanal guitars had entered a league of their own, recognized by players and collectors alike as serious alternatives to vintage and factory guitars. Some, like Traugott, found they could at last make a decent living at their craft. But the strategy by which he and others did so introduced a high degree of uncertainty into this emergent market. Not only did prices rise quickly for the work of certain makers, but there was no reliable guide to how, or even whether, price and quality were correlated. To the extent that a structure to this market can be discerned, Ford argues, it looks like a "star" system:

> We've now developed a galaxy of different levels of *stars* who carry the whole notion [of a celebrity guitar maker] higher and higher. In the early '60s, we didn't have, say, a guy like James Taylor—who plays a guitar made by Jim Olson—driving through celebrity the use of Jim Olson's guitars by a whole cadre of people who want to emulate James Taylor. And then there's all the builders whose work is like Jim Olson's who are also being dragged along with that. You can say what you want to about the quality of his instruments, but because of his association with the music star, he's become a star. He can then generate the business and get the sales figures that provide him a very good living.

Olson's meteoric rise to fame after James Taylor bought three of his guitars in 1989 is the stuff of legend among luthiers. If this amazing good fortune could to happen to an ordinary guy from Minnesota, the thinking goes, it could happen to anyone. To increase the odds, however, more than a few began building in the "Olson style"—a spherical, full-bodied shape, not wholly unique to Olson at the time.[3] Olson's coup is glorified not only for its manna-from-heaven impact on his career but for the recognition it bestowed on artisanal lutherie itself. James Taylor was one of the first mainstream artists to publicly endorse the work of an individual maker in no uncertain terms.

Before sensibilities shifted in the early 1990s, pop musicians were no more inclined to give a shout-out to their luthier than they were to acknowledge the person who did their hair or designed their clothes. Guitar makers still grouse about the near miss that occurred on late-night television when Johnny Carson asked John Denver what brand of guitar he was playing, and Denver replied by saying that it was made by "some guy in Illinois," referring to one of their own—John Greven. To be left unnamed was bad enough, but adding insult to injury, Denver even got the state wrong. Greven was living in Indiana at the time.

While celebrity endorsement is a form of marketing that benefits artisans and factory manufacturers alike, its implications for individual makers and corporations differ in important respects. Whereas large companies can usually add a musician to their stable of artists with minimal impact on their image or productive capacity, hand builders are personally linked to their endorsee and often unprepared for the demand that fame creates. Although becoming a "star" might seem like the consummation of Geppetto's dream, it can be a mixed blessing that dramatically alters how artisans relate to their customers, their instruments, and their own labor. The "celebrity effect" is never simply a function of how luthiers advertise their work or how consumers perceive it.[4] As a market phenomenon, it is driven by the emotional and economic interests that both parties have in how a maker's guitars are evaluated as cultural objects and priced as commodities.

The aura of desirability surrounding hot builders reflects the "cluster of promises" they are felt to make to people who buy their instruments. Through public presentations and private communication, luthiers narrate stories of making that describe their approach to lutherie and what consumers can hope to gain from purchasing their instruments. Beyond practical assurances about what making and playing their guitars will be like, these stories also convey a willingness to nurture clients' inchoate desires and give them sanctuary.[5] A celebrity maker holds out the tantalizing possibility of creating an instrument that will fulfill a player's wildest dreams. But the barriers to realizing this promise are formidable.

A MIDWIFE'S TALE

To hear Jeff Traugott describe the event that triggered his rise to stardom, it appears as calculated as it was serendipitous. The photographer on the *Acoustic Guitar* shoot was a friend of his, and together they worked to make the resulting images something special:

> We did all these art shots, and we took pictures of tooling and stuff—you know, we went all out. And the editors weren't telling us what to shoot. We just shot the whole process, and in that process, we came up with really unique things to take photos of. So it became something that they were excited about. It turned out to be the cover of the magazine and a twelve-page photo essay, and it was twelve consecutive pages with no ads in between, and the pictures were all either half-page or full-page. The cover is of a guitar with all these clamps. I glue my guitar up with all these clamps and it's a unique shot, but I turned it upside down, and staged it upside down, so it was a hot shot. And then I staged some shots of bending wood, making sure the steam was coming up, which is not something that you really have. So it was a sequence of building this guitar, and it was supposed to just be, you know, "a guitar bend is done this way, braces are then glued on," but instead Richard [Johnston] wrote it such that it says, "Jeff Traugott does this, Jeff Traugott builds it this way." And so when that article came out, that was it. I was already busy; I had always had orders, but my orders just shot way up at that point.[6]

Reminiscent of the Hollywood film *A Star Is Born*, the *Acoustic Guitar* article was titled "A Guitar Is Born: An Inside Look at the Making of a Steel String." In the photograph on the title page, Traugott can be seen through the glass door and window of a "climate controlled room." The room's interior is brightly lit in contrast to the shadowed area outside of it, where several power tools stand. From the outset, the reader

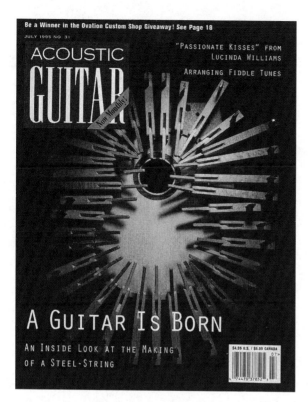

FIGURE 2.1.
"Hot shot" of a
Traugott guitar-in-
progress, turned face
up, on the cover of
Acoustic Guitar,
July 1995.

is positioned as a spectator looking into a restricted space where re-
productive labor—a "birth"—is occurring. Richard Johnston identifies
this scene of making as a "portrait" of contemporary lutherie. "We are
now in the golden age of the acoustic guitar," he writes, "Not since
the 1930s have so many great guitars been available—new, right off
the shelf." Builders are producing guitars in a "healthy climate of high
demand and constant innovation," and the steel-string guitar "dominates popular music." All this is evidence, he writes, of a revolutionary
period in lutherie:

> In the '90s, there is a new breed of guitar maker at work who builds
> instruments a few at a time. Today's builder has many more spe-
> cific tools than his or her counterpart of 20 years ago. Of course you
> can still build a guitar after an expensive trip to the hardware store,
> but one is probably all you'll build unless you become a skilled tool-

maker. In the last several years, a vast array of specialized, accurate tools and knowledge became available; and when these new resources are combined with human experience and skill, guitarists get the benefit of both the measured world of precise production and the imaginative realm of the individual craftsperson. This photo essay is a portrait of the new era in guitar making.[7]

With a nod toward the movement's origin story, Johnston calls attention to the "specialized tools and knowledge" that have become available as a result of the "new era in guitar making." Readers are thus invited to witness not one but two "births": the making of a guitar in Traugott's shop and the emergence of a new "breed" of luthiers. What distinguishes builders today from those in the past, Johnston argues, is the use of "modern" as well as "traditional" production methods in a state-of-the-art shop. It is the combination of "individual imagination" and "precision measurement" that draws the writer's praise, even as the camera's eye is attracted to embodied skill. The dialogue between visual and textual representation creates a tension between "past" and "present" ways of operating, casting the practices on display as ambivalent signs of the future.

The image that shows Traugott prebending the guitar's side over a hot pipe is an "art shot" not only because it is artfully produced but because it is readily perceived as demonstrating the art of lutherie—much more so, that is, than the now more common practice of placing sides into a bending machine. Of the hot pipe—backlit to dramatize steam rising from dampened wood—Johnston enigmatically observes, "Many luthiers still do all their wood bending this old-fashioned way," leaving it unclear whether these makers are behind the times or those who use mechanical forms take the easy way out. But the juxtaposition of the two techniques on opposing pages of the magazine says it all: Traugott, master of both approaches, has one foot in the old world and the other in the new.

When Traugott is shown hand-carving the guitar's neck, Johnston observes that this is "a decidedly old-school approach in such a modern shop." To explain the paradox, he says that Traugott is devising a fixture that will soon allow him to rough out necks mechanically before he finishes them by hand. When Traugott is depicted attaching the

FIGURE 2.2. Jeff Traugott bending wood over a hot pipe in Acoustic Guitar's article "A Guitar Is Born." Photograph by Paul Schraub.

neck to the body with a dovetail joint—a classic symbol of golden era authenticity—Johnston notes that both parts of the dovetail are "cut in a routing jig." When Traugott is shown performing the definitive act of artisanal lutherie—"voicing" the soundboard with a hand plane and chisel—Johnston emphasizes the originality of his bracing design. And when Traugott is portrayed "clamping" the binding to the body with strips of fiberglass tape—the industrial alternative to "roping" the body by hand—Johnston focuses on the precision fit and finish achieved. In each instance, recourse to "tradition" must be rationalized, while the appeal of the "modern" is taken for granted.

The paradoxical idea of a *new* "golden age"—a standard of excellence that both recapitulates and rejects the past—operates to position luthiers in the global economy as competent modern subjects. At stake is the issue of whether North American guitar makers are capable of competing in an international market that caters to cosmopolitan tastes and privileges technological sophistication over the presumed "backwardness" of provincial arts and crafts.[8] As a marketing device, the golden age concept offers potential buyers the assurance that guitars made today—by industrial manufacturers as well as artisans— have achieved the tonal quality associated with prewar instruments, while also meeting the more exacting standards of high-tech production.[9] "Traditional" construction methods are of value, in this formulation, only if they are harnessed to "modern" ends.

The transformation of tradition into a guarantee of "state-of-the-art" quality is accomplished by presenting artisanal labor as a personal service rather than a mode of production per se. The story of making that *Acoustic Guitar* tells is essentially a midwife's tale. The "birth" it chronicles is performed by Traugott on behalf of a client—and by extension, the magazine reader—who wants to *have* a guitar and participate vicariously in the process of making it. As midwives to the object of someone else's desire, luthiers are engaged in a collaborative project that turns the spectator's longing into an *event* as well as a possession. In this way, a maker's "brand" becomes a promissory note that specifies the personal service to be placed at the client's disposal. Traugott cheerfully acknowledges that *he* is a big part of what consumers get when they commission a guitar from him:

TRAUGOTT: Part of what we sell is ourselves. So I have a thing and people want that thing because it's me.

DUDLEY: And you're aware of that—that you are your own brand?

TRAUGOTT: Yeah, and I've branded myself actually quite literally for many years. Very consciously.

DUDLEY: How would you describe that?

TRAUGOTT: Well, [laughing] that's one of the secrets, that's not— [smiling] it's not a secret to me.

DUDLEY [rephrasing]: How would you describe the brand?

TRAUGOTT: The brand was to be—try to not compromise on the quality, try to stand for what I believed was the right aesthetic, and to try to focus on the tone and playability, and pay homage to the best of the past while still trying to evolve toward the best of the future.

Branding the self, as the awkward moment in our conversation attests, is both "very conscious" and "secret"—both a marketing strategy and impression management. Traugott's "presentation of self" is notable for the "dramaturgical discipline" he exercises, taking care to distinguish which aspects of his self are available for public consumption and which are not.[10] He is willing to tell me what his brand is but not how that brand is enacted. Indeed, for most builders the challenge of selling artisanal lutherie to the public involves a complex dance of accessibility and reserve. To satisfy a client's desire, they must offer as well as restrict entry to a "backstage" where the scene of making can be witnessed.

How zones of privacy are managed in dealings with customers, and what conditions are placed on the interpersonal relationship itself, varies from one builder to the next. But prospective buyers come to the handmade guitar precisely because it promises access to the site of production and the mediating presence of a skilled professional focused on their individual needs and desires. Not surprisingly, when guitar makers cite a cultural model for the service they provide, they most often mention tailors or therapists. The latter resonates with Traugott:

Having a guitar made for you is a form of therapy because the musical instrument has always been something that is special. Music is something that is unexplainable, but it makes you cry, you don't know why. It just gives you that sense of wild emotion, and you don't exactly know why. And that relationship of having something made for you, that is made with the very best materials in Old World style, it's not about that you're doing things by hand, but essentially that you are actually *taking care* of this person from the moment you talk to them to the moment that whole instrument is finished. And you don't get that [with most consumer products]. Where? I don't care how much you want to spend on a computer, you can never get it. As much as Apple hypes their products, they are still made in Taiwan, and as soon as you get them, they break down and you are frustrated, and Steve Jobs isn't coming to your house to say, "Oh, sorry, let me tweak that a little bit." And I am.

Individual luthiers "take care of" their customers in many ways, but central to their gestures of care is the effort to honor clients' wish to be involved in the making of their guitar. Details of the physical specifications and aesthetic appointments may be discussed at length by phone, by e-mail, or in person. Shop visits may be permitted to allow observation at various stages of production, and when that is not feasible, a photo journal may be kept or sent as e-mail updates. The guitar's setup will be personalized for the owner's playing style, and "tweaking" and regular checkups are offered for as long as needed after the instrument has left the shop.

But there is an important way in which the commercial relationship departs from expectations of personalized service. Unlike a tailored suit or a therapy session, a guitar is seldom so customized that it cannot reenter the market "like new," and if branded by a star maker, command a higher margin of profit for the seller than it did for the maker. Many luthiers agree to lock in the price of a guitar when they receive a customer's deposit. If an order is placed with a builder who raises his or her price an average of 10 to 15 percent a year, as was common from the mid-1990s until the 2008 recession, and if that builder has a waiting list of two or three years, customers had an incentive to wait for a guitar: at the time of delivery the price they paid would be less than the current cost of the same instrument.

In theory, this system seemed fair enough. Customers had the sense that their investment would hold its value or even increase in value over time, and builders could anticipate their income in advance, reducing uncertainty in an otherwise unpredictable trade. By the late 1990s, however, that was not how things necessarily worked in practice. By that time, an elite group of luthiers had risen to stardom, as Internet forums lit up with rave reviews and photographs of their instruments were stamped "sold" shortly after appearing on dealers' websites. As these makers' waiting lists stretched to five, six, and even ten years, price guarantees came back to haunt them. Contractually constrained or honor bound not to raise the price of guitars on their back log, these builders helplessly looked on when customers with no such compunctions turned around and put their newly acquired guitars up for auction on eBay.

With the publicity generated by the *Acoustic Guitar* article and the Internet buzz created by satisfied customers, orders for Traugott's guitars began streaming in, and then pouring in, reaching a high of thirty-one orders in one month alone—until he found himself back-ordered for eleven years. Noticing that people were "flipping" his guitars for considerably more than he was charging for them, he decided to increase his price and stop taking orders until he could pare his waiting list down to four years. As he explains it:

What happened with my instruments is they were much lower priced, and then some people sold them for incredible markups. Like one person sold one that they paid $3,000 for, and they sold it for $28,000! So now everyone thinks they can sell my guitars. [The price] went way up, and now it's coming back down to reality. So if you order a guitar from me today at $26,500[11] and you want to sell it in a week, you probably won't even be able to sell it. I'm actually telling people, "Don't make the bet." Because of this reason: there is a ceiling. The guitars that have gotten above my price range are generally vintage instruments, and so it's tough to get more than that. I think it's going to be difficult to push past this level, this price point, because the truth is now there's *so* many good builders.

By raising his asking price to what sellers could get on the secondary market, Traugott beat the speculators at their own game. Being known as a maker with pricy guitars is a dubious honor, however, and over the past decade he has worked hard to control the fallout this reputation produces. In 2008, Traugott gave a talk at the Montreal Guitar Show called "A Builder's Perspective on Finding Your Next 'Best' Guitar." Although his title appeared to support the phenomenon of what is known in the business as "guitar acquisition syndrome," or GAS, his message was quite different. Telling a packed room of guitar buffs that instruments only get better as they age, he encouraged them to choose a guitar and "stay with it" once they find one they like:

> I'm trying to change the way people think about buying an instrument like this. What I would like is for you to buy one—at $26,500, yeah. Don't buy ten. I'm trying to market my guitar as saving you money. Buy one; yeah, it's very expensive, but maybe you won't need ten. Maybe you are able to take the one that you have and really become better and better at playing. This is a lifetime guitar. This is a guitar, in one hundred years someone is going to be playing it. It's built that way. It's made light but it's made to last, and it's made to be taken apart and reworked so that you can get joy out of it for generation after generation. And that's all—that's what we [luthiers] want. I much prefer that to having speculators buy my guitars.[12]

A curious longing underlies this plea for monogamous desire. Unlike so many consumer products, Traugott argues, the artisanal guitar is made to last for generations. If buyers could appreciate its intrinsic worth, irrespective of its market value, they could become better players and discover the rewards of playing one guitar for the rest of their lives. Implicit in the wish to have people think differently about his guitars is the hope that they will recognize the special kind of labor that went into making them and value them for that reason, exactly what "speculators" seem unable to do. Yet it remains unclear whether higher prices can change hearts and minds. The logic of speculation is now built into the prices that Traugott and others charge for their instruments. The market is no longer what it used to be back in the day, builders lament, recalling a time in the not so distant past when people thought of guitars as tools to make music with, not commodities to make money on.

James Olson graduated from high school in 1968 without a clear direction in life. A self-described hippie, he never ventured far from where he grew up, a small town in Wisconsin near Minnesota's Twin Cities. His search for self led him to play guitar in rock bands, experiment with drugs and Eastern religions, and make furniture and art objects out of wood. In the early 1970s, Olson says, "I would take Salvador Dali paintings and glue them on boards of pine and then burn the edges for wall hangings and make string art. Any kind of object that you could find some way to be creative with and make, I did."[13] Although he had taken a shop class in junior high and won the school's Future American Craftsman award, he developed his woodworking skills largely on his own—or, as he puts it, "just monkey see, monkey do. But without being able to 'see,' I was just the monkey inventing."

The guitar was an object of fascination to him, and he did repair, refinishing, and inlay work on instruments for himself and his friends. When he was twenty-one, the desire to make a guitar by hand took hold, but he was stymied by the question of how to bend the sides. At his mother's urging, he signed up for a cabinetmaking course at a vocational school in St. Paul, hoping to please her by learning a trade and discover how to make a guitar while he was at it. Much to his dismay, however, the course focused on "Formica and particleboard," not the advanced skills he longed to acquire. Even more depressing was his instructor's utter lack of knowledge about lutherie. When Olson showed him a guitar, the man speculated that perhaps the sides were cut out of a solid piece of wood. "Even I knew that wasn't possible," Olson remembers. "You could tell by the grain of the wood, so he had no idea." Disillusioned with formal education, Olson dropped out of school and found a job "just punching the clock" as a carpenter with a walk-in refrigerator company.

Not long thereafter, his wife came across two books, Irving Sloan's *Classical Guitar Construction* and *Classic Guitar Making* by Arthur Overholtzer.[14] With these how-to manuals in hand, Olson made a side-bending iron and built his first guitar, sold it to a friend for "almost nothing," and immediately began itching to make another. "That's when the disease started," he tells me. He made over a dozen more, offering bargain prices to those who wanted them and scraping together the money to buy more tools and materials. He tried selling them to music stores but found no one willing to take a risk on a handmade guitar. "The only thing that existed in the guitar world back then were Martins and Gibsons and a couple of Japanese imports," Olson observes. "If it didn't say that on the headstock, nobody was interested."

A few stores agreed to consign his instruments, but after months of seeing his guitars hang on walls gathering dust, he realized that even with a 10 to 20 percent commission, dealers had no real incentive to promote them over guitars purchased at wholesale prices, which could be marked up by 40 to 50 percent. I ask him why he refers to guitar making as a "disease."

> OLSON: There was no financial future even remotely feasible in doing this. It took way too much time to make. That made them too expensive, more than [the cost of] the materials. You couldn't give them away.
>
> DUDLEY: What compelled you to build them?
>
> OLSON: It was the process. The product wasn't as important as the process. It's the creative desire. Like I had a guy where I was working, he was a pretty good guitar player himself, and he said, "Why do you want to *make* one? You know, you can *buy* them. You're crazy! What do you want to make one for?" The end result was certainly the goal, but once you had the end result, that wasn't the end. It was only the beginning. You wanted to make another one that was better, different. And then during the process of starting the next one, you're already thinking, "Wow, I want to know how to make a cutaway, and I want to know how to put that pearl around the top!" So you're excited every day to get done with work so you can go down in the basement and work on it some more, because it's the *process* that was the driving force.

Olson tacitly accepts his friend's view of the "irrationality" of artisanal lutherie, acknowledging that buying a factory instrument would be easier and less expensive than making one from scratch. By this logic, the price of factory guitars became the standard by which he judged the value of his labor. To make his endeavor financially feasible, he argues, his guitars would have to be priced much higher to cover the cost of materials *and* the time required to make them, and that price was more than people were willing to pay in the 1970s. Under these conditions, his "creative desire" was in excess of what economic rationality could justify, and as a result, his unremunerated labor was derided as a waste of time. To escape this logic, Olson emphasizes the "driving force" of the labor process itself and the inherent pleasures of experiential discovery. The need to satisfy a yearning for knowledge and craft mastery was unstoppable: "It was an addiction. It was an obsession. It was a drive that you couldn't control."

Olson is not alone in his view of guitar making as something that luthiers feel driven to do. Many use the analogy of physical and psychological disorders such as alcoholism and obsessive behavior to describe the overpowering urge to make guitars under conditions where little or no money is earned doing it. If builders have a "manly flaw" akin to their clients' uncontrollable urge to acquire guitars, it is their self-proclaimed need to *make* them no matter what the financial consequences might be.[15] While this kind of masculine generativity may not be as stigmatized as, say, unrestrained sexual drive, a similar claim of unbridled virility underlies it. Fellow makers are usually the intended audience for this confession, since they are among the few who validate an unconventional work ethic that others may consider "crazy."

The admission of excessive desire is also received sympathetically within the guitar world as a whole. For better or worse, it is the lingua franca that unites all who share the experience of a hobby or avocation that "got out of control." Olson compares his early years of guitar making to those of a musician who practices endlessly only to play for "tips at a coffee house." As he puts it, "The need to keep creating these guitars, in spite of the fact that it wasn't happening financially—it wouldn't go away. Because it's like the musician: they want to write another song, they've got a better song in them. I've always got a better guitar in me." Time devoted to honing creative skills, by this logic, cannot be measured in terms of economic return alone. Value also lies in the maturation of skill and aesthetic sensibility that is ideally reflected in the quality of the craft object itself.

Portraying lutherie as an "addiction" functions to excuse an activity that is not productive in an economic sense. Even if financial reward is not forthcoming, those who engage in unremitting labor for its own sake can claim a modicum of moral virtue. But a sobering reality subtends the desperation of this emotional gambit. In the 1970s and 1980s, hand builders endured extended periods in which little or no profit was realized or income generated. As survivors of those years often say, they were lucky to "break even" and receive enough for their guitars to cover the cost of production. Self-deprecating humor about the need to have a working wife or other sources of income is commonplace:

QUESTION: What do you call a luthier who goes out of business?
ANSWER: A guy who got a divorce.

QUESTION: What does a luthier do if he wins the lottery?
ANSWER: He continues making guitars until the money runs out.

The affective tenor of this joking behavior is rarely outright hilarity. These "jokes" are usually presented as consensus opinion within the lutherie community. In answer to a question about economic challenges, builders will say, "Have you heard the one about the luthier who went broke after his wife left him? Well, that's pretty much how it is a lot of the time." Those no longer in this situation will frankly admit that they owe their success to the support of a sympathetic life partner. Those who still rely on parental or spousal largesse tend to be more elliptical, and here, jokes and the language of addiction come in handy. Although the reality of male unemployment has become increasingly normalized in middle-class families, men who fail to fulfill breadwinner roles remain hard-pressed to legitimize activities that cannot, in aspiration at least, be justified in entrepreneurial terms.[16]

Determined to make a go of guitar making, Olson quit his carpentry job in 1977 and moved into a small shop with a harpsichord maker, relying on his wife's income as an elementary school teacher and part-time waitress to support their growing family. In 1979, he was approached by a sales representative who offered to market his guitars through a chain of music stores in the Midwest. Under the terms of the contract, the guitars would be sold at $895 apiece. Olson would receive 50 percent of that amount upon delivery, and the store and agent would receive 40 percent and 10 percent, respectively, when the instruments were sold. In order to put several guitars in every store at the same time, the agent wanted to have at least fifty to sixty guitars in stock before he began selling them.

In the meantime, Olson was not to sell any guitars on his own. Aware that at $447.50 per guitar he would not make much money, he went forward with the plan anyway, hoping that it would be a shot at something better. For the next two and a half years, Olson worked around the clock to produce seventy-eight guitars. His wife "took care of everything," he admits, as he put in seventy-hour weeks, making guitars in batches of six and rarely seeing his family. "It was a very, very hard time," he says, "but it was also exciting, because I felt like I was *doing* something."

In 1980 Olson's guitars hit the stores—and there they stayed. "They didn't sell," he remarks, disappointment still evident in his voice. "The winters came, and these small stores dry out bad, and some of the guitars cracked." The chain closed out the guitars at cost, selling them for $400 and below, and his contract was canceled in 1981. All sold eventually, and, obligated to honor the warranty, Olson had to deal with a long line of customers who expected him to fix their instruments for free. Knowing, in retrospect, that the disco decade killed acoustic guitar sales across the board was little consolation. "My life," Olson reflects, "in many ways, was falling apart." His wife joined a small evangelical church, and when he began attending it with her during that difficult year, he found in the gospel of Christ a new circle of friends and a revitalized sense of purpose. "I gave my life to the Lord in 1980, and it totally changed everything."

Leaving behind a social life that involved "smoking drugs," Olson redirected his efforts toward serving a divine mission. "I didn't care if I lived or died," he says. "I just wanted to feel that I was right with God." The church had just purchased a commercial building in East St. Paul, and Olson was invited to set up his guitar shop there, rent free, in exchange for helping with the building's renovation and providing custodial services. Soon he was earning a salary, and for the next few years, he divided his time between making guitars and cleaning toilets, vacuuming, setting up tables, and organizing Sunday school rooms. Of his spiritual rebirth, Olson says, "Something changed in me." But he is reluctant to describe what that change involved, as he has found "it's fruitless to try to explain it" to others.

OLSON: I have a feeling I probably alienated myself by just bringing this up.

DUDLEY: No, not at all. I think it's clear that this was a really important turning point in your life.

OLSON: It was an incredible turning point, and I believe that it was predestined. You wake up every morning and there's a door or a road in front of you and you either go the way that you're on or you choose this other road. It was a tremendous choice for me to make this decision, because I knew what it was going to cost.

DUDLEY: It seems like it came right at the time when you were losing hope.

OLSON: I was indeed realizing that when I woke up in the middle of the night and I walked into the bathroom, I didn't know what I was about, where I was going, what I was doing. I only knew one thing: I was realizing that I was not immortal, and that at some point I'm going to be accountable. And a court of law couldn't even find enough evidence to convict me of anything good, because I—I mean, I thought I was a good person, but I didn't *stand* for anything.

The transformation Olson describes—from a wayward youth to an adult cognizant of mortality and committed to a moral purpose—is one shared by other guitar makers, whether they speak of it in spiritual or secular terms. Yet this developmental task was complicated by the fact that careers in lutherie lacked public recognition and institutionalized markers of occupational advancement. Left to gauge the worthiness of their endeavor by the economic value of their guitars, they were acutely vulnerable to vagaries of the market. Thus, when Olson anticipates appearing before a divine "court of law" with God as his sovereign judge, he fears being found wanting and "convicted" of nothing good.

That the guitars for which he had sacrificed so much were unsold and cracking in music stores throughout the Midwest no doubt underscored the humility of his Christian awakening. Guided by Reformed theology, Olson realized that religious salvation does not depend on the value of his work in the world but is a gift bestowed by God despite his personal failings.[17] In this moral reckoning, he came to see his labor as a *response to* the gift of salvation, not an effort to earn it, and effectively decoupled his sense of self-worth from the judgment of the marketplace.

While working as a custodian, Olson built a dozen guitars a year, selling them to church members and friends for $500 to $600. By 1985, his fortune began to turn. Phil Keaggy, a rising star in the Christian music scene, bought one of his guitars and began playing it on albums and in concerts. Orders started coming in from out of state, and Olson was able to steadily raise his prices, such that by 1989, when he met James Taylor, his standard model cost $2,195. In 1992, when the growing church needed his workspace, Olson found a house with a detached building that was ideal for his now thriving guitar business. "I believe that everything is directed by the Lord," he observes. "There's very little that is circumstance that isn't orchestrated. This is the place I'm supposed to be." As he settled into his new shop, as if confirming his sense of destiny, the phone began ringing off the hook.

Within a fifteen-year period, Olson had gone from selling his guitars "at cost" to scrambling to make enough of them to satisfy demand. By 1995, his base price was $3,295 and he had collected deposits of $1,000 on 160 guitars orders. He was working seventy- to eighty-hour weeks, with a waiting list three and a half years long, and still the phone rang. "People were calling all the time, wanting to come out and visit, people bringing in guitars to get repaired, out-of-town people just wanting to see how it is done," he recalls. "I was coming apart." One night, working late in order to ship a guitar to England the next day, he was standing at the buffing wheel putting the finishing touches on the guitar. In a flash, the instrument got caught on the buffer, flew out of his hands, and exploded on the floor. Not knowing how he would make up for the lost time given his unforgiving schedule, he felt totally overwhelmed:

> I went into the house; I took a shower; I collapsed in tears. I just said, "I can't take it. Everything is coming apart." I thought I was having a nervous breakdown. My wife said, "I'm worried about you; you're not doing well physically." I also had an accident that had taken my life almost on the table saw. A board flew off the back of the blade, a wedge-shaped piece of a peg head, and went past my head with such momentum it stuck in my eighteen-foot-[high] ceil-

ing. If it had hit me in the head, it might have killed me. I had over $160,000 in deposits of people's money that I've already spent on wood, tools, a new CNC machine, a laser, and if I had gotten hurt seriously, I'm really in debt. I borrowed from all these people, and now I owe them. I am employed by all of them, and they're calling me every three weeks. We prayed about it. I believe the answer was, the next person that called, saying, "I'm sorry, I can't take another order." I wanted to make a guitar for everybody at the lowest price that I could. But I realized that I just couldn't *do* this anymore.

From that day forward, he refused to take additional orders until he had fulfilled his outstanding commitments. When prospective customers called or e-mailed wanting to order a guitar, he invited them to write him a letter, promising he would contact them when his list reopened. To his amazement, he amassed over five hundred letters from people who wanted to be on the list to *get* on his waiting list.

In the meantime, on eBay and these small Internet sellers, I started seeing Olson guitars go for double what I was getting for them, in some cases triple. The market went *crazy*. People that couldn't buy a guitar from me started buying used ones. People that had bought a guitar for $600 saw one just sell for $6,000. They're going, "Are you kidding? I'm going to sell this thing! I don't even play it." So now there's just a flood of these used Olsons. And I'm getting bashed in these news groups: "Who does he think he is? You know, selling his guitars for $8,000, $10,000, and $11,000? They aren't worth it." And so on.

The anguish of the Internet backlash was compounded by the fact that he had locked in his selling price when he took a customer's deposit. Throughout the late 1990s, in other words, Olson was delivering guitars that cost their recipients $3,000, only to watch them turn around and cash in on a feeding frenzy. His thoughts return to one incident that was particularly upsetting. In the mid-1990s, a worship leader in a church down South contacted him to say that it was his dream to own an Olson guitar, but he couldn't afford one. Moved by the sincerity of the young man's appeal, Olson cut him a deal, offering a guitar at his base price but adding a cutaway and inlaying doves on the fretboard free of charge. Three years later, no less than a week after delivering the guitar, he got a call from someone interested in an Olson guitar being auctioned on eBay for $12,500. The doves were a dead giveaway.

> So I e-mailed this kid a cursory little letter, [saying], "Congratulations, you're going to make approximately four times what I made on the guitar." He wrote me back and he said, "I'm so sorry, I was hoping you wouldn't find out. A lot of things changed in my life since I ordered the guitar. I got married and I bought a house, and I can no longer afford your guitar. I had to borrow the money on Visa just to get it from you, as I didn't want to cancel it." He says, "Please forgive me, but we need to sell." That's when the Lord dealt with me really strong. He said, "Look, you were happy when you took his order. You took it; you fulfilled it. What he does with it doesn't matter. Let it go. You just take care of what you need to do." So I did. I tried not to let it—but it did affect me. I had that happen continually.

When he began taking orders again in 2000, he raised his price to $12,500 to match the going rate on his used instruments. Ten years later, his price remains the same, yielding a manageable flow of work with twenty or so guitars on order at any given time. But the price increase was an outrage to prospective customers who had sent him letters hoping to get on the waiting list for a $3,295 guitar. Hurt by insinuations that his pricing has been anything less than honorable, Olson adopts a philosophical approach:

> When I raised my price from $1,195 to $1,395, I had people say, "You just priced me right out of the market." So you're always going to price somebody out of the market. And you know what's happened anyway? This is Economics 101. The rich always end up with the product anyway. If I sell these guitars for less, where do they end up? [In the] $11,000–12,000 price range. You go on Guitar Gal site, you go on Luthier's Collection site, you look at all those used ones that sold. They sold them in the $8,000 and above range. Who got them? The people who can afford them. So the rich get them anyway.

If the market decrees that the artisanal guitar is an object that only the wealthy can afford, Olson suggests, then luthiers cannot be blamed for selling their guitars at whatever price it has established. Yet not so long ago, when the market's verdict was otherwise, he, along with most makers, chafed at the notion that the product of their labor could be valued solely as a commodity—as an object whose worth and social destiny depended on what people were willing to pay for it. Even, or perhaps especially, when luthiers all but gave their guitars away, they harbored aspirations for the "social life" of their instruments: that as "gifts" with virtually no market value, their guitars might escape the "commodity situation" and find owners who would value them for their intrinsic qualities and be inspired by the artisanship that produced them.[18]

To be sure, customers able to afford the most sought-after instruments may also value them for their singularity and "decommodify" them by removing them from market circulation, enjoying them for a lifetime, and passing them on to the next generation as a family heirloom or gift to a young musician or museum collection.[19] But when instruments make the leap into luxury registers of the market, there is the ever-present possibility that the craft object can be converted into a monetary value greater than the original investment. Particularly when a guitar has acquired an illustrious biography on the basis of the fame and social status of people who owned it—or the reputation of guitars made by the same builder—the temptation consumers feel to cash in on good fortune may override the emotional connection they have with the instrument and its maker.

The anguish Olson felt when he learned of the worship leader's behavior was less a reaction to his sale of the guitar than it was to the young man's apparent disregard of the "gift" he had been given. By seeking to realize a greater profit than Olson himself had, this customer, and others like him, acted as a rational economic actor—recommodifying his instrument and making a speculative bet on the market and his place in it. The cultural form of the auction—whether it is manifested as competitive exchange on the stock market, eBay, or an instrument dealer's website—is arguably capitalist society's most spectacular "game."[20]

Like the cockfight in Bali, Indonesia, studied by the anthropologist Clifford Geertz, the auction generates a feeling of affective intensity or "deep play" on the part of guitar buyers and sellers, offering them a ritualized mode of interacting with and comprehending the political economy in which we live.[21] The passionate intensity with which Balinese contenders prepare their birds for combat, place their bets, and experience their wins and losses reminds us that no matter what the stakes, market competition is never devoid of emotional content nor, in the end, about money alone. What counts is the "vocabulary of sentiment" that deep play instantiates, providing participants with a visceral sense of "what [their] cultural ethos and private sensibilities look like when spelled out in a collective text."[22] While the artisanal guitar market—and the stories of making that render it sensible—may seem like a far cry from the blood sport of the cockfight, it too is an arena in which we experience the agony and the euphoria of capitalism.

ON ORIGINALITY

Sooner or later all guitar lovers make a pilgrimage to the C. F. Martin Company factory in Nazareth, Pennsylvania. Martin is the oldest maker of acoustic guitars still operating in the United States, and it also has the distinction of being managed by generations of the same family. After a night at a Victorian bed and breakfast in town, I decide to poke around the "old" factory before meeting Dick Boak, Martin's director of artist relations, at the "new" one later that morning. The old North Street factory is where Charles Frederick Martin Sr. set up shop in 1859, after starting his business in New York City in 1833.[23] Today the once rambling structure has been pared down to a two-story commercial building that contains a shipping warehouse and Guitarmakers Connection, a retail outlet that sells supplies for guitar construction and repair. Situated on a tree-lined residential street, the red brick building—emblazoned with "C. F. MARTIN & CO. INC" in large block letters—looks much as it does in photographs from the turn of the century.

Opening the front door, I inhale the pungent aroma of exotic woods mixed with the old-wood smell of the building itself. Directly in front of me are several aisles of metal shelves stacked with precut guitar parts and an assortment of small parts and accessories. The sunlight falling through large factory windows creates the atmosphere of a cozy library with an enticing collection of books. So entranced am I that when a young woman approaches to ask if she can help me, I find myself saying, "I'm thinking about making a guitar."

"Well, you've come to the right place," she says cheerfully, leading me into the adjoining room, where there is more floor space and a row of glass-enclosed cabinets that display lutherie tools. Handing me a list of things I will need to have, she asks, "What kind of guitar would you like to make?"

Inwardly I panic and begin back-pedaling furiously. I decide that coming clean immediately is the best option. "Actually," I stammer, "I'm interested in what someone would need to know if they were *going* to build a guitar." She looks at me with a bewildered expression, and I try again. "I'm writing a book about lutherie," I say, "and I'd like to get a sense of what's involved in making a guitar from a kit—if that's possible."

She tells me to wait a moment and picks up the phone to summon the sales manager. Within minutes a lanky man wearing glasses and a red baseball cap enters the room. As we get to talking, it becomes evident that Danny Brown knows a lot about building guitars, not just from kits and from scratch but from years spent on Martin's production line. He agrees to an interview, and we climb two flights of stairs to talk in his cluttered "office" space in the attic.

Brown grew up in Nazareth, in a house across the street from Martin's main plant. Although he could see the factory from his bedroom window, he says he never seriously considered working there until after a few years out of high school, when it became clear that he would have to supplement guitar playing with another source of income. In 1987 he started in the shipping department and then moved into production, where he bid on new jobs as soon as he learned the one he was on. With a stellar attendance record and a gung-ho work ethic, he eventually gained an overview of job stations throughout the factory. His avid interest in lutherie recognized, Brown was hired in research and development and, as a job assignment, was encouraged to go to the Healdsburg Guitar Festival in 1999 in order to attend lectures, meet people, and learn what he could. Once he was there, his conversations with individual luthiers made him realize how much he actually knew about guitar making. "I remember being three thousand miles away from home," he says, "calling my wife and saying, 'You know what? I know how to build a guitar!'"[24]

Inspired by the innovative work of William Eaton and Fred Carlson, Brown began making some unusual guitars:

> They impressed upon me—and this was *huge* at the time—it's not just a guitar; it's a functioning, working piece of *art*. Okay, what we're building is just a glorified box. It's basically—think about it as a rectangle or as a square that's been rounded off. And they really made me think of "Yeah, make something different." So I made some really different-looking guitars. People that see them either really like them and say, "Wow, that's really cool," or they are like "That's just really stupid" and "Why did you do that?" So they provoked a re-action, but it was one of those things, when I left the [Healdsburg] show, the people that I remembered the most were the people that were trying to be creative with their own designs.

The guitars that Brown built combined the asymmetrical shape of an electric guitar with the lightly braced top and open sound box of an acoustic. It happens that one of his creations is here, returned to him by the owner for repair after a car accident. Brown extracts it from a box on a nearby shelf. The top has been damaged and some of the binding has come off, but when he lays it on the floor to give me the view from above, its novel outline is readily apparent. It looks like a fried egg that—slipped. As he gently puts it away, I express surprise that Martin has encouraged his effort to establish an independent career in lutherie. In addition to making his own instruments, Brown offers local classes showing people how to build guitars with Martin kits. Wasn't the company concerned about his use of proprietary information? Brown shakes his head:

> I could duplicate a Martin guitar to the maximum and my guitars would never have the value or the worth that a Martin will, and that's okay. They are a big company. I mean, I build two guitars a year. There is no way that I can really harm them. I'm fortunate to be a part of [lutherie] *because* of them. So I give Martin a lot of credit, Chris [Martin IV] especially, because he could very much be that way [proprietary] and he's not. But I give my best for this company. I do believe we make a phenomenal instrument. I believe our culture

is very unique. The fact that it is still in the same family after all this time is a big deal.

Aspiring to create his own instruments yet loyal to his employer, Brown offers an intriguing vantage point on the biographical difference between artisanal and factory guitars. The instruments he builds under his own name and those he makes as a Martin employee enter the market bearing the traces of different origins and conceptions of originality. Integral to their respective "values" is the question of who owns the design ideas and labor power that goes into making them. Even if he wanted to "duplicate" a Martin as an individual builder, Brown acknowledges, it would not be "worth" as much as the Martin he makes as a Martin employee, because he is not the authorized agent of reproduction. "Famous musicians are not lining up to play a Danny Brown guitar," he admits, and he doubts they ever will. Although it is likely that they will play a guitar he builds at the factory, he does not claim individual credit for making that guitar:

> It is a Martin—it is their design. I just happened to be a couple of hands that put it together. Now if it was my guitar, my design, then I would be very proud to tell you that. But since it's a Martin, it's their guitar. It's not mine. That weird guitar that you saw? You'll never say that looks like a Martin. I deliberately do not build Martin clones. I will use their body shape, but I will not build a stock D-45 replica. I won't do it. If you want one of those, go buy a Martin.

Simply being "a couple of hands" in the collective body of workers that "puts a guitar together" does not confer ownership. That right is legally invested in the "person" of the corporation, which owns the design as well as the goods produced by the labor force it employs.[25] For an instrument to be truly his, Brown recognizes, he must also be the mind from which its design springs—and the "weirder" that design is, the more "original" and unmistakably his the guitar will be. To make a "clone," in this sense, would be to duplicate the wrong DNA—the company's intellectual property rather than his own.

In 2006, Brown was invited to exhibit his guitars at the second Newport Guitar Festival in Newport, Rhode Island. Elated by this opportunity to join the "brotherhood" of independent luthiers, he worked evenings and weekends over a seven-month period to make the three instruments he took to the show. He spent so much time preparing for the event that his wife had been ready to "kill" him. "But in the end," Brown says, "she saw that it was worth it." In what sense, I ask, had it been worthwhile?

> To me, it was to just show guitars, to be a part of the brotherhood. I have been a part of [lutherie] with Martin, but I felt like—how can I say this? I felt like I was cheating them [other builders] and cheating myself because I was a part of a big company. As much respect as I have for Martin, I have the same amount of respect for these small hand builders, because I know what they are going through; I'm doing it. So there is a certain amount of respect that's unspoken. So I felt like I had to go there to prove to them that I was worthy to be a part of their group. I know that sounds strange. But it was very important to me. I wanted to prove my worth to them, that I wasn't just a face in the corporate company.

At the Newport show, Brown suggests, he received validation for being a luthier in his own right. As long as he was identified solely as a Martin employee, his claim to artisanal "originality" felt inauthentic— as though he were "cheating" the community by attempting to pass off a corporate product as work of his own. Much to his delight, Brown sold one of his guitars to a neurosurgeon at the festival for $2,500. That a perfect stranger had come up to him in a room full of guitar makers and purchased one of his instruments was a powerful affirmation of his "worthiness" and membership in this masculine peer group. Building the guitar had been a gamble because it was made without a prospective buyer in mind—although as he worked on it, he admits with a grin, he fantasized that Dolly Parton might want it. When he subtracts the amount he spent on materials and adds up the time required to make it, Brown figures he earned three dollars an hour. But when the guitar sold, he says, "I was really happy and the guy really liked it, so that's what mattered to me." Artisanal labor, whatever its market value, has the redeeming virtue of being entirely one's own.

———

Driving over to the main plant a short distance away, I think about the uniqueness of Martin's "culture." That the company has remained in the

hands of the same patrilineage for six generations is remarkable, particularly given its embrace of free-market ideology from the 1970s onward. In 1977, a protracted labor strike registered dissatisfaction with
new management policies that severely restricted workers' autonomy.[26]
And in the mid-1980s, debt incurred through mergers and acquisitions
brought the corporation to the brink of bankruptcy. The person credited with steering the firm though these crises was the family patriarch,
Christian Frederick Martin III, grandfather to the current CEO, Christian (Chris) Frederick Martin IV. Some say that the senior Martin mort-
gaged his house to save the business, others that he vowed to stay the
course until his stock was worthless. As company lore would have it, an
old-fashioned "damn the torpedoes!" commitment to the family firm
was what distinguished Martin from other corporate casualties of the
same period.[27] In 2008, the company celebrated its 175th year.

Pulling into the factory parking lot I experience a déjà vu moment:
on the front of the sprawling single-story manufacturing plant is a
recently constructed facade that reproduces in detail the front of the
original factory. The red brick is brighter and the slate-colored roof is
only a partial one, but the two rows of windows and the painted letter-
ing, "C. F. MARTIN & CO. INC.," appears identical. The only spontaneous gesture seems to be the electric candle in each window.

Approaching the entrance to the right of the facade, I notice that the
first-floor windows are purely cosmetic and walled off from behind. To
operate the automatic doors, I step onto what appears to be the headstock of a Martin guitar inlaid into the cement. I don't fully appreciate
what is happening until I come through the glass doors, walk on a run-
ner of floor tiles that looks like a fretboard, and see the receptionist sitting behind a circular desk. As my eyes drift upward, I can discern the
body shape of a Dreadnought guitar in the ceiling tiles. It finally dawns
on me that I have entered a virtual guitar and the receptionist—with a
curved wall behind her and the image of a Martin guitar rising above
her head—is sitting in the sound hole. Suppressing a laugh, I tell her I
am here to see Dick Boak.

Glancing around the reception area, I decide the only word for its
aesthetic is *camp*, or a "sensibility of failed seriousness."[28] What else
could this be? A comic theatricality pervades the space, from the un-
dulating walls that mimic the curved sides of a guitar to the brown

FIGURE 2.3. *New facade and entrance to the C. F. Martin Company factory and museum, 2007. Photograph by the author.*

semicircle of floor tiles that imitate a tortoiseshell pick guard, which is itself an imitation of real tortoiseshell. Looking through the curved glass wall of the gift shop, I suppose that this decor may prepare the unwary for Martin baby bibs, golf umbrellas, stuffed toy guitars, and D-45 wall clocks. But how it is received by the legions of tourists who take the daily factory tour could be another matter.[29] It was largely to welcome these visitors that Chris Martin remodeled the lobby, built the new facade, and created the company museum, which opened in 2005. Coming on top of an ambitious expansion that doubled the size of the factory in 1998, the effort signaled great optimism about the company's future.[30] Yet the lobby's "walk-in guitar" also stages a magisterial claim to originality. What you have entered, the whale-sized Dreadnought proclaims, is the *body* of the corporation from which Martin guitars originate, both as a physical site of production and as a historical site of innovative design.

Boak emerges from an elevator near the end block of the "guitar" and strides over to greet me. With his gray hair, dark-rimmed glasses, black slacks, and black crew-neck shirt, he looks hip in a corporate-casual sort of way. He proposes to show me the museum before we have lunch and tour the factory, and I readily agree. The museum is located to the left of the main entrance in the space behind the new facade. Apart from the illumination of the museum cases, the space is dimly lit and inviting, quite obviously the work of a professional design firm. I pause to read the inscription on a wall plaque displayed at the entrance. It quotes Eric Clapton: "If I could choose what to come back as, it would be a Martin OM-45." I smile at Boak, he smiles at me, and we proceed to the first exhibit.

GOLDEN ERA

Although Boak has led guests through the museum many times before, he speaks about each display with an enthusiasm that seems newly inspired on the spot. His own contribution to the museum has been substantial, as it was he who organized, labeled, and installed the instruments featured in this collection. He is also the one who searched through the attic of the old factory to find the antique tools, molds, patterns, coffin cases, and other memorabilia that complement the display of period instruments. Boak has been with the company for over thirty years, and as he talks about Martin's history, I get the impression that he is accustomed to speaking for the company in matters large and small. A middle-aged man and woman have begun listening to his tour and ask if they may tag along. Boak is agreeable, so we move in a small cluster from case to case, accompanied by classic folk music from a satellite radio station.

The first four exhibits span a period of 133 years. From the birth of C. F. Martin Sr. in Mark Neukirchen, Germany, in 1796 to the stock market crash of 1929, a series of events are highlighted: C. F. Martin Jr.'s mechanization of the workshop in 1887; Frank Henry Martin's introduction of the bowl-back mandolin in 1896 and ukuleles in 1907; and the transition from gut strings to steel strings between 1912 and 1922. These cases are filled with valuable vintage instruments. Here is a circa 1820 guitar made by Johann Stauffer, the luthier with whom C. F. Martin Sr. apprenticed in Vienna, an assortment of parlor guitars from

1839 to 1873, and an eclectic collection of mandolins, Hawaiian guitars, and ukuleles.

The "most valuable" uke that Boak points out is one made by C. F. Martin III for his wife Daisy; another famed uke—signed by Arctic explorer Richard Byrd, aviator Charles Lindbergh, and President Calvin Coolidge, among others—was the first to "fly over the North Pole."[31] These, I think, are instruments with stories to tell! They are displayed with large photographs depicting people who played instruments like them—a bevy of young ladies with guitars during the Victorian era and mixed-sex social scenes of guitar societies and mandolin orchestras from the early twentieth century. Another fascinating exhibit features a workbench and hand tools from the North Street factory, offering a legible overview of how guitars were made when shop equipment was powered by a steam engine.

When we arrive at the exhibit labeled "The Golden Era: 1930–1945," however, the sense of a tangible connection to the history and socially embedded lives of Martin instruments drops away. Not only are there no period pieces in the display case, but the large photographs that accompany this exhibit and those that follow are not of anonymous musicians in the company of peers but studio shots of celebrities, a few showing the scrawled lines of an autograph. Two photographs dominate the golden era display. One is Perry Bechtel, a banjo player during the Roaring Twenties; the other is film star Gene Autry posed with a horse and a pearl-bordered D-45.

The guitars associated with these men are the golden era "archetypes" for Martin's most popular guitars: the long-scale OOO or OM (for "orchestra model") and the Dreadnought.[32] In 1929, by modifying the twelve-fret OOO model, Martin developed the new fourteen-fret model OOO with a longer string length for Bechtel—one of the first guitars explicitly designed for steel strings.[33] Players quickly embraced the longer neck, and Martin soon offered the fourteen-fret neck on all of its models. The Bechtel model is significant not simply because the OOO/OM was popular in its day but because when Clapton appeared on MTV *Unplugged* in 1992, he was playing a 1939 OOO-42.

Martin developed the Dreadnought as a prototype for the Ditson Company in 1916 and introduced it as a new model under its own label in 1931.[34] Named after a British battleship, the D-18 and D-28 (made with mahogany and rosewood, respectively) were big guitars by historical standards. Musicians had been clamoring for larger, louder guitars, but the Dreadnought took awhile to catch on, given that bread lines were forming as the Great Depression deepened. Hollywood stars, as it happened, were one demographic that could afford the new guitar. When Gene Autry placed a special order for his D-45 in 1933, it included the most elaborate pearl work that Martin was willing to do. This top-of-the-line decorative work was dubbed Style 45 as orders rushed in from other singing cowboys—who, not to be outpearled, also wanted their names inlaid, like Autry's, on the fretboard.

Neither Bechtel's original OOO nor Autry's D-45 is on display in the museum. The whereabouts of Bechtel's guitar are unknown; it may have burned in a fire in 1936. Autry's is at the Autry Western Heritage Museum in Los Angeles. That guitar, Boak tells me, is "the most valuable guitar in history, with [Autry] turning down offers for a million and a half dollars." What this exhibit features, therefore, is not historical artifacts but the contemporary commemoration of these models. In the early 1990s, Martin released two limited editions of its "signature series" vintage reissues—a Perry Bechtel OM-28 (signed by Chris Martin and Perry Bechtel's widow) in 1993 and a Gene Autry D-45 (signed by Autry) in 1994.[35]

Boak has been responsible for negotiating these and other special editions, and he is especially proud of his work on the third in the signature series, the first of several Eric Clapton models—a reissue of his OOO-42, which sold out in one day at the 1995 NAMM show.[36] The same year, Martin offered a D-18 Golden Era guitar—a replica of a 1937 Dreadnought—and it set another impressive sales record. The wave of the future, it became evident, was a return to the past. In 1996, Martin debuted its Vintage Series, a special line of golden era–model reissues.

The golden era exhibit area contains a display case devoted to the Great Depression, where the museum label notes that the factory's workforce fell to thirty employees. While a few vintage instruments hang in the display case—examples of Martin's unsuccessful archtop guitars, released in the 1930s and discontinued in the 1940s—I am unable to appreciate them, as they distract from the questions I want answered in this location: what made the golden era instruments so great and why did Martin stop making them?

The museum's largest exhibit covers the years from 1946 to 1969. But I find no information about World War II or its impact on production. Instead, this corner of the room is dominated by a photograph of Elvis Presley, which shows him with his legs splayed, holding a microphone to his face, and playing a Martin Dreadnought in a tooled leather cover. A guitar with a similar cover sits in the case. Pointing to it, Boak tells me about the artisan who made it, noting that lots of people want a guitar cover like Elvis had, even though it suppresses the tone. When I look closely, however, I see that this is not the same guitar or leather cover featured in the photograph. So why is this guitar—never touched by the King—here at all?

This instrument is a D-28 Elvis Presley Limited Edition, which includes the optional leather cover. While I may have missed the clues, I eventually realize that all of the models on display in this part of the museum are currently for sale. None is actually a historical instrument played by the artist associated with it. They are all new models issued within the last two decades as limited editions endorsed by a living guitarist or named posthumously in honor of one.

The campy, spectacular sensibility of the lobby has been extended to the museum. Each model is shown with a dramatic photograph of a performer who played it, face contorted with emotion—except for Johnny Cash, who stands stoically holding his black D-35 by the neck. Even the display of a modern factory workstation—sandwiched between Eric Clapton and John Mayer—has a droll theatricality. Showing no evidence of the computerized technology currently in use, it depicts a single job site on the assembly line. What job that might be is a mystery, however, since there is nothing on the workbench—but a shop apron hangs jauntily to one side, as if the worker has just stepped away for lunch.

Perhaps it is academic of me to expect that objects in a museum should be historical artifacts. Yet knowing that I am looking at reproductions of famous instruments subtly alters my relationship to what I see. That the artists featured here are a legitimate part of Martin's history cannot be denied. Not only did they play Martin guitars, but the music they played on them is woven into the fabric of American life. I, for one, love seeing photographs of Joan Baez and Bob Dylan and the album cover image of Crosby, Stills, and Nash sitting on that old red sofa. This is the music I grew up with, and it is why the first guitar I got had to be a Martin. But somewhere along the way the line was blurred between the history of guitar making and the marketing of celebrity instruments. As if by sleight of hand, the museum had suddenly become a high-end guitar store. That the wand was waved in the vicinity of the golden era is, I think, no coincidence.

For the prewar era became "golden" for Martin only in retrospect. Boak and I are standing in front of a publicity shot of the Kingston Trio. "When their music hit," Boak tells me, "they were playing Martin guitars, and they really did more than any other group in popularizing the Martin Dreadnought." College students formed Trio-like bands, and orders for D-28s and D-18s "went through the roof." I ask him whether the North Street factory was ready for the spike in demand.

> BOAK: Well, it wasn't ready for that. The result was that we were back-ordered for four years. Frank Herbert Martin, the bearded fellow there [in the photograph on display], he's kind of our black sheep. He's the son of CF III. He was a young man at the time. It was his idea to build a new factory to meet the demand and cut all the models down to the D-28, D-18, and D-45. Nothing else. Ramp up. It was a good idea to build a new factory, but it caused a lot of problems, and we eventually had a labor union strike that almost took us down. He was a casualty of that. He left the business, and his father stayed on as the chairman of the board, and Chris came in as a young kid in the sales department. The guitars of the early '60s are typically not thought of as the best of what we do.
>
> DUDLEY: What would you attribute that to?
>
> BOAK: A number of things. The guitar had reached such a pinnacle in the prewar era, the golden era. We didn't call it that [at first], because we didn't even *know* it was a "golden era" until musicians said, "Hey, you got rid of scalloped bracing; you're getting rid of all the special things that make the guitar right." Brazilian rosewood you can't hardly get, so we changed to

Indian. Adirondack spruce we can't hardly get, so we changed to Sitka. Scalloped bracing started lifting the tops, so we dropped the scalloped bracing and added a big bridge plate. The corners of the headstock started to become very round from the fixtures wearing out, and nobody noticed. Just little details. So when Chris Martin came in, he had a lot to do with returning to the prewar specifications and expanding the line more in the philosophy of the Depression era, when Martin specifically made guitars that were [affordable] for the common person.

I peer through the glass at the photograph of the "black sheep." In his thick black-framed glasses, mustache, goatee, and hair combed forward over a balding head, Frank Martin looks—so 1970s. His activities have earned him a separate exhibit—"Acquisition and Diversification: 1970–1985"—which is set off in an island of cases that is easily missed by visitors turning the corner, distracted by the wall of celebrity guitars. This Martin is the maverick who, as vice president and then president of the company, leveraged its assets to acquire other companies with the not-so-wacky vision of making Martin a musical instrument empire. Martin historians have not been kind to him, however, insinuating that he used the guitar company as a "cash cow" to finance risky investments and an extravagant lifestyle involving heavy drinking, sports cars, and four marriages.[37]

That Frank Martin has become the scapegoat for the fallout of that economic period undoubtedly appeals to those inclined to blame the messenger rather than the message. During the years of his reign, global capitalism was in the throes of unprecedented restructuring, and the neoliberal ideology that currently holds sway in the corporate world was the direct outcome of "chaotic" practices such as his.[38] Responsibility for the end of the golden era can be more equitably distributed. Critical changes to Martin's prewar guitars actually occurred under C. F. Martin III's watch when the United States entered World War II. Wartime shortages of raw materials, slack demand, and the loss of skilled workers to the military led him to simplify instrument construction and eliminate herringbone trim and styles with fancy pearl work. More importantly, as Boak observes, scarce woods were replaced with more readily available varieties, and guitars were fortified with thicker soundboards, braces, and bridge plates in an effort to reduce warrantied repair.[39]

During the postwar period, these labor-saving simplifications were reinforced to meet soaring demand in the 1950s and 1960s. Although Style 45 was reintroduced in 1969 and herringbone trim and scalloped braces came back in 1976, a self-conscious return to the full spectrum of refinements associated with the company's vintage models did not begin until Chris Martin became CEO after his grandfather died in 1986. With the intention of focusing "like a laser on flattop guitars," the younger Martin expanded the number and variety of instruments offered at higher and lower price points.[40] Production of the company's least expensive models was moved to Mexico, and in 1999, Martin trademarked "the newly created Golden Era concept" as the name for a line of high-end guitars.[41]

Over slices of pizza at a restaurant near the factory, Boak tells me that Martin has issued 120 signature models. Given C. F. Martin III's notorious unwillingness to court celebrities—he is rumored to have turned down Bob Dylan's request for a special guitar—the company's focus on artist endorsements is a notable about-face. Boak explains the logic behind this marketing strategy:

> It lends credence to the brand. In music magazines, kids look through the pages and they see Clapton with a Martin, or somebody that they care about. They want to learn a guitar song that John Mayer played—"Oh look, John Mayer plays Martin." Honestly, I don't think there's a tremendous amount of credence to endorsement being responsible for people buying a product. If they're just playing a D-28—I honestly don't know how many D-28s we sell because Neil Young plays a D-28. I don't have any way to quantify it. I know that it's certainly valuable. If you can be associated with one great player, it'll help your business. It's logical to assume that if you can be associated with two great players, it'll help your business by some factor more than one, and if you can be associated with 150 great players, or every musical icon in the world, that it would have some benefit.

Martin's approach to artist endorsements illustrates the delicate choreography involved in stories of making that establish a corporate brand. As a family firm, the company is invested in telling a retrospective story that creates the appearance of business acumen and seamless patrilineal succession. Not only does this "origin narrative" gloss over the contributions of wives and maternal kin, but it conflates the unruly dynamics of family life with the contractual elements of corporate stability in order to demonstrate continuity in an intergenerational enterprise over time.[42] Martin confronts an uncomfortable paradox in this regard. If prewar instruments are evidence that the company knew how to build great guitars, then how could it "forget" what it knew for almost half a century?

Rather than acknowledging an ideological shift that continues to inform managerial decision making to this day, the family's "black sheep" is called upon to explain the company's fall from grace. The effort to recruit "every musical icon in the world" is, therefore, more than a publicity stunt. Martin's story of making requires a hallelujah choir to testify to its redemption and return to the standards of its golden era—a time that becomes, in hindsight, an era of Edenic innocence when the firm made Stradivarius-like guitars without knowing it.

My tour of the Martin factory begins on the main floor. As we walk past an observation deck that exposes the lower level, I pause to look down at large banks of computerized machinery monitored by a handful of workers. That is where "parts are made using more technology," Boak explains, ushering me down the hall. "But here," he announces as he opens a door, "is where the process begins."[43] What happens to wood before it reaches the assembly line is clearly not part of the "process" Martin wants tourists to dwell on. Before my eyes adjust to activity on the shop floor, I am filled with anticipation by the seductive smell of rosewood, much as if I had stepped into a bakery.

Machines for bending guitar sides are arrayed behind a Plexiglas wall stamped with signs warning of hot equipment. Boak points out a pair of book-matched sides of American Pennsylvania cherry that are about to be pressed into shape, noting that they are part of a sustainable wood project. Antique bending irons are still used occasionally, he adds, lest the sight of mechanization unsettle me. But the human scale of the assembly work—and the relative quiet of the factory itself—impresses me as we move from one workstation to the next. With the exception of

FIGURE 2.4. *Computerized laser cutters in the lower-level machine room as seen from the observation deck during a Martin factory tour, 2007. Photograph by the author.*

the occulted CNC operations below, most of what I see could be found in any small shop, and the jobs are ones I can imagine doing myself.

My identification with the workers is enhanced by the fact that most of them are female, white, and middle-aged. After pausing to watch a woman use her chisel to flute the ends of back braces so they will fit into the body's lining, I ask Boak about the gender ratio in the plant. In the 1980s, he says, the Martin workforce began to shift away from the "good old boy, Pennsylvania Dutch, all male" club to the point where women now fill over half of the factory's jobs. "Women are more detail oriented," he observes, as if in justification.

The eclipse of Martin's male labor force came on the heels of the failed 1977–78 strike and the collapse of the female-dominated textile industry in Pennsylvania's Lehigh Valley. Martin's applicant pool swelled with laid-off mill workers at roughly the same time that the company began to retool the production process and install CNC technology, which significantly reduced the physical labor involved in cut-

FIGURE 2.5. *Martin factory worker "ribboning" a guitar by clamping freshly glued kerfing to its sides. Photograph courtesy of the C. F. Martin Archives.*

ting and shaping raw lumber. As the history of deindustrialization also suggests, women tend to outnumber men in light manufacturing industries because employers view them as docile, dependable workers who are more willing than men to accept lower wages.[44]

When we approach the station where the necks of high-end guitars are fitted to their bodies, Boak strides up to the woman working there and introduces her by name. "Susan is my favorite person," he smiles. "She's doing the neck set—it's the most critical job in terms of playability, but it's also very difficult." Susan seems accustomed to being singled out as a special point of interest for visitors touring the factory. She allows me to stand beside her at the bench to observe how she uses her centering and pitch tools to accurately position the neck. Once the angles are set, she uses a chisel to fit the neck's dovetail joint into the body's neck block.

"If you remove just a sixty-fourth of an inch too much," Boak says, "you can throw the neck significantly." After the neck is set, Susan trims the heel with a sharp paring knife to align the heel cap with the back binding. "This job is more than one hundred years old," he observes. "This is the way it's always been done." Pointing to a photograph on Susan's bench—a picture of her grandfather working at Martin in 1925—he says that intergenerational ties on the shop floor are not uncommon. The message is clear: where it matters, Martin honors the craft tradition that made its instruments exceptional one hundred years ago.

Where greater consistency and efficiency can be achieved with automation, however, Martin has adopted cutting-edge technology. Toward the end of the tour, we come upon a Japanese FANUC robot. Its job is to polish guitar bodies that have received coats of nitrocellulose lacquer. Enclosed in a small room with large Plexiglas windows, the FANUC looks like a yellow elephant holding the body of a guitar in its trunk. Bobbing its head up and down, forward and back, it presses the guitar to a large buffing wheel, shifting the guitar's position as it goes. Since the lacquer coating is quite thin, Boak explains, the robot must work in conjunction with the buffer to maintain pressure without burning through the finish to the wood beneath. That such a delicate task has been entrusted to a robot is amazing to me. But watching the FANUC in action, I am surprised by the sensitivity of its movements; and noting thick yellow dust collecting on every surface inside the room, I can appreciate the benefits to human health of having a machine perform this work.

Not far away, in a Plexiglas case the size of a telephone booth, is the PLEK fret-leveling machine. This German invention, Boak announces, "takes the guesswork out of fretting." Having spent a fair amount of time with George Youngblood learning how to dress frets by hand, I approach with incredulity. A computer-guided setup machine? The PLEK has just finished scanning the fretboard of a guitar that has been clamped vertically against one side of the booth, its headstock at eye level. The male worker operating the machine hands Boak a computer printout, explaining, "The green line is what we're going for basically." The graph shows the height of each fret at every location on the fretboard and indicates with a red line that this neck has slightly more relief than desired. All that will be needed to fix the situation is a quick truss rod adjustment.

Since Martin's procedure for installing frets is designed to catch major issues before guitars arrive at this station, the PLEK is used

FIGURE 2.6. *Robotic buffing machine in operation at the Martin factory, 2007. Photograph by the author.*

largely for quality control. Had inconsistencies been detected, however, the machine is capable of cutting and crowning frets to exact specifications within a hundredth of a millimeter. I think of the painstaking work involved in performing this operation with a straight edge and three-cornered file. To dismiss this time-honored approach as "guesswork" is misleading—skilled luthiers *know* what they are doing—but I do suspect that the PLEK does a better, and certainly faster, job than neophytes like me.

Our final stop is the area where Martin's X series is assembled. At first I have difficulty comprehending what happens here, since none of the familiar signposts are available—no side-bending machines, no spray booths or buffing wheels. All I see are stacks of what appear to be automobile tires! Boak explains that each ring consists of two sides of a guitar attached to its neck and end block, forming a perfect O. This is possible because X-series bodies are made with high-pressure laminate, a Formica-like product that can be printed with any color or graphic image, including the grain pattern of wood.

"See that lovely piece of ebony?" Boak asks, pointing at a pile of fretboard blanks. "It's not ebony; it's Mycarta—black construction paper glued in multiple layers with high-density resin." And the necks I see? They are made of Stratabond, a strong laminate that is also used for gunstocks. Although these guitars are made of composite materials, Boak says, they are still designed to "optimize acoustic tone" by using an aluminum bar, a standard bridge plate, and two pieces of graphite to reinforce the top. As Martin's least expensive line, X-series guitars take about two days to make.

Boak gives me a wooden "token" as a souvenir of my tour. It is the disk punched out of a guitar's sound hole, the Martin logo burned into it with a laser. As I look at it, I have an Alice-in-Wonderland feeling. In a factory where people are swallowed by a whale-sized guitar upon entering a new building made to look like an old one, much can seem surreal. Where new instruments are curated like historic artifacts, robots mime humans, plastic imitates wood, and work on a highly automated assembly line is presented as heir to a craft tradition, it is hard to know which is the original and which is the copy. The wooden disk I hold in my hand is surely a sign of an actual guitar, but the site of production that it links me to, and authenticates my presence at, feels far less tangible.

Boak and I walk outdoors and sit at a picnic table near the exit. The autumn sun is warm, and I imagine this to be a popular spot for employee breaks. Boak lights the only cigarette I have seen him smoke all day. Our conversation turns to the value of artisanal knowledge and traditional methods. He points to instances where Martin chooses to preserve the "old way," even when it is not cost effective. The dovetail neck is a prime example:

> Fitting a dovetail neck is a crucial and time-consuming job. The problem with it is that we would like to be able to make it *not* time consuming. But at what price? So we're doing it the old way. It takes tremendous brilliance and forward thinking to figure out a method to do it that's really efficient and produces exactly the results that you want. There are a number of guitar makers that have discovered their own methods of doing that job that are way faster than what we do. But the dovetail joint has a tonal integrity that we're not willing to give up, and our customers are not willing to have us give it up. If next week we said we're gluing the neck on instead, it might work, but the customer is not going to like it. It's a *commodity* then. It's like China.

When efficiency trumps tone, Boak argues, the guitar becomes a "commodity," the kind of product that he associates with low-cost instruments imported from China. "China," in this story of making, is shorthand for the logic of capitalism in extremis. The instruments made under this ideological sign demonstrate the consequences of market rationality taken to its limits, an undesirable state wherein preserving "tonal integrity" is not cost effective. Chinese manufacturers pose a threat to companies like Martin, Boak complains, not because their product is actually competitive but because it is a deceptive copy of the real thing:

> Our brand is very valuable because it conjures up everything that you just saw in the museum: the whole history, the evolution of the inventions, the innovations, the integrity. So the brand is important. It means that it [the Martin product] is trying to be the best that it can be in any price range. A Chinese-made instrument, under what-

ever brand, is a *commodity*. It's not trying to be the best, and it can't command the price that the best guitars get because it has no reputation. What they're striving to do is produce the cheapest, lowest-price-possible instrument. The problem is that there is confusion and disparity in the marketplace that is created by the Chinese product. This goes to guitars or toasters, I think. The confusion is the disparity between the price of the Chinese product and the price of our product that might, from external appearance, *appear* to be the same. They're not the same. Any musician can pick one up and say, "Well, it's not the same." If it were the same, we would be out of business.

Although Boak is confident that consumers can tell the difference between a Martin guitar and a Chinese import, the company is not taking any chances. Its golden age reissues, artist relations program, new visitor center, and books on Martin history all forcefully assert that the world's best guitars have been made by Martin since 1833. Yet anxiety about competition from companies that build guitars in China, where environmental protections are lax and labor costs are low, reflects the uncomfortable fact that Martin has extended its *own* brand to inexpensive lines of guitars in order to capture market share at lower price points. While musicians may realize that these guitars are not the real deal, Boak's claim that they are "the best they can be" in their price range raises the question of what it means to be the best at the low end of the market. If the standards of the prewar years do not apply, then what standards do?

What it means to be a commodity and by what criteria the acoustic guitar averts this fate is matter of controversy within the lutherie community. In contrast to the classic definition of commodification, in which an object's origin in human labor is disguised or "fetishized" by the price mechanism, guitar makers stage scenes of making that give consumers direct access to the site of production.[45] What is longed for in these scenarios is the experience of an authentic relationship with the craft object—a mode of attunement that promises to reveal the secret of what makes some forms of labor more valuable than others.

Politics of Authenticity

3

Since the Romantic era, the symbolic antithesis of Machine and Tree has served to define the essential polarities and alternatives of modern life. The Machine is understood to symbolize everything that is rigid, compulsive, externally determined or imposed, deadening or dead; the Tree represents all man's capacity for life, freedom, spontaneity, expressiveness, growth, self-development—in our terms, authenticity. Rousseau, at the very start of the Romantic age, was one of the first to use this antithesis. . . . [But] he understood that the mechanical institutions and forms of behavior which modern men were coming increasingly to dread had been created, after all, by these modern men themselves. The paradox of modernity was that the machine was an outgrowth of the tree. —Marshall Berman, *The Politics of Authenticity* (1970)*

On this chilly night in Chelsea's warehouse district, the bright lights of the gallery are the only sign of life on the block. I enter the empty lobby with some trepidation and assume a blasé stance in front of the elevator. A man wearing a black suit jacket enters the building and stands next to me. I study him out of the corner of my eye, recognition slowly dawning as I take in his puckish features and spiky brown hair. It is Tony McManus, the Scottish guitarist. A battle rages in my soul: tell him I love his music or study the elevator's blinking light? In the seconds I deliberate, the lobby suddenly fills with people and we all squeeze into the elevator.

Tonight is the launch of Pat Metheny and Linda Manzer's collaborative venture, the "Signature 6" limited-edition guitar. The invitation-only event is hosted by the Tria Gallery, which is co-owned by Metheny's wife, Latifa Metheny. I find one of the last hangers on the coat rack in the hallway and enter the exhibition area, where a lively crowd has already gathered. Lights suspended from a high ceiling illuminate a series of contemporary paintings hanging on white walls. These colorful but stark canvases are the subject of an exhibit titled "Malescapes—Contemporary Male Landscapes and Mindscapes," which explores whether "masculinity" has a "unifying theme."[1] This evening, however, the paintings provide a backdrop for the main event: the

105

FIGURE 3.1. *Pat Metheny and Linda Manzer with Signature 6 guitars
at the Tria Gallery, 2009. Photograph by Norm Betts.*

exhibition of ten guitars made by a female luthier. Looking like sculp-
tures arrayed in a semicircle on the hardwood floor, they present an
ambiguous counterpoint. Are they masculine or feminine? I am mull-
ing over this question when I spot Manzer dressed in a black sweater
and slacks, a colorful scarf thrown over her shoulders in honor of the
occasion. She is mobbed by a coterie of well-wishers and potential customers, and I wait until she is free to give her a hug.

"Guess who bought the first one?" she says excitedly. Having no
clue, I follow the direction of her gaze, trying to discern who it might
be. A throng of gesticulating urbanites has discovered the table of hors
d'oeuvres, and like a flock of pigeons pecking at a bagel, they all look
alike to me. "Paul Simon!"

I look again, and a short man in a swanky fedora comes into
view. I suppress the urge to squeal and turn to offer my congratula-
tions, but she has been borne away by others seeking her attention.
I watch Simon, clearly a reluctant celebrity, inch his way toward the
exit, hangers-on trailing in his wake. A long bench with a black leather
cushion sits near the guitars, and two people are hunched over guitars
on either end of it, trying to hear themselves play. The room seems to
be at capacity, yet more people stream through the door. Among them
are Brian Wolfe and Trip Wyeth, from Acoustic Music in Guilford. They

know Tony McManus and introduce us, giving me the chance to thank him for his beautiful music.

Soon Metheny and Manzer appear together at the front of the room. Beside them, a video screen cycles through a slideshow of images that depict the Signature 6 guitars at various stages of construction. In person, Metheny looks much as he does on stage, wiry and compact in tennis shoes and black jeans, a mane of curly brown hair and a megawatt smile. Manzer takes the microphone first, and a hush falls over the room. This project began, she tells us, when she and Metheny decided to celebrate three decades of working together by doing a limited edition of thirty guitars. The idea was to re-create the first guitar she built for him in 1982, while also incorporating Metheny's artwork and innovations the two have developed over the years.

The original guitar is a six-string flattop with a cutaway, an instrument Metheny calls the Linda 6 to distinguish it from other instruments she has built for him, some with more than six strings. Elements of the new model include Manzer's "wedge," a narrowing of the guitar's body under the arm; a "thumb notch," a groove in the heel of the neck and upper bout that gives Metheny's thumb a "soft landing" when he plays up the neck; phosphorescent fret markers that can be seen by the player on a dark stage; and a diamond inlaid at the seventh fret, to provide a tactile point of orientation. Metheny's artwork, consisting of small symbols or "doodles," is inlaid on the fretboard—a cascade of creativity that involves over two hundred pieces of luminescent abalone.

Manzer thanks the artist who did the inlay and the two guitar makers who helped her spray the finish and install the frets on the ten guitars completed to date. All three men are here, and they beam proudly when she points them out. Finally she says, "I've been working with Pat for more than half my life, and he's an extraordinary person. I'm so completely *gifted* to have been able to share my career with his, and I love him, and he's my pal. I'm incredibly lucky to have been able to do this with him."[2]

The crowd erupts with applause. Metheny takes the microphone and, as if acknowledging a band member on stage, says, "Linda Manzer!" More cheers go up, and Manzer steps to the side as Metheny says a few words and prepares to play several pieces, first on the original

Linda 6 and then on one of the new guitars. Before he begins, he asks the audience not to take pictures, video, or recordings, telling us he doesn't want to wake up and see this performance on YouTube tomorrow. I turn my voice recorder off and listen to Metheny's brilliant jazz, meditating on the bond between musicians and luthiers.

What stays with me is Manzer's turn of phrase: "I am so *gifted* to share my career with his." She could easily have said "grateful" or "honored," and her meaning would have been much the same. But her choice of words makes her sentiment explicit. I understand her to be saying that she experiences the opportunity to work with Metheny as a gift and feels gratitude for the creative energy this partnership generates. Referring to artistic inspiration as a gift taps into a powerful way of thinking about human creativity and its economic repercussions. In this discourse, as poet and essayist Lewis Hyde observes, people inspired by an artistic gift can work "in the service of art" to make that gift their own. Through a "labor of gratitude" they develop their gift to the point where it, too, may given away as a gift to others.[3] To be "gifted" in this sense is to be the recipient of a gift that links you to an expansive network of exchange in which creative gifts flow from one person to another, increasing the community's overall creativity. The "value" of a gift given in this way is not measured by economic gain but by the giver's enhanced feeling of social connection and spiritual well-being.[4]

The language of the gift, as used by Manzer and other builders, serves to articulate a "counterlogic" to that of mass production and capitalist enterprise.[5] Although individual luthiers recognize that their guitars must enter the market as commodities if they want to make a living at their craft, they rely on the logic of the gift to qualify this situation. Emphasizing the aesthetic value of their labor, they highlight the originality and singularity of their instruments to distinguish them from mass-produced guitars. Yet factory manufacturers also employ their own conception of gifted labor. Where artisans stress the unique sensitivity of the human hand and ear in bringing the best sound out of wood, industrial builders extol the human design capabilities that computerized technology and precision milling make possible. The "symbolic antithesis of Machine and Tree" that political scientist Marshall Berman wrote about in 1970 remains key to the complex politics of authenticity by which guitar makers strive to position their work as the culturally definitive expression of what it means to be human.[6]

GIFTED LABOR

In the early 1970s, Linda Manzer was attending art college in Halifax, Nova Scotia, and contemplating a career as a folk singer. Inspired by Joni Mitchell's music to make a dulcimer from a kit, she discovered a knack for lutherie and began making acoustic guitars from scratch. In 1974 she applied to apprentice with Jean-Claude Larrivée, a young builder who had been making guitars in Toronto since 1968. She remembers having to be undaunted by sexism in order to wangle her way into his shop:

> I basically harassed him until he hired me, because he didn't want to have a woman. 1974 was not the year—it was just very sexist back then. What happened was, I called him from the phone—one of my part-time jobs was telephone operator for the art school, so I would secretly call on the phone and kept bugging him. And he thought I had money, that I could afford long-distance calls. So he thought I could probably afford to work for nothing, which I did end up doing eventually. Once he said, "I can't hire you." I said, "Why?" He said, "Because I'm a *male chauvinist pig!*" I could hear his wife laughing in the background, and I thought, "He can't be that bad if she's laughing." So I said, "I don't care if you don't care." And he said, "Oh, okay." So I went to the shop and he hired me.[7]

In Manzer's case, having the wherewithal to afford a wageless apprenticeship trumped the perceived liabilities of being female. Although she remains one of the few women in lutherie, she has been a role model for others learning to negotiate male-dominated spaces and social networks. But her attraction to the craft has much in common with that of her male peers, right down to the tantalizing promise of Geppetto's dream. Guitar making, as she sees it, stems from an innate human desire, one that has become more, not less, salient in our time:

> I think it's almost primal, making a musical instrument and making some sound out of it. Like the first time I strung up a dulcimer, and the first time I strung up my first guitar, the rush is unbelievable,

that you have brought this thing to life that makes noise. And the moment I'm through with it, I hand it to somebody who can go off and make music out of it. What a thrill that is to be part of that. So that's what people are hungry for. And really, in a mass-produced world where everything is the same, individuals are desensitized in a way. The world has become smaller because of the Internet, so you can Google a house in Turkey. The thrill of exploring has changed from global to maybe people are just hungry for tangible control over their own little universe. In fact, I'll bet classical music makes a comeback because people are hungry for something with depth. In a world of so much bombardment, and being sold all the crap that we get thrown at us on the airwaves and all the media, the Britney Spears stuff, people are hungry for those sounds, the sounds of a cello, of an acoustic instrument.

Acoustic "hunger," as Manzer expresses it, is a "primal" desire to participate in a mode of cultural production that puts you in touch with making and hearing the sound emitted by wood and vibrating strings. The sequence of events she describes—receiving raw wood from trees to build a guitar that makes "noise," and then giving that instrument to a musician who makes "music"—is a scenario that involves reciprocity and a ritualized exchange of gifts. At each point in transit, the craft object increases in cultural value, as each recipient brings the vitality of wood "to life" through "tangible control" over a "little universe." Unlike classic anthropological accounts of gift giving, which portray it as a "primitive" form of economic exchange, Manzer's scenario rejects evolutionary thinking.[8] Rather than imagining globalization to be the triumph of a cosmopolitan, deterritorialized world system over the insularity of local traditions, she points to the superficiality, "sameness," and "smallness" of market culture. Against inducements to mindless consumerism, she suggests, artisanal lutherie is not a rejection of modernity but a more genuine way of being modern.

After the launch of the Signature 6 in Chelsea, Manzer presented her new guitar to the public at the July 2009 Montreal Guitar Show. In contrast to the private reception, where the main attraction was hearing Metheny play the original and new versions of the guitar, the Montreal session featured a demonstration of the new guitar and a slideshow illustrating the construction process. The performer was Muriel Anderson, a guitarist renowned for her classical and harp guitar compositions.

When I enter the convention center conference room, Anderson is sitting outside the door with a Signature 6 guitar. The room holds about forty to fifty people, and every seat is soon taken. Manzer introduces Anderson, who has arrived from the airport just in time for this demonstration. She will be making other concert appearances this weekend as part of the Montreal Jazz Festival. A petite woman with shoulder-length blond hair, Anderson takes a seat on the small stage. Tucking a strand of hair behind her ear, she laughs: "It's always fun to flirt with these guitars."[9] Meaning, I imagine, that like other artists who perform at the major North American guitar shows, she has the opportunity to play many fine instruments without the financial commitment of ownership. "So," she tells us, "I came in here moments ago, and I said, 'Well, what does this guitar want to play?' I haven't played this [piece] in a while, but this guitar just wants to play this tune."

It is a haunting piece, called "Bells for Marcel," written in honor of her friend Marcel Dadi, a finger-style guitarist who died in a plane crash in 1996. After this, she plays a composition written for classical guitar, saying that on a well-balanced steel-string guitar like Manzer's that is possible. When Anderson is done, Manzer thanks her, genuinely moved. "I am so lucky," she says. "That is exactly the reason that all the people in this show are building guitars, so that somebody can bring them to life the way you just did."[10]

The lights in the room come down so Manzer can project images from a laptop computer. She begins with photographs of the two luthiers with whom she apprenticed—Jean-Claude Larrivée in the mid-1970s and James D'Aquisto in the early 1980s. She also shows us a picture of her mother, thanking her for her lifelong support, noting that she will be ninety-two tomorrow. Telling us how she met Pat Metheny in 1982, Manzer flips through a series of photographs that show him with various instruments she has built for him over the years. The list is a musician's fantasy: a twelve-string guitar, a tiple, a miniature twelve-string, a classical guitar, a tiny classical guitar, a tiny seven-string classical guitar, an archtop, the Pikasso guitar (which has forty-two strings), a fretless six-string archtop nylon string, a fretless twelve-string, a baritone, a baritone fan-fret, a small steel string, a backup steel string, a backup classical guitar, and a sitar. What Metheny looks for in each instrument, she explains, is a "different palette—different colors to paint with musically." He gives her "very minimal instruction," she says, "and I go off and I come back six months later with something, and eventually something will come out of it. You never know. I can wait a few years, and then something will come out of it."

Displaying photographs of herself building the first ten guitars in the Signature 6 series, Manzer says that these images were taken for the embossed leather book that comes with each guitar. She invites people to ask questions whenever they wish and moves quickly through her slides, highlighting the steps involved in making these guitars. "I've never built thirty of anything in a row," she says. "I was doing what I'd never thought I would do—mass-produce something. The challenge became to make them identical." Strictly speaking, a run of ten guitars in a year is not exactly "mass production," but for Manzer, the project is a departure from making custom guitars, distinctive "one-offs," and new models in batches of three. Reproduction of the same design is made difficult by the fact that beyond standard power tools, she employs minimal technology and few jigs or fixtures. She uses a hot pipe to bend sides, a plane to calibrate the thickness of tops, and a drawknife, rasps, and files to carve necks. Prompted by a photo that shows her attaching the kerfing, a man behind me asks, "Are those just regular paper clips?"

"Yeah," Manzer replies. "I'm very low-tech in my guitar building. I've had people come in and be shocked at how low-tech I am."

Her questioner hazards a guess about the reason. "As an artist?" he suggests.

"Well," she replies, refusing the label, "I like to have a real, direct connection with what I'm doing. So this entire guitar is completely, totally handmade." A good example of what "handmade" means in her case is illustrated by the way she "ropes" the guitar's binding:

> This is a very traditional way of doing binding. I usually won't let anybody in the room. Norm [the photographer] gets super-duper-danger pay. You can see how red my cheeks are. I'm about to have a heart attack. It's surgical tubing that—you're wrapping it around,

FIGURE 3.2. *Linda Manzer "roping" a guitar's binding in her Toronto shop. Photo by Norm Betts.*

and if you let go of it, even for a little bit, either the surgical tubing [unwinds] or the guitar can spin. So both hands have to have a firm, firm grip—and you're doing really skilled labor with something that's drying and gluing. It's intense.

Manzer prefers the tubing to awning cloth, which some builders use for this purpose, because she says it gives her "more down-bearing, much better gluing, clamping pressure." She reuses the same piece of tubing for a long time, tying knots in it as it begins to deteriorate. "You get attached to the weirdest tools," she explains, "and if they work, you won't let go of them." The "traditional" aspect of this method is not the tool used but the physicality of the process, which calls for an "intense" engagement with the craft object.[11] Adherence to methods like this—and their prominent display in stories of making—puts customers on notice that they are witnessing a distinctive kind of labor.

Cultural authenticity, and by what practices one may lay claim to it, is very much at issue in the methods that hand builders use to construct their guitars and identities as artisans.[12] To promote a guitar as

FIGURE 3.3. *Manzer shaping a guitar neck by hand with a file. Photo by Norman Betts.*

FIGURE 3.4. *Manzer using a chisel to create a dovetail neck joint. Photo by Norm Betts.*

"completely, totally handmade" is to pledge that the tools the maker uses maximize, rather than diminish, sensory communication with the materiality of the craft object. Selecting a tool that becomes an extension of the maker's hand—either a tool that is itself handmade or one well worn by the hands that use it—enables "direct connection" with tone woods and manual control of the operation that the tool mediates.[13] Luthiers are quite conscious of what their choice of tools says about the kind of builder they are, and their stories of making serve to justify those decisions and authenticate their brand. That logic, for hand builders in particular, is often presented as deliberately at odds with the rationality of the marketplace.

When a man asks how much a Signature 6 guitar costs, Manzer tells us the price is $32,000. No one seems particularly surprised, but an awkward silence ensues. "I know these are incredibly expensive guitars," she offers, "and you're probably going, 'Oh my god, that's expensive!' But when I started out, the guitars I started out building, I was selling them for almost less than it cost me to make them. But I didn't care, because I loved doing it." In those years she sold her guitars through a local store, which took a third of the selling price as a commission. Even though she is now in a position to charge much more for her instruments, she insists that her work is still a labor of love:

I have the luxury of working with this incredible artist [Metheny] who—I love his music, and I'm so honored. We decided to do this because we could. But if the money went away, I would still do it, as long as I could pay my bills. That's all that has ever mattered. The real thing about what I'm doing is that I love doing it. I love standing in front of my bench sawing wood, putting it together, and tapping it, making decisions about how it's going to sound. It's a fascinating way to make a living.

It's quite hard on your body as well. People here probably don't realize how physically difficult it is to make a guitar. You can't let up for a second when you're working with power tools. If you do, you screw up, and the screw-up is royal. There's all sorts of horror stories that [luthiers] share over beers. It's hard, hard work. Sure, there's those moments when you've got a cup of tea, the sun's coming through the window, and the dust is sprinkling, and you've got this little chisel, and you've got classical music or jazz and you're listening, and it's just all really nice and peaceful. And then you switch on the band saw and dust is flying. It hurts your ears, and you've got to be careful or something falls on your foot, or the chisel hits something that hits something—like the game Mousetrap—and suddenly you've got a clamp going through the top of your guitar. It can be quite chaotic. But it's a blast. I'm very, very lucky that it chose me, and I was able to do this for my entire adult life.

True to the logic of the gift, Manzer speaks of her work as a calling that *chose her*—a gift given to her—and as a form of work she is "lucky" to participate in. When she mentions the economic hardship of her early years, it is not to justify higher prices today but to emphasize that her approach to guitar making has not changed: she still does it because she loves it, no matter how strenuous or how profitable. The language of the gift allows her to conceptualize a sphere of activity guided by values that privilege artistic exploration over monetary profit, direct connection with raw materials over labor-saving tools, and the pleasure of creative exchange over capital accumulation. To labor in the service of these values is to engage in a production process in which the "quality of the result is continually at risk during the process of making." This stands in stark contrast to industrial modes of production in which the result is "certain" or determined in advance by automated machinery programmed to execute procedures that are beyond the operator's control.[14] The possibility that a clamp can "go through the top of your guitar" in a "chaotic" scene of making underscores the skill and attentiveness required to bring a handmade instrument to completion.

Toward the end of the session, a man in the back of the room asks: "When you first started making guitars, did you have trouble selling them? Getting rid of your babies? I have made four of them, and I can't part with them." I have never heard this question asked of male builders, and I wonder if this man anticipates that a woman is more likely to share his concerns.

Manzer tells us that she kept the first guitar she made, not because she likes it but because someone told her to keep her first guitar. She describes it as a "weird Larrivée," noting that it combined Jean-Claude

Larrivée's ideas with some "bad ideas" of her own. "Instead of just copying my teacher," she says, "I had to make a change, which was probably a bad decision—but damn it, it's *mine!*" For the young artisan, altering the design she was bequeathed was the first step toward making a guitar that was truly her "own." But gratitude for her gift is expressed, she suggests, only by giving the product of her labor away:

> My feeling now is, I love getting rid of them. The sooner they go out the door the better. I finish my job, and now somebody's going to get it and with any luck they're going to create something on it. So it's their tool. I'm basically making a tool for somebody. Today somebody came to the show with his wife and a guitar that I made him thirty years ago! I was very touched by it, because he wanted me to see what it looked like. He said it was part of his soul and he spent thirty years pouring himself into all sorts of music. To have that kind of impact on somebody's life is huge, you know? So I'm glad, I'm happy, and I think most builders feel that way.

The error made by the reluctant luthier at the back of the room lies in imagining that the gift's bounty belongs to him and that by hoarding its "offspring" he can be assured of his talent.[15] What may be mistaken possessiveness on the part of amateurs, however, can be an affront to the community when it leads to imagining that the gifts offered by others are "free" for the taking, no strings attached. Just as customers may seize upon the profit to be made by selling a star builder's instrument, luthiers may capitalize on the ingenuity of others by appropriating design ideas without permission or attribution. In such cases, the impulse to possess the gift—without undertaking the labor that makes it their own or honors their debt—signals an allegiance to market rationality, wherein profit always comes at someone else's expense.

Manzer has been embroiled in just such a controversy over the use of the "wedge"—an ergonomic feature she developed in 1984 to alleviate strain on the player's arm without reducing air volume in the body of the guitar. Adhering to community norms that encourage the sharing of ideas, she was happy to make this information available, asking only that those who use it give her credit as a courtesy.[16] Over the years a number of guitar makers have incorporated this concept into their designs, often without acknowledging Manzer's claim. Some builders point to this breach of etiquette as a sign of how their tight-knit world was invaded by irreverent newcomers once a lucrative market developed. Others take the position that "independent invention" is a fact of instrument making, arguing that it is foolhardy to take credit for ideas that already existed or that other builders could come up with on their own.

While controversy over the wedge is a relatively prominent dispute, it is by no means the only one. I was told of countless intellectual property violations that fly below the public radar; aggrieved parties spoke of instances where other builders had copied distinctive body, bridge, or headstock shapes, rosette and inlay patterns, and even website content without shame or fear of retribution. Few independent artisans have the resources to obtain patents or prosecute infringements. As a result, willingness to share ideas beyond a trusted circle of peers has declined. More is at stake in these cases than the bruised egos of those whose work has been imitated without sufficient flattery. In the artisanal guitar market, the claim to originality—that your instruments are the product of your own mental and manual labor—is all that ultimately distinguishes your work from someone else's.

The narration and performance of "embodied labor" is therefore critical to how hand builders establish the authenticity of their guitars. Only by demonstrating that they are physically present in the creative design and production of their instruments can they make the case that those instruments are the product of *authentic* artisanal labor.[17] In recent decades, however, they have had to contend with the emergent reality that most manual operations in lutherie can be "copied" and reproduced by computer-driven technology. In this brave new world, the cultural distinction between "handmade" and "machine made" has become increasingly blurred. If machines can duplicate the mind's designs *and* the body's labor, how is it possible to tell from whence a guitar actually originates?[18] And why does it matter?

DISEMBODIED KNOWLEDGE

Artisans have long endured the "deskilling" of their labor by technologies that replace repetitive and physically demanding work with the untiring operation of machines. Beyond automation's economic impact lie harder-to-quantify effects: the devaluation of the physical know-how that has been rendered redundant and the eventual loss of human knowledge based on experiential practice.[19] The technology at issue for luthiers is computer numerical control (CNC), a machine tool system that has a variety of applications in guitar making. From the carving of necks and bridges with computer-controlled routers and milling machines to the cutting of tops, braces, and other parts with computerized lasers, digital machine tools have revolutionized the industry within a relatively short span of time. In the late 1980s, the steep learning curve and capital investment involved in adapting CNC to the needs of acoustic guitar making made it practical only for large-scale industrial producers. By the 2000s, however, the advent of personal CNC, designed for small-batch use by nonspecialists, has made the technology available to individual builders and hobbyists.

Bob Taylor was the first acoustic guitar maker in North America to adopt CNC, having learned about it from an electric guitar maker in 1989.[20] At the time Taylor began using his Fadal, his factory in Santee, California, was producing about two thousand guitars a year and had topped one million dollars in sales in 1988. The Fadal enabled Taylor to design and produce steel-string guitars that could be sold in the United States for under $1,000 in 1991, a breakthrough in a market where most guitars in that price range were manufactured overseas.[21] As far as the lutherie community was concerned, however, he had sold his soul to the devil:

> So I bought this machine and I started making guitar parts with it. At that time—in 1989, it was—what a sacrilege! We would call it the machine that eats men's bones and spits them into the sky! [laughing] Because that's what guitar builders thought of that kind of thing. They're just like "You're going to take all of the *human* out of it!" Now they all use [CNC] because it doesn't take the human out of it.[22]

Artisanal builders are deeply invested in the idea that an acoustic instrument made by hand is qualitatively different from one made by a robot. In the view of purists, automation of *any* procedure, no matter how routine, represents a diminution of human contact with the craft object. But a spectrum of opinion exists on the degree to which

automation is desirable and permissible, allowing individual builders to rationalize the use of digital tools for some operations but not
others. There is a slippery slope, according to this logic, between the
production of a handcrafted guitar and the assembly of a prefabricated
kit. The more operations a machine performs, the less "authentic" the
luthier and the instrument. If it takes an individual artisan going by
touch to authenticate the labor process, then computer-driven robots
quite literally "take the human out of it."

Taylor sees the matter differently. The human element in lutherie is
not simply, or even necessarily, the hand on the chisel. Rather, it is the
mind behind the design and the capacity to bring that design "to life"
in the wood:

> As with any other product, there's two ingredients [that make] a gui-
> tar good, medium, or bad. There's only two ingredients in it. One is
> its design, and the other is your ability to produce the design. Noth-
> ing else really matters. So you might be the best craftsman God ever
> put on the planet—Michelangelo. But you might make a bad de-
> sign, and so you might make a well-crafted bad guitar. Or you might
> have a really great design in mind that could really work, if only you
> could bring it to life. But you don't have the ability to bring it to life,
> because you're missing fingers, or an eyeball, or sense. So what I
> look at is, okay, I have to start with a design, and that exists in the
> ethereal. It exists in your mind. You imagine what the guitar could
> be, and then you strive to make that become real out of wood.

In Taylor's scenario, human fallibility is ever present—the design
can be flawed or the effort to realize it can be imperfect. The challenge
guitar makers confront, he argues, is to create the best design and produce the best guitars possible given the tools at their disposal. In order
to "become real," design concepts that "exist in the ethereal" must be
materialized through the use of a technological process, and some
technologies will achieve better results than others. Authentic human
making, in this view, involves using the tools and manufacturing techniques that best translate a creative vision into a material reality.

In 1972, Bob Taylor built his first guitar—a twelve-string acoustic—
with the help of a high school shop teacher and Irving Sloan's book

Classic Guitar Construction.[23] Fifteen minutes into the project, he discovered just how absorbing guitar making could be. "It was like when you fall in love, and that's all you can think about," he recalls. "I just wanted to make it; I wanted to see it take shape. It was fun, it was exciting, it was *really* something." With first-place awards from state industrial arts competitions to his credit, working with wood, metal, and electronics was already second nature, such that making the side-bending iron and the guitar's truss rod posed no problem. The following year, Taylor decided to make two more guitars, one for himself and one for a friend who was about to become his brother-in-law. Determined to decorate his guitars with mother of pearl, he went to La Jolla Shores, dove for abalone, ate the meat, broke up the shells with a hammer, and ground the pearl into usable pieces. Although this worked well enough on the first guitar, by the time he inlaid the second, he discovered that abalone was available for purchase at the American Dream, a cooperative guitar-making shop in Lemon Grove, California.

> I would go into that shop—it was like *wow!* I mean it was a little tiny hippie shop, fifteen hundred square feet of a multitenant garage-type warehouse in a little back street behind the post office in Lemon Grove. I went in there, and there were these guys; of course they were all probably in their twenties, but they looked like adults to me. I would see what they were doing, and it would just blow me away. And they were all just self-taught too. They were working with [the founder] Sam Radding. You didn't really work *for* him; you worked *with* him. He had the ultimate little late '60s, early '70s co-op going there.

The quaintness of this "little" shop—enhanced by the miniaturizing gaze of memory—drew Taylor in with a feeling of destiny. He showed Radding the guitars he had made, and the older man declared him to be "on a roll." When a bench opened up at the Dream the summer after Taylor graduated from high school, he threw himself into guitar making full time. As the socially conservative son of a navy sailor, he sometimes felt out of place working side by side with free-spirited hippies, but self-consciousness was dispelled by immersion in his work.[24] In exchange for use of the shop's tools, molds, and materials, each builder gave Radding half of the money he made on every sale.

With American Dream guitars selling for $375 apiece, take-home pay was meager but proudly earned. Taylor made his income stretch, he reports, by renting a house with three roommates and subsisting on a steady diet of liver and onions.

Although Radding gave general directions to his crew, each man was largely on his own, working at his own pace and level of skill. As a result, despite sharing a common design, instrument quality varied from one person to the next. Radding's guitars were hands down the best, but Taylor quickly distinguished himself as an able second, bringing a strong work ethic into a shop known for its relaxed attitude on that score. When Radding decided to sell the Dream in 1974, Taylor and two other builders, Kurt Listug and Steve Schemmer, pooled their resources to buy it. They originally named their enterprise Westland Music but changed it to Taylor Guitars a year later when they decided to drop the parts and repair aspect of the business and focus exclusively on building guitars for direct sale to stores.[25]

The "crudeness" and the inconsistent quality of the shop's guitars bothered Taylor from the beginning. Close study of a Martin guitar made it clear to him that there was room for improvement. "I sold one of my motorcycles and bought a brand new D-18," he recalls. "I took it home and I was just like, wow! This compared to my guitars? I couldn't believe how nicely that guitar was made." Factory guitars had always seemed too "industrial" to him, particularly inexpensive Japanese imports, which "reeked of heaviness, quickness, lack of finesse, and down-and-dirty mediocre work." In contrast, Martin's dreadnought proved that "precision and beautiful craftsmanship" could be accomplished in a factory. He looked at his guitars with a more critical eye and concluded that they "looked like they belonged in a craft fair"—a cultural location that, in his view, lacked the sophisticated fit and finish associated with a high-quality instrument:

> I was real inspired by that [Martin]. Because you looked at it and you go, "Wow, this thing's lined up! The braces fit perfectly, and there's a standard. They figured out how to do this collectively, and somebody out there knows what it's supposed to look like, and they're ensuring that everybody that works on it makes it look like that. They're making the whole dream come true, basically. You've got in

your mind what you want this to be, and then you go at it and you don't have the skill, so it ends up being something *less* that what you started out wanting it to be. I would look at those guitars and I'd go, "Well, this is *exactly* what they hoped it would be." When I saw those guitars in those early days, I began—every single time I made a guitar—I thought, "Okay, I've got to (a) improve my skill, but (b) I've got to start making some tools to help me get this done better." So I started then on the tooling path.

Taylor rethought his construction procedures from beginning to end and developed jigs and fixtures to standardize the results of specific operations. Identifying the joint between the body and the neck as the guitar's "Achilles' heel"—an angle that was difficult to get right the first time and hard to correct later on—he replaced the traditional dovetail with a "bolt on" neck that solved both problems. In 1977, Taylor signed on with the distributor who represented Jean-Claude Larrivée and several other guitar makers. As with all such arrangements, however, the security of having a purchasing contract came with lower profits. Even at the rate of ten guitars per week, the revenue generated by the company's two models—which brought net returns of $150 and $380 per guitar—was barely enough to pay bills and break even, let alone provide income for three partners. After two disappointing years with the distributor, Taylor returned to selling directly to dealers. By the early 1980s, however, sales figures headed seriously downhill.[26]

Refusing to throw in the towel, Taylor and his partners pared their business down to basics, lowering the shop's output and investing in machinery to streamline the production process. Kurt Listug hit the road as the company's traveling salesman, and by mutual agreement, he and Taylor bought out Schemmer's share of the business in 1983. The electric guitar's dominance in the music of the period made selling acoustics difficult for all makers, but Taylor had an advantage. His guitars had a reputation for "fast" necks with a low profile and low action, a playability feature that appealed to rock musicians who "crossed over" to perform acoustic sets in shows that were otherwise plugged in. When Taylor made a purple twelve-string guitar for Prince in 1984, the company captured the attention of players who wanted an acoustic sound but eschewed the "granola" guitars associated with "old folkies."[27] As orders flowed in from high-profile rockers who wanted guitars in other colors, Taylor caught the wave and rode it to profitability. In 1987 he moved to a five-thousand-square-foot plant in Santee, California, where he put his first CNC machines into production. Five years later, enjoying unprecedented success, the company moved to its present location in El Cajon.

———

When Taylor considers the impact of CNC technology on guitar making, he stresses the precision it has introduced. Unlike earlier machine tools, digital milling is able to duplicate geometrical designs that mechanical routers and shapers could only approximate. Complex forms can be now be reproduced, he says, with an accuracy and a consistency that are "impossible" for the human hand to achieve:

> When the CNC came in, you were able to actually make what you wanted to make for the last seventy-five years of building machines to make guitars that always failed and didn't quite get there. So it was like "Wow, we've finally arrived. Here's a machine that can rival what a person can do, and it can do it the same each time." Even doing it by hand—with all the craftsmanship in the world—never really made it the way you wanted it to be, and if you made two guitars, they were always somehow different.

As Taylor sees it, computerized automation has ushered in a "whole new way of making guitars." The new technology has altered not just how the guitar is made but how it is conceptualized. Despite the outward appearance of a preconceived design, he points out, guitars are traditionally constructed "free form" around the sides of the instrument:

> The reality—you know, when you pull the curtain and see the man behind the curtain—you find out that guitars don't actually fit together. They're just made one piece on top of another piece, and they turn out the way they turn out. Making a drawer slide well in a dresser is a lot harder than making a guitar, because you have a hole and you have an opening that thing has to fit in. When you build a guitar, you bend some sides, and they turn out the shape they turn out. Then you glue a back on it that's bigger than that, and a top on it that's bigger than that, and you rout the thing flush, and you put

some binding on it. So nothing really, actually *fits*. It doesn't have to fit, because everything's bigger than the last piece.

Hand builders are like the Wizard of Oz, Taylor suggests, projecting an aura of knowledge and power, all the while trying to conceal the fact that they cannot specify in advance the exact measurements of their guitars' component parts or final dimensions. In contrast, builders using CNC can make the "whole dream come true" by virtue of digital imaging and precision tooling. Mastery, in this story of making, involves producing identical copies from a design that specifies the size and shape of each part before a single piece of wood is cut. Valorizing knowledge of this kind influences how labor is organized in the factory and privileges those who design computer programs over those who physically assemble mechanically reproduced parts. Artisanal builders, from this perspective, lack the technical capabilities that true mastery requires. The problem, Taylor argues, has to do with the limitations of embodied knowledge:

> In statistics and manufacturing, a lot of times people say to measure is to know. Guitars have never been able to be measured before because they were so crude and made in such low quantities that people kind of think they know what they do, but they don't really. If a person who's really making guitars by hand is honest with the facts, they can't really tell you exactly what the shape or the specifications of their design is because they're going at it by hand. That doesn't mean that your eye isn't really sensitive. It really is, and believe me, the handmade guitars that I see out there are just wonderful. But try and make a hundred of those, or eighty thousand of those, and it all breaks down.

To "go at something by hand" is to gauge accuracy according to the visual or tactile standard set by a straight edge, template, or sensory memory. Although this form of measurement might seem "objective" enough, Taylor argues, it is open to "subjective" interpretation. As an example, he cites the problem posed by cutting along a pencil line. Do you cut to the right, to the left, or down the center of the line? With every repetition of that operation, the width of the pencil lead, the thickness of the saw blade, or the mood of the maker can alter where the cut is made. Artisanal "knowledge" is thus linked, for better or worse, to the perspective of a sentient subject embedded in the labor process. In itself, the subjectivity of embodied knowledge is not necessarily a bad thing. It only becomes a cause for concern when it "breaks down" under the demands of mass production. Judged by industrial values, the artisanal guitar fails to satisfy expectations of product *interchangeability* and the uniformity on which that depends. At issue is not artisans' inability to "measure" per se but the obstacle that their way of operating presents to commodification and the efficient accumulation of capital.

In contrast, the standard of measurement offered by CNC is nothing if not objective. Because computer-assisted design allows makers to specify the "paths" in space that a laser or router will travel, the operations governed by that program will always be executed in identical fashion within ranges that are imperceptible to the eye. Guitars produced this way gain a uniformity made possible by the digital tools that mediate human labor, and the maker's orientation to the craft object becomes disembedded and disembodied, as the labor process itself can now be viewed from afar. Taylor likens this technological breakthrough to landing on the moon:

> I remember when we were developing what we call the NT neck for New Technology. We were having a meeting of the minds, and we were arguing about a particular measurement. After a while I said, "Do you guys realize that we've been arguing over two-thousandths of an inch for the last hour—about which is the right measurement? I mean, let's just stop and bask in that for a minute. That is like landing on the moon for guitar builders! Because ten years ago, we couldn't have even *perceived* ten-thousandths of an inch, let alone argued over two."

Like an Apollo 11 astronaut whose spacecraft allows him to land on the moon and see planet Earth for the first time, Taylor exults in the triumph of a technology that conquers similar spatial distances, writ small. Like the Blue Marble photograph, the capacity to perceive "two-thousandths of an inch" signals the hope and promise of modernity: that human history can be written as a story of progress in which the mind transcends the materiality of the body. In this view, CNC makes possible a form of knowledge that marks the limits of manual labor, remaking the builder into an agent of production who rises above the labor process and the physical limitations of those embedded within it. As disembodied knowledge, high-tech guitar making is a spatial project to be managed rather than a temporal process to be experienced.[28] On a global scale, it allows manufacturers to oversee and profit from supply, production, and distribution systems that encompass ever-larger geographical domains.

But the use of digital milling embroils its proponents in a politics of authenticity that pivots on the issue of embodiment. Taylor recognizes that his reputation among some luthiers suffered as a result of his unrepentant embrace of automation. This realization hit home, he says, in 1999 when he was driving with his colleague Dick Boak to a 1999 meeting of the Association of Stringed Instrument Artisans:

> We're driving to upstate New York from Martin Guitars, and we're talking about things and I go, "Dick, you know that I totally realize that everybody at these meetings thinks that I know a lot about machinery but I know nothing about guitars." I go, "I know that" He looks at me and he goes, "Wow, I'm surprised that you would be aware of that." You know? So his answer was just pure confirmation of where I realized I had arrived in the minds of a lot of my peers. Where they thought, "Well, we're *real* guitar makers, but Bob's not."

Taylor refers to this moment as the "grain of sand" that lodged itself in his mind, as if into the soft tissue of an oyster, irritating him until it became the "pearl" of a new business venture. In 2006 he created R. Taylor as a company separate from Taylor Guitars but located at the El Cajon site. In the R. Taylor workshop a crew of five men, each with over ten years of factory experience, make guitars in limited numbers. Where the main plant produces three hundred guitars a day, R. Taylor builds three hundred guitars a year. "And we've tripled the labor hours that go into a guitar," Taylor says. "It's amazing what you can do when you do that." Tacitly acknowledging that the finer points of the craft require time, R. Taylor builds a guitar in thirty to forty labor hours—more than the ten hours per instrument in the factory, but far less than the one hundred or more hours typical of an individually handmade instrument.

Like other boutique companies, R. Taylor seeks a middle ground between artisanal and industrial modes of production. Component parts are still cut and milled by CNC, but greater attention is given to such details as selecting choice wood, hand-shaping braces, and using non-kerfed lining. "It's taking our formula," Taylor explains, "but building features into the guitar that just would never work in a factory." In the artisanal market, he realizes, customers are looking for something that robots cannot deliver:

> There's so much of what you might call *performance* in guitar buying. I mean, it's kind of like, hey, you don't really want a poncho, but gosh, you're in the Andes and somebody made one. Now you're buying a poncho because somebody wove that thing! You know? Well, you're not really buying the poncho. You're buying the performance of making the poncho. You know? I come home, it's like, I have a *poncho*? [*laughing*] But this lady *wove* it, in the Andes! Well, the thing is, I think we're all susceptible to that, and people who are buying guitars, they like that too. They want to know from whence it came. How it got there.

Handmade goods are appealing, Taylor suggests, because they answer a wish to know how things are made and by whom. That longing finds its ultimate expression in travel to sites of production where human agents can be found at the putative origin of a production process. The R. Taylor concept acknowledges this desire by giving customers the opportunity to witness, in reality or imagination, a "performance of making" that locates the origin of its guitars in a small shop of dedicated builders. As in the example of the Andean weaver, the dramaturgy of artisanal commerce requires that the embodied labor of the maker be made visible and *theatricalized* within a comprehensible work process.

Only through visceral identification with the human agent at the site of production can consumers feel confident that they know "from whence" the craft object has come.[29] Only by imaginatively substituting our own bodies for that of the maker can we enter into an artisanal scenario of decommodification and, through an economic transaction, corroborate its magical effect: the authentication of the craft object as an expression of an authentic self. Buying a poncho simply because "somebody wove that thing" affirms not just the authenticity of the artifact produced by human hands but the authenticity of the self that was co-present at the site of production. Like the poncho, however, the artisanal guitar is a souvenir not simply of a culturally distant location but of a temporally distant way of operating that postindustrial capitalism has deemed obsolete.[30]

UNRECOGNIZED LABOR

"I am very practiced at defending a robot in a handmade guitar factory," Richard Hoover says as we embark on a tour of the Santa Cruz Guitar Company.[31] He has just shown me a rack of tone wood, where we paused to admire the chocolate-brown figure of some choice Brazilian rosewood. "This is sort of like going into the kitchen of the restaurant," Hoover announces as he opens the door to the room containing his CNC machine. "You've enjoyed the ambience, and then you go, 'Oh, I don't know if I want to be in *here*.'" The new-age monster I've heard so much about looks docile enough in its Plexiglas-enclosed cabinet. Nothing is currently being milled, so the Fadal's machine head is not moving, and a darkened computer monitor sits on a shelf beside it. A middle-aged man is bent over a table vise filing an ebony bridge. Hoover introduces us and identifies me as a professor of anthropology. "So look study-able!" he commands, and we all laugh. I learn that guitar parts shaped by a computerized router still have rough edges and milling marks that must be finished off by hand. The Fadal is used sparingly, Hoover explains, primarily to reduce repetitive stress injuries:

> We still make the most *handmade* guitar of anybody anywhere. A lot of the processes that we do are repetitive, and contrary to the *lutherie* stuff we do, the dimensions are supposed to be the same each time. Here is a great example—fret slots. [He shows me a freshly cut fingerboard.] This is a machining operation where you want it accurate within three decimal points for intonation on the guitar. It's amazing how a craftsperson can develop the hand/eye skills to do this kind of work very accurately. But after a few hundred, why? It not only can expose you to repetitive stress, but if you do the same thing over and over again, your brain shrinks and you start looking

for something else to do. So our crew are all guitar makers, or aspiring guitar makers, and they didn't come [here] to work in a factory or just to get a job; they want to be guitar builders. So by taking this kind of process that's repetitive and potentially injurious and giving it to a robot, we free everybody up to do their stuff.

I regard the Fadal with new interest, trying to look past the warning stickers that show a hand losing its fingertips. Although it is in "the kitchen" at Santa Cruz, it appears to have been assigned the scut work that no one else wants to do, a robotic *chef de plunge*. Hoover reserves the term *lutherie* for operations that are *not* supposed to yield the same measurements every time, while subscribing to an industrial model of product uniformity for everything else. In this scenario, computerized reproduction not only "saves time" but reinvests it in luthiers by "freeing" them from the drudgery of handcrafting identical widgets. That such parts must be made in large batches, rather than as part of a multifaceted work process, is taken for granted.

Yet the "brain-shrinking" aspect of cutting fret slots or shaping bridges is arguably due not to the activity itself but to a division of labor in which the repetition of an isolated activity constitutes a "job." The rationale for CNC technology is thus made manifest in the organization of work on the shop floor. No one wants to do the Fadal's labor, because it is monotonous, and no one needs to do it, because the machine can do it faster and more consistently than any builder could. What remains unspoken is the ground ceded to automation as conceptions of what constitutes the *human* in performances of making come to exclude an ever-larger spectrum of craft and industrial labor.

Hoover "got the bug" for guitar making in 1967 when he disassembled his first guitar, a forty-seven-dollar Harmony. With the help of his mother, a reference librarian, he read everything he could find on the subject of lutherie, most of which, at the time, was about the violin. His foundation in traditional methods expanded when he learned to make classical guitars in 1972.[32] Hoover soon focused his energies on the steel-string guitar, and in 1976, with partners Bruce Ross and William Davis, he established the Santa Cruz Guitar Company.[33] Although Hoover is now the sole proprietor, he has remained true to the founding vision of creating a "boutique" guitar company, one that would be a team effort, he explains, but stay "within the boundaries of lutherie" rather than emphasizing efficiency and being "the next Martin."

The boutique concept, as Hoover describes it, involves bringing knowledge of violins and classical guitars to bear on "controlling the sound" of the modern steel-string by "thinking about voicing, tuning, and making the guitar sound like you want it to." Among other things, this means voicing each guitar individually—attending to the density and flexibility of the wood used for each soundboard, manually graduating the thickness of each top, and varying the shape of each brace to achieve the desired tonal qualities. To recruit his team of fourteen builders, Hoover hires graduates of American lutherie schools. Despite regular turnover, a number of his employees have been with the company a decade or more.

The CNC room contains a small office that looks out at the Fadal through a large glass window. Hoover leads me inside and introduces me to Adam Rose, a senior luthier who has worked at Santa Cruz for twenty years. Rose is seated at a desk in front of an illuminated computer screen. He is working on a peghead inlay pattern created by Craig Frazier, the illustrator who designed Santa Cruz's distinctive company poster. Using a CAD/CAM program to draw the two-dimensional image, Rose is refining instructions that will enable the Fadal to hollow out the negative space on the peghead for the inlay as well as cut the positive image out of shell. The carbide bit that does this work is ten-thousandths of an inch wide. "Two and a half hairs," Hoover says, emphasizing the delicate work the machine can do—while also replacing the need to cut shell by hand and reducing the danger of carpal tunnel syndrome.

Rose calls up a three-dimensional design on his computer, and the outline of a guitar neck appears on the screen. Removing a wooden neck from a rack where necks of various sizes and shapes hang on the wall, he tells me that this neck was "hand carved by one of our really experienced neck carvers." The shape, he points out, is a complex one. Although a mechanical drawing could easily reproduce the relatively straight contour along the barrel of the neck, it would run into difficulty at either end, where the heel and headstock flare out in subtle curves. To capture these forms, Rose uses a three-dimensional mouse to "digitize"

FIGURE 3.5. *After taking precise digital measurements of a hand-carved neck, Adam Rose creates a CNC tool path for the resulting model, allowing the Santa Cruz Guitar Company to produce exact copies on a CNC milling machine, 2009. Photograph by the author.*

the handmade neck, taking measurements at various points along the neck and then applying a graphic surface to those points in space.

"We can actually look at that surface on the screen, as you see, and turn it," he says, clicking his mouse. Before my eyes, the neck shape appears in a web of radial lines and rotates, as if turned by an invisible hand. "It's pretty much like looking at it in hand," Rose continues, "and you can really see if you've got any lumps or bumps." With a few more clicks, he adds a network of blue lines, explaining that these are the actual tool paths. When the program is linked to the Fadal, the milling process can be watched in real time on the screen.

I shake my head in amazement and say, "That's just too cool." Rose grins and leans back to entertain the counterargument:

Some people might look at that and say, "Oh well, you are just making *robot* guitars." But actually, once we get the shape that really matches this [handmade neck], the one that we machine is going to be *closer* to this than the next one that we carve by hand, because this machine is accurate to a tenth of a thousandth of an inch. So we can take our time to get exactly the handmade shape that we want, and then by digitizing it, we can just repeat it forever. What that allows us to do is, we have standard models, so if someone orders this guitar and they like that neck, we'll make them that neck on the machine. But if they want this guitar and they say, "Well, I like a little bit flatter profile on the barrel of my neck," this buys us the time to have one of our master carvers do that by hand.

In the bright glow of the computer screen at Santa Cruz, CNC appears to be a tamed beast. Rather than taking the "human" out of lutherie, it works in concert with its handlers and honors them through acts of faithful reproduction. Yet as the digital neck demonstrates, relying on this workhorse comes with a cost. If the machine's copy of a handmade neck is more "accurate" or "closer to" the original than the "next one carved by hand," then the CNC copy becomes the standard by which subsequent handmade necks are judged and found wanting. Because the machine-made copy can be "repeated forever," it obviates the need to make necks by hand, except when a unique shape is required— although any new shape may itself also be standardized.

The "deskilling" that computerized machining represents is not readily apparent. Rose is skilled at lutherie and at translating that knowledge into CAD/CAM designs, and the need for "master carvers" to fit some necks to players' hands may always exist. Rather, the cost exacted by CNC is that the manual skill required to make necks and other guitar parts is no longer recognized as legitimate labor in its own right—as human "know-how" that has a clear and quantifiable value in today's market economy. As machines take over the performance of an increasing proportion of manual labor, the know-how that artisans possess "takes on the appearance of an 'intuitive' or 'reflex' ability, which is almost invisible and whose status remains *unrecognized*."[34] What counts is not the artisan's embodied skill but the programmer's ability to tell machines how to replicate its results.

By restricting the use of CNC to repetitive operations, Santa Cruz has cordoned off a sacrosanct space for the performance of what Hoover suggests is "authentic" lutherie. In that space, a dedicated group of artisans and apprentices performs labor that remains largely unrecognized outside of the lutherie world. That work involves the time-consuming operations that distinguish high-quality artisanal guitars: individually voiced soundboards, handset dovetail neck joints, and the use of nitrocellulose lacquer.[35] To these practices, Hoover has added a wood-seasoning process that uses a climate-controlled shed to duplicate several years of seasonal cycles in three to four weeks, and a commitment to sustainable forestry that involves using wood from reclaimed logs and responsibly harvested timber. Like other boutique builders, Santa Cruz is also a training ground for those pursuing careers in guitar construction, repair, and restoration. Touring the shop, I observe over half a dozen young men engaged in various aspects of the work process, each operating with relative autonomy. Through a hybrid combination of automation and hands-on lutherie, Santa Cruz produces up to seven hundred guitars a year, carving out a viable space for artisanal labor in a market economy.

Boutique guitar shops represent the middle ground between one-person operations and industrial manufacturers. Holding the line against pressures to speed up the pace of production while also maximizing labor-saving efficiencies, small companies like Santa Cruz, Collings, and Bourgeois produce instruments that have become a staple of high-end dealers, who extol their blend of handcrafted quality and economic value. Within each shop, however, finding the right balance between market rationality and artisanal values is an ongoing exercise in negotiating the affective and material aspects of the production process.

On a warm September day, I sit on a pile of logs outside the rough-hewn workshop of Froggy Bottom Guitars, eating a lunch I packed for myself that morning. A black Labrador retriever lies on the ground beside me, eyes fixed on the vanishing meal. I think twice about drinking my iced tea—having been informed by Andy Mueller, as he walked off into the woods, that there is no plumbing in the shop—and share the last bite of my sandwich with my new friend. Mueller has worked with Michael Millard since 1994 and became a full partner in the company in 2005. Beyond Mueller and Millard, the company employs two or three men and commissions the art of Petria Mitchell, who engraves wildlife images on the heel cap of every guitar. Among the skills that Mueller brought to the business was an ability to program computer-controlled machinery, and in 1996 he was tasked with integrating CNC milling into what was otherwise a fairly low-tech operation. Even so, with a production rate of about one hundred guitars a year, Froggy Bottom remains one of the smaller boutique shops.

Limiting the company's growth takes deliberate effort, Mueller told me. But he and Millard are determined to create an environment in which everyone "involved in the process can understand and appreciate every instrument as an *individual* instrument." He was proud to say that he could "call to mind every guitar we've made for every individual or dealer" over the past year or so. When I asked him why this is important, he replied:

> I came into guitar making as someone who loved to build things, and as a musician. I've never been interested in making tremendous numbers of anything. You maximize production to maximize profitability or, as part of that, affordability. While I love the idea of making affordable guitars, [you also have to] keep the spark alive in terms of being interested in making them in the first place. If they were things—I finish it, I ship it out, I go, "Great, we're going to make payroll this week, yippee skippie!" I mean, making payroll is important, but it would be depressing if I was making things that I couldn't keep my head wrapped around, or if there were instruments showing up on my bench and I thought, "Who is this for anyway?" or "Where the heck did this thing come from?" We push that threshold. If we did three guitars a week instead of two, it would be difficult to have enough integration in the whole process to understand every instrument. So we're right at that limit. If they became generic, then I would find something to make that I didn't care as much about so that I could tolerate them being generic. I'd make end tables or something, if it was going to be about the numbers rather than about the instrument's identity.[36]

As a collective and individual goal, "keeping the spark alive" means organizing labor on the shop floor in such a way that everyone has a hand in making each guitar and no one is stuck repeating the same subset of tasks for an extended time. Acknowledging that this is not "the most efficient way to run the business," Mueller insisted the tradeoff was worth it. If guitars became "generic" objects without individual "identities," then "the creativity would be lost" and he would no longer want to make them. To prevent the commodification of guitars as well as human labor, he suggested, a goal greater than efficiency must enter the company's calculation of profit, payroll, and affordability. That goal must be to satisfy the artisan's desire to "understand" the craft object and realize its singular characteristics.

The dog dozing at my feet runs up to greet Michael Millard as he pulls into the driveway. From a distance, Millard is an imposing person, with the beard, shoulder-length hair, and ambling gate of a reclusive mountain man. Up close, however, there is a wry smile behind the whiskers and a suppleness to his bearing that I later learn reflects his training in martial arts. He leads me up an external stairway to the second floor of the workshop, where we sink into threadbare furniture. When our conversation turns to the shop's CNC machine, Millard tells me that he "resisted" getting one for many years.[37] Aware that using fixtures and machines for repetitive operations "always limits the constant refinement of your own skills," he proceeded cautiously, weighing every "compromise" made in the name of increased efficiency. Of particular concern to him is the way automation can cause builders to "lose touch" with their guitars and "degrade" the satisfaction of their work:

> I've known a lot of people who have set out to do what I've set out to do, which is to make guitars. Almost everybody, in order to feed themselves, has narrowed down their scope and made it into a *business*—and they kill the goose that lays the golden eggs. People will make guitars until they make one that makes their socks go up and down, and then they clone that guitar and keep making it. Before they know it, they're bored or unhappy. The methodology that we use in this shop, in terms of both interpersonal communication with ourselves, our clients, and suppliers and the physical methodology for building the instruments, is, by intention, limiting in terms of how many guitars we make. We fight this all the time. I steadfastly refuse to go to places wherein we are backing ourselves, unwittingly, into

a corner that in the future will narrow our scope and our connection with the instrument.

A shared sensibility informs Millard and Mueller's view of guitar making, despite the personality differences one might expect between someone who studied English and psychology in the 1960s and an avid student of physics in the 1990s. For both men, artisanal lutherie requires establishing a mode of connection—among coworkers as well as between artisans and the craft object—that would be "killed" in a production-oriented "business." If guitars are "golden eggs," then the "goose" is the authentic self—the bearer of the gifted labor that produces, but does not "clone," singular objects of great value. To "fight" commodification, the Froggy Bottom team uses minimal jigs and fixtures so they can "experiment" with the specifications and appointments of their instruments. The computerized router is reserved for repetitive work such as roughing out necks, which are then "finished," Millard says emphatically, "with these things"—holding out his hands—"and this"—gesturing toward his eyes—"and this"—pointing to his head. Building guitars, he explains, is "like being married," insofar as it requires constant attention and care:

> Part of it is spiritual or emotional. If you're so busy that you begin not talking to your spouse or your partner, you're in trouble. If you're so busy that you're not connected with each guitar, you're in trouble. You'll notice right away. There is an intimacy to our lives that we require in order to do the work that we do—because we're asking ourselves to be intimate with the guitars. It's necessary; it's absolutely essential. We need to know each guitar.

Millard's emphasis on the singularity of his instruments defies an industrial rationality in which an object's value depends on its conformity to a preconceived ideal of what that object should be. A mass-produced guitar is summoned into existence by a market culture that demands interchangeability; the artisanal guitar is called forth by a desire for singularity. Hand builders seeking "intimate" knowledge of each instrument are, in effect, asking of each guitar in progress, "Who are you, and what do you want to become?" As if relating to a sentient subject in formation, they communicate with the instrument throughout its construction, using the information gained to bring a unique entity into existence.[38] Yet luthiers are hard-pressed to translate these intuitive conversations into the authoritative discourse of scientific measurement and control. As Millard attests, knowing how to make guitars is not the same thing as being able to account for that knowledge:

> The guitar-making thing—this is something I haven't said to very many people. Guitars, in terms of how guitars work—I was born with that. I had to pull it out of myself and so on, but everything that I do with guitar making, virtually everything—I just know how guitars work. I couldn't tell you how. I'm the same way with dogs. I'm the pied piper with dogs. I know how to make guitars dance, pirouette left, and spit wooden nickels. I just know how to do that. Please, I'm not bragging. I've never met anyone in my life, anybody who knows or can answer [the question] "Hey, how do you do this?" It just works. It's a God-given gift.

Drawing on the language of the gift, Millard describes his intuitive knowledge as an uncanny ability to communicate with guitars as if they were nonhuman animals. As self-fashioned "guitar whisperers," hand builders claim that while they must work to realize their talent—or "pull it out" of themselves—the gift itself is given to them by God as an aptitude they are "born with." Making an artisanal guitar, in these accounts, involves developing an authentic self in relationship to human and nonhuman others. Guitar and self have innate potential for cross-species communication, and both come into being as the realization of Geppetto's dream—a sentimental imaginary in which the generativity of embodied labor is made evident in the vitality of craft objects that "dance, pirouette left, and spit wooden nickels."[39]

RITUAL KNOWLEDGE

When *Hootenanny* was launched by ABC television in 1963, the folk music craze was in full swing. Taped on college campuses to the rhythmic claps and warbling voices of students singing along with featured acts, the show brought an eclectic group of musicians into American homes, drawing a national audience that peaked at eleven million viewers per week.[40] Among the program's early fans was a high school junior in Morristown, New Jersey, who had formed a Kingston Trio–like band with two of his friends. "*Hootenanny* was on and Earl Scruggs came on," John Greven recalls. "That was the first time I'd ever heard anybody pick a banjo with three fingers, and it just blew me away! All that testosterone had someplace to *go*, finally."[41] Like other enthusiasts who wanted a good banjo in the 1960s, Greven got a prewar tenor banjo and converted it into a five-string with a new neck. Not content to stop there, he began working on his friends' instruments and "just kind of got hooked."

The "dream" of making acoustic stringed instruments for a living stayed on Greven's mind, but he dismissed it as "totally insane" because "nobody did that back then." Resolving to pursue an established career, he studied biochemistry at Cornell until he became disillusioned with "the lab coat thing" and transferred to Oregon State to study forestry—only to discover that this, too, was not his "calling." All the while, he was playing banjo and guitar semiprofessionally in bluegrass bands and doing repair work for other musicians. Describing a dilemma shared by other luthiers of his generation, Greven characterizes his search for identity as a struggle to reconcile "opposite" sides of his brain:

> I went through the science program in high school and college. My expectation was to become some kind of research something or other. I have a very strong left-brain component, but I also—I draw, I paint, I do music. I'm very right-brained. So I'm kind of in between the two. But my practicality said, "You need to get a real day job, so let's go to science." And the music always took the back seat.

The notion that certain cognitive functions are located on different lobes of the brain became popular in the 1970s. Inspired by neurological studies that suggest there is some "lateralization" of linguistic and mathematical functions, the concept of a divided brain is commonly used in popular culture to explain why some people excel in the arts and others in the sciences.[42] This idea is appealing to luthiers who believe that their cognitive predisposition to make guitars is a genetic inheritance, as it allows them to temper the objectivity and control associated with postwar masculinity with the intuitive spontaneity thought to characterize femininity.[43] But this understanding of himself, Greven admits, benefits from the clarity of hindsight. At the time, with college on hold and in need of an income, he "fell into" repair work and started building guitars and banjos in Ithaca, New York, and later, in Chattanooga, Tennessee. "It wasn't part of the plan," he laughs. "There *was* no plan."

In 1969, destiny came knocking in the figure of George Gruhn, proprietor of Gruhn Guitars in Nashville. On his way through Chattanooga, Gruhn would visit the town's guitar shop to eye instruments for sale and work under way on the bench. Noticing the fine decorative carving and inlay that Greven had done on banjos and guitars he repaired, Gruhn offered him a job restoring prewar instruments and making custom guitars. Thus began an extraordinary education in the history of acoustic sound:

> I was at the epicenter of the best of the old instruments coming out from the woodwork. People would bring in these '30s vintage, one-of-a-kind Martins, and we'd get to work on them, repair them, restore them, and play them. And *hear* these great guitars—hundreds and hundreds of the best guitars on the planet. One of the things that really bothers me about current builders is that very few—about half a dozen of the hundreds that are out there—have ever actually had anything remotely resembling that kind of exposure to the old instruments. To me that is critical. How do you know what you're doing, if you're not able to relate it to what has already been done? You don't have any idea what the potential of these things is until you've played the best. Like if you're a violinist and you happen to play a Strad once, it spoils you forever. Same thing with guitars.

Getting that vintage sound "in his ears," Greven feels, laid the foundation for all he has accomplished since. "Exposure to the old instruments" provided a customary sound to aim for and a paradigm within which to explore the sonic potential of new designs and production techniques.[44] To be "spoiled forever" is to gain an aesthetic sensibility on the basis of playing instruments that the music world has judged to be "the best." Without an aural and tactile appreciation of what it means to realize a guitar's full "potential," contemporary luthiers are at a disadvantage. For the knowledge that guitar makers need, Greven asserts, can be gained only through sensory experience:

Honestly, if you sat down with Red Smiley's 1939 D-45 and played one chord, you would know exactly what I'm talking about. Because it would be so different from anything else you'd picked up and played, it would stand out in your mind. You'd hear that sound. I hear it today, thirty years later! It's an epiphany of sorts. It's just a visceral auditory experience to pick up one of these great guitars.

The specificity of Greven's memory—not just of a golden era sound in general, but the voice of one instrument in particular—reflects a basic quality of the "working knowledge" that he and other hand builders use on a regular basis.[45] While skill at woodworking is necessary, they say, it is not sufficient for building a guitar. As important is the ability to "sculpt sound" by attending to the physical properties of wood and learning how subtle changes in the shape, design, and weight of a guitar's component parts influence the sound it makes. For builders working in the vintage tradition, capturing the sound and feel of iconic prewar guitars is the goal for every new instrument. Striving to make guitars that sound as good as the old ones on day one, they hope to build guitars that will also improve in tone as they age. To settle for anything less, in Greven's view, is tantamount to building "furniture with strings." The guitar maker's quest is to build an instrument light enough to conduct the strings' energy efficiently, but not so light that it develops structural issues or a "raucous, nasty sound" devoid of overtones:

> The guitar is very inefficient. Many years ago a physicist calculated a 5 percent efficiency for a guitar. Which means that the string energy driving this whole system is losing 95 percent of its energy in the materials and only 5 percent is converted to actual sound. So with that level of inefficiency, you better build a guitar that's as efficient as you can make it to get the most out of it. It's a function of mass. If you take these little tiny strings, which don't have a lot of mass, and drive them, hit them with a flat pick or whatever, start them rotating, all that energy has to drive the entire guitar. The more mass you put on there, the less efficient it becomes. That's why in the very best of the old guitars, the air inside the box weighs more than the guitar does. They're just light as a feather. The downside is they're fragile. So a lot of them haven't survived. In the future, modern ones built

that way may not survive either. But they'll sure sound good while they do.

The presumption of the guitar's "inefficiency" imbues the luthier's work with the fatefulness of an existential drama. If the way to achieve the most desirable sound is to remove as much "mass" as possible, then the resulting guitar will necessarily be a "fragile" creation, not likely to "survive" as long as one more heavily built. To actualize the voice immanent in every guitar, therefore, the luthier is a conscious architect of the guitar's eventual demise.[46] Makers who err on the side of caution and overbuild their instruments, Greven observes, produce guitars that are heavy and lifeless:

> When you pick up a great guitar, whoever made it, whenever it was made, you know it. It's *alive* in your hands; it has a great voice. You can do anything you want with this guitar. It just rewards you with this wonderful sound — this richness, this bigness, this clarity and sustain — all these qualities that you want in a guitar. When I pick up most modern guitars, there's just not much there. It's strings, it's wood, it's called a guitar, it looks like a guitar; but there's just not much *there* there.

The "tone" of gifted labor, Greven suggests, can be transmitted across generations in the form of a voice that affirms the presence or "thereness" of a guitar's lively materiality. Attuned to the failings of instruments built during the postwar years — a period akin to "the dark ages," he says, when manufacturers cranked out "really bad, overbuilt, funky things" — Greven has found a market niche by honoring the "phenomenal, lightly built, *real* musical instruments" of the past. With a high-profile following among Nashville guitarists, including pop star John Denver, Greven soon developed a national reputation. But it was the popularity of his instruments in Japan that enabled him to survive the economic slump of the 1980s. Guitarist Isato Nakagawa was a long-standing fan, and his endorsement generated a steady flow of international orders. When Nakagawa's show-stopping protégé, Kotaro Oshio, hit the world music scene in 2000 with a Greven guitar in hand, that stream swelled to a river.

Located in Portland, Oregon, since 1999, Greven operates a one-man shop and offers twelve different models. With over two thousand guitars to his name, he makes forty to forty-five guitars a year at the surprisingly high rate of four to five a month. While he has sometimes taken on apprentices for three- to five-year periods, he currently works alone. Wondering how he maintains this level of productivity, I hazard a guess: does he use computerized milling? "Oh, no, no!" Greven replies, "This is a CNC-free zone! I don't believe in that stuff." Not only does he prize the flexibility to make "custom tweaks on the fly," but he disavows the "abject, absolute, precision duplication" of mass production:

> I call it the ten thousand monkeys syndrome—ten thousand monkeys, ten thousand word processors, and theoretically you'll come up with a line of Shakespeare. It's the same thing with guitars. You build eight to ten thousand guitars a year, there are bound to be some really good ones in there—maybe ten or twelve or twenty. The rest of them will be kind of okay, and there'll be some duds. But you get a hand builder who takes every single piece of wood and considers all of its properties and the construction, and maximizes to the best of his ability what those woods will do for the guitar, it's *got* to be a better instrument, more than likely.

As Greven sees it, CNC randomizes the likelihood of making a great guitar. Like monkeys incapable of distinguishing one keyboard symbol from another, computerized routers and lasers make no distinction between the pieces of wood they process. Raw wood is cut into identical shapes and sizes regardless of the natural variation in cellular structure that occurs within the same species and even within the same tree. By ignoring the variables that hand builders attend to most closely, he argues, mechanical reproduction results in a bell-shaped distribution of guitars that may look the same but vary significantly in sound quality. Only human makers who treat each piece of wood individually—"considering all of its properties" and "maximizing what it does for the guitar"—stand a chance of making an instrument that rivals the Bard's opus. This is true, Greven asserts, even when the operations are routine:

> GREVEN: Honestly, it's just a matter of having done it so long and so many times, it's [become] easy. When I go to make—

like—a bridge, I know exactly the steps. I don't have to think about it: just grab a chunk of wood and I go through the process, and ten minutes later I've got a bridge. I don't have to measure anything; I just do it. It's like once you learn a complex dance routine—it's just *you*. It's yours, and you don't have to think about it anymore. You just *do* it. You develop an inherent, intuitive sense of what works. It's like breathing; it's an *autonomic* process. [*laughing*] Scary, huh?

DUDLEY [*laughing*]: A little bit. I mean, is there still pleasure in it?

GREVEN: Oh, I love it! It's a gas. It's so much fun. I go down to my workshop and it feels like I'm playing most of the time.

DUDLEY: So even though it's become a routine, that hasn't taken anything away from it?

GREVEN: No, it *is* a routine—it has to be to do this kind of work at this level in this kind of quantity. But it's not only forever challenging, it's always interesting because there aren't very many absolutes in guitar making. None of us really *know* what we're doing. We're constantly experimenting. Every guitar is an experiment, and in that respect, it's exciting. Every guitar is exciting. You never know exactly what you're going to get. We can kind of tweak it and tweak it and *guess*, but until you put the strings on and string it up and play it, you have no idea. That's true for every guitar maker out there. They won't tell you that probably, but that's really what we're doing. We're constantly expanding the envelope with each and every instrument.

To portray guitar making as a "complex dance" is to underscore its aesthetic dimension as an embodied activity. As a physical performance, knowledge in lutherie takes the form of a cultural "repertoire"—a system of "re-presentation" that transmits individual and collective memories and values by materializing them in a stringed instrument.[47] What is remembered or "known" by experienced hand builders is less a set of instructions and measurements than a way of operating and interacting with the tools and materials of their craft. The practices of "guessing" and "tweaking" are a ritualized mode of "experimentation" that allows makers to "expand the envelope" of their repertoire with every instrument they build.

Artisanal knowledge is thus a process of discovery rather than a demonstration of prediction and control. Luthiers who view every guitar as an experiment take their cue from the scientific practices of the eighteenth and early nineteenth centuries: not Enlightenment science, which sought to bend the material world to human will, but romantic science, the countermovement of that period that deplored the subjugation of "Nature" and emphasized the essential unity of human and nonhuman phenomena.[48] Like romantic scientists, artisans strive to communicate *with* the nonhuman through patient observation, sensory interaction, and self-awareness. Learning to recognize the "the character of the sound" immanent in wood, Greven observes, simply "takes a ton of experience":

> When you pick up a top and you tap it, you get a certain *ping* tone that tells you the character of the sound of the finished instrument, provided you don't screw it up and overbuild it or something. But you don't know exactly what that character is unless you've been able to build enough guitars with different top materials and have archived that sound in your head to where you know instantly, "Oh yes, this is going to sound like that." It just takes a ton of experience—or some kind of photographic mind for sound. It's not exactly intuition. If you build a whole bunch of guitars, and you pay attention to what you do with each of those guitars and listen to the product when it's done—archive that sound—and then go to the next one, and the next one, and the next one, you eventually come up with a massive acoustic database in your head of all the things you've done to these guitars over the years and which one worked better than others—and you keep moving in that direction.

The "archive of sound" that Greven refers to is a doubly embodied one—it exists in the maker's ears and memory as well as in the wooden body of every instrument. An "acoustic database" is a form of cumulative knowledge that depends on disciplined practices of attunement as well as exposure to the repertoires and instruments of others. Within the North American lutherie community, information sharing—whether conceptualized as freely circulating knowledge or as the inspiration of teachers, musicians, instruments, or pieces of wood—is, at base, a system of gift exchange. Unlike market exchange, the obligation to repay a debt is a voluntary act, not an enforceable contract. What sets hand builders apart from industrial makers is not the desire for authenticity per se but the extent to which that desire extends to their relationship with wood. The voice of the tree, as Greven might put it, is a gift that must be honored, not "screwed up" or squandered through overbuilding or mechanical reproduction. The key to an authentic way of operating, he argues, is recognizing that artisanal knowledge has no final destination or "endpoint."

> GREVEN: There's a passion to this. All the guys that I know from [the early] period still have it. I mean, decades later they still love it. We feel very fortunate. It's a totally involving thing. It's mind; it's art; it's just left brain, right brain. It's this perpetual not-knowing and wanting to know, and working towards knowing and never fully getting there. It's just fascinating. Not only do you have the accumulation of hand skills, which take many years to develop, it's this feedback between what your hands are doing and your ears are hearing and your eyes are seeing. It's a totally involving process, and forever changing. It's evolving as well as involving. There is no endpoint particularly.
>
> DUDLEY: What is evolving?
>
> GREVEN: Your perceptions and your skills and your understating of what it is you do. I think it takes a couple decades to get to a point where you can articulate what it is you do and why you do it, and you never quite nail it down. It's like, "Oh, this is approximately how it is." That sort of squishiness, that lack of certainty keeps us going, I think. How do you articulate intuition? It's like talking about sound. People talk about the sound of their guitars all the time. It's like talking about wine. It's kind of you put a corral around the wild horses, but you never quite touch the horse.

In a consumer market awash in prefabricated guitar kits made by CNC machines, hand builders of steel-string acoustic guitars can find it hard to make the case that "what they do" takes decades to learn. And the difficulty of "articulating intuition" can be lost on neophytes who imagine that paying their dues simply means purchasing the right equipment. As members of the older generation prepare to pass the chisel on to those who will survive them, the politics of authenticity that shaped their repertoire hangs in the balance. Transmitting embodied knowledge—and the political sensibility that informs it—is no easy affair. Now that the world's most desirable vintage and artisanal instruments are housed in private collections, accumulating a sonic archive can be difficult. But the greatest problem lies in the ritual performance of craft knowledge itself. Despite a plethora of schools and instructional aids, the enactment of lutherie's repertoire involves an awareness of material realities that cannot be named: the "wild horses" that elude the "corral" of language and representation itself.

Scenes of Instruction

The body's features are a register, a site of [social] interaction.
Consequently, what is drawn out of the person [in an initiation ritual]
are the social relationships of which it is composed: it is a microcosm
of relations. In this sense are the capacities of the body revealed. And
if the body is composed of relations, if it shows the imprint of past
encounters, relations are not in state of stasis. Awareness of them implies
they must be attended to. These internal relations must either be further
built upon or must be taken apart and fresh relationships instigated.
—Marilyn Strathern, *The Gender of the Gift* (1988)

Alan Carruth has the twinkling eyes and graying beard of someone who could play a convincing Santa Claus. His workshop in Newport, New Hampshire, occupies the front room of the old dairy barn attached to his house. A small wood stove heats the shop during the winter, but on this day in June 2007 it is covered with sawdust. I stand at Carruth's workbench, watching him distribute a handful of blue glitter on an unfinished guitar top. The braced soundboard lies face up on pieces of foam that are mounted to wooden blocks. With his left hand, Carruth picks up a speaker cone attached to an electronic signal generator. When acoustic testing equipment was hard to come by in the 1970s, his father, a retired electronics engineer, helped him build and sell twenty of these devices. Turning the dial with his right hand, he adjusts the frequency of the sound wave it generates. A low tone is emitted from the speaker, which he holds several inches above the soundboard. "When you get just the right frequency," he explains, "you can see the glitter moving here, up there, a lot of places."[1]

Before my eyes, the glitter begins to gather in areas that are not vibrating at the same frequency as the rest of the top. Gradually, a straight line forms above the sound hole and a large circle takes shape across the lower bout. "This pattern indicates a resonant frequency of this particular top," Carruth says. "What it's doing is it's telling us something about the way the mass and thickness are distributed in this top. It's telling me how the bracing and the top are working together." Every soundboard, I learn, resonates at up to eight or ten different frequencies, forming distinctive patterns at each one. Through years of experi-

FIGURE 4.1. *Alan Carruth demonstrates his plate-tuning technique on a braced top, the glitter forming a straight line and circle pattern, 2007. Photograph by the author.*

mentation and meticulous record keeping, Carruth is able to recognize the patterns associated with the sound of particular guitars and uses these shapes to guide his voicing of new ones. His research on this diagnostic technique—called "free plate tuning"—has made him the go-to person for information about the physics of sound in acoustic guitar construction.[2]

I begin asking Carruth questions that reveal how little I know about guitar acoustics. Deciding that a review of "how the guitar works" is in order, he reaches for an instructional prop he calls "the corker": a guitar body that has no neck or strings and has two rows of holes along the treble side, each hole plugged with a cork. "The basic sound-producing mechanism of the guitar is what acousticians call a bass reflex action," he tells me. "The lower part of the top is going in and out, producing sound the way a loudspeaker does." He raps on the top of the guitar and says that what we're hearing is primarily the frequency of the air rushing in and out of the sound hole. "That accounts for most of the power output of the guitar," he says. Apologizing that he "can't talk without drawing pictures," he leads me over to a worktable, where I sit on a metal stool and watch him draw on a wall-mounted chalkboard. The line is an "output spectrum" that shows the amplitude of the guitar's resonant frequencies between 50 and 350 hertz.[3]

Straining to understand the principle he is illustrating, I find myself participating in one of lutherie's scenes of instruction—a social situation in which makers attempt to represent what they know to students, fellow luthiers, prospective clients, or the general public. The classroomlike feel of Carruth's shop is no accident. Twice a week throughout the year, he offers guitar-making instruction to students who work at their own pace. But luthiers who enact these scenes are not necessarily tuition-collecting teachers. Since the early 1970s, guitar makers have gathered to exchange information and create an archive of craft knowledge in their guitars, journal articles, instrument plans, and specialized equipment. In an effort to counteract the secrecy of guilds and the proprietary claims of manufacturers, they have developed a pedagogical model that celebrates the ingenuity of autodidacts and inveterate tinkerers. To "teach" in this sense is to share what one has learned through experience and self-directed study. The Guild of American Luthiers, publisher of the quarterly magazine *American Lutherie*, states this principle in a note to prospective authors: "The "right way" is a myth. Everyone has something to tell and something to learn. The more one knows about lutherie (or anything), the more one realizes how much more there is to know. We exist to provide a forum of information exchange between Guild members, and we are interested in publishing opinions, designs, and methods which are backed by experience."[4]

Carruth's knowledge of acoustics comes not from his bachelor's degree in sociology—"That and a dollar will get you a cup of coffee almost anyplace!" he jokes—but from his ongoing fascination with lutherie, which began when he was in the navy in the late 1960s. Once out of the service, he finished college and began studying classical guitar making.[5] Like most of his contemporaries, he began teaching what he knew as soon as he learned it, assisting his teacher with classes and eventually leading courses of his own. Motivated by the need to make ends meet and the excitement of sharing their passion with others,

FIGURE 4.2. *Carruth's "corker" guitar and graph depicting*
the bass reflex, 2007. Photograph by the author.

many guitar makers find that teaching, lecturing, and writing about their craft helps them articulate what they are doing and why.

For most practitioners, however, the information exchanged in public forums is rarely about instrument building alone. Through the process of representing their embodied knowledge—to one another, a general audience, or an inquiring anthropologist—makers define what it means to be a luthier and a member of the lutherie community. Understood in this way, scenes of instruction are staging grounds for artisanal values and the production of a culturally distinctive sense of self.

QUESTIONING NATURE

Looking at Carruth's graph of the bass reflex—he is embellishing it with a dotted line to show other resonant frequencies—I begin to grasp the story it tells. With a few deftly placed lines, he has created a visual representation of what the guitar is (an air pump) and how it operates (pressure changes in the sound box cause the wood to resonate at a range of frequencies). Modes of air resonance other than the bass reflex generally operate to subtract from the total output of this primary mode, I learn, and this effect appears as little dips in Carruth's graph.

"But what happens," he asks, pausing dramatically, "when you open up a hole in the side of the guitar?" Over the past decade, a growing number of builders have been cutting "side ports" in their instruments—a craze that has captivated steel-string and classical guitar makers alike.[6] Opinions differ, however, on what effect ports actually have. Most agree that they function as a monitor, amplifying the sound to the musician's ear. But some builders argue that ports also make the instrument louder to the audience, while others are not persuaded. Carruth is in the latter camp, having put the question to the test in a series of experiments on the corker.[7]

He taps the belly of the guitar twice with his thumb. He pops out two corks from the upper bout and taps again. The difference in volume is infinitesimal. "What this opening does is vent the main air resonance," Carruth tells me. "So what you end up with is less pressure change inside the box from that resonance." This reduces the loudness of the output at that resonant frequency when measured by a mike in front of the guitar. However, in a traditional guitar, he says, there is always air sloshing around that does not get expelled through the sound hole. When a side port is opened up and a microphone is placed close to this port, the main air resonance shows a gain of several decibels.

"This is what people hear when you pull out the corks," he explains. "But what you get is an increase of 1 or 2 percent, and when that's averaged out across the whole spectrum, it's nothing to write home about." The human ear is designed to detect small differences, he says; think "the rustle in the bush that's the tiger." Side ports have caught on, he concludes, because people assume that if the player hears an increase in volume, the audience must too.

Being a damper on others' enthusiasm is not a role that Carruth relishes, and he shrugs good-naturedly when discussing opposing views. What aggravates him is the fact that side port advocates offer no evidence to support their position. "In this kind of a situation," he observes, "somebody who can talk a good line can go a long way on almost nothing, because nobody really knows."

In a community where there is no "right way," competing claims jostle for attention on the Internet, at annual meetings, and in lutherie publications. Few mechanisms exist to adjudicate disputes, let alone advance a "science" of lutherie. For Carruth, this has been a disappointment. From the start of his career, he was drawn to experiments on free plate tuning with violins and guitars. This work seemed to be the wave of the future: a scientific technique that promised to take the guesswork out of instrument voicing. As a visual indicator of soundboard density and stiffness, pattern-based tuning offers a check on the fallibility of human senses — a concern for Carruth, who incurred partial hearing loss aboard an aircraft carrier while in the navy.

In its heyday, research conducted by the Catgut Acoustical Society turned heads in the guitar world as makers began to think about the physics of their instrument in scientifically informed ways.[8] But free plate tuning has never caught on widely among guitar makers. The specialized equipment, time-consuming process, and meticulous record keeping it requires have limited its use to all but the most empirically minded. Interest in its general principles nonetheless remains high, so Carruth undertakes his experiments as a labor of love on behalf of the lutherie community. In addition to helping fellow luthiers understand the acoustic properties of stringed instruments, his work legitimates the intuitive aspect of artisanal ways of operating. What hand builders do, he argues, goes beyond the limits of "rational" explanation:

> Guitars are very complicated boxes. They are much more complicated than they might seem to be. The result is that while a physicist can deal with them at some level, they do some fairly complicated computer modeling studies that really don't get all the way there. We [luthiers] are dealing with all of the little details around the edges that are difficult for the physics guys to look at — that are way too complicated or at the edge of being understandable in a *rational* way. All the little nonlinearities and the interactions that are complicated — but they are, in fact, what makes the difference between merely good guitars and really fine ones. It's all those little things.

Computational physics can take one only so far when faced with the materiality of a "complicated box." Where "rationality" fails, however, empiricism can persist, as artisans employ sensory perception to go beyond what can be known scientifically. "The elephant in the room," Carruth observes, "is that the ultimate judgments are subjective, and it really is a lot of little things that are very hard to define." In this craft epistemology, luthiers rely on subjective experience—tactile information, hunches, and suppositions—to deal with phenomena that cannot be understood objectively. "Anybody who is getting consistent results *knows* what they are doing," Carruth points out. "Even if they can't tell you what they are doing in an objective sense or a scientific way, they know what they're doing." Subjective knowledge may not be amenable to culturally authoritative modes of representation, he observes, but it can be conveyed in a "story":

> The human mind is such a wonderful thing in terms of dealing with huge quantities of information and making sense out of disparate kinds of data that in a rational sense would be hard to deal with. The artificial intelligence people say that all the things that are easy for computers are hard for people, and all the things that are hard for computers are easy for people. And it's really true. The hardest thing to do, to get a computer to do, would probably be to walk down the street in a city—something on that level that almost any three-year-old can do with a little supervision. Because we're used to dealing with all this kind of fuzzy stuff and making some level of sense out of it, whether or not it's rigorously mathematically provable that it is *true* or not. This is why we have myths and legends. Somebody said that the human mind is a story-making machine—that you look at what's going on and you make up a story about that and try to account for what's happening by making up stories. The role of science is to try to figure out which of those stories is more likely to be true.

The art of walking through city streets requires the ability to process "fuzzy" information under changing or unique circumstances and act spontaneously when necessary. It can also be an experience of uncertainty, of not being exactly sure where you are or where you are going.[9] Nonetheless, in Carruth's scenario, the jaywalking luthier, not the "rational" computer, is more likely to "get all the way there"—arriving at the desired destination by whatever route "accounts for what's happening," however circuitous or unorthodox. Likewise, the accounts that guitar makers give of their improvisational practices express a subjective grasp of material reality, not a "rigorously, mathematically provable" truth. Before these stories can be accepted as "true" representations of reality, however, they must be supported by experimental evidence or testimony of the finished instrument. In the meantime, he laments, the imagination soars:

> Unless you have some kind of a reality test, you can come up with all kinds of stories. There's way too many invisible pink unicorns in lutherie. There's way too many people saying way too many things that are just not true. There is a very well known classical builder who, in an interview in *Guitar Player*, said the way the guitar works is that you pluck the string and the sound comes off the string, and it goes in through the sound hole and bounces off the back, gets kind of dispersed, and comes out through the top. The top is porous and the sound comes through the top, and that's why you have to use something like French polish finish on the top, so the sound can get through. I just looked at that and I thought to myself, "Well, where do I start with this guy? In terms of physics, he is so far off in left field that it's pathetic." That's the tip of the iceberg. There's just a lot of this stuff out there.

The danger of "pink unicorns" is not that they exist but that they proliferate unchecked. Nor is the problem that the guitar is an endless mystery. This is a subject upon which even laconic builders can wax poetic. Rather, stories with no empirical basis flout the key requirement of knowledge claims within the lutherie community, that they be backed by experiences others can replicate, and its ethical corollary, that they be developed in consultation with the raw materials of the craft. Carruth is exasperated with his imaginative colleague not simply because his story is "untrue" but because there is no common ground for the dialogue he wants to "start with this guy."

To preserve and bequeath their cultural repertoire, guitar makers must be able to communicate what they know in terms that translate into actual practice. Looming below the "tip of the iceberg" is the mortality of subjective knowledge and the threat its loss poses to the future of the community. Unshared intuitive ways of operating follow the maker to the grave, forever lost to the collective consciousness of the group. The only hope for the survival of a living craft tradition lies in a pedagogy that makes its repertoire accessible in a language others can comprehend. Like a unicorn, experiential know-how is rare: it cannot be possessed on demand or invented to fulfill a wish of mastery. It must be pursued patiently and, as medieval legend has it, with the mind of a maiden who can coax it to sleep on her lap.

———

The Healdsburg Guitar Festival is a not-to-be-missed extravaganza in the lutherie world. Established in 1996 and held every other year since 1997, the three-day event in mid-August draws over one hundred North American guitar makers to California's Sonoma Valley. In addition to the exhibition of artisanal guitars of all styles and shapes, the Healdsburg show—named for the location of its original venue—features demonstration concerts and instructional workshops by well-known musicians, and begins each day with a ninety-minute lecture given by a top builder.

On this morning in 2007, I am accompanied by my wife, Maria Trumpler, a historian of science. She has been persuaded to attend the talk but not the show itself, steadfast in the belief that touring local vineyards holds greater appeal. We stop at the ticket table to see if this odd request can be accommodated. Luthiers Merchantile International is the festival's chief sponsor, and I wave to LMI's general manager, Natalie Swango. She greets us warmly and, taking the situation in hand, allows us to enter the theater.

Today's speaker is Mark Blanchard, a builder in his early fifties. Blanchard's presentation is projected onto a large screen that dominates the stage of the darkened auditorium. "My topic today is Chladni pattern-based voicing," he tells us, a soft light from the podium illuminating his face and mustache.[10] "I am only going to talk about the methods I use, because those are the only methods I really know anything about." A portrait of Ernst Chladni—a German physicist who lived from 1756 to 1827—appears on the screen. Blanchard describes Chladni's research on "free plate resonance," showing us pictures of the circular metal plates Chladni used in the 1780s to create geometric patterns out of sand.[11] The plates' homogenous metals allowed Chladni to predict the frequencies at which sand would form distinctive shapes when the plates were made to vibrate with a violin bow.

Given the variable nature of wood, Blanchard explains, no universal formula exists for guitar tops. Nonetheless, "through sheer per-severance," he says, "I have managed to crack some of the code and find ways to use Chladni patterns in a fairly simple way, day to day at my workbench." Blanchard's introduction to free plate tuning came in 1996, when he took a two-day workshop with Alan Carruth, whom he describes as having an "intense and very lovable nutty-professor type of energy." Skipping the "equations and theories" that his teacher is fond of, he proceeds to show us how this approach to guitar voicing works in everyday practice.

Aware that his audience is filled with fellow luthiers and avid guitar players, Blanchard introduces Chladni top voicing by comparing it to a testing procedure everyone is familiar with. The patterns that appear at certain resonant frequencies, he suggests, are simply visual represen-tations of the sonic information guitar makers derive from "tap tones." Most builders will tap on the surface of a soundboard while voicing it, listening for two or three different resonances or "singing" tones to indicate whether an optimal thickness gradient has been achieved. To produce these tones, they must find places where the top is *not* vibrat-ing, such that holding the top at these "nodes" allows it to resonate freely when tapped. The significance of the Chladni technique, Blan-chard argues, is that it makes tap tones legible to the careful observer:

The Chladni patterns are to tap tones what the written word is to spoken language. They are just a written representation of some-thing audible. We can think of individual patterns as words; each one has meaning, a definition—it tells us something about the top. But as with language, where arranging words into sentences will produce meaning beyond the definitions of the words themselves, a set of Chladni patterns will have meaning beyond what the patterns tell us individually. It did take me time to learn the language, but as familiarity with the patterns increased, so did my ability to extract data from them.

I exchange glances with the historian of science sitting beside me. Maria wrote her dissertation on scientific experimentation in Ger-many at the end of the eighteenth century. During this period, she ob-serves, researchers associated with the romantic movement in science saw their experiments as ways of "questioning Nature," believing that

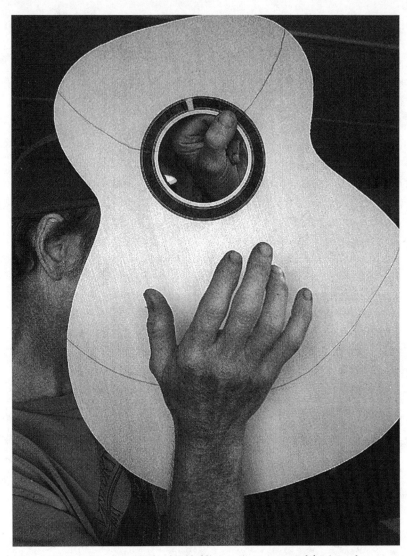

FIGURE 4.3. Mark Blanchard holding a guitar top at a nodal point and listening for "tap tones." Photograph by Mark Blanchard.

"Nature," figured as a woman, would reveal herself to those who asked the right questions.[12] To romantic-era scientists, Chladni's vibrating plates were the quintessential demonstration of how nature's "secrets" could be deciphered by patient and persistent experimentation.[13] Luthiers who use plate tuning techniques—the "glitter people," as they are sometimes called—have clearly taken a leaf from the romantics' notebook when they conceptualize tap tones as a "spoken language" and Chladni patterns as "written words." Although Blanchard does not identify *who* is speaking and writing this language, he implies that it is the wood itself:

> Over the years I have generated thousands of these patterns, and I still find it quite thrilling. It is as if the specific frequency of sound coming from the speaker is a key that unlocks a hidden secret. Indeed, the top is revealing something about its inner structure. The shape, mass, and stiffness distribution unique to that top will affect the shape of the pattern and the frequency at which it occurs. As with a fingerprint, the patterns produced by a given top seem to be unique; no two are exactly alike.

Pattern voicing legitimizes the artisan's intuitive approach to the presumed singularity of every instrument. As a distinctive set of "fingerprints" emerges in the whorls of sawdust that collect at each modal frequency, the guitar comes into being as an "individual" and active agent in its own right. Through careful record keeping, Blanchard has identified ideal frequency ranges for ten modes between 50 and 500 hertz. Using his initial Chladni patterns to thin and graduate the top, he optimizes each mode by removing wood in selected areas, effectively lowering the frequency at which a pattern appears.

As it happens, thinning a top does little to affect the original shape of a mode—a lesson, Blanchard admits, he learned the hard way.[14] But time spent voicing the soundboard is invaluable. Not only does it increase the likelihood of building a great guitar, he says, but it offers an opportunity for playful discovery of an instrument's inner character:

> It is the top that makes the [guitar's] sound. By taking time with the unbraced top, I know that it is right, that it is in its optimal state for making a guitar that might sound the way I want it to. I know this

because I've tried different things, kept records, and been shown that all my favorite guitars had tops about like this. In addition I am now very familiar with this top. The knowledge I've gained by working with it—by tickling it with my signal generator, flexing it, tapping it, and thereby getting it to reveal its secrets—will inform my decisions when I start the bracing.

Like a baby or coy lover, a soundboard is thought to "reveal its secrets" under the persistent ministrations of the luthier. Builders' language of discovery often employs the narrative conventions of a fetishized romantic encounter, positioning the guitar maker as both desiring to know and wishing to disavow sexual difference. Producing a guitar, in this scenario, fortifies the maker's masculinity by enabling him to project feminine aspects of himself onto the craft object. Yet as the give-and-take of Blanchard's "tickling" suggests, the process of making is experienced as much more interactive than classic accounts of feminine passivity allow. His wood may be eroticized, but it is not objectified.[15] Quite the contrary: it directs and corrects the luthier's every effort.

Once the modal frequencies are where he wants them, Blanchard records a final set of patterns for the unbraced top. These figures provide reference points that guide how he carves the braces. Stiff and heavy at the outset, new braces have the effect of "distorting" the modal shapes of the free plate. Unshaved braces "disrupt" the smooth movement of sound waves in the top, Blanchard explains, resulting in an "inefficient" transfer of energy and "thuddy" tap tones. The goal of sculpting the braces, he says, is "to restore the modes to their undistorted shape while retaining the structural integrity required to handle the string tension of the finished instrument."

To do this, he carves the braces until the top's distorted patterns come to resemble a set of "target modes" he has developed over the years. Giving us an example of how modal patterns can be altered in the desired direction, Blanchard shows us the "infamous 'ring and a half'" mode that appears on X-braced soundboards. Ideally, the nodal line should form a circle in the lower bout, but sometimes it remains open on the bass side. Closing the ring is not easy, since patterns do not indicate exactly where the braces should be shaved. "But," he smiles,

FIGURE 4.4. *Blanchard taking notes on Chladni patterns. Photograph by Mark Blanchard.*

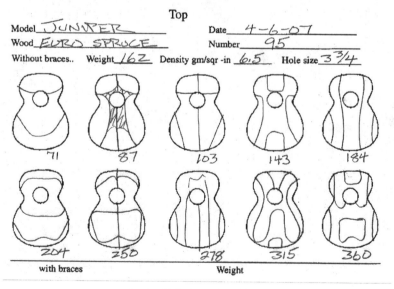

Top

Model _JUNIPER_   Date _4-6-07_

Wood _EURO SPRUCE_   Number _95_

Without braces..   Weight _162_   Density gm/sqr -in _6.5_   Hole size _3 3/4_

71   87   103   143   184

204   250   278   315   360

with braces   Weight

FIGURE 4.5. *Blanchard's final set of patterns for an unbraced top.*
Photograph by Mark Blanchard.

FIGURE 4.6. Blanchard sculpting top braces to alter the shape of modal patterns.
Photograph by Mark Blanchard.

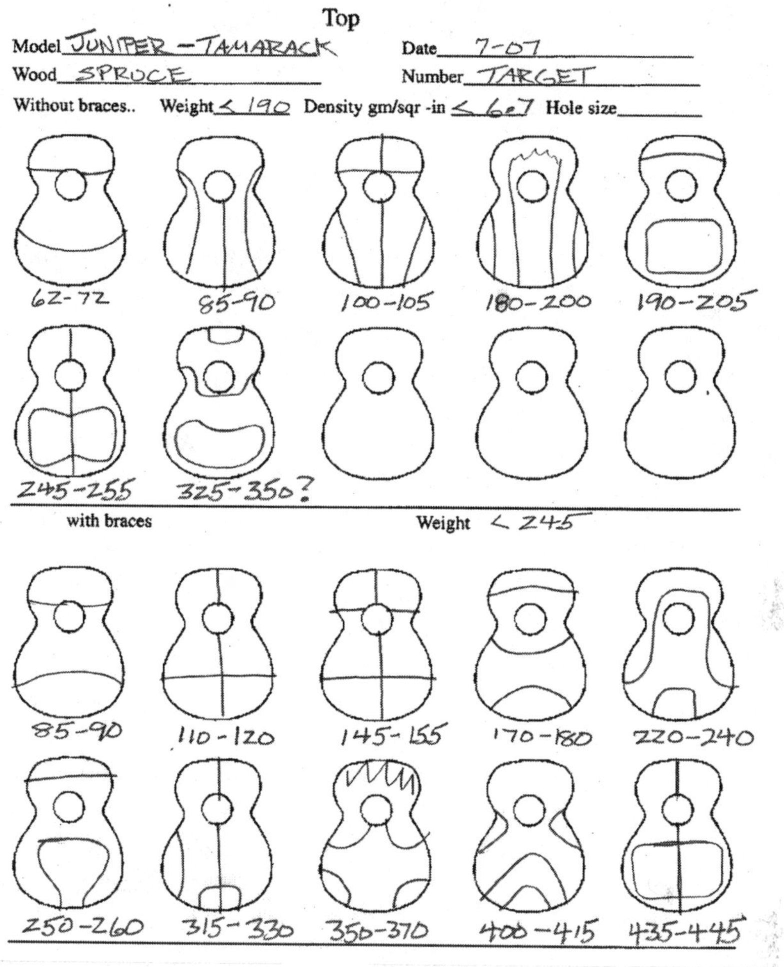

FIGURE 4.7. Blanchard's target mode patterns.
Photograph by Mark Blanchard.

"there is a little trick to finding the right spot": "And the trick is — to *guess!* That's right, good ol' trial and error. Take a little bit of wood off somewhere and check the mode again to see if it caused the mode shape to change in the direction you want it to go. If nothing happened, or it moved the wrong way, try another brace. Eventually, you will find the 'hot spot' that does what you want it to do." Attentive "trial and error" — posing questions and listening to the wood's response — is the hallmark of artisanal ways of knowing. Motivated by the desire to communicate with their wood, hand builders enable it to "speak" in a language they can understand.[16]

Although pattern-based tuning is by no means everyone's cup of tea, the habits of mind it requires and the commitment to empirical inquiry it sustains are central to the luthier's craft. As Blanchard concludes, "Whether we tap, listen, and remember, do deflection testing and record the deflections,[17] or just build and let our intuition develop over time, the idea is to gather information that we can correlate to the tone of the finished guitar and use that information to inform us as we build. Chladni patterns are just one way of doing that."

The practices by which luthiers gather empirical information, whether through pattern tuning or other techniques, provide them with a way to narrate and visually represent material realities that are not otherwise amenable to human comprehension. Their efforts to reveal the hidden, indwelling, or "immanent character" of a guitar's tone result in a story of making that serves to rearticulate that tone. In this sense, tone can be understood as a "hyper-relational concept of *feeling* that encompasses an attitude," affective orientation, or "'set toward' its audience and the world."[18] The feeling-tone of the artisanal encounter is one of surprise, unfolding discovery, and uncertainty, allowing makers to question the "nature" of culturally authoritative knowledge itself.[19] As Blanchard makes clear, the goal of his experimentation is not to arrive at a definitive pattern or design: "I guarantee [my target modes] will be different in another year. It is an ongoing, never-ending evolution. I still do a lot of experimenting with the structure of my guitars. I'm constantly trying to make them better, and as I make new discoveries, my Chladni formula changes."

Artisanal guitar making is a cultural site where a romantic sense of wonder and passionate engagement with the nonhuman world thrives as a viable alternative to the economic and scientific rationality that dominates the contemporary political landscape.[20] Yet as a living repertoire, the uncertain status of artisanal knowledge presents a pedagogical dilemma. If there are few settled truths in lutherie—if the craft object is open to continual revision and the process of making is subject to "ongoing, never-ending evolution"—then what do guitar makers actually "know," and how can it be communicated to others?[21]

CRAFTING SELVES

On summer days in 1973, sixteen-year-old Fred Carlson could be found sitting "stark naked" outside an old dairy barn near Montpelier, Vermont, making banjos and sanding dulcimers in the company of his similarly unclad mentor, Ken Riportella. "The image in my mind is really pretty charming," Carlson says with an impish grin. "There was nothing bad about that—it was very innocent."[22] We are talking at the 2007 Healdsburg Guitar Festival, sitting outside in the shade of a covered walkway. Occasionally the sound of low-flying jets from the Sonoma County Air Show interrupts our conversation, causing us to look up and protect our ears. Carlson is a man of small stature, bedecked today in pants that feature a pattern of suns, moons, and stars, and a hat that sports a peacock feather. His flair for the dramatic, nourished by a lifelong love of the theater, extends to the fabulous, one-of-a-kind stringed instruments he is known for.

Over that summer of artistic awakening, Riportella lived in a tent on the hillside behind the barn. As part of a countercultural experiment, he had persuaded his student to join him in seeing how long they could go without wearing any clothes. Carlson lived in a local commune and attended an alternative high school during the school year. When he and another student expressed an interest in making dulcimers, the school's director had found them a teacher in the person of Riportella, a Goddard College student who made "psychedelic dulcimers." Among Riportella's teaching qualifications was his stint as a welder of gongs for a musicology professor who built "every instrument in the world," most notably a Javanese gamelan orchestra out of sheet metal.[23] Riportella tutored his charges in the basics of dulcimer construction and wood acquisition, pointing them in the direction of Dumpsters outside a door factory and a motorcycle shop where they scavenged for

FIGURE 4.8. *Fred Carlson at the Healdsburg Guitar Festival, 2007. At the left is The Flying Dream, a thirty-nine-string "Harp-Sympitar" (six unfretted sub-bass harp strings, six main strings, twelve sympathetic resonating strings inside the neck and body, and fifteen treble harp strings positioned diagonally across the top) made in 2003. To its right is an eighteen-string "Sympitar" (six standard guitar strings, and twelve sympathetics inside the neck and body) built in 1996. Photograph by the author.*

plywood "door skin" and packing crates made of Philippine (lauan) mahogany. After the class was over, Carlson befriended his teacher, finding in him the support and inspiration he needed to begin designing and making instruments from scratch:

> [Riportella] was not a trained musician or a trained instrument builder. And really, he didn't teach me anything directly other than by the way he did things, because he didn't know that much, except that he was very inspired. He was a wonderful artist, very talented, and knew more than I did, basically. I just watched him, and he would give me ideas about my drawings. Since he did a lot of drawing, I learned very early on to draw out instruments and try to

imagine how they would work. I was just making things up. He took me to the Metropolitan Museum of Art in New York. I was just completely blown away. I can't tell you; it almost brings tears to my eyes to think how moving that was to me—to realize that there was a whole world full of musical instruments. I just wandered around and drew little sketches of things. I wanted to make a *pipa*, a Chinese lute, in the worst way, not knowing anything about it. I made one out of plywood and lauan mahogany. It didn't play very well. It had these long, high frets. But I carved little faces in it and stuff. I was not musically sophisticated at all, but I was very visually oriented, so I'd pick up on the design elements and things like that.

The capacity to "just watch" and learn through observation is the foundation of an artisanal apprenticeship.[24] As Carlson recognizes, Riportella provided very little direct instruction apart from "the way he did things." What Carlson absorbed from this mentorship was not a body of knowledge—Riportella "didn't know that much"—but a way of seeing and thinking about the craft objects he longed to make. By creating a visual representation of an instrument's actual or imagined features, he was able to test that design against the functional reality of its materialization. Carlson's visit to the Metropolitan Museum of Art "blew him away" not only because it exposed him to instruments he had never seen but also because it overwhelmed the scene of instruction with possibilities he was unequipped to handle. As he wandered around drawing what he saw, he practiced a mode of attunement that may have worked with a dulcimer but was, as yet, no match for a *pipa*.

In 1975 Carlson came upon a flyer advertising a guitar-making school called Earthworks in South Stafford, Vermont. The school was about an hour's drive from his commune—close enough not to trigger the anxiety attacks he suffered away from home but far enough to be a challenge. Established two years earlier by Charles Fox, the six-week residential school—later renamed the Center for Guitar Research and Design—was the second of its kind in North America.[25] Invoking the spirit of the *Whole Earth Catalog*, Earthworks—a complex of three yurts—catered to a generation of youth attracted to the idea of meeting their material needs with their own hands. The course's eight-hundred-dollar cost was a large amount for Carlson, whose monthly contribution to the commune rarely exceeded the fifty-dollar allowance sent by his father. "I was really being supported by other people," he admits. His parents were estranged, and both had left the commune. But his father had set aside two thousand dollars for him to put toward college, and he let Carlson use this money for tuition, living expenses, and a basic set of tools.

The course began in November, and the student body consisted of Carlson and five other men who slept in the yurts and prepared common meals together. Charles Fox lived with his family in a log house and began each morning with a demonstration of the procedures students were to execute that day.[26] Having been a high school art teacher, Fox had a knack for distilling the complexities of guitar making into a "simple set of rules" that students could easily digest. "This is his gift," Carlson avers, "and it's still his gift." Documenting Fox's instructions for future reference, he filled a "big, thick notebook with copious notes and pictures of everything." Looking back, he says that the most valuable lesson he learned was a "way of thinking about the guitar-building process":

> What [Fox] taught me is almost still what I do, in a certain way. I'd been doing it [making instruments] for long enough that all I needed was the recipe. It's like being a cook and knowing how vegetables work, knowing how much you have to cook them, and knowing what tastes like this, but just not having the recipe. Then someone gives you a recipe, and suddenly you can make a quiche or whatever it is. So I had this recipe and this recipe book. I used that book with every instrument I made for years. I was very dependent on it, even though I was—well, I really wanted to be an artist. But I knew that I needed to spend a while just following the rules and learning what they were. So I did that for a few years, and I made a few instruments that were pretty traditional. Ever since then, I've been trying to figure out how to stretch beyond that.

Carlson's affirmation that Fox's gift is "still a gift" speaks less about the fact that Fox continues to teach guitar making from his home in Portland than about the way Carlson still values that gift over thirty years later. For the "recipe" he was bequeathed was not a static document. Coming to Fox's school already familiar with the materials, methods, and aesthetics of his craft, he was given a way of putting those ingredients together. Making that gift his own, however, required a labor of gratitude—a period of "following the rules" before he could "stretch beyond" them to realize his own gift. This labor began when Carlson realized that what he recorded in his notebook was not an inviolable set of procedures:

> The funny thing is, I went back [to the school] a number of times to visit, because it was close enough and I eventually learned to drive. I could go and visit while his classes were in session. And he taught it differently every time! I would go and look at what he was teaching, and he was teaching something completely different than he taught me. They had a whole different way of bending the sides, different ways they were doing things, but they all worked. That was the wonderful thing.

Rather than being dismayed by the new methods Fox used, Carlson delights in his improvisational approach. As a performative repertoire, a "recipe" is an organizing logic for what "works"—a logic that leads, in practice, to the development of alternative techniques. Longing to enjoy a similar freedom from his rule-bound notebook, Carlson came to focus on its underlying wisdom concerning the physical requirements of a vibrating string:

> Everything starts with a straight line on a piece of paper—that was what [Fox] taught me. That's still what I do. I love that. I take a big piece of poster board and start with a straight line, and then everything is anchored to that straight line. That is the center of everything—center of the string access, center of the neck, center of the sculpture. But I started trying to take that and then work it and get asymmetrical, and very early on I became more and more asymmetrical. Eventually I got to a point where I realized that I really wanted to lose the rules. I really wanted to be an artist in a way where I wasn't imprisoned by the rules.

During the late 1970s Carlson's instruments began to attract notice, and he found camaraderie in the emergent lutherie movement. The Smithsonian included one of his guitars in its groundbreaking "Harmonious Craft" exhibit, and he met his life partner, Suzy Norris—an artist and violinmaker—at the 1979 meeting of the Guild of American Luthiers in Boston. Carlson and Norris, together with Riportella, founded the Vermont Musical Instrument Builders Cooperative, a workshop that pooled resources and made the work of a small group of artisans available to the general public.[27] Through that workshop, Carlson came to know Daniel Hecht and Alex de Grassi, two artists who recorded with Windham Hill Record Company. By the 1980s, Carlson was designing unusual guitars with sympathetic strings, instruments that would eventually be introduced to a mainstream audience through de Grassi's virtuoso music. In 1989 Carlson decided the time had come to leave his commune, and he and Norris set off for Santa Cruz, where her parents lived. In the tumult of that move, the Earthworks notebook was lost.

In the early 1970s, Ralston Purina's sixty-foot fiberglass cow was touring Europe when a renegade political group kidnapped it and threw it into the ocean. In 1974 the cow washed ashore in Peggy's Cove, Nova Scotia, sorely in need of a new paint job. Answering an ad that said, "Wanted: Artist to paint cow," Tony Duggan-Smith, a student at the College of Art and Design in Halifax, showed up for work game for anything—although detailing larger-than-life bovine anatomy atop a scaffold was not, he tells me, a possibility he had considered. Chatting over breakfast before the opening of the 2009 Montreal Guitar Show, Duggan-Smith tells me about juggling careers as a guitar maker, songwriter, and professional guitar player. And on this drizzly, overcast morning he speaks rapidly, animated by life's ironies before taking his first sip of coffee.

The cow-painting episode would have been just another crazy gig were it not for the local entrepreneur in charge of the project. Rufus Stewart also happened to be a guitar technician who had moved to Halifax from Montreal to set up a guitar shop. Duggan-Smith began hanging out with Stewart in his spare time and eventually came to the realization that instrument repair was more compelling than art school, especially at a time when conceptual art ruled the gallery scene in New York City. Midway through the academic year, Canadian folksinger Bruce Cockburn performed in Halifax, and Duggan-Smith struck up a friendship with members of the sound crew. Before he knew it, they had persuaded him to leave school, jump aboard their van, and come with them to Toronto. We share a good laugh recalling how easy such things were to do at the impetuous age of twenty.

Before leaving Halifax, Duggan-Smith had acquired a Larrivée guitar from Stewart in a trade for his Les Paul and a Gibson Southern Jumbo. Shaped like a classical guitar but built for steel strings, the handmade Larrivée had the best sound he had ever heard in an acoustic guitar. There was only one problem: "the neck was really big, like a log," a feature that made the guitar hard for Duggan-Smith to play.[28] When he got to Toronto, he went to Jean-Claude Larrivée's shop to see if something could be done. Larrivée handed the guitar to his assistant and asked him if the neck was too big. After playing a Cockburn piece on it, the assistant said the neck was fine. In a public relations gambit unimaginable in today's custom guitar world, Larrivée gave the guitar back to Duggan-Smith and told him, "You'll just have to get used to it."

Duggan-Smith went directly to the Toronto Folklore Center and sold the guitar. The center eventually hired him to repair guitars, and he relished the opportunity to hone his skills. Like other folklore centers operating across North America, Toronto's was a hub for folk musicians and countercultural ferment. Its owner, Eric Nagler, had left the United States in 1968 to protest the war in Vietnam and in 1972 was tried and acquitted of draft evasion.[29] In 1975 Larrivée came to the center hoping to find a new apprentice, and Duggan-Smith was offered the job:

At that point people were writing to Larrivée from all over the world [saying], "Please take me on as an apprentice!" He was well known as a classical maker because he was Edgar Mönch's apprentice and he was really good. But I hadn't even thought about working for him. I said, "Well, how much does it pay?" He looked at me and said, "It doesn't pay anything; it's an apprenticeship. You come and you get experience, and the payment is that you learn how to build guitars." I said, "You've got to be kidding! Are you out of your mind?" But all of these people [who worked for him] had been working there for nothing because they really wanted it. I said, "I can't do that. I don't have a trust fund; I have to make a living." So he ended up paying me what I got paid at the Folklore Center, which wasn't a whole lot of dough, but it was enough to live on.

Duggan-Smith says he was "no revolutionary union leader," but his coup led Larrivée's other shop assistants to demand and receive modest salaries as well. That these negotiations took place when they did—at a time when Larrivée was planning to expand his six-person shop into a factory—reflected a turning point in North American lutherie. During the mid-1970s, several American hand builders were in the process of adopting industrial production methods.[30] Among this group, only Larrivée had served a traditional apprenticeship.[31] When he switched his focus from classical to steel-string guitars in 1971, Larrivée had begun taking on apprentices himself—beginning with eighteen-year-old Grit Laskin, who worked with him for two years before setting up his own shop. Those who were lucky enough to find apprenticeships in the early 1970s could expect to learn the craft in exchange for their labor. Yet as Duggan-Smith observes, this contract unraveled when production levels rose and work became more specialized:

> The reality is, working with Jean [at that time], everyone was taught very narrow, specific things. Nobody was taught everything. A real "true" apprenticeship is a staged thing where you learn the whole process, and Jean was never about that. He was a smart guy. He knew that if you teach somebody everything, they're just going to learn it all and split. So you'll keep people longer if you just teach them a little and they have to observe everyone else to try and get a sense of the rest of the process.

For those who hope to make guitars themselves, Duggan-Smith argues, "understanding the process is everything." When Larrivée moved to a larger facility in Vancouver in 1977, four of his Toronto apprentices—including Linda Manzer and Duggan-Smith—made the trip with him.[32] In the new location, Duggan-Smith was assigned to installing frets during the day and doing inlay work at night. Although he is proud of the inlay he did on special "presentation" models, he felt overworked and underpaid and soon returned to Toronto. From the late 1970s to the early 1990s, he did instrument repair and restoration, designed sets for film companies, and launched his career as a musician.

Drawn back to lutherie in 1995, Duggan-Smith received a grant from the Canadian Council for the Arts that allowed him to study archtop guitar building with Manzer, and he continues to work with her on a part-time basis today. Reflecting on this formal apprenticeship, what stands out in his mind is how she taught him to see the guitar. Rather than focusing on isolated aspects of construction, he says, she encouraged him to conceptualize the process as a whole:

> It's understanding the elements as a whole that is the skill, that is the magic. A lot of people make stuff, whether it's a guitar or anything else, and they only understand a few of the elements. They have a percentage of the elements under control, but they don't have the whole. It's like science or anything else. The people who suddenly see the big picture are the ones who can actually do something that takes off. Because the magic or the mystery of stuff is big; it's never totally finite, you know.

Not getting hung up on the details—like the pitch of a tap tone or the precision of a miter joint—allows him to "see the big picture" and intuitively grasp how the instrument works as an integrated system. The critical difference between artisanal and industrial ways of apprehending the "whole" production process has to do with the temporal and sensory modalities by which it is grasped. The factory manufacturer's knowledge is displayed in a visual design prior to the instrument's production, which is then carried out by a large group of workers, each of whom has only a fraction of the "elements under their control." The artisan's knowledge, in contrast, engages all five senses and is physically demonstrated throughout the construction process, which is under the control of an individual or a small shop of builders from beginning to end. To be "full of mojo," Duggan-Smith asserts, a guitar must come into being "organically" by virtue of intense, prolonged contact with its maker's body:

DUGGAN-SMITH: Linda is incredibly strong, and she's fearless as well. She has no fear. She just gets down and just does it. She's a dynamo, and it's fantastic to watch. People have this presumption of a woman guitar maker and all that stuff, but she is such a frickin' beast in the workshop, it's incredible. I've spent a lot of time with Linda and I've learned a lot from her, from watching her. I've gleaned a lot from her just because of how *physical* she is with guitar making.

DUDLEY: When you say fearless, what do you mean?

DUGGAN-SMITH: She's not thinking, "I'm making a terribly expensive guitar." That thought is never in her head. It's "I've got a piece of wood in my hands and I'm on the way." It's not a precious thing. It's just her doing her stuff. It's like when you see glass blowers with piles of glass and spinning stuff, and you go, "Oh my god, it could just fall off and break!" It's like that, where she's in a flow and it's raw and it's really energetic. I love that.

Being too cerebral—measuring and weighing every piece of wood, obsessing over each "precious" detail—risks missing the forest for the trees. An act of creation, Duggan-Smith implies, must be a fully embodied process. To describe Manzer as a "beast in the workshop," as I hear it, is to express awe at the physicality and affective intensity with which human and nonhuman agents interact in the "flowing, raw, and energetic" performance of artisanal labor. As Duggan-Smith is keenly aware, much of what Manzer knows cannot be conveyed in words. "Not everyone can tell you what they're doing," he points out. "Some of the best builders, the best artists in the world, can't analyze it and take it apart and teach it to you. So you have to be able to watch it happen and just physically get a sense of it." In this kind of apprenticeship, lutherie's repertoire can be transmitted only to those who are skilled at disciplined watchfulness.[33] As Duggan-Smith puts it, the onus is on the student to be receptive to this form of pedagogy:

> You have to have the ability to stop talking about yourself and shut up. Because we're all like that—the ego is at work. We're all trying to pitch ourselves and make an impression. Sometimes you have to shut up and just take it all in, and not everyone's good at that. That's one of the most important skills, if you really want to become a great guitar maker: to stuff your ego in a suitcase and literally just be able to look at stuff. I think a lot of people get knocked off along the way because they can't do that. They don't realize that some learning is not what you're used to. Some is subtle, and it's very slow.

Lutherie's scenes of instruction, in this account, are fashioned largely in the eyes of the beholder, not the instructional techniques of the beheld. Learning an artisanal repertoire in situ involves "stuffing the ego in a suitcase"—focusing the mind on what is happening in the present and imagining one's body in another person's shoes. The ability to learn in this "unusual way," Duggan-Smith suggests, is integrally connected to how the craft is eventually practiced, as those who fail to develop this skill "get knocked off along the way." The alert observation of the master, in this sense, is a dress rehearsal for the attentiveness that must eventually be trained on the craft object itself.

That this form of learning is "subtle and slow" is one reason why apprenticeships are so hard to come by today. Didactic techniques that offer quick, measurable results are far more compatible with the economic interests of students and potential employers. But for hand builders who approach guitar making as more than just a job, the acquisition of ritual knowledge holds out the promise of transforming habitual ways of "pitching" and experiencing the self.[34]

ON EXPERIENCE

A gust of wind lifts the awning of the Mexican restaurant, offering a brief respite from the midday heat. Seated on a patio overlooking the road that cuts through old South Phoenix, Arizona, I am having lunch with five men in their twenties and thirties, all instructors at the Roberto-Venn School of Luthiery. The school is located a block away on a strip of land pinned down by a few thirsty trees. Its horizontal sign rests on a flat roof that covers a wide front porch, making the single-story office building look like a saloon in a Hollywood movie. Near it sits a corrugated steel Quonset hut that houses the classroom and student workshop. Most of the machine tools are outdoors in a shaded workspace. Before the school occupied this site in 1986, the previous owners operated a junkyard—a past life that is not difficult to visualize today.

The Roberto-Venn instructors, all recent graduates themselves, are engaged in a lively debate about whether Guitar Hero and other video games decrease or improve hand skills. We have been talking about the characteristics of the student body over time and whether current students come prepared to do the work required. Finally one man says, "As you've probably noticed, most of our students tend to be guys." I ask if they have ever had women or students of color in their classes. The memories of older instructors are consulted, and a consensus emerges that there have been approximately eight women and two African American men over the past fifteen years.[35]

Given that two classes are offered every year, each with an average of thirty to thirty-five students, the social homogeneity is hard to miss. "For whatever reason," one instructor offers, "RV is not a big draw for women and blacks."

I ask why this might be. In the uncomfortable silence that follows, my mind flashes back to the pornographic magazines that I saw piled up by the only toilet in the school.

With a shrug, one of the younger instructors speculates, "It's just not culturally encouraged." Others chime in, agreeing that culture has a lot to do with it, pointing out that it is "more acceptable" for boys to take shop classes and play in bands—two activities that give them familiarity with machinery and guitars.

Like most luthiers, Roberto-Venn instructors rely on the concepts of "experience" and "culture" to explain why some people pursue lutherie and others do not. In this scenario, the kind of person who wants to build guitars is typically someone who plays guitar, is handy with tools, and comes from a white European ethnic group in which artisanal craft has traditionally been valued. This understanding of cultural experience allows makers to affirm their aptitude for lutherie without questioning the forms of exclusion that have historically underwritten their sense of opportunity. From this perspective, the fact that the majority of aspiring builders are white men like themselves is totally beside the point: they simply happen to be people whose genetics and socialization have predisposed them to love guitars.

But there is another way to think about experience. It can be "that which we seek to explain," rather than the "origin of our explanation."[36] From this angle, the question becomes not "what kind of person builds a guitar?" but "what kind of experience does a person *have* when building a guitar?" If lutherie is "learned from experience," then what exactly is learned? And why is that experience desirable? For experience can be a mercurial teacher. Not everyone "learns the same lesson or learns it the same way," the historian Joan Scott observes. "Experience can both confirm what is already known (we see what we have learned to see) and upset what has been taken for granted."[37] What fledgling builders hope to learn through lutherie's scenes of instruction, I suggest, is a culturally meaningful way to be white, male, and economically self-sufficient in a postindustrial society.

———

Don Windham's first day at Roberto-Venn was, as he puts it, "totally weird."[38] At the start of every term, students and instructors introduce themselves, telling everyone where they are from and why they came. Windham grew up in a "mostly black and Mexican neighborhood" in Oceanside, California. He was, by his own reckoning "irritable and soured by a lot of stuff" and "mad about something" he has yet to "figure out." At thirty-six, he has now taught at Roberto-Venn for the past ten years. But on that first day, listening to a performance by William Eaton, the school's director, he felt he had entered an alien universe:

> Later that day we had this demo in the lecture room where Bill [Eaton] had set up all his gear and was playing—he's kind of a new age musician. So he's playing like that kind of new age-y stuff, and he was telling us to close our eyes and imagine ourselves in a *cave* and stuff. And I just felt completely out of place. I'm looking around at all these hippies, and I'm like "Oh man, I'm surrounded by hippies! Should I be here? Is this really the right thing for me?" Anyway, it turned out being okay, but the first day was an odd day. I had a pretty small comfort zone back then.

Sizing up the other students, many of whom were "wearing tie-dye," Windham decided that he was the only one who "looked like a Mexican biker from the 1960s," and he refused to join Eaton's sonic journey to the ancient past of stringed instruments. His aversion to "hippies" dated to unspecified encounters he had while working at a head shop in high school. Windham does not identify as Mexican American when talking with me, but he is aware that others may perceive him as such on the basis of his appearance and hometown—cultural markers he has tried, with some ambivalence, to distance himself from. Telling me that his "small comfort zone" was a "security thing," he offers a psychological account of his biker persona. "I was just an insecure guy," he explains, "which was why I had a huge mane of hair and a big beard. I just didn't want people to talk to me that much." Joining the navy at eighteen, he says, was an effort to separate himself from his friends and the rough character of his neighborhood: "One of the reasons I wanted to leave [Oceanside] when I got out of high school is because I already had friends that were arrested and in jail. I just felt like if you stayed in your town, that was the path that a lot of us were going to end up on. And I didn't want to get sucked into that, because I just wasn't interested in going to jail for something that was totally stupid probably."

Nonetheless, when Windham got out of the service, he returned to his old haunts, resuming his social life as a bass player in bands that ranged from "weirdo instrumental bands" to "skuzzy punk rock kind of stuff." He got a job as an auto mechanic and enrolled in the local community college, his tuition paid by the military. Apart from his philosophy courses, however, nothing truly interested him. He had hoped to avoid his father's fate—marriage after high school, and an exhausting job in a machine shop—but as he racked up lackluster grades, he felt destined to fix brakes for the rest of his life. "I still was very negative from the time when I grew up," he observes. "I just didn't feel like there was much hope for a lot of things." But when he learned about Roberto-Venn from a friend who joined him on "guitar hunts," the vision of working in a pawnshop repairing and reselling guitars took shape in his mind. With a stroke of resolve, he sold the 1949 Chevy he was rebuilding and moved to Phoenix, determined to use his savings, a loan, and military benefits to bet on an alternative future:

> WINDHAM: I was not happy about where I was working or just any part of it really. I developed a drinking problem [in the military]. So I felt like everything—like I always fucked up what I did. As a mechanic I never ruined anybody's car or caused any issues—I never had a guy drive away and have a tire fall off or anything. But I just always felt like either I wasn't doing what I ought to be doing or to the level I ought to be doing something or that I just didn't feel like I was accomplishing anything. But when I came [to RV], that was something—we built a couple guitars, and I got through those guitars, and that was an accomplishment. I didn't think it was going to be as hard as it was.
>
> DUDLEY: That what wasn't going to be hard?
>
> WINDHAM: Building the guitar itself. It was mentally challenging. The hand skills thing wasn't that big of a deal, because you're

going to develop hand skills and stuff, and I did okay. But I just was surprised at the end that I really felt like I had *done* something, and it had been a while since I'd really felt like I had done something. So that was something that sort of opened a door for me.

To say that the experience of building a guitar is "hard" and "mentally challenging" is to recognize that it involves more than manual dexterity or technical proficiency. The sense of "accomplishment," especially upon the completion of a first instrument, involves attaining a social status associated with refined tastes and self-mastery. For blue-collar men like Windham, who rebuild cars and motorcycles without hesitation, exacting work with wood can seem quite esoteric. Windham is chagrined to admit that when instructed to bring his own chisels to school, he brought a set of "cold chisels"—appropriate for metalwork and second nature to a machinist's son, but not the correct implements for lutherie. Moreover, his exposure to woodworking projects in a seventh-grade shop class had led him to believe that making a guitar would be fairly simple:

> In my mind, it all seemed like it was going to be relatively easy. But what you find is that every aspect of it has its difficult part, no matter what you're doing. There's always something that if you don't pay attention to this little thing then you're going to miss something bigger. And that was one of the things that filtered over into my everyday life, in that if you don't pay attention to the little stuff, something bigger is going to get missed, and that definitely was a good lesson learned.

Under a high-intensity lamp, even the smallest of tasks is linked to the success of the finished product. Things are not as straightforward as they seem, and behind every detail is "something bigger" that may be "missed" or unrealized altogether. From this vantage point, constructing a guitar is an exercise in "paying attention" to the relationship between the self and the craft object and how the capabilities of one are reflected in those of the other. "The thing that building a guitar teaches you," Windham says, "is patience and limits. You learn the limits of yourself, even in something as small as gluing something together and having a good seam." No excuses can alter the fact that a seam has been done poorly, and becoming a luthier means accepting the need to redo it "instead of getting mad and leaving it behind."

Learning to accept personal limits, Windham argues, is the first step toward developing knowledge and skill. "The cool thing about learning limits is that they're not always the same," he says. "So maybe today I can't do that, but if I work at it, sooner or later I'll be able to get it." That a consciousness of limits and possibilities for growth "filters over" into daily life points to the ways in which the "subject" of the "lessons learned" in lutherie is as much the self of the maker as it is the guitar on the bench:

> They told us that you'll learn a lot about yourself going through the class. I didn't believe them at first, but at the end, you realize it's true. All that creativity and everything that you put into your guitar, that's all coming from—it might be something you've seen, but you take something in and you hold on to it for a little while, and then you get the chance to put it back out. That stuff is coming from within you, regardless of whether it might be similar looking to something. You're trying to express whatever it is.

Making a guitar, Windham suggests, involves a growing awareness of one's own creative potential. While some might discount the originality of what he does—most RV students build variations on standard models—he realizes that creativity is not simply a matter of the guitar's design. It is also involves developing aesthetic gifts by "taking something in," "holding on to it," and then "putting it back out." Lutherie is an "art," he contends, because he puts himself, physically and emotionally, into the material composition of his instruments:

> I can draw okay and stuff, but I don't consider myself an artist in that sense. I can't take feelings and translate them into color or something. But I know the feelings that go into all the guitars that I make, and the ups and downs of building that guitar, the frustration and stuff. Hopefully all of that, all those vibes or whatever get ingrained into all that wood from the sweat you might drip on it, just the hand contact all the time—that's what makes it like the art that I make. Even though it might look like the same [Gibson] J-45 shape some-

body else might build, inside that guitar, there's a lot more—there's all this part of me in all that stuff. That's what makes it the expression [of yourself]. It's not like putting a model together. It's not A and B and C and D. You run into all these little issues, and you get frustrated with yourself. You have to turn to yourself and be like "I have to do this, this is what's going to make this okay." You're thinking through every process and really spending a lot of time with it and a lot of heart with it, if you care about it.

Reflecting on the "door that opened" for him when he graduated from Roberto-Venn and became an assistant instructor, Windham speaks of feeling less emotionally inhibited and "bound up in my own world." Where he used to make jokes about hippies, he came to see them as "just like normal guys," except that "they are quite a bit more open about emoting." He was "not a very emotional guy," but over time that has changed. He now believes that "everybody's kind of the same at the core of it all: everybody's looking to exercise some creativity." He shakes his head in bemusement at the "tight" person he used to be:

It took a few years before I looked back and realized that it really was a corner to turn for me personally. A lot of other guys have a nickname for me, which is Don and the Opinions, because I have an opinion about everything. But my opinions were a lot more closed in. I wasn't open-minded. Even though I could sit around and talk to somebody in the context of a class, I didn't give a shit about other people. Coming through Roberto-Venn sort of opened me up to being able to care about other people a little bit more. Just hanging out with these people that were quite a bit more open to other people and open to other ideas and stuff. It's my being able to be more open to people instead of just letting them know what might seem like an intimate detail of my life, but only a surface detail when it boils down to it. Being able to be more honest with everybody, and myself included: that was kind of what the corner was.

Learning to "hang out" with an ever-changing group of instructors and students who vary in terms of class and cultural style allowed Windham to be more accepting of difference and more authentic in his relationships with others. Not only did his animus against hippies dissipate, but whatever anxieties he felt about his own class and ethnic identity also seem to have been allayed. The school, as a collective mentor, has given him a gift he feels obligated to return. "I feel like I owe Roberto-Venn something," he explains, "because it changed something in the core of me, just gave me a new way to look at everything." Wistfully, he imagines moving on to other things. "I don't care if they don't remember who I was," he declares, "but hopefully [Roberto-Venn] will still focus on what's important, which is showing people a new light. It's an important place, however small it might be." In 2010, spurred by his growing connections to the music scene in Phoenix, Windham left Roberto-Venn and opened his own music store and repair shop, where he sells his handmade Haymaker guitars.

MAKING POWER KNOWN

During a period of intense soul searching in 2004, Jason Kostal awoke from a dream with an epiphany:

> I woke up—it was about two o'clock in the morning—and literally said, "I want to learn how to build guitars." What was interesting was my desire wasn't to learn how to build guitars to do it for a living. It was a desire to know how something is made and how it's put together. As a performer, I was collecting guitars at the time, and I felt like I was spending really good money on a lot of instruments and didn't really understand why one guitar was worth more than another. So I was drawn to this industry without really wanting to be in the industry. I just wanted the information. I craved that knowledge.[39]

At the time, Kostal was enrolled in an MBA program at Emory University. After eight years of military service as a Special Operation Forces officer in "all of the world's major hot spots," he was preparing for a job in corporate America. Were it not for the operation tempo endured by his generation of West Point graduates—which faced more deployments than any other since the Vietnam War—remaining on active duty would have been a serious option. As it was, his duty to the country had been honorably fulfilled, and he felt that the time was right to explore other futures. His "craving for knowledge" about lutherie did not come out of the blue. As an adolescent, Kostal had studied fingerstyle guitar at the Wisconsin Conservatory of Music in Milwaukee; at

West Point, he had often performed as the opening act for musicians on campus and at venues in and around New York City. Although he had set aside the dream of being a professional guitar player, music remained a constant source of meaning in his life.

Unbridled curiosity led Kostal to take a guitar-building class with Atlanta-based maker Kent Everett. In the course, students watched Everett demonstrate the process of making a guitar, taking notes and asking questions but not actually building their own instruments. His appetite whetted for the real thing, Kostal began to make guitars in his spare time, consulting with Everett when necessary. In 2005 he accepted a position in retail management at a Fortune 500 company in Salt Lake City. After a year of disillusionment, however, he chose to follow his heart.

"I felt like 'Wow, I'm too young to spend the rest of my life doing something I don't enjoy,'" he explains. "I felt like I had sacrificed a lot of what was important to me while I was in the military, not values or anything like that, but just—*time*." Kostal quit his job, packed up all of his belongings, and moved to Phoenix to join the spring 2006 class at Roberto-Venn. He was hired as an assistant instructor that fall, and it is in that capacity that I meet him two years later. "I gave up an amazing salary and a job that on paper looked unbelievable," he reflects. "I gave that up to find my happiness, and this is the first time in my adult life where I wake up every single morning excited to start the day."

Kostal is aware that his decision to become a guitar maker may seem odd to some. Falling out of step with the Long Gray Line, he worried that he had "let the institution down by not being the CEO of Coca-Cola right now." Yet when he attended his tenth class reunion in 2008—"the largest congregation of type-A overachievers ever assembled"—he was surprised to find that these friends were the ones who most appreciated the courage it takes to do something one loves. Every one of them gave him a pat on the back and congratulated him on "breaking the code" and daring to live a life that makes him happy. The satisfaction gained, however, has been less the freedom to *be* himself than the permission to nurture an underdeveloped aspect of himself:

> My life seems very outside the cookie-cutter approach to most people, but because it's the only thing I've lived, it seems very comfortable

to me. I don't possess the flaky musician mentality that's very common. In some ways that helps me. But it also hinders me, probably. Because what I find is that a lot of the people on the other side of the spectrum possess more creativity, whereas I'm more of an analytical, driver kind of person. I hope that with time, the artistic side of my building becomes more prevalent in what I'm doing. But for right now I'm still kind of a floundering type-A personality that's trying to find my way in this world.

Kostal's career trajectory is outside the norm because it flies in the face of how power is reproduced in a society that aspires to global dominance, economically and militarily.[40] In this political regime, pursuing a "cookie-cutter" model of social advancement typically involves excelling at elite forms of higher education and military combat in preparation for positions of authority and wealth in exclusive sectors of the labor market and national government.[41] To opt out of this meritocratic system is to set oneself adrift from the institutions that permit economic mobility and confer occupational status in a postindustrial era. Yet Kostal's longing to demonstrate a different kind of personal efficacy does not represent a total rejection of neoliberal ideology. Insofar as he is on an entrepreneurial quest to realize an inner "spectrum" of capabilities and succeed in the marketplace as a "company of one," he has taken its valorization of economic independence to heart.[42]

Lutherie's scenes of instruction serve to initiate its participants into an occupational alternative to mainstream articulations of power. An alternative path, however, is not necessarily an incompatible one. Most luthiers, whether male or female, seek to achieve the personal efficacy and material self-sufficiency traditionally associated with middle-class masculinity. Artisanal instruction, seen as an initiation rite, is therefore a process that demonstrates to its participants what this identity consists of and how to claim it. Puberty rites, as anthropologist Marilyn Strathern argues, "make explicit the practices by which people 'know' and classify their attributes." What matters is not whether these capabilities are intrinsically "male" or "female" but how the ritual *makes known* to its members *what* is "male" or "female" by showing them how "to draw out of the body what it is capable of."[43]

The transmission of lutherie's performative repertoire has a similar challenge: making known to the student—and by extension, consumer markets—the habits of body and mind that produce not just viable but economically valuable instruments. In this regard, however, not all scenes of instruction are the same. To learn what goes into building a "world-class" guitar and how to bring this capability out of the self, Kostal observes, a special kind of initiation is required:

> The guitar-building schools are a great wealth of knowledge for learning how to build a basic guitar. But they can only take you so far. What I found is, when you go to guitar shows you are seeing world-class guitars. But there is no source of information out there that says how you get from the basic knowledge to the world-class knowledge. There's books on how to build a better basic guitar, but there's nothing that says, "Here is what you have to do to sell a guitar in the high-end boutique market. Here is what you have to do to make that guitar." Every one of the guys [in that market] has learned that through years and years and years of trial and error. For me, I would like to cut that learning curve down, or at least be further along in my education as I begin that learning curve.

After two years at Roberto-Venn, Kostal feels that he has reached a "plateau." He recognizes that the information he needs to bridge the gulf between where he is now and where he wants to be cannot be found in a book or a school. Yet he is unsure of what this additional knowledge consists of or how to acquire it, short of dedicating a lifetime to the experiential process of "trial and error." Like a Gimi initiate in Papua New Guinea standing outside the charmed circle of elders who wield the power of the community's magic flutes, Kostal senses that there are craft secrets yet to be divulged.[44] In the fall, he will attend a guitar-voicing class taught by Ervin Somogyi in Oakland, California. He feels confident that this experience will move him forward on his "learning curve." Then, lowering his voice so as not to be overheard, he confides to me, with evident elation, that Somogyi has invited him to interview for an apprenticeship.

On the last day of most North American guitar shows, Ervin Somogyi stands out in a crowd. With stately grace, he strolls around from table

FIGURE 4.9.

Ervin Somogyi, resplendent
in his robe at the Healdsburg
Guitar Festival, 2009.
Photograph by the author.

to table dressed in a floor-length robe that features images of guitars in red and gold. Some call him "the Yoda of the lutherie world" in recognition of his role in training up-and-coming builders as well as his penchant for dispensing pearls of wisdom. How individual makers receive Somogyi's tour of the exhibition area I can only guess. For many, his rounds must be a humorous affectation. But judging by his detailed postshow critiques, e-mailed to a select cadre of builders and clients, I imagine that not a few makers hold their breath as he passes by, wondering whether their work measures up in his estimation.

In a consumer market where no formal arbiter of artisanal value exists, cultural authority is granted to those who receive top dollar for their instruments. Not only do these guitar makers command the attention and (sometimes grudging) respect of their colleagues, but their work also sets standards that ambitious builders hope to achieve and long to surpass. Lest it be forgotten, Somogyi's perambulations remind the vigilant that guitar shows are in toto a scene of instruction in which status distinctions among luthiers make visible the hand of the market in their community.

As one of the few luthiers who have an active apprenticeship program, Somogyi has devoted considerable time to teaching guitar making as an artisanal craft. When he first began taking on apprentices, the decision made financial sense. "For many, many years I worked alone," he recalls. "I didn't make enough money to hire anybody, so it seemed natural for me to take on people who would work in exchange for instruction."[45] But as apprentices came and went—some experiences positive, others less so—he sought to clarify what was otherwise a loosely organized set of expectations. Among other things, he became more selective, deciding to consider only those who had guitar-making experience—a prerequisite that, by the 1990s, could be fulfilled by attending one of the many lutherie schools in North America.

Avoiding rank beginners spared him the chore of remedial instruction and constant worry about accidents with power tools. "Along with everything else," he explains, "I actually have a business to run, and I need to guard a certain minimal cash flow. If I take somebody on who is going to be totally useless for six months, it will affect other people in my life." Even with prior training, however, apprentices require a substantial commitment of time and energy. Their negative impact on productivity, Somogyi observes, is the primary reason that apprenticeships have become so rare:

The attitude that one needs to have in order to effectively take on apprentices and train them is an attitude of dedication and devotion to the craft, we might call it. You are going to give up a focus on productivity and making money, because apprenticeships are very inefficient. At first I didn't know that, but it has become very clear. One of the satisfactions is planting seeds and watching the next generation grow, and people carrying on the torch, and passing things on. The downside is that whatever you are doing through the process of the apprenticeship and its own learning curve builds on itself, takes on momentum, and once things are going and people know what they are doing, they leave. Then you have to start over again. It's really interesting. But it's absolutely part and parcel to how it has to work.

Passing the craft repertoire to future generations through on-the-job training, Somogyi tells us, is not economically efficient. Only by appealing to the logic of the gift can he rationalize the decision to offer apprenticeships. As a form of gifted labor on behalf of the lutherie community, investment in the education of the young is not only re-payment for gifts received but an act that should, in theory, obligate the next generation to take on a similar labor of gratitude in return. Yet the ideal of intergenerational continuity bumps up against the realities of competition in a capitalist society. Unlike transfers of ownership within a family firm, the transmission of intellectual property in an artisanal apprenticeship is rarely a contractual agreement backed up by the force of the state and the informal sanctions of kinship.

No barriers of trademark infringement or filial duty prevent an un-grateful apprentice from setting up shop in direct competition with a former mentor. Moreover, the scene of instruction may itself be a site of struggle over what kind of knowledge is to be given and received. Should the master wish to impart a way of life when the apprentice wants to be given foolproof techniques and exact specifications, both parties are doomed to frustration. Likewise, if the apprentice wants to accelerate the transfer of knowledge, heedless of the need for mutual trust and sacrifice, the craft workshop will be a stage for subterfuge, not the bestowal of a gift.[46]

The greatest failure of transmission occurs with young builders who are increasingly willing to use computerized machinery for operations that would otherwise be performed by hand. While technical compe-tence is required to use CNC programs effectively, the manual skill needed to reproduce complex designs is correspondingly devalued. As a result, fewer luthiers seek—and offer—training in traditional wood-working techniques. As an artisan who identifies primarily as an "art-ist," Somogyi is the first to admit that his approach to lutherie would be considered "inefficient" even if he did not take on apprentices:

A lot of the young rising stars in this business are people who are very left-brained and technical whizzes, which is fine, but that's not what I do. They are not interested in the nontechnical things, and I am. I recognize that there are lots of nontechnical dimensions to the work. My approach is shockingly inefficient. I produce wonderful results that people admire, but nothing is done quickly. I would make a lot more money if I streamlined and standardized and focused my approach more narrowly. I don't know whether I am doing it "right" or "wrong." But having the attitude that I've taken has implications. In this culture, I'm not really supported in being the artist, if I may call it that. People admire me, but most people will not emulate this; they'll go the other route.

By distinguishing himself from "left-brain" luthiers, Somogyi calls attention to the inner capabilities—the "right-brain" creativity—that give his instruments their economic value and aesthetic allure. Indeed, for him, "shockingly inefficient" is something of a personal trademark. His hand-carved headstock and bridge shapes are impressive precisely because they cannot be reproduced on a CNC machine. Varying by model and the specific requests of clients, Somogyi's instruments often feature stunning feats of labor-intensive handwork, from segmented rosettes and complex inlay patterns to intricately carved artwork—and, on a masterpiece called the Andamento, spectacular mosaic tile.

Far from being "streamlined and standardized," much about Somogyi's work is executed in defiance of the very idea of a mass-produced instrument. Even his tables at guitar shows make no concession to utility. Instead of resting his instruments on simple metal guitar stands as most builders do, he supports the necks of his guitars on prongs that are dressed in ladies' evening gloves, effecting a haut couture presentation. With a wry audacity unmatched by other makers, Somogyi also distributes instrument case stickers that read, "My other guitar is a Somogyi."

At the 2009 Healdsburg Guitar Show, I have the chance to talk with Jason Kostal about his apprenticeship-in-progress. Kostal has been working with Somogyi for about six months and is still in the early phase of a three-year commitment. That morning during Somogyi's public "Voicing the Guitar" lecture, he was the behind-the-scenes assistant who set up and moved the elaborate stage props that Somogyi used to illustrate his presentation. He has the bleary eyes of someone operating on insufficient sleep, but he speaks with eloquence and energy as he fills me in on what has happened since we met at Roberto-Venn. Recalling the voicing seminar he took the previous November, he conveys a sense of Somogyi's unorthodox pedagogy:

> When I took Ervin's [voicing] class, I walked away very frustrated because I'm one of those "I want answers people" and Ervin's approach was very much "I'm going to provide a whole bunch of questions." It wasn't until after I went home that I realized he had actually given me a gift by forcing me to think through my own building process and apply what I already know to make it even better, and that's his teaching style. "Sure," [he will say], "I can tell you what I do, but what I do is for my Modified Dreadnought guitar." But if you go build a parlor [guitar] and you try to do this, it's not going to work. So his response is often to get you to do the *discovery* learning. That's where there's been sort of a close hold on information. It's not "I don't want to share it with you," it's "I want you to get to my answer through your own hard work, and I'm going to guide you and direct you along the way, if you start to fall off the path. But you are still going to get there through your own interaction [with the materials]."[47]

Rather than providing "answers," Somogyi offers provocative "questions," offering students a "gift" by showing them how to draw out of themselves "what they already know." This mode of instruction is well suited to an artisanal orientation that involves an intimate relationship with craft materials, not the application of formulaic solutions. But it also places novel demands on those unprepared for a style of learning that is as much about aspects of the self as about the acoustic properties of wood. Of his "interview," which involved two weeks in Somogyi's shop over Christmas, Kostal says, "It was one of the more difficult things I've been through as a woodworker—just intellectually, creatively." In addition to lengthy discussions about his interest in lutherie, he was given a series of tasks that required careful planning and patient handwork. On the first day, Kostal was given a rough-cut wooden block that was laminated together from scraps. His assignment was to make a three-inch cube that was perfectly square using only hand tools—planes, files, rasps, scrapers, chisels, hand saws, and sand paper:

> That was one of those things where my mindset would have been "Well, I'm just going to go over to the belt sander and make a cube." But now you are doing it with a chisel, and you have six different pieces of wood—some end grains, some cross grains—so as you are chiseling, the chisel is not cutting cleanly. So essentially you have to learn how the tool works; you have to learn how to apply it to the material. And as you start to get really close to that three-inch mark, you have to start thinking through: "Okay, I can't make a mistake on this, so how am I going to do it? How do I set it up? What measurements am I taking to ensure that everything is staying square?"

Although he was given no time limits, Kostal resolved to finish every task by the next morning, even if it meant staying up a good part of the night. Over many long hours, he had ample opportunity to contemplate the contrast between the artisanal practices he was being asked to perform and those that characterized his prior "mindset." Where he had previously relied on a range of power tools and jigs, he was now entertaining the idea that "the artist touches every piece of wood and does most work by hand." With each task he undertook, he saw more clearly how the hand skills he was asked to demonstrate translated directly into the process of making an aesthetically distinctive guitar.

As an example, Kostal describes his most difficult assignment: making one of Somogyi's signature headstocks—a complex design that features parabolic curves, bevels, and a flared point. He realized that producing something that merely *looked* like the real thing would not be good enough. "If his bevel is an eighth of an inch," he observes, "yours can't be ten-thousandths of an inch more than that. He was actually checking to see, did I recognize all these different facets of it?"

By the end of the week, Kostal was unsure of how well he had done. Somogyi's demeanor throughout had been cordial but matter-of-fact, offering no clue to what he was thinking. Only on Sunday, over breakfast before Kostal left for the airport, did Somogyi invite him to become his apprentice. Looking back, Kostal feels that even if the apprenticeship had not worked out, the two weeks spent in Somogyi's shop were invaluable. "I actually felt like a better luthier, like I had better hand skills, when I walked away from that interview," he says, "because I went home feeling much more confident about my ability to use hand tools to do things that in the past I would have used power tools to do." His perception of his own capabilities had been altered, and returning to Phoenix with a newfound sense of personal efficacy, he "threw all the routers away" and bought himself "a bunch of really nice chisels."

Lutherie's scenes of instruction offer participants a way to experience the self and the material world that supports a visceral feeling of discovery and personal empowerment. Unlike industrial productivity, artisanal efficacy is not predicated on increasing efficiency or founding a family business. Hand builders are focused on actualizing an entrepreneurial self through the performance of a cultural repertoire that is collectively, not corporately, owned. Learning to reproduce the craft object by hand involves drawing a range of resonant frequencies out of tone wood and a spectrum of physical and psychological capabilities out of the artisan. Ultimately, unlike the industrial alternative, operating artisanally involves cultivating an openness to personal transformation through intimate contact with nonhuman materiality.

The divergence of artisanal and industrial production in lutherie is a relatively recent phenomenon. As a material object and icon of authenticity, the steel-string acoustic guitar came into being in the early twentieth century at the crossroads of art and science, handcraft and mechanical reproduction, folk music and consumer culture. The power that it makes known reflects the ongoing struggle for human dignity in a market society where the knowledge in greatest demand is not, by and large, embodied. In this political context, lutherie instantiates a longing not to opt out of economic competition altogether but to defy the commodifying logic of postindustrial capitalism. Sprung of a preindustrial mode of production, the artisanal guitar is nonetheless able to rival, if not surpass, the best of what high-tech factories have to offer. Its origins obscure, its existence a paradox, it presents an irresistible lure to anyone who wants to know how it came to be a singular work of art in a gloved hand.

Guitar Heroes

In general, all personal possessions invoke an intimate connection with their owners, symbolizing personal experience that, even though private or secret, adds value to the person's social identity. . . . But there are possessions in which prestigious origins, successions, or an edifying authority connected to the past like gods, divine right, ancestors, or high status make these particular possessions differ from other things even of the same kind. In societies with complex political hierarchies, precious possessions may accumulate historical significance that make their economic and aesthetic values absolute and transcendent above all similar things. . . . In this way, certain possessions become subjectively unique, removing them from ordinary social exchange as they attain absolute value rather than exchange value. —Annette Weiner, *Inalienable Possessions* (1992)

Standing in the bright light of a small stage, Ervin Somogyi blinks behind wire-rimmed glasses as he looks out at the fifty-some people, mostly luthiers, who have gathered to celebrate his book launch. He holds the first volume of a two-volume set—*The Responsive Guitar*—in his hands, while its counterpart, *Making the Responsive Guitar*, rests on a table nearby. Also displayed on the table is a guitar Somogyi built in 1980 for the Windham Hill guitarist Daniel Hecht. This evening, the Hecht guitar will be formally donated to the National Music Museum at the University of South Dakota for inclusion in its permanent collection of musical instruments. Wine and cheese have been laid out for the occasion, and those present recognize that this is a significant moment both for Somogyi and for the North American lutherie movement. The radical idea that the flattop steel-string guitar, a common folk instrument, could—if built one at a time by hand—become a work of art has been vindicated, and its progeny are now entering the annals of history and repositories of material culture.

The event is held at the 2009 Montreal Guitar Show, after the close of the day's exhibition. Invitations were issued in advance, lending an atmosphere of intimacy and exclusivity to the proceedings. Jacques-André Dupont, the founder of the show, is the first person Somogyi thanks for making this reception possible. Somogyi begins his remarks by describing the impetus for his book:

> I've been building guitars longer than most people in this room, maybe anybody in this room. And it's been my life's work. I've built guitars, I've repaired guitars, I've sold guitars, I've bought guitars, I've thought about guitars, I've dreamt about guitars, I've had nightmares about guitars, I've fantasized about guitars for most of my adult life. And in the process of doing all of those things, I've paid quite a bit of attention to what are they really, how do they work, and why do they have different voices.[1]

The book he has written is an answer to those questions. Unlike other books on the market, he explains, his text goes beyond "*how* does Somogyi make a guitar?" to include "the thinking behind it." So compelling was the latter problematic that his exposition of it grew to fill a separate volume of its own. As he describes the many topics his book covers, I am intrigued by the last two he highlights: how to evaluate guitars and market them. "Once you put your last tools down and put the strings on your guitar, here you are with this resplendent, shining instrument: how do you know if it's any *good*?" There is a set of "neutral criteria," he says, by which judgments about a guitar's tone and mechanics can be made. Knowing what they are, and developing the critical capacity to tell when an instrument falls short, is how a luthier learns to build a better guitar. These also happen to be the criteria that discerning customers bring to a potential purchase.

Somogyi segues to "selling guitars" by observing that, more often than not, new builders fail to think about what they will *do* with their creation until after they have made it. For such makers, he has compiled a helpful list of do's and don'ts—which, I later discover, runs to no fewer than 226 suggestions.[2] His pedagogical desire to emphasize the marketing, not just the making, of artisanal guitars reflects the heightened self-consciousness that luthiers now bring to the business of selling their instruments. Where pioneering builders faced the challenge of persuading customers to buy handmade guitars *instead* of vintage and factory instruments, today's "market makers" must channel existing demand toward their guitars in particular.[3] To do so, they must position their product as one that shares a set of desirable attributes with other instruments in its class—Somogyi's evaluation criteria—yet also stands out as having unique qualities in its own right.

In this respect, the market for artisanal guitars is an "economy of qualities"—an arena of economic competition in which participants vie with one another not through price wars but through the strategies they use to "qualify" or distinguish the qualities of their instruments from others in the marketplace.[4] Hand builders typically qualify their work in relation to mass-produced instruments by highlighting practices of singularization: how they customize their guitars to buyers' preferences and bring out the unique voice of each instrument. But if the "personal touch" is a strategy of qualification that characterizes *every* artisanal guitar, how do luthiers set their work apart from that of their peers? What does market competition look like within a community where an ethos of mutual support and information sharing is supposed to prevail?

The answer lies in the form of market making that unfolds at events like Somogyi's reception. The book he unveils is a documentation of his personal repertoire as well as a contribution to the craft's public archive. It is also a strategy of qualification. As a stylized story of making, Somogyi's book enters the marketplace as an ancillary product to his guitars, one that enhances his brand and increases his stature within the community. Self-published in an elegant hardcover edition, it will circulate among builders, collectors, and serious enthusiasts as his "gift" to the craft. For those builders who labor in gratitude to make the gift their own, the value of the information it contains will likely exceed the price of the book ($265), which Somogyi charges to defray the cost of publication, not to make a profit. In this sphere of gift exchange—inseparable from the market itself—luthiers' reputations are burnished and a strategy of qualification is made manifest.

An international cadre of wealthy collectors drives the market in which luthiers now participate. As individuals, these elite consumers exert a significant influence on the demand for certain instruments and the work of particular makers. Together with the museums, dealers, and artisans who benefit from their largesse, major collectors promote a set of activities that take the form of what can be called "tournaments of value." These ritualized economic events stand apart from regular market exchange by virtue of their "agonistic, romantic, individualistic, and game-like ethos."[5] Like the emotionally riveting "deep play" that brings guitarists of all classes into the market for vintage and handmade instruments, these events provide occasions for contestants to display their cultural acumen and elevate their social status.[6] But tournaments of value are, by and large, playgrounds of power and privilege. At stake at this exclusive level of market making is nothing less than the "disposition of the central tokens of value in the society in question."[7] The artisanal guitar, and the dream of masculine independence and creativity it instantiates, has become such a token in North America.

Somogyi turns to the guitar on the table. "I have been in this field of work for more than forty years," he says, "and I'm now looked on as somebody who is significant, who's important, who knows a lot, who's made contributions, and to the extent that those things are true, many of them started with this guitar here." Establishing this instrument as an originary site from which the arc of his own career can be traced, he proceeds to identify it as a point of reference for North American lutherie as a whole.

During the 1970s, he explains, most of the instruments that hand builders made were copies of Martin's Dreadnought, because that was what customers wanted. Not until Will Ackerman founded the Windham Hill Record label in 1976 did musicians' preferences begin to change. The guitarists that Ackerman was recording—Alex de Grassi, Michael Hedges, Daniel Hecht, and himself, among others—were having an impact on public perceptions of what solo acoustic guitar music could be. These were musicians, Somogyi observes, who wanted instruments that could do things that the steel-string guitar had never done before:

> With Windham Hill, a new standard was brought to the fore. The recording artists needed a guitar that sounded good, recorded well, played in tune all up and down the neck, and that played evenly, so that the sound you got playing [in first position] was comparable to the sound you got further up on the neck. Furthermore, these were fingerpickers. This was a new breed of musician. These were people who sat when they played. So a guitar that had a favorable center of balance became important. The Dreadnought lacks that. It's de-

signed to be played standing up with a strap around your shoulders; it has a very shallow waist that slips and slides around on your lap and tends to be a little top-heavy. So all these factors came together with the Windham Hill label.

Located in Oakland, California, Somogyi had several years of experience building classical and steel-string guitars when Daniel Hecht came to him looking for an instrument more sophisticated than a factory Dreadnought. The instrument that Somogyi designed for Hecht was his first Modified Dreadnought or MD model. Constructed with a narrow waist, Florentine cutaway, and traditional materials—Brazilian rosewood, European spruce, mahogany, and ebony—the "Mod Dred" soon became the guitar of choice for several Windham Hill players and has remained one of Somogyi's most popular and readily identifiable models.

But it is not Hecht's fame that makes the Modified Dreadnought a historically significant guitar. The primary character in Somogyi's retrospective account is the innovative instrument itself. His narrative is not about the endorsement of a noted artist but the genealogy of the artisanal guitar itself. "The guitars that we see in the exhibition halls [at the guitar show today]," he asserts, "are the brothers and sisters of this one here." Acknowledging that other guitar makers of his generation have also redesigned standard models—hence their instruments are siblings, not offspring—he nonetheless positions himself among the first to have done so successfully, placing his work at the forefront of a sea change in how luthiers and their clients think about the guitar.

The Hecht guitar reentered Somogyi's life when, in the course of normal business, it came to Paul Heumiller, owner of Dream Guitars, a boutique dealership near Asheville, North Carolina. After learning that the guitar was available for purchase, Somogyi tells us, he "persuaded Heumiller not to treat it as another commercial item but to consider donating it to a museum." Huemiller obliged, but it was some time before they found a receptive curator and host institution. The problem, Somogyi deadpans, is that he is still alive. "They really need you to be dead before they want to lavish any attention on you. I'm dying as fast as I can, but . . ." The audience laughs appreciatively, and one man shouts out, "Slow down!" Appearing genuinely moved, Somogyi intro-

FIGURE 5.1.
Alex De Grassi and
Daniel Hecht with
Somogyi's "Mod
Dred" guitars, 1980.
Courtesy of Ervin
Somogyi.

duces Heumiller and André Larson, the museum director, who will "be taking care of my baby, as it were."

Heumiller speaks briefly before handing the microphone to Larson. "Ervin, as many of you might know, is my favorite builder," he confesses. "I personally play a Somogyi, and it's one of my babies. So when this one came up, I knew that we just had to do something special with it."

Larson, a retiring man with a stately bearing, gives us a snapshot of the material archive that Somogyi's guitar will join. Lest anyone think that a public institution in the middle of "flyover country" is of no consequence, he informs us that the National Music Museum is in possession of an astonishing 14,500 musical instruments, dating from the sixteenth century to the present. Its acoustic guitar collection is arguably among the finest in the world, containing a guitar made by Antonio Stradivari (only four are known to survive), several seventeenth- and eighteenth-century Italian guitars, and an assortment of Martins, Gibsons, and instruments from lesser-known builders. The Hecht guitar, we learn, will be exhibited in a gallery of "great American guitars," which also features archtop guitars made by John D'Angelico and James D'Aquisto, along with their complete workshops, including drawings, notebooks, workbenches, and original tools.

"It's a great honor and privilege to accept this instrument as a premier example of a great American maker," Larson says in conclusion. "We look forward to having many of you make the pilgrimage one day to Vermillion, South Dakota, to see this instrument in its new home." As Larson makes his way back to his seat, Heumiller stands up to extend recognition to Bill Tippin, the luthier who services instruments for Dream Guitars.

Hecht played the guitar with a double-capo machine, which was operated by two foot pedals that allowed him to change keys in the middle of a song.[8] The wear and tear to the neck, combined with the rigors of international travel, had taken its toll. "But Bill did quite a bit of restoration work," Heumiller says, "and brought it back to a life where hopefully it will be ready to go on for decades more." With that parting thought, the reception is brought to a close by Michael Watts, an English fingerstyle guitarist, who performs a mesmerizing piece of his own on the Hecht guitar.

As he plays, I find myself wondering what kind of "life" this guitar will have in the museum. On the one hand, among such august company, it will declare to all who see it the evolution of a craft tradition that remains vibrant to this day. On the other, encased in glass, contemplating the flattened noses of the curious or the droopy eyes of the bored, it will fall silent. Perhaps it will be loaned out for special performances, or perhaps, like Stradivarius violins in captivity, it will be "exercised" periodically by volunteers or museum employees. Whatever its fate, this much is clear: it will now circulate in a rarefied sphere of gift exchange in which its value is no longer determined by the market.

When anthropologists encounter this kind of "decommodifica-tion"—the strategic diversion of a commodity out of market exchange into a noncommercial realm—they tend to think of the "Kula ring," a system of ceremonial exchange among Massim islanders in Papua New Guinea. Originally described in Bronislaw Malinowski's classic text *Argonauts of the Western Pacific*, the Kula ring has become paradig-matic in anthropology for how power and fame won through the ritu-alized exchange of gifts influence and depend on trade in ordinary com-modities.[9]

In the Kula, men of economic means exchange valuable shell gifts with one another, linking the islands of the Massim archipelago into a trading circuit in which shell necklaces move in one direction and shell armbands in the other. As shell gifts travel from one man to the next, they acquire a "biography" that reflects the social status of the men who give them away and the reputations of those who receive them. Be-hind the scenes, through related commercial trade, Kula players create strategic alliances with a network of men on other islands, reinforcing or redirecting the paths along which shell valuables will flow.

In this gift-giving system, Kula partners are not in competition with each other; rather, they compete with traders on their *own* island to forge ties with influential men in other communities. For skillful players in this tournament of value, "immortality" is achieved by maintaining trade networks over the years it takes a particular Kula shell to make a complete circuit of the islands and return to them. Their names will remain part of its biography for as long as it remains in circulation.[10]

To the extent that Somogyi's book and the donation of the Hecht gui-tar are ritualized "gifts," circulating as they now do in a privileged realm connected to, but separate from, the artisanal guitar market itself, a central principle of the Kula is operative in lutherie. In both cases, the use of economic resources to divert commercial goods into networks of gift exchange is the means by which social preeminence is gained.[11] This is not to suggest that such diversions are purely self-interested but to underscore the fact that without such tactics, guitar makers would be hard-pressed to expand the scope of their enterprise beyond their own circle of acquaintances. The Guild of American Luthiers' public exhibitions were an early foray into this cultural realm, well before a market for artisanal instruments had been established. Today there are several international guitar shows that extend the scope, effectiveness, and duration of makers' social networks. Like setting off for another island in an outrigger canoe, primed for adventure, trade, and a shot at stardom, builders participating in lutherie's tournaments of value introduce the artisanal guitar to a sphere of circulation in which it becomes more than a musical instrument.

ZEN OF DIVERSIONS

"Why anyone in their right mind would come to a seminar called 'Guitar Collecting as a Zen Practice,' I'll never know."[12] With a self-deprecating laugh, Jeff Doctorow welcomes the two dozen of us who have come to hear his presentation at the 2009 Montreal Guitar Show. I, for one, found the title of his talk irresistible. What could possibly be Zen-like about amassing a collection of over one hundred guitars that is valued at one million dollars?

My path has crossed Doctorow's several times before, at public exhibitions and private events where he can usually be found behind a luthier's table or in a quiet corner hunched over a guitar. In his mid-fifties with a goatee and closely shaved head, Doctorow does have something of a monkish mien, especially when he expresses a profound lack of interest in the monetary aspect of his acquisitions. "I'll say right off the bat," he announces: "I have never, and will never, buy a guitar as an investment. For me, that has absolutely nothing to do with it. They are first and foremost *musical* instruments, not financial instruments."

People who invest in guitars as if they were commodities on a futures market, he says, tend to lock their guitars in closets, never playing them or letting them grow as instruments. To him, this is nothing short of criminal. However, he is not offering his collecting philosophy as a model for anyone else to follow. "I'm just sharing some of my experiences as the journey has progressed, and it's been a great and fun journey." Never having set out to be a collector, he refuses that label, wanting to be known as a "guitar enjoyer" instead.

Doctorow was a drum player as a child, but upon hearing Jimi Hendrix and Jerry Garcia, he immediately switched to electric guitar. After college, he played guitar professionally, supporting himself by giving lessons when he was not on the road. At the age of twenty-six, "tired of depending on other people for a livelihood—whether it was club owners, band members, or agents," he went to work at his father's publishing company, where he demonstrated a knack for selling magazines and ad space. With a steady income, his "compulsive addictive and acquisitive nature" was given free rein, and before he knew it, his motley assortment of guitars had become a collection.

Starting out with vintage instruments, he did "crazy things," he says, that "now seem silly in retrospect"—like collecting every model of Fender electric guitars in Lake Placid Blue. Not until he stumbled upon artisanal lutherie did he identify an approach to guitar collecting that felt right to him:

> It's a very visceral gut reaction. If I pick up a guitar, I will know in maybe ten or fifteen seconds if it's the right guitar for me—if I want it, if it speaks to me. It could be the sound, it could be the look, it could be the playability; it usually is all of the above. And it's really that quick. I'm not talking about money or price or anything like that. I'm just talking about the direct connection to the guitar. You just *know*. You don't have to think about it. I try to leave my brain out of it as much as possible. It's a very emotional, passionate, *magical* thing. Part of the fun of it, I think, is that guitars seem to me to be living, breathing things. There are tons and tons of great guitar builders out there, but I think it's a little bit like sports. On any given day any one team can beat any other team, no matter how many championships they've won. I think on any given day a great guitar builder can build a very mediocre guitar, and, the flipside of that, an unknown guitar builder can all of a sudden pop out a brilliant guitar. So that's part of the fun; that's part of the discovery of it.

Perceiving an element of risk in the guitar market—that extraordinary guitars are "discovered," not guaranteed by a maker's reputation—Doctorow revels in the sport of identifying which ones "speak" directly to him. Being hailed by a "magical" instrument, as he expresses it, establishes an immediate preconscious bond—"you don't have to think about it"—that preempts financial considerations. Yet his preferences, along with those of other collectors, directly influence the careers of individual artisans and the price structure within which they operate. Indeed, were it not for these well-to-do patrons of the craft, an international luxury market for North American guitars would not exist today.[13] By diverting selected guitars from market exchange into his widely acclaimed collection, Doctorow does more than survey contenders in lutherie's tournaments of value. He picks winners and losers, and in so doing sets standards of evaluation for the market itself.

As a friend and benefactor to hand builders, Doctorow has donned the mantle dropped when Scott Chinery died of a heart attack at the age of forty in 2000. A self-made multimillionaire at twenty-nine, Chinery invested a large portion of his wealth—earned through the sale of ephedra-based bodybuilding and weight-loss products—in vintage and handmade guitars that numbered over one thousand at the time of his death.[14] Prone to dramatic gestures—in 1989, Chinery purchased the Batmobile for $180,000—his involvement in the lutherie community solidified the stature of a top tier of up-and-coming builders. In 1992 he commissioned Linda Manzer to build an exact replica of the Pikasso guitar she made for Pat Metheny in 1984. After Chinery died, the Pikasso II found its way to a West Coast dealer and is now a crown jewel in the Doctorow collection.

In 1996 Chinery commissioned twenty-two luthiers to make him their best archtop guitar. Inspired by the blue sunburst archtop made for him by the late James D'Aquisto, Chinery asked participating builders to finish their instruments in the same shade of blue. "All of these great luthiers saw this as a friendly competition," he said at the time. "As a result, they went beyond anything they'd ever done and we ended up with a collection of the greatest archtop guitars ever made."[15] As a tournament of value from the outset, Chinery's Blue Guitar collection was exhibited at the Smithsonian Museum of American History in Washington, DC.[16] Showcasing magnificent instruments as well as producing demand for the artisans who made them, Chinery's project set a precedent for how well-heeled investors could single-handedly shape the market for custom-built guitars.

Doctorow's collecting strategy has led him to purchase some of the most idiosyncratic instruments in lutherie. Among the builders who have caught his eye is Steve Klein, an innovative maker based in Sonoma, California. In the 1970s, Klein caused a sensation in the lutherie world when he began experimenting with design concepts influenced by the iconoclastic acoustic theory of Michael Kasha.[17] Combining Kasha's ideas about the differential frequencies of vibrating plates with his own artistic vision, Klein produced a series of head-turning instruments—from acoustic guitars with unusual bracing patterns, asymmetrical bridges, and offset sound holes to electric guitars that feature revamped ergonomics, headless fretboards, and harp strings. In the late 1990s, Doctorow bought two of Klein's guitars and struck up a friendship that led him, in 2003, to bankroll a book about Klein.[18] "Publishing that book opened a lot of doors for me," Doctorow recalls, "and I became known. It was the beginning of my name getting out there as a collector and general man about the guitar world."

Among luthiers, Doctorow's stature in the community was sealed when he acquired Fred Carlson's Flying Dream after seeing it exhibited at the 2003 Healdsburg Guitar Show. As he tells it, his connection to the Dream was instantaneous:

> I was like a little kid! I'm walking along down the aisles and I saw a whole bunch of people staring at it. I kept circling around, getting a little closer each time, and after about an hour I got up the nerve to go up to [Carlson] and say, "Could I pick that thing up and play it?" I'd never met Fred before, and he's become a friend of mine. I was just lucky to see it at the Healdsburg show. I became obsessed with that thing. It was just so unique and yet so musical, and everything that was weird about it was weird for a reason and it all seemed to make sense. It's a thirty-nine-string instrument with a regular guitar neck, six sub-bass strings like a harp guitar, a whole bunch of treble strings like a Japanese koto. But the thing that flipped me out was there was a set of twelve sympathetic strings that ran through the neck through a hollow tube that vibrated sympathetically when you played any of the other strings on the guitar. So you don't even have to know what you're doing—you can just bang on it and it goes zzzzzz!

A sense of childlike wonder and openness to spontaneous aural gratification is, I come to realize, what "Zen" means to Doctorow. Experiencing the craft object as a gift—"I was just lucky to see it"—allows him to undertake an exploration of its features in which each discovery is a thrilling delight. Breaking with economic rationality, and imaginatively retracing the process of making, allows him to participate in the lutherie market at the level of ritualized exchange: offering the monetary gift of patronage while leaving considerations of financial risk to collectors with less fanciful dispositions. Which is not to say that calculation played no role in his decision. Doctorow is no doubt betting that the value of Carlson's instrument will rise. But the pleasure of playing enchanting instruments, validating talented builders, and establishing a robust social network, he explains, is not incidental to collecting—it is the point:

> It's really been a journey for me, and it's really been a lot of fun. And that's why I do it, *that's* what I'm trying to get out of it—just the pure enjoyment and the satisfaction and the good karma. That's maybe why I keep going back to some of the stories and some of the things that have happened as a result of what I've done. I'm fortunate in that some of my favorite guitar players are now good friends of mine as a result of this hobby of mine. By the way, I think that guitar collecting is a metaphor for life in general. There is something much more than the guitars. It's really hard to describe. It's almost like tapping into some sort of flow and being just part of something—I'm not quite sure what that is. Maybe it's really just the human spirit.

Collecting guitars can be a "metaphor for life" precisely because it participates in the creation of an art world in which cooperative activities are organized by a collective desire to endow artisanal labor with cultural value, allowing it to flourish against the odds in a technologically advanced society. Through such modes of exchange, the objects circulating within those worlds come to have a value that is determined by social practices, not by an abstract economic rationality.[19] Thus when Doctorow describes his activities as "tapping into a flow" larger than himself, I believe he is talking about what it feels like to take guitars out of the commodity state and redeploy them in a cultural realm where they can be apprehended as signs of the "human spirit" and stand for the creativity made possible by gift exchange writ large.

As noble as this heightened sense of purpose may be, it is not without its detractors or attendant risks. Because diverted valuables must remain outside the market to perform their existential magic, the threat of "recommodification" is ever present. When Doctorow comes to the end of his presentation, a man in the audience asks him if there is ever any "turnover" in his collection. Does it just keep growing, or does he ever sell some guitars to buy others? Sighing audibly, Doctorow replies:

> If I see something that I really like and feel that I must have, if I need to — especially nowadays [during the Great Recession] — I will have to trade or sell a couple of guitars to get that next one. It's never "Eh, this guitar sucks, I'm bored of it." It's [sold] only if it is a stepping-stone to something else. But I do once in a while sell a guitar. My wife and I owed a large tax bill and she was on my case — you know, wives and guitars is not a good subject — and I was able to quickly sell one guitar that paid the whole tax bill, so that shut her up for a couple months — [laughing] sorry, couldn't help it! Once I buy or trade for a guitar, I do so with the intention and the expectation that I'm going to play it and love it for a lifetime and hopefully never have to get rid of it. That's why flipping guitars for money doesn't really work very well for me.

That the demands of the domestic sphere can intrude upon the sanctity of the lutherie world underscores the precariousness of its market diversions. Even if the guitar reenters the commodity state only briefly, its status as a ritual object will have been cast into doubt, as the intimacy guaranteed by the sentimental promise to "love it for a lifetime" comes to an end with the estrangement of a price tag. That the drama of recommodification is often staged as a conflict between men and women in a marital relationship points to what is ultimately at stake in such transactions. When the unlucky instrument is thrown back into the market to fulfill domestic obligations, its owner must confront the fact that the economic interests of the family do not always coincide with bids for personal immortality in the realm of gift exchange. At such moments, the artisanal guitar and the masculine independence it represents can unceremoniously return to the familiar form of the commodity.

ECONOMIC CITIZENSHIP

The first Healdsburg Guitar Makers Festival was held in August 1996 at the Villa Chanticleer, a charming hilltop resort in Sonoma wine country. In a departure from exhibitions held by the Guild of American Lu-thiers, "Healdsburg" was from the start intended to be a commercial exposition. Organized by Todd Taggart, president of Luthiers Mercan-tile International (LMI), along with guitar makers Charles Fox and Tom Ribbecke, the festival featured sixty-eight exhibiters, many of them customers of Taggart's former company, Luthiers' Mercantile. In 1994 the transnational corporation that owns Theodor Nagel, a German tone wood company, acquired Taggart's deeply indebted mail-order busi-ness. In the turbo-charged "new economy" of the Internet boom and high-tech startups, however, LMI enjoyed a swift recovery as demand for handmade guitars soared.

With Silicon Valley a stone's throw away, the time seemed right for a three-day event designed to benefit luthiers and raise the profile of the show's sponsors, LMI and String Letter Press, publisher of the recently launched *Acoustic Guitar* magazine. With self-conscious zeal, festival organizers aimed to redefine artisanal guitar making in the eyes of the general public.[20] For the first time in the commercial guitar world, the focus was not on celebrities who play particular brands of guitars but on the artisans who make them. In a rave review, the *Economist* stated this novel idea succinctly, dubbing Healdsburg's top makers "gods of the craft."[21]

That a reporter for a London-based financial news weekly would be on the scene at all was a sign of changing times. As prices of desirable instruments in the vintage market rose beyond the reach of many in-vestors, the work of contemporary hand builders had become more at-tractive with each passing year. But standards of evaluation in this new market were slippery, and the process by which "gods" were anointed was cloaked in mystery. If befuddled collectors and high-end con-sumers were afraid to trust their instincts, guitar makers themselves were beset by status anxieties. All yearned for a mechanism that would make the rules of market competition clear.

Healdsburg 1996 was thus the first iteration of what has since be-come a rite of passage for guitar makers and a premier arena for col-lective market making. By placing builders in physical proximity to one another, allowing customers and makers to size up the competition, the lutherie community institutionalized a forum for economic ex-change that had not existed before. Now, instead of marketing their wares through costly distributors or in the company of other artisans at regional craft fairs, they entered a tournament of value in which they vied not just for sales but for the good opinion of an elusive coterie of collectors, dealers, and journalists who exercised growing influence over public perceptions of their instruments.

Standing in a grove of giant oaks and redwoods at Villa Chanticleer, marveling at the panoramic view of the Alexander Valley, was Michael Keller, a guitar maker from Rochester, Minnesota. Keller had been a Luthiers' Mercantile customer since 1978, the year that Todd Taggart and Tom Peterson bought Lewis Luthier Supply from Bill Lewis in Vancouver. Keller had recently moved from Portland to Minnesota to be near his wife's family while they raised their own. Staying connected to the lutherie community through Luthiers' Mercantile had been a lifeline for Keller, who feared that, professionally speaking, he had "fallen off the edge of the earth." Between the guild's quarterly journal and phone conversations with Taggart, Keller stayed in touch with the social network that supported his business. Yet nothing had prepared him for Healdsburg. "It was just so incredibly beautiful, up on the side of this hill," he recalls. "They had this giant barbecue for all the builders, and the vibe was just like *Wow! We've arrived!*"[22]

The sense of "arrival" that Healdsburg conferred came from being recognized as artisans who make something of economic value in an increasingly global and technologically sophisticated market. Like knights in a medieval melee or jousting match, guitar makers were invited to showcase their talents in a "friendly competition" that raised public awareness of their craft—a common goal that benefited all. Prizes were awarded to the "best" makers in the form of customer sales, but everyone present was feted as a pioneer at the vanguard of the North American lutherie movement.

For individual builders, the payoff could be significant. Although Keller did not sell any guitars at that first show, he considers it a pivotal moment in his life: "The Healdsburg show was the absolute kickoff for my professional career on a national level." Rubbing shoulders with guitar makers he respected and being treated as an established builder himself validated his work and allowed him to see himself as a serious contender on a playing field that promised economic success and cultural acceptance as a productive member of society.

To desire recognition on a "national level" is to understand that having a "professional career" involves enacting a legible trajectory—a structured sense of *going* somewhere in life, from "kickoff" to touchdown. For luthiers who entered adulthood in the 1970s, achieving this kind of identity has been fraught with uncertainty in moral and economic terms. Opting out of, or being unable to claim, the national recognition that came with being Vietnam veterans, college-educated professionals, or skilled blue-collar workers made it difficult to imagine what progress or achievement looked like. Keller's first encounter with a well-regarded luthier suggested that the route to respectability led to the nation's capital. He traces his interest in lutherie to a talk given by Jeffrey Elliott at Portland State University in 1976:

> The national acoustic guitar scene was starting to heat up. Jeff Elliott was one of about fifteen people who had been accepted to the Smithsonian's handmade acoustic guitar show called "The Harmonious Craft." That was the first time a major institution in the United States was bellying up and acknowledging that some serious instruments were being made in the United States. It [the lutherie movement] was certainly in its infancy at that time.

In this vision of national belonging, professional success is signaled by the fact that the "infant" artisanal guitar actually went to Washington, where it commanded the attention of the nation through one of its "major institutions." Pilgrimage to Washington narratives have long been a staple of how American citizenship is popularly understood. The story of "going to Washington," as literary scholar Lauren Berlant argues, "depicts both real and conceptual distances that occupants of the United States have felt the need to traverse: not always because they want to usurp the space of national mastery, but sometimes because they seek to capture, even fleetingly, a feeling of genuine membership in the United States."[23] For luthiers whose income-earning potential was still in question, the Smithsonian's imprimatur assuaged ongoing anxiety about their ability to claim full economic citizenship.

At issue during the early years of the movement was the legitimacy of the financial choices that builders made. While their pursuit of economic autonomy was in keeping with the entrepreneurial ambitions of other men of their race and class, the fact that they persisted as self-employed artisans through years when they were barely able to support themselves, let alone a family, raised more than a few eyebrows. "A good citizen is an earner," political theorist Judith Shklar has observed, "because independence is the indelibly necessary quality of genuine, democratic citizenship."[24] From the Great Depression forward, gainful employment—and the "family wage" it once garnered—has been the primary grounds upon which workers claim citizenship in the United States.[25] To forgo this form of participation in the polity, even if only temporarily, set luthiers apart from mainstream rationality.

Guitar makers found in the lutherie movement the validation withheld by society at large. When Keller reminisces about the guild's 1977 convention in Tacoma, which he attended with his wife and newborn baby, he exults in "all the countercultural funniness" that transpired camping out at Tim Olsen's parents' house, where Olsen's sister and brother-in-law were living in a teepee in the backyard. It was an exciting time, he says, when he felt part of a "real community" that was bound together by its economic marginality:

> The guild was a galvanizing factor, because the music stores didn't care, and the factories didn't take us seriously. Nobody saw what was coming, and it very much felt like we were outside the loop—outside the commercial realm. We weren't involved with the "suits," if you know what I mean—the guys running the factories and the big, huge importing concerns. It definitely felt like another world, not in a serious sense, but it felt like our world, you know? It was like it didn't belong to anybody but us. I did many, many craft shows, art festivals, and Renaissance festivals. I have hundreds of artist friends—knife makers, jewelry makers, potters, pewter artists, you name it. It all felt counterculture; it all felt outside the mainstream. I remember feeling like we weren't depending upon music stores; we weren't depending upon the popular media; we weren't depending upon even the public's acceptance. It was just that everybody—most of the people I met—just liked doing it.

Nothing could be further from "the suits" and the "commercial realm" they signified, it seemed, than an art world identified with the European Renaissance, a past in which artisans, not corporations, enjoyed pride of place.[26] But living outside the "mainstream" depended on a conceptual opposition between work done for personal fulfillment and that which was "publicly accepted." For early builders, this tension was often negotiated in gendered terms, as a spouse's work outside the home became the family's mainstay. As Keller acknowledges, "The only reason I survived is my wife has always been very independent and strong—she's always wanted to have her career." Without the paycheck and medical insurance she earned as an elementary school teacher, he says, "I would never in a million years have been able to continue making guitars, because there was a time when I couldn't give my stuff away."

Although Keller derived an income from repair work, his failure to fully assume a breadwinner's role left him open to the criticism of family members who wanted to see him finish college or enter a line of work that conformed to their idea of responsible masculinity. The more serious he got about building guitars, he recalls, the more vocal they became about the error of his ways:

My family saw that I was really doing things—that I was a decent, grounded kid, working a job, married with kids. I wasn't dealing drugs, wasn't an alcoholic, wasn't a thief or a burglar, I was just kind of just—you know? It was so outside of my parents' and family's experience. My stepfather—my parents got divorced when I was very young and my father disappeared, but my mother remarried—my stepfather was always just [saying], "Ah, the hell with this guitar stuff! You need to be a machinist; you're so good with your hands!" To his dying day he thought I made the biggest mistake of my life. They'd say, "Oh my God, you've got so much talent—be a machinist!" But still, they came around eventually, once I started getting some recognition, after about ten years—when I started popping up in a few magazines here and there and when I started exhibiting at shows.

To be "outside the experience" of your own family is to manifest nonconformity in the intimate realm of marriage and reproduction, where normative ideas about proper citizenship have increasingly come to be defined.[27] Making an irrevocable "mistake" in this morally charged realm, Keller suggests, is tantamount to engaging in dissolute or illegal behavior. What finally quelled the worries of kin was not an intrinsic change in the nature of his work but the public rehabilitation of the character of his product in popular culture. Not until his instruments started "popping up" in national media did relatives stop viewing him as an unspeakable cipher alone in his shop. As Keller sees it, his personal success reflected the renaissance of artisanal guitar making in the nation as a whole:

When Columbus landed in America in 1492, there was no America. But in Europe, instrument making, especially violin making, was already fairly well developed. When America was founded in 1776, there had already been a four-hundred-year history in Europe alone of handmade instruments. The violin market was astronomical in Italy, in France, in Germany in the 1700s. So the United States has had a lot of catching up to do as a very young country. We didn't *have* a history, you know? So when the country was starting—I'm sure there were a few instrument makers, probably in Boston and places—but by the time I was born in the 1950s, the industrial revolution was happening and factory production owned the world. And the United States is kind of playing cultural catch-up in a certain way. That's how I see the instrument-making market: it's just catching up with what existed in the rest of the world on some level.

Keller frames his quest for national belonging as connected to the country's aspirations for recognition on a world stage. Using the state of lutherie in the United States as a measure of the nation's relative "infancy," he positions his labor as masculine nation-building that endows his country with a "history" and the ability to compete on a global scale. In this scenario, the dominance of "factory production" arrested the development of the craft until the 1960s, when Keller's generation stepped in to rectify the situation. The sense of acceptance luthiers began to savor in the 1990s was especially sweet. Not only had they matured in skill over the twenty years following the Smithsonian exhibit, but their handmade product had become a force to be reckoned with by industrial makers. The game of "cultural catch-up" with the Old World was being won by the New, and for this the United States and Canada had their own homegrown artisans to thank.

Much, therefore, was riding on the second Healdsburg show in 1997.[28] The venue was the same, but the number of exhibiters had gone up and organizers were anticipating a larger turnout. Keller spent several months of the preceding year preparing for the festival, building two guitars with the competition in mind. "One of the last things my wife said to me at the airport before I left," he remembers, "was 'I hope you sell something!'" In reply, he joked that he should have brought a bale of hay and overalls to distinguish himself from everyone else. "Nobody knew who I was," he explains. "I didn't have the stature or visibility of Steve Klein or Jeff Elliott, Grit Laskin or Linda Manzer, but I was getting good."

On the first day, shortly after the doors opened, a Portland lawyer who collected guitars came up to Keller's table, played his instruments, and walked away. Over the next hour, Keller saw him moving around the room playing other guitars until he came back and asked point blank, "How much for everything on the table?" Keller told him. The man asked if he could get a discount for buying two, and Keller said it was too early in the show to consider discounts—whereupon, the man pulled out his checkbook and asked Keller to ship the guitars. Stunned, Keller called his wife. "She about died," he says, reliving the moment. "She said, 'How's it going, honey?' I said, 'Oh, I just sold my guitars—*both of them!*'"

Word of Keller's coup spread quickly. In addition to being known as "the hit from Minnesota," he found that he had more orders waiting for him when he got home. The next show, which had now become a biannual event, was held in 1999 at the Wells Fargo Center for the Arts in Santa Rosa, and it resulted in even greater success for Keller. "I took a bunch of orders," he says, "and all of a sudden it was like I could make a living off this one show." Over the next six years, orders continued to roll in, and Keller's work appeared in *Acoustic Guitar* magazine and a book on handmade guitars published by String Letter Press.[29] But superstar status continued to elude him. He sensed that he should be doing something else to achieve it but could not figure out what that might be:

> How do you get your name out there? I mean, how did Jim Olson get famous? Well, he went after James Taylor, Leo Kottke, Paul McCartney, and gave them all guitars. That's a really valid way to do it, because the buying public loves to follow famous people. But, other than that, how do you create the buzz that builders like Linda Man-

zer has or John Monteleone has—besides just doing good work? It's a mixture of luck, it's a mixture of marketing—and I was always really bad at marketing.

His break came in 2004, when a wealthy guitar collector from Miami Beach approached him at the Healdsburg show with an unusual request. Henry Lowenstein was looking for a luthier to build him a small-bodied guitar that he could play as degenerative arthritis wreaked havoc with his arms, shoulders, and hands. He also wanted the instrument to be inlaid with an intricate pattern involving three thousand separate pieces of pearl so that when he was no longer able to play it, he could derive pleasure from simply looking at it. Lowenstein told Keller that he had been dreaming about this guitar for ten years but had not yet found someone willing to make it. Keller later learned that Lowenstein had talked to others at the show who declined the commission and recommended him.

Flattered but apprehensive, Keller discussed the project for almost two hours before agreeing to take it on. "What he was asking me to do was very risky," he points out. "He was talking about three or four months of my life and twenty-five thousand dollars worth of effort, and what if he didn't like it? But he took a liking to me and said, 'You're my man.' He brought his wife over and had his picture taken with his arm around me."

When Keller finished the instrument, Lowenstein flew him to Miami to deliver it in person, paying for an additional seat on the airplane for the guitar. The reception he received that evening was extraordinarily gratifying. Lowenstein and his family had all been tracking the progress of the guitar by viewing the photographs that Keller regularly posted to a gallery on his website. When Lowenstein finally took the guitar out of its case, Keller says, "He *loved* it, he was just 'Holy crap!'" The family threw a celebratory dinner at which Keller was the guest of honor, and Lowenstein's brother formally thanked him for all the happiness that he had brought to the family.

Before Keller left, Lowenstein told him that the editor of the *Blue Book of Acoustic Guitars* wanted to do a feature story on his "dream guitar."[30] This turned out to be the career-changing event that Keller had been waiting for. "When this article came out in the *Blue Book*," he says, "it just exploded for me. All of a sudden I was hot. I was a world-class builder, building a twenty-five-thousand-dollar guitar for a very serious collector and being featured in one of the most respected books in the world." His newfound fame has caused him to ponder the curious nature of stardom. As doors once closed swung open, he realized with dismay that professional success often depends on the actions of a few well-placed gatekeepers:

> I've been here [in Rochester] for twenty-five years, and the newspaper suddenly goes, "Whoa, what do you mean this guy's in the *Blue Book*? Get a reporter out there!" You know, whoa! And then they wanted pictures of Henry's guitar, and then when I did that Bauhaus [a bold new model]—oh man, they wanted pictures of that too. That showed up in a magazine and a book, and all of a sudden now I've got credibility. Now I'm not just some flake-o hippie, you know, dragging one leg around the shop, muttering to myself, [*in a low growl*] "Guitarrrrs, guitarrrrs." It's true, though, and that makes me mad. Now that's pitiful to me. No matter how good your work is, it takes somebody else saying it's good. Now that—that bothers.

The belief that good work should speak for itself is a cornerstone of an artisanal ethos. Advertising, currying favor, and "branding" oneself may be necessary evils in a market culture, but when all is said and done, guitar makers agree that the quality of the instrument should be self-evident to discriminating players. Indeed, just as the privileges and prerogatives of white masculinity are often felt to be innate characteristics of the person, "good craftsmanship" is held to be an intrinsic property of the craft object, not a quality that can be conferred by others. Yet as luthiers have discovered, a sense of national belonging does not come automatically. Those who triumph in lutherie's tournaments of value must confront the unsettling fact that stars are not born—they must be made.

THEATER OF BRANDING

That morning in April 2008, the main entrance to the Miami Beach Convention Center could have been mistaken for an airport. Throngs of luthiers carrying guitar cases and venders towing trunks on casters flowed through a wall of glass doors. The guitar show didn't begin until 10:00, but I had arrived early to attend a 9:00 seminar and misjudged the time it took to walk from the hotel. A guard was stationed at the base of the up escalator, permitting only those with badges to ascend to the second floor, where the exhibition was held. I drifted across the lobby to a table displaying albums by musicians who were here to perform on luthiers' instruments.

As I picked up a CD to look at its cover, I noticed an open door at the back of the lobby that revealed a darkened auditorium. On a metal stand by the door was a small sign that read "Foreclosure Auction." No one was entering or leaving at this hour, but a custodial cart parked nearby suggested that the room had been readied for use later that day. The irony was sobering. At a time when Florida was reeling from massive defaults on subprime mortgages — and the federal government was months away from bailing out leading Wall Street firms — the organizers of this show hoped to attract public interest in guitars priced between five thousand and fifty thousand dollars. The times were hardly auspicious, it would seem, to be launching a guitar festival in southern Florida.

But significant outlays of money in lutherie are rarely driven by market logic alone. Between 2004 and 2008, three major exhibitions for artisanal guitar makers were introduced to supplement the biannual show in Healdsburg, each one founded by an individual with an idiosyncratic vision. The first to appear was the Newport Guitar Festival. Held in Newport, Rhode Island, at the same time as the Newport Folk Festival, the show debuted in August 2004 and ran again in 2006. "Newport" was organized by Julius Borges, a Massachusetts-based guitar maker, who sought to create an event where luthiers, accustomed to working alone, could relax and enjoy the camaraderie of their peers, much as they had at Healdsburg before that venue became "too crowded."

In keeping with this nostalgic desire, a key sponsor of the Newport show was Todd Taggart, now the owner of Allied Lutherie, a wood supply business he started after leaving LMI in 2000. The goal, as Borges describes it, was to throw "an amazingly good party with a lovely guitar show attached to it."[31] From its inception, he says, it was a low-budget affair:

FIGURE 5.2.
Program cover for
the second Newport
Guitar Festival,
2006. Reminiscent
of Healdsburg's
"Beauty and Tone"
photomontage, the
singing mermaid and
moonlit harbor conjure
a seductive field of
human/nonhuman
desire that is fraught
with danger.

My favorite thing about Newport is, it was like I was Mickey Rooney in one of those movies, you know, [saying] "We're going to put on a show! We'll get a barn, and we'll put up posters, and it's going to be great!" You know, and really, it's just a little tiny thing. I didn't have any money. The budget was the table fees that came in and then some sponsorship money. That's what I had to work with, something in the fifty-thousand-dollar range. We just wanted a show, and I tried to figure out a way that we could do it. The way it worked was if they [guitar makers] didn't cooperate, we didn't have a show. And if you don't have the heavy hitters—they all know who they are—you don't have a show.

In the end, the big-name luthiers came through, giving the show a feeling of gravitas and exclusivity. This was enhanced by its venue: a Hyatt Regency on a private island in Narragansett Bay that could be reached only by boat or by a long causeway. Shuttle boats to the Newport Folk Festival docked nearby, drawing in diehard folkies, while proximity to Boston and New York City appealed to enthusiasts unlikely to blink at the cost of staying at a luxury hotel.

Although Borges had demonstrated that there was demand for a guitar show on the East Coast, the effort involved in producing it was more than he could handle on a permanent basis. Recognizing this, two entrepreneurs stepped into the breach: Jacques-André Dupont founded the Montreal Guitar Show in July 2007, and Henry Lowenstein acquired the Newport Guitar Show and moved it to Miami Beach in 2008.

While smaller guitar shows have emerged to help builders reach regional markets, the Montreal and Florida shows represent explicit attempts to enhance the competitiveness of North American luthiers internationally. Both shows are significant departures from Healdsburg and the original Newport insofar as the individuals who run them are not directly involved in the production of artisanal instruments, either as material suppliers or as builders. Dupont and Lowenstein are guitar collectors with the resources to act as impresarios who can front—and take calculated risks with—substantial amounts of investment capital. As events that might eventually make money for investors through advertising fees, table charges, and ticket sales, these shows were designed to compete with Healdsburg as the main stage upon which lutherie's "theater of branding" occurs.[32] As tournaments of value, all three shows have developed distinctive "brands" or strategies for promoting the work of individual luthiers and introducing the general public to the economic and aesthetic value of artisanal guitar making.

Now in its sixteenth year, the Healdsburg brand is the benchmark against which the other shows position themselves. Its imagery draws upon LMI's location in Sonoma wine country. Along with its trademark phrase "The Luthier's Art," the Healdsburg Guitar Festival makes an explicit analogy between guitars and wine and a corresponding argument about how handcrafted guitars should be valued.[33] Like appreciating fine wines and their terroir, LMI suggests, connoisseurship of the guitar is a matter of developing a discriminating palate for "tone."[34] The show is an extravagant "guitar tasting" in which visitors are invited to refine their "ear" as they play—and listen to professional musicians

FIGURE 5.3.

The Luthier's Art features luthier profiles and high-quality photographs of instruments exhibited at the fourth Healdsburg Guitar Festival, 2001. The curves of rosewood and koa guitars are depicted as rolling "vineyards," visually linking the "terroir" of wine and "tone" of exotic wood.

play—a wide variety of instruments made from different species of wood. To the consternation of some, LMI makes no overt distinctions between luthiers based on their reputations or level of experience. Novices are assigned to tables next to more experienced makers, with nothing other than the price of their instruments—and sometimes not even that—to distinguish them from masters of the craft. Making such distinctions would undermine the "goodwill" that LMI's business manager Natalie Swango cites as the show's primary purpose:

> [The event] is not profitable; it will never be profitable because we don't put any of our [the staff's] labor into the cost. So we make money on the books, but there is no labor accounted for in that. And we put in so much time. Like we're starting in September for next year's show, and it's huge, just huge. So every time my boss goes

"Oh, we did pretty well at that," I say, "No, no, we didn't do pretty well at it." We love it; I'm not saying we shouldn't do it. It's a gesture of goodwill; it brings us business. But it's goodwill, I mean, that's the biggest part of it. It brings us clientele; it gives us exposure; it gives our customers exposure. It just promotes guitar making in general, and that public awareness is part of what has, I think, caused the resurgence of interest in the craft.[35]

Healdsburg celebrates the *activity* of making guitars and the raw materials out of which they are made, irrespective of the status of individual makers. Just as a tour of a winery would be incomplete without an opportunity to view the grapes, LMI sets aside a large room for the display and sale of wood and other building supplies. Swango estimates that 75 percent of LMI's customers are hobbyists, noting that established builders prefer to buy wood directly from the source when possible, thereby eliminating the "middleman" and cost markup. "Promotion of guitar making in general" may lack the selectivity that certain builders and collectors desire, but what is lost in exclusivity is gained in the support given to the ambitions of amateurs and professionals alike. Because LMI has no economic incentive to pick winners in its tournament of value, it has created an event in which the opportunity to compete is open to all.

The Montreal Guitar Show is based on a very different premise.[36] Central to Jacques-André Dupont's approach is the idea, expressed in English with a lilting French accent, that "luthiers are not exhibitors— they are *stars*."[37] By this he means that they should be treated like the jazz celebrities he routinely deals with in his job as vice president of the Montreal International Jazz Festival. Like Healdsburg, "Montreal" is limited to one hundred makers and participation is by invitation only. But advertising the show successfully, Dupont argues, requires recognizing that not all stars burn as brightly:

I wanted to start working on creating a luthier star system. When I was sitting in the first [Montreal] show and looking at how people were behaving in the show, I realized that there were stars there. So what I realized is that I needed to enhance that—to put more lights on these guys, because these guys will be the shining stars. They will receive a lot of visibility, and they will bring more attention to the show, and that's good for the starting luthiers. So this was very important for me that I would get the stars and that they would have what they deserve as stars. This would also help the younger guitar makers or the ones that are still yet to be discovered.

Making status distinctions among artistic types preternaturally alert to slights real and imagined is no easy task. But the underlying rationale—that lesser-known builders will benefit from the publicity generated by "shining stars"—performs double duty, assuaging bruised egos and big ones alike.[38] Nonetheless, "creating a star system" requires identifying the makers whose instruments are desirable to experienced collectors. To do this, Montreal's promotional materials feature images of instruments that organizers suggest already have been or could be removed from ordinary exchange to circulate in the nonmarket realm of lutherie's art world. Whether in advertisements or in the design of posters, programs, and T-shirts, the decision to feature some makers' instruments more prominently than others inscribes, in a visual field, the aesthetic expertise of the show's organizers.

Montreal's first T-shirt, for example, featured images of twelve guitars, each identified by the name and email address of the maker. The 2008 program cover depicts the silhouette of a generic guitar that is composed of countless smaller guitars, suggesting that the work of many builders is represented. But the posters available for purchase at the show reverse this imagery: each contains a large image of a selected maker's instrument against a galaxy of infinitesimal guitars. I suspect that my reaction to this enticement was not unusual. I bought the poster of a luthier whose work I admire and asked him to autograph it. This allowed me to take home an image in lieu of the prohibitively expensive real thing.

Even when the imagery promoting the Montreal show does not identify individual luthiers by name, the makers of the selected guitars are evident to anyone familiar with their distinctive styles. Through promotional efforts such as these, Montreal positions itself much as an art gallery or auction house would: as a place where cognoscenti of the craft can find guitars of the highest quality and inexperienced consumers can trust that the instruments they see have aesthetic and economic value. Dupont is conscious of the marketing clout he exercises on luthiers' behalf—and, he readily admits, he is happy to use it:

> These guys basically need a marketing team behind them, and that's my forte. I try to find a way to work for them and make sure it works. If you open next month's *Premier Guitar Magazine*, you'll see an ad that I purchased, and this ad will feature five guitars from luthiers coming to the show. I'm not featuring my logo and saying, "Come see all the great luthiers." I'm saying that, but I'm saying it by "Here are some examples." For a luthier who has a guitar in our ad, that's a real value, because he doesn't have to pay for that [advertising]. Also, it's a message I'm sending to the whole industry saying, "At the Montreal Guitar Show we put the luthiers on top; we feature them and they're the stars of the show." Of course I don't show their face, because it's their guitar that is featured.

The decision to show guitars, not faces, is a not an established convention in lutherie. In 2009, for instance, the program covers for the Montreal Guitar Show and the Healdsburg Festival adopted opposing representational strategies, the former looking like a surrealist's dream, the latter like a high school yearbook. What makes the absence of faces an element of Montreal's brand is not the focus on guitars per se—Healdsburg's 2007 poster was also a collage of guitars—but the fact that a three-dimensional perspective is used to foreground some images against the backdrop of others. To act as luthiers' "marketing team" means explicitly promoting their work as art, not just as tools for music making.

"I see guitars like people see sculpture or a great painting," Dupont tells me, "and I invest in this field like people will invest in art."[39] Emphasizing visual as well as sonic aesthetics, he describes guitar collecting as an act of patronage. In doing so, he invokes the mystique of a craft that depends on royal sponsorship for its survival:

> For me, there is something noble about making something with your hands. I'm always impressed with people that have those skills, which I don't have at all. And I like the image of the Geppetto thing, the image of someone in his workshop, which is all messy—and this is just a perception—with tools, pieces of wood, dust, and a candle.

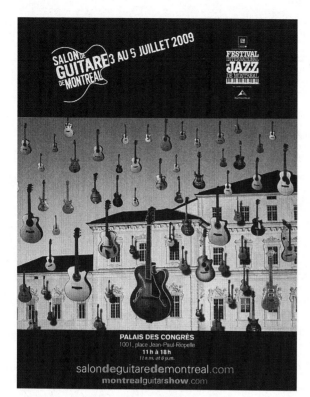

FIGURE 5.4.
Program cover for
the Montreal Guitar
Show, 2009. A
surrealist's dream
of lutherie's "star
system."

[Laughing] I like to say when I look at a tree, "This is a guitar, or "This is a violin." And like Geppetto, who gets his log of wood and makes a puppet, these guys have the same approach in a way. So basically I find this very romantic. It's the old days and I—for me, to look at a piece of wood and see the finished product is magic. I feel blessed that I have the money to give to an artist. And that's part of the romance thing. Like, you know, a noble was able to commission— which we don't do anymore—a painting in the older ages.

The "romance" of guitar making, Dupont suggests, is made possible by the noblesse oblige of those who recognize and support it. Were it not for the economic sensibility that accompanies this sentimental vision, Geppetto's cluttered garret and primitive light source would remain simply that: a site of impoverishment. The affective promise of this tableau, as Dupport apprehends it, lies in the exchange that takes place between patron and artisan. If the artist is gifted with a talent that is culturally undervalued, then a patron is someone "blessed" with the power—not unlike Pinocchio's Blue Fairy—to right that wrong.

"There's a romantic thing," Dupont insists, "to having a conversation with someone and saying, 'Would you do a guitar for me?' What I say to them is 'Do something that you'll be proud of and I'll be excited.'" The client in this scenario is not "buying" a commodity but the performance of making a singular work of art. That this exchange is likened to the patronage systems of "older ages" underscores its perceived departure from the current socioeconomic order. In Montreal's theater of branding, those who lack the hand skills to perform the "noble" art of lutherie can enact the "nobility" of aristocratic gift exchange, in which the monetary gift of the patron is amplified by the gifted labor of the artisan and the commodity situation of the craft object may be bypassed altogether.

Florida's Newport Guitar Show, which ran for two years before being suspended indefinitely, tried to market handmade guitars quite differently. Henry Lowenstein, an international lawyer and guitar collector, rejected the elitism of other guitar shows and the exclusivity of NAMM—the music industry's trade show, which caters to dealers, purchasing agents, and industry insiders. He parlayed skills developed running a music store and duty-free shops into what he envisioned as a "NAMM show for the general public."[40] The focus of his promotional strategy was on increasing the number and economic diversity of people who attend high-end guitar shows. On the theory that reaching a large audience requires appealing to a mass market, he included guitar accessories and less expensive acoustic and electric guitars in the same event that showcased the work of artisans.

Thus at the 2008 show in Miami Beach, factory instruments filled a large display area on the main floor of the convention center, while hand builders were located on the second floor. Effectively dividing the site into a "bargain basement" for the proletariat and an upper level "salon" for the well-to-do, Lowenstein drew upon a principle of retail marketing that has shaped the design of department stores since the 1870s—a use of class distinctions that is "calculated to stir up feelings of social inadequacy and envy and meant to inspire impulsive buying."[41] In this case, however, placing markers of class in close proximity to one another was also intended to cultivate the notion that handmade guitars *are* luxury goods—signs of social status that belong in the same market register as high-end cars and watches.

The brand developed by Florida's Newport Show was tied to the imagery and activities of the venues in which it was held. Although guitars made by individual builders are featured in the show's advertising, these images are dominated by a revamped version of Newport's original logo. The ethereal mermaid who once strummed her guitar in a moonlit harbor was exposed to the light of day and depicted wearing dark glasses, suggesting a cross between a blonde beach babe and a blind black musician. While the mermaid logo may signal the siren's song of consumer desire, the show's locations—the Miami Beach Convention Center in 2008 and the Seminole Hard Rock Hotel and Casino in 2010—made it clear who the relevant publics were and what kind of transaction was encouraged. By attracting sponsors with deep pockets and consumers who enjoy car shows and slot machines, Lowenstein hoped to introduce the artisanal guitar to a mass market: "If you turn a [guitar] show into a tea party for just the few, the proud, and the most distinguished, what you're going to get is a very, very small show, and one that doesn't have the resources to carry that message out to the world. This is what caused me to want to do the [the Newport] show in the first place. I went to a Healdsburg show and I said, "Oh my god, *nobody* knows about this!"

That he, a consummate consumer of luxury goods, had not known about the lutherie world until a severe case of arthritis sent him on a quest for a custom guitar is evidence, he asserts, of an untapped reservoir of wealth among those in his market demographic. Nonetheless, he says, some luthiers have had to be dragged kicking and screaming into this way of understanding their economic self-interest:

They said, "Well, if Gibson's going to be there, I don't want to be there." Why? Because they are used to being so overwhelmed by Gibson's advertising. It's stupidity. You ride the coattails of whoever you ride the coattails of. Someone's going to come here because there is a Gibson Les Paul, and then they are going to walk upstairs and they are going to see a one-of-a-kind guitar for twelve thousand dollars. Are you going to spend twelve thousand dollars for a guitar

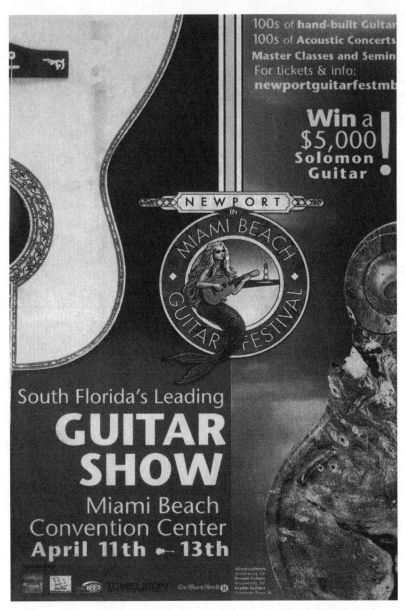

FIGURE 5.5. *Newsprint program cover for the Miami Beach Guitar Festival, 2008.*
Newport's mermaid dons dark glasses for South Florida's sun.

that anybody can have? No. So both of them can survive. We have the big car show here at the Miami Beach Convention Center. "Okay, we need a Honda for the kids," so you see all this. But I'm really coming to see the Lamborghinis and the Ferraris and the Lotuses and stuff like that. But [the luthiers] are saying, "Well, we're not going to show our cars if you've got Hondas over there in the other hall." What kind of stupidity is that, right? I put up with it, but I have no patience for it anymore. Either they are going to survive or they are going to die—and they really will. There are people who could not afford to come to this show even when offered a free table! Could not afford to come here!

Lowenstein does not entertain the possibility, at least not publicly, that something other than poverty or "stupidity" might cause artisans to balk at his business model. As he sees it, the capitalist marketplace should be an inclusive public sphere in which barriers to the accumulation of capital are overcome. To realize this inclusiveness, he sought to facilitate the flow of information across various segments of the guitar industry. Idealizing the marketplace as a democratic space, he hoped to show that free-market capitalism could operate to the advantage of consumers of all classes and firms of all sizes. Invoking the mantra of neoliberalism—that what is good for capital is good for everyone— Lowenstein states with Darwinian conviction that artisans who refuse to engage in cross-marketing will "die" for want of commercial success.[42] Florida's Newport was an attempt to create a venue in which they could tap into the international luxury market. As he puts it:

There is going to be a cachet to American-built guitars, just like I want a German or a Swiss watch and I want French perfume. As the Chinese make more money selling us their cheap guitars, they are going to have more money to spend on our expensive guitars. However, you've got to take our guitars and put them into the luxury industry so that when they have the money in China to buy the guitars, we are perceived as having the things they want to buy. If we are just a bunch of scattered people who are selling guitars for twenty-five thousand dollars who they have never heard of, they are not going to do it. But if they click on luxury.com, and they see, "Oh, yeah, if you really want something good from America, you get a Keller guitar," what are they going to do? They are going to order a Keller guitar. People don't understand that. But I'm looking—if I were a chess player, this is ten moves away. Right? That's where it's all going.

Lowenstein's game of chess assumes a global political economy in which winners understand the rules of the market and think several moves ahead. As a national iteration of a transnational tournament of value, Florida's Newport aimed to establish the artisanal guitar as a luxury object, its value derived through comparison with other luxury goods. Promoting the unapologetic commodification of artisanal instruments, the show emphasized not only the class of goods within which they should be valued but also their capacity to function as "incarnated signs" of elite "taste" that could be recognized by anyone alert to the symbolic dimension of consumer culture.[43]

But how do handmade guitars come to have luxury value? How do you put a price on social distinction? To answer such questions during the festival, Lowenstein appeared on a panel called "Guitar Marketing 101." Handmade guitars can be approached as commodities, he explained, if you focus on a set of "objective" criteria. Instruments will typically have good investment value, he pointed out, if they are made by a maker with a famous pedigree and low productivity and if they feature rare woods, novel innovations, and elaborate ornamentation. "Tone," in his view, is not a reliable indicator of value because it is "so subjective." The only way market value can be placed on an instrument's tonal qualities, he argued, is if respected musicians play others like it, thereby testifying to its "reputation for being a great-sounding guitar."[44] Thus, as an exercise in creating a new theater of branding in lutherie, the South Florida show attempted, despite communal misgivings, to rationalize the market for the artisanal guitar.

INALIENABLE POSSESSIONS

On a chilly morning in March 2011, I glance up at the banner draped across the entrance to the Metropolitan Museum of Art. "GUITAR HEROES," it announces in bold letters: "Legendary Craftsmen from Italy to New York." Invoking rock icons and the video game inspired by them, the museum obviously relishes this opportunity to attract a demographic unaccustomed to setting foot in a venue redolent of old masters. That this marketing feat is achieved with a display of lutes, violins, and guitars that date from Italy's "golden age" of lutherie to the new golden era today makes me smile. Twenty-five years have passed since the first Healdsburg show demonstrated the commercial value of artisanal guitars. Now their aesthetic value is being acknowledged at the pinnacle of the international art world.

In the bustling lobby, I spot my colleague Jean-Christophe Agnew, a historian of capitalism and American consumer culture. As a member of the museum, he procured tickets to a lecture on the luthiers featured in the Met's show, and we agreed to meet beforehand to see the exhibit. Snapping on our visitor's buttons, we wend our way through a maze of art-bedecked hallways until we come to the designated gallery. Signs map out a prescribed path through the exhibit, informing us that supplementary information, interviews, and musical performances can be downloaded as a digital application.[45] Not wanting to be antisocial, I resist the temptation to pop in my ear buds. But as J-C and I become absorbed in what we see, the appeal of the Met Guitars app becomes clear: looking at stringed instruments in glass cases can be oddly unsettling. Just as the Martin Company pipes classic folk music into its museum and every major guitar show offers "mini concerts" and "listening rooms," the exhibit's curator recognizes people's desire to hear the instruments on display.[46]

But the absence of guitar music in the exhibit itself has a disquieting effect on me. Try as I might to shake my impatience—wow, a guitar made by Antonio Stradivari in 1700![47]—I become increasingly aware of the insistent *visuality* of the exhibit and the European origin myth it propounds.[48] Looking but not hearing, unable to touch the guitars or excite their strings, museumgoers are asked to appreciate lutherie as a fine art, as if what is sculpted were the wood itself, not the sound it makes. Exhibited as artifacts of virtuoso making, not vehicles of inspired playing, the guitars are presented in a state of suspended animation, eliciting an anticipation of aural gratification that must be deferred or denied.[49]

In this acoustic desert, our attention is directed instead to the "voice" of the curator who—through the exhibit's labels, catalog, and multimedia application—enunciates the story that these instruments have been gathered to tell. That narrative is one of origins: a sweeping historical saga of the intergenerational transmission of an "ethnic" craft tradition. To appreciate the talent possessed by some of the world's greatest guitar makers, the exhibit suggests, all we need to do is look at violins made by Andrea Amati in 1559 and Antonio Stradivari in 1711, bowl-back mandolins made by Italian immigrants to New York City in the 1800s, and archtop guitars made by three Italian American builders between the 1930s and today to see an unmistakable family resemblance.

The pivotal figure in this genealogy is John D'Angelico (1905–64), the son of immigrants from Naples. D'Angelico grew up in Little Italy and learned to make Neapolitan mandolins in a lutherie shop owned by his great-uncle Raphael Ciani. When the popularity of this mandolin style waned, D'Angelico began making reproductions of Gibson's L-5 archtop guitar. Eventually he developed his own design aesthetic, creating instruments with art deco and New York–themed motifs that now rank among the world's most valuable vintage guitars. Although D'Angelico's instruments were "copies," the curator observes, "he was such a great maker [that] they immediately had their own level of sophistication, their own sound quality. He just had the generations of quality in his manufacturing."[50] And it is this ethnic patrimony, the exhibit argues, that D'Angelico passed on to James D'Aquisto, the young man who became his last apprentice.

The section of the exhibit dedicated to D'Aquisto (1935–95) is dominated by a flat-screen monitor that shows, in a continuous loop, excerpts from a 1986 documentary, The New Yorker Special: Handcrafting a Guitar. The film features D'Aquisto building one of his best-known models at his Long Island shop in the late 1970s.[51] Shirtless in a white tank undershirt, looking like a young Marlon Brando in A Streetcar Named Desire, he is virility personified. Drawing closer, I can hear the film's audio track at low volume. Against the backdrop of shop sounds and piano music, a man is speaking. The voice is D'Aquisto's, with a telltale New York accent, dubbed onto footage that cuts between scenes of making and archival photographs of himself and D'Angelico.

Transfixed, I realize that this disembodied voice, detached from the image of the man on the screen, hovers above an empty workbench displayed with a sparse assortment of tools and equipment.[52] The intended effect, I presume, is to encourage the visitor's fantasy of being inside

FIGURE 5.6. James D'Aquisto in his Farmingdale, Long Island,
shop, 1977. Photograph by Tim Olsen.

D'Aquisto's shop and present at the site of production.[53] But as I turn to catch up with J-C, I am struck by the vulnerability of the male body made visible in this ghostly tableau. Although the filmic voice-over creates an illusion of presence—D'Aquisto's speech seems to be coeval with that of the exhibit's curator—the virtually empty workbench signifies his absence. To luthiers who have seen this film, the sight of his exposed body—lacking protective gloves, glasses, and a respirator in the spray booth—is a portent of his fatal epileptic seizure at the age of fifty-nine and a reminder of a time when the toxicity of wood dust and guitar finishes was widely underestimated.[54]

The visual transition from D'Aquisto's instruments of the 1990s to John Monteleone's of the same period is virtually seamless, so similar are they in appearance. Although Monteleone, born in 1947, never served an apprenticeship, he and D'Aquisto were well acquainted, and both were at the forefront of the "artistic turn" in the lutherie movement. The sculptural qualities of their guitars and mandolins is evident in the playful citations of historical elements and the novel shapes of their headstocks, fretboard extensions, pick guards, sound holes, and tailpieces. Under museum lighting, the polished contours and surfaces of spruce, ebony, and maple appear wrought from clay or stone, and the grain and intricate shell inlay look as if they could have been applied by brush. As guitars built to be enjoyed as much by the eye as the ear, they reflect contemporary aesthetics in lutherie as well as the growing influence of wealthy patrons who no longer "collect guitars" but commission artwork.

At the end of the exhibit, J-C and I come upon the quartet of guitars, completed between 2002 and 2006, that Monteleone calls the Four Seasons. Each one is unique and designed to evoke in sound and decorative detail a different season of the year. Displayed in freestanding cases that permit viewing "in the round," these instruments are a career-culminating show of virtuosity. Not only are their exteriors exquisitely appointed, but "sound ports" in the bass side of each guitar reveal an interior scene consistent with its seasonal theme.

In Monteleone's allusion to Antonio Vivaldi's 1723 violin concertos I hear the luthier commenting on his own genealogy. His "voiceover," like D'Aquisto's filmic one, blends with the exhibit's metanarrative, amplifying a structure of desire that locates the origin of lutherie today in a European craft tradition. In the Four Seasons, as in "Guitar Heroes" as a whole, artisanal mastery is associated with the Italian baroque, and this heritage is visualized as the property of white ethnic bodies. Thus in Met Guitars, Monteleone is heralded as "the living embodiment of [a] long tradition of Italian American craftsmanship."[55]

———

The Four Seasons—Winter, Spring, Summer, and Fall—are arrayed in stands on the stage as Jean-Christophe and I find seats toward the back of a rapidly filling auditorium. After being introduced by a colleague, Jayson Kerr Dobney, a curator in the Met's Department of Musical Instruments, strides up to the lectern. Most people, he says, associate the term *guitar heroes* with great guitar players. "For the exhibition we wanted to flip that around. We wanted to say, 'No, in many cases the *real* guitar heroes are the makers, the craftsmen who give life to this tradition and, in many ways, are heroes to some of the players.'"[56] Dobney's entertaining talk is punctuated with samples of music and interviews with musicians talking about D'Angelico, D'Aquisto, and Monteleone. All of the featured guitarists are white men,[57] except for a video clip of Mary Kaye, a 1950s Las Vegas lounge singer, performing with her D'Angelico—"lest you think," Dobney tells us, "that guitar playing is only a boy's sport."

Nonetheless, the testimonials that he presents uniformly revere and romanticize an inchoate connection shared between men, whether as master and apprentice or maker and player. The excerpt Dobney plays us from *The New Yorker Special* is instructive in this regard. As in the exhibit, D'Aquisto's voice is heard speaking over images of himself and D'Angelico:

The first time I met [D'Angelico], I walked in the shop and he had just finished a brand-new guitar, a big blond New Yorker. And it was really unbelievable. I never saw anything like that. He says, "You want to try it?" He says, "Be careful!" I sat down on the stool and he put it in my hand. I played a couple of chords on it. I couldn't believe the sound out of it. One Saturday I says, "Geez, I could come here every day." He says, "Oh no you can't!" Because he was in a bad mood that particular day; that's the kind of person he was. So I was "Oh, okay, anything you say." And he must have liked me because I never come on smart or a wise guy or anything like that. So I guess he finally decided, "I guess we'll try him." As a teacher he'd show you something and he'd say, "This is how I do it. You can do it either my way or your own way, but it better come out as good or better than I can do it." I guess I molded to actually the way that he wanted me to be.[58]

The elements of this narrative—a ritual object placed in the young man's hands that augurs a future foretold, and the attentive obedience that he offers in exchange for instruction in an arcane art—lend it a mythic quality. The master's inscrutability and gruff tenderness become, in D'Aquisto's account, the affective means by which the craft repertoire is bequeathed. The desire to become a luthier, as represented here, is a longing for, and sentimental realization of, masculine intersubjectivity. The "unbelievable sound" of D'Angelico's guitar instigates the apprentice's wish to simultaneously produce a similar tone in his instruments as well as hear the inscrutable voice of his mentor. As a mode of nonverbal attunement, this desire enables D'Aquisto to divine D'Angelico's true feelings despite "bad moods," allowing him to bond with a taciturn father figure and eventually express himself in the craft object.

D'Aquisto's attitude to D'Angelico draws upon the structure of feeling that infuses lutherie's scenes of instruction more broadly. Just as he "molds" himself to his teacher's expectations through imitation and empathy, hand builders attend to the voice of wood and the wishes of clients in order to create a guitar's distinctive tone. The bodily discipline and intuitive performance of the craft repertoire become, in this scenario, the same affective disposition that enables the transmission of an ethnic patrimony.

The sentiments expressed in narratives of ethnic succession and nonverbal rapport between men are as compelling to players as they are to makers. Among the videos that Dobney shows is one of Mark Knopfler, the British guitarist, performing a song called "Monteleone."[59] Before playing the piece, Knopfler describes what led him to write it:

There's a tradition of great violinmakers in Italy, Stradivarius and Guarneri and Amati in Cremona in Italy. And there's a tradition of making these f-hole guitars in New York City by Italians, and it's sort of a strange parallel—D'Angelico, D'Aquisto, and now a man called John Monteleone. And I met John Monteleone, and it was like meeting Stradivari—I'm sure it was like that. He's like Leonardo da Vinci in a way, and he set about building me a guitar, which is an archtop guitar with f-holes like a violin. I don't have it here. It's a beautiful thing. But when he was making it for me, he'd send me little e-mails, and he'd say things like "The chisels are calling, it's time to make sawdust." I realized, of course, that he has this compulsion to be with his chisels and his work, and it was inspiring.

As the meditative, waltzlike piece begins, the swelling sound of a violin gives way to Knopfler's world-weary voice and solo acoustic guitar. Creating a portrait of lutherie as work that yields tangible and singular results—wood shavings and a beloved instrument—he repeats the refrain "The chisels are calling" several times to underscore the sense that Monteleone is spiritually "called" to his craft. But the song is not simply a sentimental paean to manual labor. Knopfler also offers a European origin story for contemporary lutherie when he riffs on the "strange parallel" that exists between Italian American archtop guitar makers in New York City and Cremonese violinmakers in Italy.

Collapsing the historical relationship between Monteleone and Stradivari, the singer claims that meeting one maker today is no different from meeting the other one four hundred years ago. Knopfler underscores this portrayal of a timeless, unchanging craft and the eternal recurrence of masculine generativity with references to the cyclical nature of "seasons go[ing] by to the songs in the wood." By using personal pronouns—"My finger plane's working, gentle persuasion / I bend to the wood and I coax it to sing"—he tacitly identifies himself with the luthier and locates his own work of "crafting songs" as coextensive with Europe's "great tradition" of stringed-instrument making.[60]

Dobney gestures toward the Four Seasons guitars on the stage. "I've seen how players like Mark Knopfler are inspired by guitars like these here," he observes, and how this "wonderful circle" of inspiration prompts luthiers, in their turn, to innovate and create such master-pieces. Then, announcing a surprise guest, Dobney invites us to "please welcome the *living* guitar hero John Monteleone." The guitar maker, a tall man with a neat beard and regal mane of gray hair, mounts the stage to enthusiastic applause. He raises his hands in thanks and speaks in a deep, resonant voice:

> I know firsthand that the beauty of [lutherie] is that the entire sub-ject deals with intimacy, and that is something that's shared be-tween the musician and the maker. You can see it obviously in these [video] clips. Every musician just has a passion that is probably equal to my own. And then there is the excitement when you hand an in-strument over to a musician for the first time. It's one of your in-struments; of course, you're very proud. There's a lot that comes with that. But then there's that moment that you hand it to a musi-cian and something very *magical* happens. And I love to watch it, if it's a good instrument. Hopefully, everything works out great, and usually it does. But to see the smile on their face when they just set these strings into motion for the first time! They've played it once, they fool around; then they play a few pieces that are familiar to them. And I love to watch their expression. It's that full-circle con-nection that gives purpose to every ounce of energy you put into building that thing for this person.

It is precisely this "intimacy"—this knowledge of "how musicians feel about the instruments"—Monteleone goes on to say, that distin-guishes artisanal makers from industrial manufacturers. Individual lu-thiers, he explains, "sit down with the musician and understand what his or her needs are, and what their desires and dreams are. It is my job to try and turn that idea and those wishes—that *desire*—into a reality." A player's creative desire, in this telling, is an amorphous longing that can become a material reality only through the mediation of a skilled hand builder. A shared "passion" for music allows Monteleone to access mu-sicians' feelings by hearing them play and "watching the expression on their faces." Evoking the ultimate scene in a story of making, he high-lights the moment in which—without words—a "full-circle connec-tion" occurs, as maker and player recognize each other's gifts.

Were lutherie's "magic" reducible to such moments, we might be inclined to think of it as an ineffable affair, an encounter between two individual dispositions that happen to be in harmony. But to conceive of the craft in these terms, however romantic, is to miss the larger field of play in which those transactions take place. As a tournament of value, the Met's "Guitar Heroes" makes explicit—in a way other guitar shows rarely do—how high the cultural stakes are when it comes to which instruments are removed from commodity exchange and why. These are instruments that can be called upon to symbolically represent and materially instantiate the patrilineal genealogy that gives them value. As signs of a "mystical" bond between men across time, they commemorate the "heroism" of intergenerational power.

What kind of heroism, in the end, is this? In one sense, it is the courage to defy the inevitability with which high-tech automation presents itself. Handcrafted objects that become permanently tied to gods, ancestors, and discriminating owners demonstrate an ethical fortitude in the face of commodity exchange: the capacity of their makers to profit from market transactions without being reduced to their economizing logic. Like treasured shells in the Kula ring of the Massim archipelago, such instruments may become "inalienable possessions" with an "absolute value" that overrides their market value.[61]

In another sense, however, the celebration of artisanal lutherie as a heroic endeavor perpetuates a simplistic vision of European history and hegemony. As cultural artifacts made famous by virtue of their circulation in elite registers of the market, handmade stringed instruments can be used to underwrite a *collective* story of making. In this master narrative, they participate in a storyline that authenticates not just extraordinary instruments but "legendary craftsmen" who legitimate European imperialism. And this legacy, occulted by masculine sentimentality, haunts guitar makers to this day.

Ghosts of Empire

Everyone knows a commodity: it is the material good of capitalist production and the object of consumers' desire. Commodities seem so familiar that we imagine them ready made for us through every stage of production and distribution, as they pass from hand to hand until they arrive at the consumer. Yet the closer we look at the commodity chain, the more every step—even transportation—can be seen as an arena of cultural production. Global capitalism is made in the friction in these chains as divergent cultural economies are linked, often awkwardly. Yet the commodity must emerge as if untouched by this friction.
—Anna Lowenhaupt Tsing, Friction (2005)

The docklands of Manhattan's Battery District were a forbidding yet fascinating world to young guitar makers in the 1960s and 1970s. Here, at the port where cargo was unloaded directly from merchant ships into commercial warehouses, was a primary source of raw materials for lutherie. Prowling the docks in search of African ebony, Honduras mahogany, and Brazilian rosewood, luthiers could experience firsthand the trade in wild plant and animal species. Dockmasters were known to carry weapons as protection against smugglers and thieves, and the cavernous warehouses enclosed an international market in goods that brimmed with the spirit of a bazaar, replete with glass aquariums featuring an arresting array of vagabond reptiles.[1] A discerning eye for quality tone wood in the roughhewn form of a billet or split log was essential, as importers were rarely knowledgeable about an instrument maker's needs, let alone inclined to spend time on customers who purchased wood in small quantities. Early steel-string builders learned to navigate the docks by following in the footsteps of classical makers whose skill at wood selection and long-standing relationships with vendors proved indispensable.

When guitar makers reflect on the changes they have seen in lutherie over the past five decades, trips to the docks and other supply depots are cited to demonstrate how hard it used to be to acquire not only information about their craft but also the materials and specialized equipment necessary to practice it. In their recollections, the search for wood and tools, and the stamina required to obtain them, takes on the feel of an expedition to the margins of civilization. Writing in 2000, in the tenth-anniversary issue of *Guitarmaker*, William "Grit" Laskin describes a trip to the docks he took as an apprentice to Jean-Claude Larrivée in 1971.[2] At eighteen, Laskin was new to lutherie, but Larrivée, a few years his senior, had made the trek before with his mentor, the German luthier Edgar Mönch.[3] Laskin opens his account with an arrival scene that highlights the discomforts they endured:

> We drove to New York (ten hours from Toronto) in an old and empty van. We arrived late in the night and parked on a side street somewhere in lower Manhattan. A hotel was not even a consideration. We rolled out sleeping bags across the slatted metal floor of the van and tried to get some sleep. The unending drone of passing traffic didn't make it easy. By sunrise, the stares of passing pedestrians curiously checking out the van's curtainless windows was our incentive to get moving. At a nearby very-greasy spoon we ordered breakfast and took turns in the grimy toilet splashing our faces with water.

While the hardship of penurious travel has long been a badge of honor among the young, Laskin's emphasis on the primitive conditions of this excursion also sets up a compelling tension between the mission-oriented luthiers and the natives who "stare" inquisitively at them and their vehicle. Borrowing a classic trope from the travelogues of Victorian-era anthropologists and explorers, he imagines how strange he and Larrivée must look to those they encounter, temporarily inverting or suspending the symbolic opposition between the savage and the civilized.[4] In this cultural imaginary, the intrepid travelers have entered a social universe in which they are simultaneously empowered to act—to "order breakfast," for instance—yet also at the mercy of circumstances—"greasy spoons" and "grimy toilets"—that are marked by a loss of the standard of living they enjoy at home. Their encounter with the "uncivilized" extends to the behavior of their interlocutors:

> The first stop on our agenda was a wood dealer down at the docks. We were hoping to buy some Ebony billets, small trimmed log pieces coated in wax. Once we entered the yard office we were treated as if we were no better than insects. We were young, scruffy, and our purchase (maybe $2,000) would not even qualify for their petty cash. I

watched Jean squirm in frustration but hold his tongue. Eventually, most likely because we apparently weren't going away, they sold us some wood. We loaded three shockingly heavy billets into the van and left the docklands. Only three intersections away, coming to a sudden stop, the waxed logs slid forward in the van with such momentum that they rode up and crushed the centre dash. So much for the radio.

Putting up with rude or humiliating behavior on the part of local gatekeepers was the price they had to pay, Laskin suggests, for getting what they wanted. Stubborn persistence and holding their tongues was the key to prying desirable resources out of the possession of those who saw them as little more than pests and had no need for their money. At this point in the narrative, it would appear as though Laskin and Larrivée had the upper hand vis-à-vis the island's inhabitants—until, that is, the ebony logs wreak their havoc, symbolically leaving them cut off from the outside world. With their "sudden stop," the scene turns decidedly ominous as they venture further inland in search of the esoteric tools they hope to find at the H. L. Wild store:

We walked into a very "tired" storefront that was so dark we weren't sure at first that they were open. We entered a shadowland of dust covered tools, glass display counters so dirty you could hardly make out what they contained, walls hidden behind aged dark oak drawer cabinets and a loud TV casting its pale flicker into the gloom. On one counter sat a china plate filled to overflowing with fresh chicken livers. Two cats, to whom human customers like us were at best irrelevant, energetically gorged on the livers, whiskers dripping chicken blood. A cautionary growl emerged from deeper in the store. A full-grown German Shepherd bared his teeth and likely would have lunged had not his metal neck-chain been in the grip of one of the Wild brothers.

From the docklands to a "shadowland" shop of horrors, we are transported to a place that is simultaneously primitive and modern. Although punctuated by the "pale flicker" and "loud" presence of contemporary telecommunications, this zone of commerce is also "aged" and "dust covered"—visibly "tired" of keeping up with the times. No longer mere "insects," Laskin and Larrivée have become, through the eyes of indigenous beasts, "irrelevant" interlopers, if not unsuspecting prey. Laskin's juxtaposition of savage and civilized imagery alternates rapidly—between the "china plate" and "bloody whiskers," the "metal neck chain" and "bared teeth"—producing the startling apparition of a shopkeeper who is both wild and Wild himself.

Although the two "scruffy" luthiers were ultimately successful in their quest, crossing the Canadian border at midnight with their bounty secure in the van, Laskin concludes with a "final image of the trip" that raises the question of exactly *what* they have succeeded in doing:

> The Customs Officer asked us: "Purpose of the trip?"
> "Visiting friends," we said.
> "Anything to declare?"
> "Nope."
> "What're those black things there?"
> "Ballast for the van," Jean answered. "You know, for traction in the snow. They just slid forward and can you believe the mess they made of the dash?"

Poker faces and a quick wit saved Laskin and Larrivée from import duties, but their capacity to dissemble in dialogue with customs agents implicates them in a larger system of geopolitical borders and national identities. At ease in the borderland between the United States and Canada, they are able to reenter their country with undeclared merchandise hidden in plain sight—a feat that would have been unthinkable, then and now, for travelers lacking their racial profile and citizenship status. As for the "black things" that lay between the front seats and on floor of the van, they are invisible to the nation-state at this historical juncture. They arouse no suspicion and pose no obvious danger, save the damage that has been done to the luthiers' vehicle. Yet even in this private sphere, the logs' ability to "make a mess" can be imaginatively harnessed to order and stability—offering, as Larrivée claimed, "ballast" and "traction in the snow."

Laskin's anecdotal account is intended to remind fellow luthiers of the lengths to which they once had to go to acquire the materials and tools of their trade. When seen from the vantage point of the last century's end—when guitar makers could purchase these items with a phone call or click of the mouse—it certainly seemed, as Laskin concludes, that lutherie had "come a long way." But the expedition he describes expresses more than nostalgia for adventurous consumption. Embedded in his tale is a tacit recognition that the resources luthiers use and cherish have historically been harvested from colonized regions of the world and shipped to imperial centers in Europe and North America.

The prototype of today's artisanal guitar is a creature of the Renaissance. The five-course guitars presented to royalty in Spain, Italy, and France in the sixteenth and seventeenth centuries showcased the reach of sovereign empires through the exotic materials that composed and adorned them.[5] In the New World, the Industrial Revolution did little to displace this concept of elegance. Early nineteenth-century guitar makers, operating factories powered by steam, tapped into Atlantic trade routes to distinguish their top-of-the-line models with ebony, mother-of-pearl, ivory, and tortoiseshell, reproducing aristocratic tastes for well-to-do Americans.

Taking their cue from Spanish guitars and golden era instruments, pioneering hand builders have adopted an aesthetic that values traditional materials over the perceived compromises to tone and beauty associated with the celluloid plastics and laminates that came into widespread use in factory guitars in the 1950s.[6] Ever since the 1975 Convention on International Trade in Endangered Species (CITES) banned global trade in elephant tusks and sea turtle shell, however, artisanal makers' use of classic materials in vintage instrument restoration and new guitar construction has put them on a collision course with domestic and international law.

Updates to the convention, combined with America's own environmental protections and restrictions imposed by exporting countries, have made it increasingly difficult, if not impossible, to import, export, or travel with guitars containing ivory, tortoiseshell, Brazilian rosewood, and certain types of abalone without requisite permits and declarations. In this regulatory regime, crossing national borders with contraband materials has become a criminal offense, and guitar makers' moral innocence is no longer taken for granted. Today, confronted with escalating post-9/11 security concerns, North American luthiers find themselves "haunted by empire" as they attempt to negotiate zones of commerce where the legacy of colonialism exerts an un-acknowledged force.[7] The craft's long-standing love affair with exotic tone woods now subjects guitar makers to the discipline of a neoliberal government that has renewed imperial ambitions.

CROSSING BORDERS

In September 2009, a shipment containing over seventy-six thousand dollars' worth of ebony arrived at the port of Newark, New Jersey. Noticing that the wood lacked the import declaration form required by a 2008 amendment to the Lacey Act, US Customs and Border Protection reported the violation to US Immigration Customs and Enforcement, and the negligent importer promptly filed the correct paperwork. The following month, however, acting on evidence that the ebony in question had been illegally harvested in Madagascar, agents of the US Fish and Wildlife Service raided the Gibson factory in Nashville, seizing computer records, pallets of ebony parts, and several guitars.[8] Gibson denied any wrongdoing, pointing to its support of environmental certification programs and its long-standing relationship with the distributor—one of the world's largest tone wood suppliers, Theodor Nagel and Company of Hamburg, Germany.[9]

Gibson and Nagel allegedly ran afoul of Madagascar's regulations concerning the harvest and export of ebony and rosewood. It was this breach of foreign law, prohibited under the newly amended Lacey Act, that triggered the American government's scrutiny of the shipment's chain of custody.[10] Of the environmental legislation to affect North American guitar makers over the past three decades, the Lacey Act amendment has had the greatest impact. Where CITES acts to curtail or restrict trade in specific species of plants and animals, Lacey authorizes federal surveillance of international transport involving virtually all undocumented plants and plant products.[11]

Signed into law in 1900, the Lacey Act was originally designed to preserve wild birds by criminalizing interstate transport and sale of poached game. Over the last century it has been amended several times, extending its coverage to a wider variety of animals and plants as well as to wildlife obtained in violation of other countries' laws.[12] Lacey's recent update, enacted as part of the 2008 Farm Bill, targets illegal logging by expanding the category of protected plants to include timber. It further requires that all commercial imports involving raw lumber and wood products be accompanied by an import declaration.[13] Together with the convention treaty and the Endangered Species Act, both of which mandate permits for the species they protect, the Lacey documents required to cross United States borders with lutherie materials and finished instruments have effectively criminalized not just poachers and wildcat loggers but the mobility of an unauthorized class of goods that makes up the artisanal guitar.

Guitar makers were slow to grasp the implications of the newly globalized regime of customs interdiction and border control. Not until 2007 — when Brazil proposed that the convention should restrict trade in pernambuco wood — did luthiers realize that the future of their craft could be in jeopardy. In a single stroke, panicked bow makers and touring musicians worried about confiscation of their bows were thrust into the bare-knuckled politics of rainforest destruction and the black market in endangered species. Lest anyone in the guitar world underestimate the significance of a crackdown on violin bows, vintage dealer George Gruhn and guitar historian Walter Carter pointed out that if similar measures were adopted for mahogany, it "would all but kill international guitar trade."[14]

At issue for Gruhn and Carter was not whether to list pernambuco in appendix 2 of the convention. Like most luthiers, they support conservation efforts. Rather, they objected to the clause that would subject *finished* goods as well as raw lumber to international regulation. While restrictions on finished goods are mandatory for species in appendix 1 (e.g., Brazilian rosewood, ivory, and tortoiseshell), Brazil's proposal marked the first time that this higher level of scrutiny would be applied to products in appendix 2. Given that Latin American big-leaf mahogany has been popular in guitar construction since the early nineteenth century and listed in appendix 2 since 2002, there was reason to be concerned about where such a precedent might lead.

The National Association of Music Merchants (NAMM) led the industry's charge against the pernambuco petition, lobbying government officials and launching a letter-writing campaign. In apparent capitulation to this protest, Brazil annotated its proposal to exempt finished goods, and the US Department of the Interior assured musicians traveling with bows that they would be allowed to enter and exit the country unmolested.[15] Happy ending notwithstanding, guitar enthusiasts saw the episode as a harbinger of outrages yet to come. Scenarios in which fanatic bureaucrats could seize golden-era instruments were the most fearsome. In their widely read piece on pernambuco, Gruhn and Carter described the multiple convention violations that would be incurred if a 1965 Martin D-28 were sent or carried across US borders to England or Canada, and the alarm they sounded reverberated throughout the lutherie community.

Although a vintage D-28 was made before Brazilian rosewood was listed in 1992, it would still be subject to the appendix 1 ban on finished goods. Even if its owner had the foresight to apply for a permit to import or export a pre-CITES instrument—paying a single-shipment processing fee and waiting over sixty days for final approval[16]—the guitar's original saddle and nut, made before elephant ivory was listed in 1975, would still violate restrictions on ivory "reworked" after 1947. Moreover, if the owner were in possession of a tortoiseshell pick, that too would be illegal, unless it could be proved that the pick had been made over one hundred years ago. The days of "slipping by" customs inspections were over, the authors warned, noting ominously that among the contraband goods prominently featured on the government's website was a Brazilian rosewood guitar.

In October 2007, Brazilian police arrested twenty-three members of a "gang" accused of illegally harvesting and exporting thirteen tons of Brazilian rosewood, most of it to the United States.[17] Caught in the dragnet were customs agents on both sides of the border who were charged with tipping off smugglers to impending raids and failing to notice the doctored export permits on rosewood concealed in shipments of less valuable timber. Observing that this "rare" tropical wood was "prized for use in making fine guitars and other instruments," the Associated Press announced that the US Fish and Wildlife Service, in partnership with Brazilian authorities, had also executed a federal raid at an undisclosed location in Massachusetts. The search warrant was sealed by court order, but among luthiers, the target of the government's investigation was rumored to be a Brazilian middleman from whom several highly regarded builders regularly acquired wood.

In a 2008 Fretboard Journal article on the dangers of traveling with a Brazilian rosewood guitar, John Thomas, a lawyer and guitar player,

FIGURE 6.1. *Stepped-up customs enforcement of the CITES Treaty, enhanced by heightened post-9/11 airport security, strikes fear in the hearts of guitar lovers, Fretboard Journal, Fall 2008. Illustration by Robert Armstrong.*

described himself "standing in the security line at the airport, sweating bullets, with a large object strapped to [his] back."[18] Channeling the angst of a generation of hippies familiar with illegal substances, he invoked "Flying into Los Angeles," Arlo Guthrie's 1969 song about smuggling drugs past a customs agent. Thomas enumerated the conditions under which US border guards could confiscate guitars. Condemning the "Orwellian" logic of conservation law enforcement, he regaled readers with "horror stories":

> What happens if your guitar doesn't contain any CITES substances, but the government seizes it anyway? You have to prove that the government was wrong. That's right: As long as the USFWS [US Fish and Wildlife Service] can show that it had "reasonable grounds" to believe that your guitar's headstock overlay, for example, was Brazilian rosewood, you'll have the burden—not the USFWS—of proving that it's really ebony or Madagascar rosewood. You'll have to hire an expert to testify at a hearing in the federal courthouse in Washington, D.C. And even then, just how are you going to prove exactly when your guitar's ivory saddle—the one you scored off of eBay—was actually fashioned into a saddle? You simply can't.

At the time of the article's writing, only two instances of federally seized guitars had been reported. In both cases, a Canadian dealer had sent instruments to American factories for warranty repairs without declaring the white abalone shell—prohibited under the Endangered Species Act—allegedly contained in their inlay. The US Fish and Wildlife Service impounded the guitars; and according to Thomas, the dealer was fined $225 per violation and forced to forfeit the guitars, despite the strong possibility that agents had misidentified the type of abalone they contained.[19] The article's takeaway message was clear: draconian environmental laws were inflicting an undue burden on guitar owners, who, forced to leave their guitars at home, would have to "take up the kazoo instead."

Outside the lutherie community, the fracas over CITES and the Lacey Act can appear self-indulgent, if not evidence of retrograde environmental politics. To onlookers, the solution seems simple: if the documents necessary to import or export banned wood cannot be produced, then the desired trade or travel should not occur. Even within the music industry the predicament of artisans has been downplayed. In a 2010 webinar sponsored by NAMM's Public Affairs and Government Relations office, designed to help builders understand and comply with Lacey regulations, luthiers' concerns about the legal status of their preconvention Brazilian rosewood were largely dismissed. The following exchange between NAMM's legal advisor James Goldberg and English lute maker Paul Thomson was typical:

THOMSON: You mentioned the use of old woods, but not from the point of view of exporting to the United States, as I do occasionally. The point I'd like to make is that I have no way of verifying that these timbers were legally harvested, because they were bought so long ago. Also, if the Lacey Act is to prevent the importation of illegally harvested timbers, there must be a system of certification in place for suppliers of timber, or else how can anything be proven?

GOLDBERG: That's one of the difficulties of enforcement which makes me say the concern about criminal enforcement is really very slim for the folks that are on this call. The bigger problem for you, Paul, if you're shipping wood to this country, in terms of unfinished product, is to make sure that the import declaration that accompanies it, or that is filed by the importer at this end, contains the best guess as to what the genus and species of this product . . .

THOMSON [*interrupting*]: No, I'm shipping finished instruments.

GOLDBERG: Well, same thing. You have to make an educated guess as to the genus and species and the country of origin of the wood.

THOMSON: That's not the problem. I'm saying I bought the wood a long time ago.

GOLDBERG: To be honest with you, I wouldn't worry about it. First of all, the chances of enforcement are slim to none. In any inquiry question, the government's not going to be able to prove when this wood was harvested, and if you have any record that shows that you bought it ten, twelve, fifteen years ago, I think that solves your problem right there.[20]

Now it may be that the "old wood" Thomson had in mind was not endangered and that he had receipts for transactions conducted "long ago." But he would not have been the only luthier to approach this opportunity for legal advice with circumspection, aware that anything he said would become a matter of public record. What is striking about Goldberg's response is the trust he places in the rationality of the law and the government agents enforcing it.

That confidence is of a piece with the neoliberalization of border control in the United States more broadly. Captivating conservative legislators in Washington, DC, and statehouses across the South, this policy regime emphasizes "self-deportation" as the logical response to legally enforceable demands for citizenship papers on the part of immigrants without them.[21] The showpiece for this ideology is Arizona's 2010 immigration act, which empowers police to stop and arrest anyone unable to prove legal residency.[22] As immigration scholar Alicia Schmidt Camacho observes, this approach to the transnational mobility of labor consigns the over ten million unauthorized migrants already living in the United States to legal limbo, placing them under the constant threat of deportation while also barring pathways to naturalization. Under these circumstances, she argues, the human rights of the undocumented are routinely violated as federal and state governments practice the "lawful violence" of deportation.[23]

The new Lacey Act institutionalizes a similar logic. Criminalizing the failure to produce import documents at the border, it gives agen-

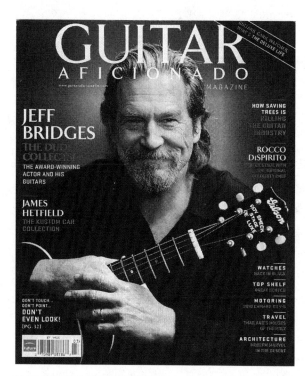

Guitar Aficionado's
eye-catching cover
line (Spring 2010)
suggests that the
guitar industry, and
the luxury market
it supports, is being
"killed" by overzealous
environmental
regulations.

cies of the US Departments of Homeland Security, Agriculture, and the Interior sweeping powers to detain and impound shipments suspected of containing illegal wildlife. As in the immigrant community, outcry among luthiers has focused on the fear that authorities will subject an entire population—in this case, a class of commercial products— to unwarranted scrutiny. Citing an instance where customs officials sawed into guitars to identify the wood they were made of, Bob Taylor expressed guitar makers' anxiety in a 2010 issue of *Guitar Aficionado*. Cued up by the sensational cover line "How Saving Trees is Killing the Guitar Industry," the article quotes him as saying, "Customs agents will certainly be looking out for particular species of wood as a result of the Lacey Act. . . . There's a high alert on several varieties of wood now, so they'll be doing what you could call '*species* profiling.'" [24]

That exotic tone woods and racial groups can be treated to the same techniques of governmental control speaks volumes about the biopolitics of national sovereignty in an era of "free trade" and global enterprise. Like the undocumented migrant, the guitar made of proscribed materials is now trapped in a twilight zone of indeterminate "rights," neither certifiably legal as a commodity nor at liberty to circulate freely in an international market. Common to both spheres of law enforcement is a political rationality that has increased the risks of crossing US borders without proper authorization, regardless of whether the target is a "nonnative" species of plant, animal, or person.

Neoliberalism, as philosopher Michel Foucault pointed out, is an approach to governance that seeks to manage, not eradicate, criminal activity. Toward this end, policymakers use the mechanism of law to affect the "economics of criminality" and the "market milieu" in which people are said to "choose" among possible behaviors, weighing the advantages of committing a prohibited act against the likelihood and consequences of being caught. In this political regime, governmental intervention induces individuals to "control" their own behavior by bringing the power of the state "to bear on the rules of the game rather than on the players."[25] Aimed at altering the economic calculations that importers and migrants make—by not seizing every Brazilian rosewood guitar or deporting every illegal immigrant—neoliberal border policies leave the field of play open to confusion, inconsistencies, and abuse.

ROUTES OF TRAVEL

Since its modest beginnings in a Toronto shop in 1968, Larrivée Guitars has become a transnational corporation with a retail presence throughout Europe and North America and production facilities in Vancouver, British Columbia, and Oxnard, California. Of his far-flung enterprise, Jean-Claude Larrivée says that manufacturing and marketing have been the "easiest part of globalization to deal with."[26] The greatest challenge, he observes, has been acquiring raw materials—a mission he has pursued energetically ever since developing the "recipe for the Larrivée sound" in the 1970s. To this day, he maintains an extensive travel schedule, personally sourcing all of the wood his company buys.[27] When he considers the legacy he will leave his sons, John Jr. and Matthew—who currently manage his Canadian and American operations, respectively—he points to the relationships he has established with venders around the world:

The biggest problem [facing guitar makers today] is acquiring materials globally. That's becoming tougher and tougher because there are embargoes on certain woods and you can no longer just transport wood like you used to. Now it's much more complex and harder to get. And that's the reason why I travel so much: in order for me to get these materials without agents, I have to go to the source. I spend more time in India than I should. I like the food, but that's about it, you know? And I select wood—I select every single piece of wood that the company uses; I'm the one that does that. But it's very rewarding, because [then] I know that every piece of wood I use in the guitar is the right piece of wood. I think it's really important that you know your sources, and little by little I'm teaching my sons to understand this stuff, and I've created a path for them so if something ever happens to me they have a path to follow. The big thing is learning all about the sources, where they are from, who you are talking to, how you deal with that person. And then they have children and grandchildren, and it's changing to the next generation— as it is for me and as it is for my suppliers. Most of my suppliers are lifelong friends, right? They know me; they know what I like.

Like network entrepreneurs who facilitated information exchange in the 1970s, Larrivée is one of several builders and timber merchants who opened the routes of exchange along which resources vital to guitar making now flow. No less integral to the renaissance of guitar making than the craft's professional organizations, the creation of an international market in wood intentionally selected for lutherie has given manufacturers and hand builders access to instrument-grade materials that would otherwise be difficult to find. Wood hunters like Larrivée have largely been focused on procuring lumber for their own use, but some realized that profit could be made by selling processed wood to other builders.[28] If information was power to those weaned on the *Whole Earth Catalog*, then "knowing your sources" was a critical corollary. Long before that phrase was codified into law as a safeguard against illegal logging, it encapsulated a savvy business strategy: maintaining a network of suppliers through face-to-face contact was the surest way to procure the raw materials desired.

Few luthiers understood personalized sourcing better than Bill

Lewis. In the mid-1960s, Lewis was employed by George Bowden at the Mediterranean Shop in Vancouver. He gave guitar lessons, repaired classical and flamenco guitars, and shipped western red cedar logs to Bowden's guitar-making factory in Palma de Mallorca, Spain.[29] In 1965 Lewis spent several months abroad managing the factory and deepening his knowledge of the industry. When Bowden turned his Canadian operation over to his son a year later, Lewis opened his own retail and repair shop in Vancouver. In addition to running the store, Lewis built guitars in a workshop down the street and, with his brother Jack, harvested and milled cedar for instrument building. Well known in the burgeoning lutherie community through friendships with Michael Gurian and Jean-Claude Larrivée, Lewis began supplying wood to artisanal builders and eventually launched a second venture, Lewis Luthiers' Supplies, which put out its much-anticipated mail-order catalog in 1974.

The softcover manual was a compendium of guitar-making know-how that introduced readers to a one-stop shop where virtually everything needed to make a guitar by hand could be acquired. Unlike earlier retailers, who carried an eclectic selection of lutherie supplies and assumed their customers knew what to do with them, Lewis provided detailed information about his products and instructions for their use. His "boxed material system" consisted of all the parts necessary to build several sizes and types of guitars and was explicitly aimed at "non-professional builders." In the introduction to his catalog, Lewis articulated a business philosophy that was as collaborative as it was commercial:

> Instrument building is a marvelous avocation combining craftsmanship in the working of wood and other materials with music, visual art and the science of design. It covers so much area that someone with wide interests can truly lose himself in as many of its different aspects as he chooses. With us, it's a way of life—and it's a joy to be able to share this satisfying activity with you. We have depended on you for new information about special items and sources, and particularly, for word-of-mouth advertising. We hope to continue in this way and appreciate any help you can give us. If you have ideas for new tools and/or supplies, please write us and let us know. On the

other hand, if you need information about musical instruments, etc., maybe we can help out or at least point you in the right direction.[30]

That Lewis felt he was "sharing" an "avocation" is as noteworthy as how he was doing it. Just as he was not making a living solely by building guitars, he did not expect that the majority of his customers would be either. Rather, the catalog was conceptualized as a gateway into a "way of life"—a field of cultural activity in which the presumptively male practitioner could "truly lose himself" while relying on the support of fellow travelers. To emphasize the challenge that guitar making presented, Lewis distinguished his boxed sets from the "prefab" dulcimer kits he also sold, the latter requiring no more than a knife, sandpaper, and glue to assemble.[31] "Although the [boxed sets] could be described as kits," he writes, "they are really just boxed selections of rough wood and parts. They do not have the pre-finished, ready-to-glue-together, modular set-up of kits." Those wishing to move beyond "kit building" would need to already have, or make an upfront investment in, the tools needed to achieve a professional degree of fit and finish.

Those tools could be found in Lewis's catalog, along with user-friendly tips about such things as sharpening blades and using hand scrapers. And the payoff was evident. Of the completed Dreadnought shown beside the boxed contents of a Mahogany Jumbo, Lewis notes, "A professional would build a guitar worth $300 to $500 [in 1974 dollars] from these materials." Stirring curiosity and latent ambition, the depiction of boxed sets presented a tantalizing prompt for readers to wonder how these pieces could be combined to produce an object worth more than the cost of its parts. Holding out the promise of saving money, doing something cool, and learning to build professionally, Lewis's marketing strategy made building a guitar accessible to a generation of would-be luthiers who might never have considered it otherwise.

Lewis's *Catalogue for Musical Instrument Builders* also offered a way of thinking about "sources" that remains salient today. From the cover image—a forest coastline viewed through the sound hole of a guitar—to the black-and-white drawings and photographs of tools, wood, and finished instruments, the only sign of human agency to be found in the catalog is in pictures of Lewis and his coworkers on the job. Know-

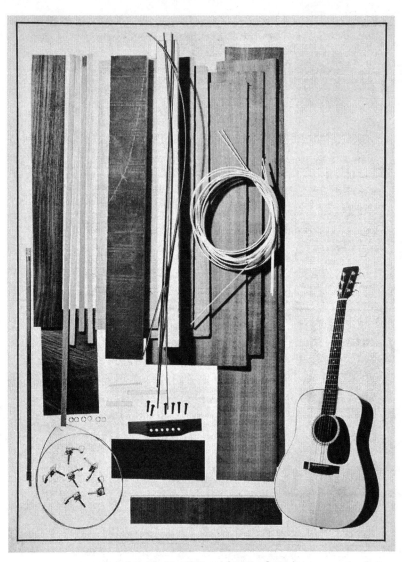

FIGURE 6.3. The "Boxed Material System for Mahogany
(or Indian Rosewood) Jumbo Guitar" as displayed in Bill Lewis Music's
Catalogue for Musical Instrument Builders, 1974.

FIGURE 6.4. *The full-page photograph on the inner back cover of the* Catalogue for Musical Instrument Builders *shows Bill Lewis (third from right) and his logging crew harvesting spruce; his brother Jack (far left) holds the chainsaw.*

ing one's sources, it suggests, involves feeling personally acquainted with the people who bridge the gap between mist-shrouded trees in the wilderness and the box of rough-hewn wood delivered by parcel post.

Whether Lewis is depicted sawing top sets from a billet of spruce or tap tuning a soundboard, his self-portraits invite the viewer to engage imaginatively in the production process. The closing image of the catalog—a shot of Lewis and his crew gripping woodcutter's equipment in front of a giant tree—establishes his presence at the origin of the supply chain. To the extent that making a guitar by hand implies that it is made from scratch, knowing one's sources allows builders to conceive of their work as the continuation of a labor process that is rooted in unmediated contact with the material world, even if they do not wield the chainsaw themselves.

On a hot day in 1972, Gulab Gidwani was dismayed to find himself on a slow train to a remote region of India. To hear him tell the story, he was the hapless victim of good intentions gone awry. Born in Pakistan and raised in Bombay (now Mumbai), he had gone to America to earn a degree in mechanical engineering and was hired by the US Navy to design ammunition machinery. The job was a good one, and he had never considered leaving it. But vacationing in his homeland that summer, he opened a telegram that changed the course of his life.

The Gibson Guitar Company was desperately seeking a source of ebony in India, and Gidwani's younger brother had promised a friend who worked at Gibson that he would enlist the assistance of a family member. As a favor to his brother, Gidwani agreed to help, assuming it would involve nothing more than going to the large lumber market in Bombay and asking around. Had he been trying to find teak, his quest would have been over, as suppliers of wood for the furniture industry were plentiful. As for Indian ebony, however, the merchants he spoke with told him they had never seen it. Believing that his duty was honorably fulfilled, he sent his brother a telegram saying that there was "no ebony in India."

Gibson refused to take no for an answer. Shortly thereafter, Gidwani received a package containing samples of ebony that the company had been buying from India before it "lost [its] source." Armed with this evidence, he went to the regional office of the Indian Forest Service and showed the agents what he was looking for:

> They told me, "Sure, there is ebony in India, but you have to go about two thousand miles from Bombay to the eastern part of India, and in the forest, you will find some ebony over there." I asked them, "Do you know any dealers who can supply the ebony?" And they said, "No, we don't know anybody like that. This is not a commercial wood in India; there's not much produced. There's not much market for it, so there is no business in this. But if you are insistent that you want to see ebony, you have to travel the distance." And by now I had got curious myself. I wanted to know, what is this thing that people in the USA want—but over here, *nobody* wants?[32]

The three-day journey by rail brought him to a transfer station where he boarded a "narrow gauge" train, a mode of transportation so slow, he says, that a person could keep up with it at a steady jog. Seven excruciating hours later, he arrived at what felt like the last outpost of civilization:

> This was all in the middle of summer. In the eastern part of India, summers are pretty hot. Like if you put a pot of water on the asphalt, you will see steam coming out of it. The temperature goes anywhere up to 120 degrees. And those trains were not air-conditioned; they got the steel roof, but in the first class, they have showers. The only problem with the shower is that the tank of water is on top of the roof and you are taking a shower only with hot water and nothing else. So sometimes it's very uncomfortable, but believe it or not, after you take the shower, you feel a little cooler. Only after five minutes, you know, you want to take another shower! So it was a weird situation. I never imagined I would be in a situation like that. In the many years I lived in Bombay, I had never gone to the eastern part of India. I thought Bombay was the world, that everything was in Bombay. You don't go anywhere. The ocean is there; the mountains are nearby; we have everything.

Or almost everything. Gidwani found what he was looking for in a remote area of Orissa near the Bay of Bengal.[33] There ebony was being harvested along with a variety of other hardwoods for use as durable and relatively inexpensive railroad ties. A single tie could be purchased for forty rupees (about $8.50 in 1972). Knowing that Gibson would be using the wood to make fingerboards, Gidwani gave the mill operator two hundred dollars and instructions to cut the logs into slabs of a more manageable size. With several gunnysacks of ebony in hand, he returned to Bombay, dispatched his cargo, and enjoyed what remained of his vacation. When he returned to the United States, however, he was summoned to Chicago, where Gibson's corporate owner was headquartered. The top brass wanted him to become their ebony supplier and were prepared to make it worth his while:

> They said, "Can you supply us the ebony?" I said, "No, I've got a regular job to do. I'm not in the lumber business; I don't have a sawmill. I don't have anything to do with any wood." Then they say, "Well, we can sweeten the pot for you. We can give you $25,000 an order for each month over the next four years." Realistically, I should

have told them to post a bond, if that's what they wanted to do. I was kind of naive; I was not a businessman. I just knew that a big company was giving me an order for four years and it comes to quite a bit of money. So I said, "Okay, I'll leave my job and I'll arrange to get you the ebony." That was my downfall.

Gidwani returned to India and, with a loan from his mother, set up a sawmill in Bombay. Through brokers in Orissa, he arranged to have ebony logs culled from local harvests and transported across the country to his mill, where he could process them and ship factory-ready wood to the United States. He operated under a contract in which Gibson agreed to pay for each shipment and clear it with customs as soon as it arrived. For the better part of two and a half years, everything went according to plan. And then it all fell apart.

Gidwani received notification from his bank that the import documents on a shipment sent six months earlier had not been picked up and no payment had been made. At this point four more containers were en route to the port in New Jersey, and no one at Gibson would tell him what was happening. Caught off guard and forced to borrow money to cover his outstanding debts, Gidwani flew to America to deal with the situation. What he discovered would come as no surprise to victims of corporate restructuring the 1990s, but in 1975 the claim of insolvency by a company with a household name still had the power to shock.

Reeling from the default of his only customer, Gidwani decided that he had invested too much in his company to let it fail. Instructing his employees in Bombay to continue sending him ebony, he began to advertise his business within the nascent lutherie community. Meanwhile, however, pallets of ebony were accumulating in his garage in violation of residential zoning laws. In the midst of this situation, he got a call from John Woodrow, a senior partner at the Stewart-MacDonald Company in Athens, Ohio.

Stew-Mac, as it is affectionately called in lutherie circles, was founded in 1968 by Creston Stewart and Bill MacDonald, designers of a five-string banjo that sold for less than one hundred dollars. To finance their operation, they sold banjo and mandolin parts to repair shops and hobbyists through their Banjoists' Supplies Catalog. Woodrow's purchase of ebony for banjo and mandolin fingerboards, together with orders that began flowing in from other luthiers, kept Gidwani's newly established Exotic Woods Company afloat. Today Gidwani's inventory in Sicklerville, New Jersey, is valued at over one million dollars and consists of fifty species of wood used in musical instruments as well as pool cues, gunstocks, and custom cabinetry.

Like guitar manufacturers before them, those in the lutherie movement have relied on cultural intermediaries to extract natural resources from near and distant lands. Intrepid entrepreneurs like Gulab Gidwani opened up routes of global connection that constitute what anthropologist Anna Tsing calls "resource frontiers." A key feature of these regions of "resourcefulness," she argues, is the "magical vision" they bring to the existing geographical terrain which "asks participants to see a landscape that doesn't exist, at least not yet."[34] While it is likely that some merchants in the early 1970s knew that eastern India—along with Sri Lanka, western Africa, and Indonesia—was an excellent source of ebony, local loggers and brokers had to be primed to "see" and separate individual trees from the other hardwoods that share its forest habitat. Sawmill operators also had to be willing to process this wood in ways that produced a commodity of value on the world market. When Gidwani talks about his relationship with indigenous sources in India, Madagascar, and Cameroon, it is the process of cultural translation that he accentuates:

When you have to deal with the whole world, trying to buy wood from various countries all over the place, dealing with various different cultures, everything does not work the same as it works over here. Here the people just make a phone call and say, "Send me this"; they get it—while in many other places one has to run around, sometimes in the forest to select trees; sometimes one has to go see some sawmills and see what junk they are producing and want to sell you, and you've got to try to make them work, train them, so that next time they can at least meet part of the demand, if not all of your demand. Because if you try to tell them exactly what you want and expect them to do, many cultures don't permit that. We are not used to that here, but one has to understand all different ways of operating. And the way they operate is, they want to sell you something and [wonder,] "Why don't you want to buy that?" If you want to buy that, then you are in trouble. And if you explain to them a lot, you know it will never happen, so it ends up being that you have to have compromises; you give them the specifications but don't expect that. So you have to learn to live with what the world is ready to give you, and that's the way it goes.

Making "compromises," as Gidwani puts it, is part and parcel of negotiating the divergent economic systems brought together by resource frontiers. As Tsing shows in her study of logging in Kalimantan, Indonesia, the "friction" that occurs at sites of global exchange can be found at virtually every step in the chain of production that carries a commodity from the rainforest to the end consumer. In this sense, a "resource" is not a natural aspect of the landscape but a cultural object that must be imagined and then "made" as it travels from point to point in a supply chain. Likewise, a resource frontier is "not a natural or indigenous category," Tsing observes. "It is a traveling theory, a foreign form requiring translation."[35]

To say that the entrepreneurial activities of North American guitar makers impose an external vision of economic development onto vulnerable environmental zones is to recognize, with Gidwani, that native interlocutors do not necessarily endorse or benefit from the dynamics of capital accumulation that have made the United States and Canada imperial powers on a global scale.[36] "Learning to live with what the world gives you" is, therefore, not just a pragmatic business philosophy but a tacit acknowledgment of the unruly forces that global capitalism has unleashed.

FRINGES OF LEGALITY

Tethered to a "hookah" air pump and the Volkswagen engine that powered his floating suction dredge, Chuck Erikson spent the early 1980s in the Sierras mining for gold. Like other amateur prospectors, he was drawn to the snow-fed creeks by the surge in gold prices between 1979 and 1983, when the value of a single ounce soared to $850 in January 1980.[37] In his case, the adventure was also prompted by the industrywide depression in sales of acoustic guitars, mandolins, and banjos. As he weighed gold nuggets at the end of a day and tallied the economic return on his labor, lutherie and his place in it seemed to belong to another time.[38]

Erika Banjos—the instrument-making, inlay, and shell supply operation he had started in 1965 in Van Nuys, California—had been dismantled. The shell-processing equipment was in storage, and the banjo jigs and fixtures had been discarded when no buyer could be found. The call of the wild beckoned, offering a proving ground for masculine self-sufficiency. "Living in the gold camp and moving rocks in the river was a pretty primordial experience," he says. "Some of those guys were pretty rough, but they respected you if you were a hard worker. Friends who would come looking for me would ask for the big guy with the Bible and the big gun."[39] Enjoying modest success as a miner, he cobbled together a living year round by recycling scrap metal and making gift-shop curios, among them the distinctive signs that prospectors used to mark their claims.

In its heyday, Erikson's business had supported several employees and a thriving trade in the raw materials used for inlay, including abalone, rare hardwoods, tortoiseshell, and elephant, hippo, and fossilized ivory. Known for his precision machining of shell as well as his original classification and grading system, Erikson had established a name for himself in the relatively small world of artisanal inlay, filling a narrow but vibrant market niche. He banked on this reputation when a broken wrist forced him to sell his share of the mining claim and reenter the shell trade in 1985.

When Gibson opened its acoustic guitar division in Montana in 1989, the company purchased Erikson's business with the intention of meeting its need for processed pearl and becoming a supplier for the industry. Assuming that Gibson would be a major consumer of shell, Erikson began collecting large quantities of red abalone from fisheries and sports divers in northern California. A year later, when Gibson decided to keep its inlay work in-house, Erikson was released from the noncompete clause of his contract and free to market shell on his own. He soon found a buyer looking to purchase abalone by the ton: a South Korean merchant who manufactures shell laminates and buttons for the furniture and fashion industries.

The globalization of Erikson's enterprise coincided with an environmental crisis. Abalone—a marine mollusk harvested for its meat as well as the "nacre" or iridescent mother-of-pearl that lines its inner shell—was rapidly disappearing from California's coastline. Overfishing, combined with "withering syndrome," a disease that appeared in 1985, had severely depleted populations from Baja California to Oregon, threatening two species with extinction. California closed all abalone fisheries along its southern and central shores in 1997, and white and black abalone came under the protection of the Endangered Species Act.[40]

Nonetheless, between 1988 and 1991, when Erikson was trolling beaches and state parks along the north coast, sport fishing of red abalone was legal. With an abalone stamp card and fishing license, divers outfitted in wetsuits, masks, and snorkels were permitted to take a limited number of animals for personal consumption, provided they observed regulations concerning open season, minimum size, and the prohibition against selling their catch. As the 1980s came to a close, however, environmental law enforcement, which was evolving in tandem with stricter prohibitions, could be inconsistent and self-contradictory. Uncertainty in the system created wiggle room for a wily entrepreneur.

Erikson acknowledges that the abalone shells he acquired during this period were obtained at the fringes of legality. With a flair for lawyerly detail, he insists that he was not "buying" either the animal or the shell:

> I would set my truck up over in Fort Bragg or Gualala or all around the coast where the divers were in the summer. I'd get a ton to a ton and a half of shells from the sport divers. Fish and Game came by and said, "You can't buy shells." I said, "Well, we've been buying them for years and years and years and nobody's ever enforced the law." They said, "Well, we realize that, but we don't want you guys down by the beach where the divers come in. If you're up here in the parking lot, that's okay." But at the time, there were a couple other guys buying shells that were really pushing it. They tried to make those guys stop, and they didn't; so they just shut us all down, and said, "Well, we're going to enforce the law now." Well, I kept going over there, but I changed the sign on the top of my truck that said "buying abalone shells." I changed it to "cash for abalone shells."

What I did was I didn't *buy* the shells; I *donated* for the shells. I had little pieces of paper printed up that said, "These shells were freely given to Chuck Erikson, were legally taken, and the animals were already consumed." We'd sign it and put down the diver's license [number], and they'd give me the shells. Then, if I went to the guy's house, they'd find several hundred bucks sitting in the washroom from me or something.[41]

As Erikson sees it, he was adopting the same rationale that governed the disposal of shell at state parks. At MacKerricher and Van Damme Beaches, sport-caught shell left in the campgrounds was brought to the visitor's center, where, for a donation of two dollars, anyone could acquire shell and take it out of the park. Erikson was himself a frequent benefactor to those parks, giving them one hundred dollars if they had fifty shells and asking the docents to write him a receipt showing that he had acquired the shell legally. When California's Department of Fish and Game challenged the source of his shell and attempted to put him out of business, he argued that he had received it in exchange for donations, just as he did at state parks. According to Erikson, the agents he spoke to were inclined to accept this argument until it was vetoed by higher-ups:

They said, "We had a meeting, and we've decided that you cannot donate for shells; and in fact, we've informed Van Damme and MacKerricher that if you ever come in and try to donate for those shells, if they let you have the shells, we'll shut them down." In their own state park! So I would still go in and get them, I'd just go in incognito and get them and get my receipt from them. So I was playing a game with the courts, you know. I was actually having to get shells on the weekends when Fish and Game was pretty much closed. I would meet people at their homes, get the shells, put them on a truck, cover it with a tarp, put a chainsaw and some firewood on top, so it looked like I was carrying a load of wood. I would not park anywhere in town. If I needed to go to the market, I would park a block away in a residential area so I would not be seen. I carried a scanner with me, and twice I evaded roadblocks they set up in the middle of the night to catch me going home with a load of shell. It was like running hooch in the old days! I'm playing this cat-and-mouse game with Fish and Game.

Like those who "ran hooch" during Prohibition, Erikson was violating a governmental policy that forbade the sale of a commodity for which there was active market demand. Although bathtub gin may have been a "homemade" product in a way that wild-bred abalone is not, the animals that divers pry from underwater rocks and bring to the surface are also "produced" by human agency and smuggled into the market under similar conditions of resourcefulness. From this perspective, California's ban on buying and selling abalone shell in the late 1980s adopted the logic behind much of today's environmental legislation as well as national policy regarding immigration and traffic in narcotics.

What these spheres of law enforcement have in common is the government's effort to break commodity chains at points where the targeted products or people enter the market as "commodities"—as labor or objects exchanged for money.[42] In effect, the government seeks to discourage capitalist enterprise that involves restricted persons and goods by placing a legal barrier between buyers and sellers at critical junctures in the supply chain. The neoliberal twist, which has increasingly characterized public policy since the late 1970s, lies in the effort to alter the economic environment in which people choose to break the law. By criminalizing the conversion of abalone into cash, Fish and Game turned abalone into an "unauthorized" commodity—a good that is risky to buy or sell—in order to make it less desirable to prospective consumers.

Erikson sees the matter differently. Just as the gold nuggets he extracted from mountain streams were rightfully his to sell, he reasons, abalone lawfully taken from coastal waters belonged to the individuals who invested time, money, and skill into acquiring them. If it was legal for divers to catch and eat abalone, it should have been legal for them to sell him the byproduct of that activity. To support this view, he points to the precedent that already existed in the salmon industry, where California allowed the entrails of sport-caught salmon to be sold commercially. Fishers who took their salmon to canneries were free to sell the guts "out the back door" to buyers who used them for high-quality fertilizer.

"As a Christian," Erikson explains, "I think we were put here—part of Adam's job was to tend the garden, not waste it! It's built into us that we need to take care of the ground we're sitting on—use it and don't abuse it—and I really believe that." Mustering the courage of his convictions, he petitioned California Fish and Game in January 1991 for the right to operate openly under state supervision:

I called Fish and Game and said, "I want to make a formal presentation to argue to buy these shells legally under your control. You can put a quick tie tag on them. Then you can audit me and my books; you can check the shells on my truck at any time; I'll work with your lawyer." When I went down there [to the regional office], I took all my books and showed how many tons of shell I'd bought illegally over the last four to five years, what I'd paid, how I graded, what I was getting for my market in nacre. I also took a banjo with some inlay. I said, "Here's what's being done with this shell that you want to take to the dump. The Indians have traditionally used it from prehistoric days, and now you say, conserve this resource. I am conserving it! You're saying, 'Take it to the dump.' That's not conserving the resource! These animals were taken legally, and you want to throw away the part of the animal that makes these inlays?" I gave them the records of all the illegal stuff I'd been buying, and they could've just arrested me on the spot. So it was kind of scary, but I thought, "I'm just going do this and we'll see what happens. I'll risk it."

In the end, Erikson says, he persuaded the commissioner of the supervisory board to authorize a trial program, but protest on the part of local field agents scuttled the plan. "So that's politics," he shrugs. Looking at him now, with his bushy white beard, black top hat, and tuxedo jacket worn over a T-shirt and blue jeans, I can easily imagine Erikson winning over a roomful of bureaucrats with his swashbuckling personality. We are at the 2008 Newport Guitar Show in Miami Beach, sitting at a table under a sign that reads, "The World Renowned Duke of Pearl."

Since 1992, when Erikson rolled out his new business venture, he has been known as the "Duke of Pearl," an appellation that derives from the 1960s, when customers would enter his Van Nuys shop singing a sendup of the doo-wop hit "Duke of Earl."[43] Dangling from the posts of his sign are small leather pouches made from the bodies of poisonous cane toads, and arrayed around us on the table is a colorful array of inlay materials, including an amazing variety of shells, beetles, butterfly wings, and peacock feathers, as well as the shell laminate called Abalam that Erikson developed and patented with his colleague Larry Sifel.[44] Also displayed at the table is a guitar made by Grit Laskin that features an amazing wedding portrait of Erikson and his wife—dressed as the Duke and Duchess of Pearl—inlaid on the ebony fingerboard.

After Erikson lost his battle with Fish and Game, his business transformation involved more than adopting a royal persona. Instead of being a source of raw shell on the world market, he became the US importer and distributor of inlay materials that his Korean partner sources around the world and processes to his specifications in factories in South Korea and Indonesia. To make this operation work, Erikson says, he had to "retrain Asian workers to Western standards" and the needs of inlay artists in the North America. "Cultural things had to be overcome," he observes, to get workers to understand his instructions and execute them properly. Once that hurdle was cleared, the quality of the product has been high, a fact he attributes to the reputable character of his partner—"the only honest Korean," he says—and working conditions in the factories that this man operates:

> They're not Nike kids. They've got dust protection. We're overpaying them. When they had labor riots in Indonesia several years ago, I checked with the factory. They said there was one guy here—out of the hundred and some employees—that tried to make problems. I said, "Well, what happened?" They said, "The other employees took care of him." I don't know what that means! But the fact is that we're paying about a third more than the prevailing wage rate in our factories in South Korea and Indonesia, treating them really well. I just made a trip over there in October [2007] with the factory manager from Pearl Works in Maryland, and he couldn't believe how clean the factory was, no dirt, and you couldn't hardly smell the shell. The workers were happy and chatty. They didn't tense up when we walked by with the managers; the managers were real amiable. So it's nice to know that nobody's getting abused over there.

That Erikson extends his concern about the "abuse" of the environment to the well-being of workers in Southeast Asia testifies to the global consciousness he shares with others in the lutherie community. Among artisans who appreciate the distinctive properties of the organic materials they use, anxieties about sustainability go hand in hand with the awareness that these resources are harvested in parts of the world where governmental control is weak and indigenous labor is subject to exploitation. Yet as more aspects of artisanal production are outsourced to international venders, labor relations that constitute links in lutherie's supply chains have become illegible and difficult to monitor. To say that a foreign workforce is "overpaid" if wages are slightly higher than the abysmal going rate presupposes a concept of pay equity that is lost in translation.

Thus although Erikson's visits to Seoul and Jakarta have assured him that the workers who process his orders are "happy and chatty," the phantom of "Nike kids" hangs over the scene—pointing, however obliquely, to the rapaciousness of global capitalism and the unsavory practices that lurk beneath surface of transnational enterprise. As *Life* magazine revealed in a 1996 cover story about child labor in Pakistan, companies such as the American-based Nike, founded on the strength of a superstar brand, are not above dealing with shadowy sources that operate at the edge of legality—in this case, contractors who force children sold into bondage to work for six cents an hour making soccer balls for the world market.[45]

Yet if distance from one's sources offers the alibi of ignorance, political pressure has increasingly been brought to bear not on foreign suppliers, who frequently operate under the auspices of corrupt officials, but on the demand side of tainted products, whether that be importing companies or end consumers. As the anti-Nike campaign demonstrated, grassroots activism aimed at tarnishing a company's brand—protests at the point of sale that bring awareness of sweatshop conditions home to the shopping mall—is a potent weapon in the service of moral outrage.[46]

Wildlife advocacy groups such as Greenpeace have used similar strategies to track down consumers of irresponsibly harvested forest products and hold them accountable for the devastation wrought by their vendors.[47] Indeed, it was precisely this approach to illegal logging

and trade in endangered species of timber that empowered the Environmental Investigation Agency, a nonprofit research organization, to drum up broad-based support for the 2008 amendment to the Lacey Act.[48] By requiring accountability in the commodity chain, the agency and other environmental groups have successfully enlisted US sovereignty to impose territorial barriers to the global circulation of unauthorized goods.

The post-2008 spotlight on import declarations has ushered in a newly aggressive era of law enforcement. In March 2010, a special agent of the US Fish and Wildlife Service appeared unannounced at Erikson's door to question him about the two businesses he runs: Duke of Pearl, which supplies inlay materials, and Chainsaw Chuck, an online antiques dealership, which specializes in items made from exotic woods and animal parts. The agent initially told him that she was conducting a "routine check" of import/export permit holders. But her detailed questions about butterfly wings and beetles Erikson had recently acquired from Costa Rica and Malaysia made him suspect that the agency possessed information it could have gained only through access to his private e-mail correspondence.

"Within a few minutes," he reports, "it became apparent that this was anything but a 'routine' investigation!"[49] Although he held valid licenses and could produce "some form of a paper trail" for almost all of the ivory and tortoiseshell he has bought since 1965, he was threatened with bankrupting fines and confiscations. Only the good "heart" of the agent, he believes, prevented the government from throwing the book at him. In the end, he was fined $4,050 and forced to relinquish a valuable turtle shell. His alleged offense was the sale of "antique" tortoiseshell—the material out of which guitar enthusiasts fashion "new" tortoiseshell picks. Under the CITES treaty, buying, selling, and commercially reworking appendix 1 species are illegal, even if the material was obtained prior to the date of the ban and purchased on the open market.

THE NEW IMPERIALISM

News of a late addition to the June 2011 symposium of the Association of Stringed Instrument Artisans ricocheted through the lutherie community with lightning speed. Chuck Erikson and DC-based guitar maker David Berkowitz had organized a three-hour panel on CITES, Lacey, and the Endangered Species Act that would feature officials from the Department of Agriculture, the Fish and Wildlife Service—and, in an eleventh-hour surprise, the Environmental Investigation Agency. The event was held at East Stroudsburg University in Pennsylvania, and organizers reserved a large lecture hall for the event. As word spread, however, so did a sense of caution and mistrust. Not everyone was thrilled with the idea of having federal agents milling around the exhibition area. In a memo to Craig Hoover, Fish and Wildlife's Chief of Operations, Erikson sought to clarify the matter:

> We are, after all, welcoming all of you as guests for the very reason that while eager to become voluntarily compliant, not many in the industry clearly understand the issues or how to actually accomplish that goal. It's entirely likely that a few vendors and builders may show up with very old uncertified "legacy" rosewoods, or ivory string nuts and bridge saddles made from estate materials. But using the occasion to bust people wouldn't exactly win friends and encourage cooperation! We're willing to partner with APHIS [Animal and Plant Health Inspection Service] and F&W, but if this will cause problems, in all fairness we need to advise attendees to leave those items at home.[50]

With reassurances from Hoover that agents would not use their participation in the symposium "as an opportunity to take any enforcement actions," planning for the panel went forward. In conjunction with the panel, Erikson wrote an article about environmental laws of concern to luthiers. In that piece, he revealed that his run-in with Fish and Wildlife was, in fact, the impetus behind the panel. When confronted with multiple citations for trade in illegal wildlife, he argued that his violations were committed "unknowingly" and that he had exercised "due diligence" by obtaining appropriate licenses, maintaining records of his transactions, and, to the best of his ability, staying abreast of new regulations.

To support his claim, Erikson polled thirty similar businesses in the lutherie community to confirm that his understanding of import/export restrictions was equal to, if not better than, that of his peers. When asked to divulge the names of those he contacted, however, he refused.[51] To resolve the impasse and forestall the possibility of cascading prosecutions, the parties agreed to public outreach: Erikson would disseminate regulatory information through his article, and agency officials would attend the symposium to inform luthiers how to become "voluntarily compliant" with laws governing endangered species. Despite these conciliatory gestures, the incident gave legs to the collective suspicion that guitar makers were embroiled in nothing less than a federally orchestrated witch hunt.

———

The auditorium is abuzz with nervous energy. I find a seat between George Gruhn and Natalie Swango of Luthiers Mercantile International. As Gruhn tells me about various people in lutherie who have had run-ins with the agencies represented on the panel, I watch the four speakers assemble on stage. Two are middle-aged men in casual attire who could easily pass for luthiers, but the others look a tad out of place at this convocation of aging hippies. One is a tall man wearing a crisp uniform and badge; the other is a young woman from the environmental organization, which, someone near me declares, is "the cause of this fucking amendment!"

The chatter dies down when Erikson steps to the podium, looking subdued and penitent without his top hat and tails. He alludes briefly to his encounter with law enforcement, noting that copies of his article are available at the door. He emphasizes that his problems stemmed from a lack of knowledge. "There was just a lot of confusion," he confesses. "I didn't know I was confused, but I was." Speaking for the audience at large, he says: "Today, hopefully, we're going to walk out of here knowing what the laws are—and what we need to do to stay out of trouble."[52]

Each agency representative gives a presentation that lasts about half an hour. George Balady, from the Department of Agriculture's Animal and Plant Health Inspection Service (APHIS), is the exception. He goes on much longer, occasionally leavening the stupefying legalese of Lacey prohibitions with folksy banter. Conceiving of their mission as amplifying the law through a laborious recitation of its aims, each speaker casts himself or herself as an intermediary between legislation delivered from on high and the subjects it is intended to discipline.

"Don't shoot the messenger," Balady exclaims, when boos and

hisses follow his joke that Lacey declaration forms have become luthiers' "favorite document." So oppressive is the atmosphere of patronizing simplification — "we've tried to break this down into plain English so it's not too horrible for people" — that I start to feel restless and bored.[53] Not until a short break is called, and I climb over the back of my seat to talk with guitar makers sitting two rows behind me, do I realize what a luxury my boredom is. Far from bleary-eyed, this group is alternately fearful, angry, and despairing.

"I might as well slit my wrists right now," says one, with no trace of melodrama in his voice.

"I have wood that I've had around *forever*," another points out with rising indignation. "I bought mahogany from people who had it for sixty years; the people before them had it for forty years — it's almost a hundred years old! There's no chain of custody for this; people don't *have* receipts for this wood!"

Nodding in grim agreement, a third offers, "I have a lifetime supply. I bought a lot of wood that was supposedly properly documented and procured, but I don't have anything in writing. In fact, I just bought a set [of wood] off of eBay, and the seller said it was certified, but I didn't get anything to prove it."

The overriding affect is one of helplessness. As I listen to a harrowing story of how a valuable guitar sent from Canada to a customer in the United States was damaged when Fish and Wildlife inspectors detained it to examine the shell used in its inlay, it becomes clear that simply "knowing what the laws are" will not render their enforcement any less opaque or arbitrary. The regulatory regime that luthiers face is not a unified system administered by the US government but an intimidating patchwork of domestic, international, foreign, and tribal laws. This policy maze is further complicated by the political struggles that underlie it.

By authorizing the United States to crack down on unauthorized trade internationally, the Lacey Act enforces a vision of wildlife conservation — supported by the US forest products industry — on foreign governments perceived to be "too weak" to protect their own resources. As the history of African ivory has shown, the imposition of elephant management plans in the name of "conserving nature" is often "a not so subtle form of intellectual colonialism."[54] Not only are local decisions about resource use overruled, but the economic rationality of poaching, illegal harvesting, and smuggling is chalked up to a "failure" of self-government. Policing the global environment has thus become a technology of the "new imperialism" that extends the reach of the American government far beyond its territorial limits.[55]

That this new regulatory apparatus rests on documentation becomes increasingly apparent as the morning wears on. As one panelist after another hammers home the importance of keeping written records of every transaction that involves wildlife products, I begin to see how artisanal ways of operating confound the economic rationality that Lacey is designed to enforce. A key concept in determining whether a violation of law has occurred is "due care." Showing us a slide on the topic, George Balady explains it this way:

> What is due care? According to the Ninth Circuit pattern of jury instructions, due care means "the degree of care which a reasonably prudent person would exercise under the same or similar circumstances." Okay? I said in order to be convicted you have to knowingly do x, y, and z. That doesn't mean you can suddenly go "Okay, well, I'm never going to ask anybody a question ever again. I'm just going to take the stuff and [say], 'I didn't know, nobody told me!'" You have to have taken steps to *prove* that you tried to find out if the material was illegally made. Now, if you run into a bunch of master liars, you [can] say, "Oh, I called so and so on this date, they said x, y, and z; here's the paperwork, this is what they sent to me," et cetera, et cetera. So keeping these kinds of records is going to keep you at least in a minimum of trouble, if not completely out of trouble. It will minimize your exposure.

The distinction between "knowingly" and "unknowingly" committing a crime turns on the ability of the accused to demonstrate their effort to comply with the law. At the core of this distinction lies the court's assumption about what steps a "reasonably prudent person" would take to ensure that the wildlife products he or she buys were legally procured. A "reasonable person," in this discourse, is one who seeks to "minimize the risk of exposure" to criminal sanctions by attempting to clarify the commodity chain at the point of purchase.

"You can ask, 'Where was the tree cut down?'" Balady suggests.

"'What species is the tree? How much material are you sending me? How old is the material?' Ask any question you want of your suppliers—but ask." Standards of due care vary, he adds, depending on the knowledge that someone in a given occupation can be presumed to have. "You folks are experts at producing instruments, so you have to exercise more extensive due care than someone you just grabbed in from off the street." Paradoxically, due care can be substantiated only by a paper trail, yet even with written records, the consumer is never "completely out of trouble."

The shaky legal status of documentation is related to how underlying violations of the Lacey Act are conceptualized. Because illegal logging is virtually indistinguishable from legal commerce—in the forest, at the sawmill, on the ship, or at the port—there is the ever-present danger that traffic in unauthorized wood and wood products may flourish undetected. The final speaker of the morning captures this nightmarish scenario in a single image (see fig. 6.5).

Anne Middleton represents the Environmental Investigation Agency and the Forest Legality Alliance, an international program that aims to reduce demand for illegal forest products.[56] A central goal of the alliance, she explains, is to work with its members—Taylor Guitars is one—to develop compliance strategies that will alleviate the burden of regulatory requirements. With this olive branch she defuses a degree of pent-up hostility, and scattered applause erupts when Chuck Erikson introduces her as someone who plays bass in a bluegrass band. But when she explains the legal reasoning behind the Lacey Act, a stunned silence falls over the room:

> What this graph basically depicts is that regardless of where the illegality occurs in the supply chain in Lacey . . . it taints the supply chain with that illegality and anywhere along there an actor can be held liable. So if you're over here on the right side of the supply chain, on the retail end or on the building end, if an illegality occurred way back in the forest or anywhere between the forest and your product, you can be held liable for that illegality.[57]

In this vision of global capitalism, trade in unauthorized commodities is a direct threat to legal commerce. Much as a toxin released into a river has consequences for those downstream, illegal logging is held

THE LACEY ACT: LEGALITY FROM STUMP TO SHELF

The Flow of Tainted Goods: An underlying violation to the Lacey Act can occur at any step along the supply chain. Colored circles represent examples of underlying violations. The illegal act "taints" the supply chain.

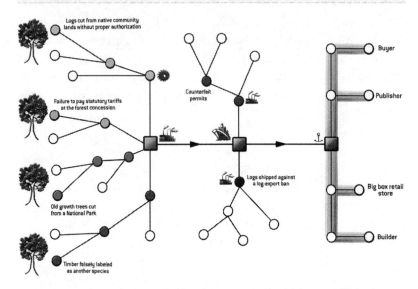

FIGURE 6.5. *The Lacey Act holds end consumers (at the right) accountable for the underlying violations (at left and center) that "taint" the supply chain for forest products. Courtesy of the Environmental Investigation Agency.*

to "taint" every link in the supply chain. An anthropologist would be remiss not to call attention to the fear of "pollution" and desire for "purification" that this flow chart represents.[58] But even ritual mechanisms such as the Forest Stewardship Council (FSC), which tries to certify the legality of every transaction from stump to store, are not fail-safe. As Middleton tells us, certification is simply a way of demonstrating due care:

> If I'm certified, does that mean I'm Lacey compliant? No, the US government does not recognize certifications like FSC to be a silver bullet. That being said, the steps that one goes through in order to become certified are essentially exercising due care. So just because you have a [FSC] label on your product, the US government isn't going say, "Oh, great, you're Lacey compliant." If they go through

their work of due process and find that in fact it's not legal, you're still in trouble. However, if you go through these steps, that, in essence, is exercising due care.

The realization finally dawns that full compliance with documentation requirements will never expunge the presumption of illegality from the exotic materials that guitar makers use. Although the arrows on the agency's chart suggests that contamination originates in distant lands and at points in time prior to the final sale, it is the ongoing investment capital, corporate enterprise, and domestic interests moving in the *other* direction that create the resource frontiers within which illegal activities have market value. But this flow of activity is not represented or considered to be part of the problem.

The new imperialism, every bit as much as the old, is haunted by the resourcefulness it unleashes in the territories and spheres of exchange it penetrates but cannot control. Where older empires conceptualized the threat of pollution from their colonies primarily in terms of racial "impurity" and miscegenation, today's imperial powers are concerned with impediments to the accumulation of capital, whether they consist of restricted access to resources or the inefficient operation of global markets. Unauthorized traffic in wildlife is the fly in the ointment that casts the legality of all such trade into doubt, giving rise to charges of rainforest rape, species extinction, global warming, and the abrogation of indigenous rights. In an effort to cleanse international supply chains of illegality, however, the US government, acting in concert with other nations, is prepared to throw artisanal guitar makers under the bus. By a curious twist of fate, it is luthiers, as well as exotic wildlife, who are endangered.

Once the floor is open for questions, the number of people clamoring to speak makes it apparent that the panel will need to reconvene after lunch in order to accommodate everyone. Even so, over half an hour elapses before someone finally asks the question that I sense is on everyone's mind. Roger Sadowski, a member of the community since the 1970s, poses the question:

SADOWSKI: I think I speak for a lot of builders here, so let's
just get this out of the way. Speaking for myself, my personal

stash of wood, I bought Brazilian rosewood wherever I could.
I bought from guys in parking lots out of the trunk of their car
or whatever. The bottom line is I can just forget about using that
stuff, is that correct?

HOOVER: No, that's not correct. You can use it domestically
without any requirement whatsoever. There's no Lacey
requirement, no CITES requirement, et cetera. Domestic activity
is still available to you.

SADOWSKI: But forget about selling it to anyone else?

HOOVER: The burden is on you to show documentation to prove
that the specimens you have were obtained prior to 1992.

SADOWSKI: But if I can't do that, forget about it.

AUDIENCE MEMBER [interrupting]: So [it's legal] only if he sells
in the United States of America? We're talking about a very fine
instrument! What if the musician who buys it goes to England?

HOOVER: He can't take it out [of the country] without a
preconvention [CITES] certificate.

AUDIENCE MEMBER: There is no preconvention certificate! The
wood he bought forty years ago. He can only manufacture the
instrument and sell it in the States? But what if the person he
sells it to leaves the country with that instrument to perform?
What you're saying is, he's not bringing it back in?

HOOVER: What I'm saying is that the material is covered by the
convention. The requirement is that it has to be accompanied
by a preconvention certificate. In order to issue a preconvention
certificate, we're going to have to make a finding that the
specimens were lawfully acquired. That's it. That's the answer to
that question.[59]

The finality of Hoover's reply and the trace of impatience in his voice
have an electrifying effect. Bodies lean forward, eyes flash, and people
mutter to one another under their breath. George Gruhn seizes this
moment to underscore the absurdity of requiring musicians to obtain
a certificate — assuming they can get one — every time they travel. "The
problem is," he stands up to say, "there are literally *millions* of these instruments; we're not talking about a few."[60] Unlike consumer goods
that break or become obsolete overnight, he explains, guitars can "last

literally hundreds of years." Before 1970, virtually every major guitar maker used Brazilian rosewood. Martin alone made over a quarter of million guitars with Brazilian rosewood prior to 1992. "There's millions of these things and musicians are playing them." Pausing to let the full weight of this reality sink in, Gruhn adds, "And they are oblivious to the fact that, when they travel, they are international felons!"

Hoover looks startled and raises his hands to hold off an onslaught. "Let's take a step back," he proposes. Noting that Brazilian rosewood and ivory were banned twenty years ago, he observes, "None of these problems happened yesterday." The government could have done more to inform the music industry about the law, he concedes, and luthiers may have engaged in "activity in contravention of these requirements." But that was then, and this is now. The point, he reiterates, is "to figure out a way to get those activities into compliance."

Tempers are flaring and emotion is running high when we break for lunch in the campus cafeteria. I sit with Linda Manzer, a few tables away from Craig Hoover and the other Fish and Wildlife agent. As we poke at uninspiring vegetables from the salad bar, she tells me that one of her Metheny-Manzer models was detained by Hoover's agency a few months ago. The Indian rosewood guitar, adorned with eye-catching fretboard inlay, was en route from Toronto to a special exhibit on hand-crafted guitars at the NAMM show in Anaheim, California. Evidently NAMM, as the importer, had neglected to submit the required declaration form.[61]

Manzer spent several anxiety-filled days on the phone with personnel at Federal Express, who later sent her a box of chocolates in apology. In the scheme of things, a shipping delay might seem like a minor snafu, were it not for worry of damage to a $32,000 guitar. But Manzer remains shaken by the episode and what it portends for her and other artisan guitar makers:

> I have a thirty-five-year supply of wood. I have Brazilian rosewood and now I can't use it. I know I obtained it legally. I know that I got a lot of it from a guy that bought it—who died, and his wife, ten years after he died, sold me the wood, and I've had it for at least fifteen years. So I know it's in compliance, but I can't certify it. I paid a lot of money for it, and this was my nest egg. And it's really beautiful

wood. It just seems stupid not to be able to use it in some way. I feel like beautiful wood—I save some of it for years, waiting and thinking about what I'm going to do with it to make the best use of it, to make something beautiful. And that's what I feel like is being taken away. You know, Roger [Sadowsky] made that joke, we might as well blow our brains out? I understand exactly what he meant. I don't want to blow my brains out, but I don't want to *play* anymore. If [complying with regulations] outweighs the magic, then it's like—maybe that [second] golden era, that fun community thing, is now over.[62]

Manzer notices that two chairs have opened up at the table where Hoover sits. Since none of the morning's panelists discussed compliance issues north of the border, she takes this opportunity to ask about Canadian law and allows me to tag along. Hoover listens impassively to her account of the NAMM shipment, commenting only that as the "broker," Federal Express bore some responsibility. He glances at his watch when she brings up the problem of her undocumented wood. As we walk back to the auditorium together, Hoover writes the name of his counterpart at the Canadian Wildlife Service on one of his business cards and gives it to Manzer.

The panel discussion picks up where it left off. But this time it is Anne Middleton who wonders what has changed since trade in ivory and Brazilian rosewood was banned. "What happened in the last couple of years? What is the straw that is breaking the camel's back? Why is, all of a sudden *now*, everything so complicated?"[63] The obvious answer—that until April 2010, when Lacey's declaration requirements went into effect for stringed instruments, commerce involving acoustic guitars was regulated in theory but not in practice—is clearly the elephant in the room. No one appears willing to acknowledge this.

"I'm not going to go back to 1992," Hoover says. "My first question would be, how many people in this room have applied for, and been rejected for, a preconvention certificate for Brazilian rosewood?"

A collective intake of breath follows. After a few beats, a woman in the front row sighs loudly. "Nobody here is that stupid to apply for something that they know they can't document," she observes. "So that's not a good question."

Hoover fires right back, "It is a good question—because until you understand what the bar is that you have to meet, what are we talking about?" The US Fish and Wildlife Department's Branch of Permits, which issues the certificate, he suggests, might be willing to take a sworn affidavit as evidence of compliance. Although he admits that he does not know what the criteria for qualification might be, he reminds us that no one will ever get a permit if they don't apply for one. "Right now, we seem to be talking about a theoretical problem because you're not even *willing* to go in there . . ."

I am not the only one who hears the implicit taunt in Hoover's statement. Several people begin talking loudly at the same time, but one voice prevails. It is Michael Gurian, now a manufacturer who supplies the lutherie community with custom marquetry, shell inlay, rosettes, and purfling:

GURIAN: You know *why* they're not willing to go for a permit? There's a fear factor. [*Hoover tries to interrupt.*] Let me finish. It goes through this industry like a hot knife through butter when they hear that all of the Brazilian rosewood for Spanish builders was confiscated and absorbed, taken away from builders. Now I know a lot of these [people], I'm very friendly with a lot of these builders. One of these companies, they had a warehouse filled with Brazilian rosewood that was from the '30s, the '20s. They took it all away.[64] How do you have documentation . . . ?

HOOVER: Who's they?

GURIAN: The Spanish government or whoever—the powers that be.

HOOVER: Okay, well, we're not in Spain. So let me answer the question for the way we would do it here. You come into the Branch of Permits because you want to export some Brazilian rosewood. You provide documentation—let's say it doesn't meet the bar. You provide a sworn affidavit, and the Fish and Wildlife Service decides that the sworn affidavit is not going to be sufficient to issue you a preconvention certificate to allow you to export that item. The sole ramification of that process is that you will not get a permit. It doesn't mean that the office of law enforcement will be notified to go in and kick down your door. The burden remains on the Fish and Wildlife Service to show that the wood was unlawfully obtained or unlawfully imported. Your inability to show that you obtained it in 1960 is not that evidence. So what I'm saying is, until you attempt to get preconvention certificates for that material and are denied, we're talking about a theoretical problem. I understand the fear factor. I answered this question about five times during lunch. What I'm telling you is that if you are denied a permit, it is not proof of illegal activity on your part.[65]

When pressed on whether it was conceivable that a certificate would be issued solely on the basis of a sworn affidavit, Hoover concedes that he does not know. From his vantage point, voluntarily subjecting one-self to the government's disciplinary gaze is a straightforward matter of risk assessment: the chance of having an application rejected does not outweigh the possibility that it might be approved. For artisans, how-ever, the risks are much harder to calculate. The United States may not be Spain, but both governments operate in a global context where national sovereignty is exercised on behalf of trade policies that benefit a narrow spectrum of economic agents who enact the appropriate rationality. Artisans, and corporations like Gibson, are not among them.

Given the prevailing policy regime, some in the lutherie community have argued that guitar makers should be exempted from Lacey's declaration requirements on the grounds that they are custodians of a cultural tradition. Earlier in the day, before the symposium's panel broke for lunch, Henry Lowenstein, a lawyer and founder of the South Florida Guitar Show, forcefully articulated this position:

When you talk about guitars not being able to go across borders — guitars are a basic part of our culture. This [law] is stopping not a business, not an industry; we're worried about cultural exchange. We're worried about the cultural exchange of music, the cultural exchange of our national heritage. Those are all, by the way, things that are basic to the documents that form the CITES treaty. If you look at the United Nations' documents from which all these [regulations] spring, there are cultural exemptions — that people are allowed to preserve their cultures based on national cultural exchanges.... This is a serious cultural issue. I believe there is a way to [exempt] all of these things so we don't seize guitars for a dot [of shell inlay], so we don't kill our cultural heritage for a dot that's on the guitar.[66]

Thinking of artisanal guitar making as "national heritage" appeals to the idea that Canada and the United States have a craft tradition, one that extends and possibly even surpasses the stature of lutherie at the end of the European Renaissance.[67] Yet to argue that the craft's practitioners and artifacts must be exempted from market regulations in order to preserve that "culture" is to equate the predicament of North American luthiers with that of Native Americans, First Nations, and other indigenous peoples whose claim to sovereignty predates the constitution of the settler nation that has imposed its governance on them. As bearers of "cultural heritage," in this reasoning, artisanal guitar makers should be exempt from the political rationality that is "killing" them because they occupy a different social "tense," or temporality, which gives them a prior claim to national belonging.[68] Not only are they exemplars of a "past" way of life, Lowenstein suggests, but maintaining the national character of the United States and Canada depends on their survival in the present.

The politics of social tense rarely bode well for alternative social projects that seek recognition for their unique cultural practices. More often than not, as anthropologist Elizabeth Povinelli argues, the struggles of indigenous people result in a "temporal suspension of judgment" in which recognition is neither granted or denied, "suspend[ing] or bracket[ing] social differences that cannot as yet enter into the communicative rationality and moral sense of the late liberal public sphere."[69] The US government has relegated luthiers to precisely such a zone of uncertainty. By goading individual builders to adjudicate the legality of their preconvention rosewood on a case-by-case basis—with no formal guidelines or official accountability—the Fish and Wildlife Service has effectively deferred a decision to the indefinite future, leaving guitar makers no choice but to operate at the fringes of legality.

Were we simply witnessing an instance of social abandonment and economic dispossession that affected the livelihood of a relatively small number of people, the injustice done, it seems to me, would still be too high to countenance. But the shock waves of this political impasse extend far beyond the workshops of North America's most revered builders. What the Lacey Act and other legislation of its ilk promote is the consolidation of power in a governmental apparatus that legitimates differential modes of social belonging in the name of national security. Policing international trade and travel through the demand for documentation at the borders, the federal government has mobilized post-9/11 surveillance technologies to protect a range of economic interests by consigning whole classes of people and things to the status of unauthorized citizens and commodities.

In this context, holding out hope for politically popular "exceptions" misses the point.[70] Guitar makers labor under a cloud of suspicion because they insist on working with wood and other materials that were declared endangered within their lifetime. No matter whether they acquired their supplies legally in the past or on the "gray market" today, their persistence in the present is taken to be not just anachronistic and "irrational" but disruptive of the historical fiction that policy makers cultivate. In this fantasy, imperialism was the sin of European aristocracy, not North American settlers who fought to free *themselves* from the colonial yoke. But the millions of ornately appointed instruments—in collections, circulation, and yet to be built—tell a different story. They are ghosts of empire that the neoliberal state disavows; and for that very reason, they deserve to be heard.

Conclusion
Pinocchio's Body

> "And the old Pinocchio of wood — where could he have gone to hide?"
>
> "There he is over there," replied Geppetto; and he pointed to a large
>   puppet propped against a chair, its head turned to one side, its arms
>   dangling, and its legs crossed and folded in the middle so that it was
>   a wonder that it stood at all.
>
> Pinocchio turned and looked at it; and after he had looked at it for
>   awhile, he said to himself with a great deal of satisfaction:
>
> "How funny I was then, when I was a puppet! And how glad I am now
>   that I've become a proper boy!"
>
> — Carlo Collodi, The Adventures of Pinocchio (1883)

In August 2011, for the second time in two years, federal agents raided the Gibson guitar factory in Nashville. Once again, agents were responding to inaccuracies on import declaration forms, and once again, computer records, guitars, and pallets of imported wood parts were seized. In 2009 the manufacturer had been charged with buying illegally harvested wood from Madagascar, and that case was still under investigation. In 2011, it appeared, the company had imported unfinished wood products from India — the ebony and rosewood "blanks" from which fretboards are made — in violation of Indian export restrictions. Expressing outrage at the "arrogance of federal power," Gibson CEO Henry Juszkiewicz held a widely televised press conference in which he all but threatened to move his factories — and the American jobs they created — to a low-wage zone overseas.[1]

The ensuing hue and cry — taken up by Tea Party sympathizers, Republican presidential hopeful Newt Gingrich, and apoplectic Fox News commentators — focused a national spotlight on guitar making and the Lacey Act. At issue for Gibson and its supporters were not the law's declaration requirements per se but what Gingrich called the Obama administration's "vendetta" against Gibson, a display of "big government attack[ing] a small business" for the whole world to see.[2] In this spirit, the incident became fodder for 2012 presidential and congressional campaigns. Tennessee representatives Jim Cooper (Democrat) and Marsha Blackburn (Republican) introduced legislation that took

aim at what they called Lacey's "unintended consequences." Among
other things, their proposed "RELIEF Act"—the Retailers and Entertainers Lacey Implementation and Enforcement Fairness Act—would
eliminate penalties for violations that were "unknowingly" committed
and exempt wood acquired before 2008.[3]

Country music stars spoke out in favor of the act, while environmentalists unilaterally condemned it.[4] Although the bill advanced out of
the House Natural Resources Committee on the strength of Republican
support, it died a quick and quiet death when Republican House leadership—facing fierce opposition from the US timber industry—canceled
the vote scheduled for July 2012.[5] Equally anticlimactic was the government's resolution of its case against Gibson one month later. Declaring
progress in "protecting the world's natural resources," the Justice Department decided not to charge the manufacturer with any crime, settling instead for a fine of $300,000 and a "community service payment"
of $50,000 to the National Fish and Wildlife Foundation.[6]

As the episode lurched toward its denouement, no one came closer
than Henry Juszkiewicz to naming the problem that divided public
sentiment on this issue. On Gibson's website and in an editorial for
the *Wall Street Journal*, he put his finger on the contradiction inherent in
the Lacey Act's rationale. Noting the federal government's "increasing
tendency" to penalize and prosecute infractions of "rules and regulations," Juszkiewicz implored policy makers to "stop criminalizing capitalism" and incarcerating "entrepreneurs" for violating "obscure foreign laws."[7]

Few scholars of globalization and the new imperialism have stated
the contradictory aspects of free-market ideology as succinctly. As a
political rationality that promotes markets in anything that can be
commodified, neoliberalism advocates a freewheeling capitalism that
operates with minimal regulation. Yet as a system of governance that
represents a territorial nation-state, it must also protect and advance
the economic interests of its own citizens, especially those at the helm
of domestic and transnational industries.[8] Through disciplinary legislation, the federal government is called upon to produce citizens who
act as risk-calculating entrepreneurs in every sphere of their lives; yet
at the same time, it is entreated to "free" its citizens, and the markets

in which they operate, from burdensome "rules and regulations." In the end, Gibson's prosecution illustrates the paradoxical effects of neo-liberalization.

Through the Lacey Act, the United States has fortified the competitiveness of the American timber industry and its labor unions by closing loopholes in the black market for illegally logged wood.[9] Environmentalists and industry leaders have found common cause in the recognition that banning the sale of endangered species and monitoring cargo at international ports actually does very little to prevent unauthorized commerce. To reduce illegal flows of capital and commodities, they argue, the federal government must also regulate the behavior of "law-abiding" citizens who consume forest products. Lacey accomplishes this by criminalizing the importer's failure to exercise "due care" in determining the legality of wood harvested in other countries.

Artisanal luthiers have largely been excluded from the public debate over environmental regulation.[10] Their relatively small numbers, arcane practices, and marginal economic status make them vulnerable to the whims of customs agents and all but invisible to policy makers. Not only is their predicament underplayed by government officials and representatives of their own trade organizations, it is overlooked by environmentalists who prefer to work with major manufacturers attempting to certify their procurement of legally logged wood.[11] Nonetheless, hand builders continue to make world-class guitars from their dwindling supplies of preconvention rosewood. These instruments, along with the millions of Brazilian rosewood guitars already in circulation and in private collections, deserve our attention. How we choose to value the precious resources they embody is a measure of our ability to imagine a democratic counterrationality to the prevailing policy regime.[12]

THE VOICE OF TREES

In the aftermath of the second Gibson raid, I had the opportunity to talk with Alfredo Velázquez, a Florida-based guitar maker and son of the renowned Puerto Rican luthier Manuel Velázquez. His reaction to the media frenzy helped me understand why Lacey's punitive force falls primarily on independent artisans, not major manufacturers:

VELÁZQUEZ: Everybody, all my guitar maker friends, they were calling me [to say], "Did you hear what happened at Gibson? Oh my god, are we going to be affected by this?" It's like, well, we're *already* being affected! A big corporation can survive, but it's people like us, the makers who treat guitars more as an art, who take guitar making to the next level, we're the ones who are affected.

DUDLEY: What makes you different from a large factory?

VELÁZQUEZ: I think it's how we integrate ourselves with each piece of wood. How we calibrate and fashion the wood the way we want it, not to have a general look or have a general effect. Each instrument, we personalize it the way we want to. And I tell everybody this: the reason why my father is so admired is because he leaves a piece of his soul in every guitar that he made.

DUDLEY: What does that mean, to leave your *soul* in an instrument?

VELÁZQUEZ: He grabs a piece of wood and he's like—how do you say it?—he *talks* to it, very romantically. It's just a very romantic point of view. He talks to it, and he listens to what the piece of wood wants to be. Because he will look at one piece of wood—and not only looking at how it looks, but how the grain is going to go—he literally will just take an hour or two hours, and sometimes I've seen him take almost a whole week just looking at the same piece of wood, [asking,] "How am I going to glue this? How am I going to take care of it?" And then when he starts working on it, he has general measurements, but after he gets it up to a certain point, that's when he starts going by touch, calibrating it the way he wants to.[13]

Speaking in English to me and in Spanish to his father, who still works in their shop at the age of ninety-five, Velázquez makes it clear that his father's "romantic" orientation to lutherie is also his own. That orientation, articulated in similar terms by most hand builders, involves a lively, interactive encounter with the wood out of which guitars are made. Whether artisans consider their work to be an "art" or a "science"—and many insist that it is both—they invariably point to a relationship with wood in which a conceptual division between the self as an active "subject" and wood as a passive "object" is routinely dissolved. To "talk" to a piece of wood and "listen" to what it "wants to be" is to engage in a dialogic process that renders the animicy of wood sensible through practices that expand the luthier's repertoire and ability to engage with a diffuse array of material phenomena.[14] Integral to this "conversation" is a two-sided field of awareness in which questions and answers can emerge from either the builder or the wood—or, escaping "language" altogether, are experienced as the tone of the encounter itself.[15]

The practice of "going by touch" is thus the hallmark of practices through which guitar makers *feel* their way beyond predetermined measurements and remain open to *being* touched and led elsewhere by the willfulness of wood.[16] In this way, artisans' emphasis on "integrating" themselves with the craft object undermines a basic premise of commodification: the assumption that goods derive their value not from their existence as a sensuous object with a social function but from their market price. To "leave a piece of one's soul" in a guitar, I suggest, is to recall the animated field of desire that produced the instrument in order to disrupt or subvert its commodification.[17] Rather than feeling alienated from a product in which their labor has been concealed, hand builders maintain a sense of kinship with each guitar *despite* its commodification at the point of sale. This ongoing attachment to, and identification with, the craft object is precisely what makes the criminalization of its mobility an affront to their professional integrity.

"We have many requests from Europe and Asia from people who have purchased instruments," Velázquez explains. "They want the historical value of their instrument to be maintained, so they only want either my father or myself to work on the instrument." But apprehension about fines and confiscations has forced him to stop importing Velázquez guitars for repair and restoration:

> What I'm worried about is not what [wood] I'm going to build with, but these instruments that have *already* been built. How do you say it? That people who own these instruments will be *reprimanded* because of having these instruments. As much as I would love to have

Brazilian rosewood, people will adapt [to other woods]. But these older instruments that have already been built, it's like, who is going to be able to take care of the import and exportation? People who bought them as investments, they're going to be fined or they're going to be reprimanded because of just owning a Brazilian rosewood instrument! How are these old instruments going to live, going to be left for the next generation, if they're being restricted and people are not able to take care of them appropriately?

Anthropologists have argued that material goods can be said to have a "social life" insofar as their routes of travel within the marketplace endow them with a "biography" over time.[18] When Velázquez refers to the "living on" of Brazilian rosewood instruments, however, I hear him saying something more, something that asks us to consider their intrinsic vitality as a form of life and the moral obligations that this recognition entails.[19] By emphasizing the aliveness of these instruments — and the intergenerational projects of transnational kinship groups — he calls the legitimacy of the reigning political order into question:

[The effect of the Lacey Act] is like taking the canvas away from the artist, from a painter! How can [policy makers] be so ignorant about the wood that we appreciate, that we love to use, and that we create with? I've seen my father have new creations, and all those creations are wonderful. They're like little sisters to me. [laughing] I have a lot of sisters to take care of! The thing is, he always thought of them as daughters, as a piece of him. And the ones that I create, they're my daughters. And whenever I get one of my father's instruments [to restore], it's like seeing an old family member.

It might seem easy to discount guitar makers' talk of begetting wooden offspring as anthropomorphic hyperbole artfully laced with sentimental notions of gender and kinship. But I think there is more to it than this. Not only do they deploy sentimentality in the service of a nondominant conception of masculine generativity; they use it to actively contest the commodity situation itself. If we take artisans at their word, claiming kinship with guitars reminds us that hearing the tone of things has political implications. If we acknowledge the shared materiality of people and guitars, we must recognize that our mutual survival depends on the politics of animacy and environmental conservation. In this sense, the tone of the artisanal guitar invites us to hear the urgent story it has to tell.[20]

That story, like *The Adventures of Pinocchio*, concerns the fate of forests and the craft object in a global marketplace.[21] Pinocchio's perilous travels through the social landscape of an industrializing agrarian society—the unscrupulous characters encountered and the grotesque bodily transformations endured—are, in my reading, a parable of the commodity situation, as through extended misadventure the puppet's body is conscripted to purposes other than his maker's own. At the end of his journey, Pinocchio looks back upon that body, relieved to have escaped it, and ridicules its pretensions to self-animation. The commodity state, in this narrative, need not be a permanent one. Geppetto's dream comes true, we could say, when the artisan's work leaves the marketplace and lives on as an inalienable possession of someone who cherishes it as a member of the family.

The sun is low on the horizon when the taxi drops me off in front of an old industrial building several blocks from the Toronto side of Lake Ontario. I press the buzzer for unit 12 and am soon greeted by William "Grit" Laskin and led up the stairs to his shop on the third floor. In 1992 Laskin and eleven other artists and artisans collectively purchased this massive brick building, once a mattress factory, and divided it into a dozen spacious studios. Noting the sign on his door—"Warning: Handmade Guitars Only Beyond this Point!"—I am ushered through a small office, an anteroom with machine tools, and then into the main workspace. My eyes are drawn to two large windows that look out over neighboring rooftops onto an early evening sky.

Like many one-person shops, Laskin's is organized around a central worktable that is accessible on all sides. On it the unfinished neck of a guitar rests on support blocks. I step closer to admire the inlay in progress. On the headstock Laskin has inlaid a dialogue bubble that reads, "What is your desire?" In the center of the fretboard is the face of a Japanese anime character. "This particular character was a princess who comes into somebody's life by accident," Laskin explains, "because he happens to dial a wrong number. This is capturing the moment when she shows up and he's just knocked for a loop. She's come

FIGURE 7.1. *What Is Your Desire? fretboard inlay-in-progress in Grit Laskin's shop, Toronto, Ontario, 2006. Photograph by the author.*

out of a mirror, and that's exactly what she says, *What is your desire?*"[22] Composed of ivory, red coral, yellow spiny, Tahitian black pearl, blue lapis, and green gaspeite, the inlay is visually exciting, as the shells' "chatoyance" gives a sense of motion to the scene.[23]

Laskin's name is synonymous with an approach to guitar inlay that treats it not as a decorative element but as a medium of artistic expression in its own right. Coveted by collectors and players around the world, his instruments now circulate as luxury goods, and several are in the permanent collection of musical instruments at the Canadian Museum of Civilization. In June 2012 he was appointed to the Order of Canada, an honor bestowed on citizens who "have devoted lifetimes to the betterment of humanity's mind, body, and spirit."[24] While there are a number of inlay specialists in the lutherie community, few have developed an aesthetic signature to the extent that Laskin has, making his work recognizable at a glance. Unlike many, he never repeats his original designs, and he inlays only his own guitars. "The guitar has got to be a good tool first," he maintains. "Even if the inlay is stunning, the woods are beautiful, the joinery is perfection itself, if it doesn't sound good and play well, it's a complete failure."[25]

Although Laskin refers to the guitar as his "canvas," the images he "paints" are almost always composed in collaboration with his clients. By sharing the "themes of things that are important in their lives," they give him ideas to work with; and out of this autobiographical material, which he calls "the novel," he distills the "short story" or "song" of his visual narrative:

> Something is art when it exists to communicate. So I try, within the limitations given to me by my clients, to create inlay designs that have something to say. They tell a story, they evoke a mood; they use visual metaphors to convey meaning. I feel my designs succeed best when they are the visual equivalent of a good song, one whose poetry has a surface meaning graspable from the first hearing but that also contains deeper meanings perceivable on repeated listening. I want the client to take delight in viewing the inlay for many years.[26]

The stories told by Laskin's designs are wide ranging in imagery and thematics. As befits a builder who is also a visual artist, guitar player, singer-songwriter, and novelist, however, his artwork is frequently a reflection on the creative process itself—a subject he occasionally signals, as if with a wink, by representing himself in the design. A well-known Laskin inlay is explicitly about the art of guitar inlay. The Puppet-eer was created in 1995 for Larry Sifel, one of the lutherie's pioneering inlay suppliers. Sifel requested a design "on the theme of inlay," and Laskin came up with the following narrative:

> An imaginary "Inlay Muse," represented by an aged golden woman, is the puppeteer that controls me. As the puppet, my hands create inlays that give pleasure, represented by the embracing, laughing couple. Larry stands below them—and beneath their "plane" on the fingerboard—cradling samples of the various shell and stone he at one time supplied to me. His left hand is placing a missing piece of the inlay, symbolizing the crucial role of the supplier. On his T-shirt are engraved the words, "I Ain't Marchin' Anymore," the title of Phil Ochs's antiwar anthem.[27]

The subject of the Puppeteer, as I interpret it, is the nature of gifted labor. With a nod toward realism, Laskin made the "samples" that Sifel holds out of the same kind of materials he supplied. Laskin's self-portrait, however, plays with magical realism—and even speculative realism—in its representation of his relationship to the "Inlay Muse." Artists have long depicted their source of inspiration as a lovely maiden or goddess, but Laskin's Muse is not a passive object of contemplation: she is actively pulling the strings. Her maturity and ambiguous ethnicity, combined with the T-shirt's slogan, pointedly reverse imperial hierarchies of gender and race. In this scenario, the artisan is simply the "body" through which the gift of creativity passes, and mastery involves the realization of one's own gift, not the exercise of power over others. Laskin's scene of making *speculates* about a process in which inlay materials, muses, and humans machinate with one another to produce a collective aesthetic experience.[28]

Laskin's puppet and puppeteer also stage a clever reprise of Geppetto's dream. If the old woodcarver personifies the craft wisdom marginalized by industrialization, then the "golden woman" is a similar figure—and one who also wields the Blue Fairy's power—in a postindustrial age. Her puppet, like Pinocchio, is half "wood" and half "human," but here the duality suggests the artisan's intimate relationship with his craft materials, not the difference between the commodity and the gift. Unlike the body of the "old" Pinocchio, whose strings were pulled by the "monstrous" forces of industrial capitalism, Laskin's creative labor is performed in the service of his Muse for the benefit of those who appreciate the tone and beauty of his instruments, expressed in sonic and visual odes to artisanship.[29]

A few years before completing the Puppeteer, Laskin explored similar themes in a "children's fable" published in *Guitarmaker* magazine.[30] While children may have been the nominal audience for the piece, in a periodical written by and for practicing luthiers, its de facto readers were other guitar makers. This fable can thus be read, I propose, as a mythic story of making—one that offers an "origin" narrative for the artisanal guitar and the lutherie movement itself.

"The Princess Trees" is cast as a scene of instruction in which a fictional luthier named Rosalie recalls a "legend" she was told by her guitar-making instructor. The legend posits a time in the past when the

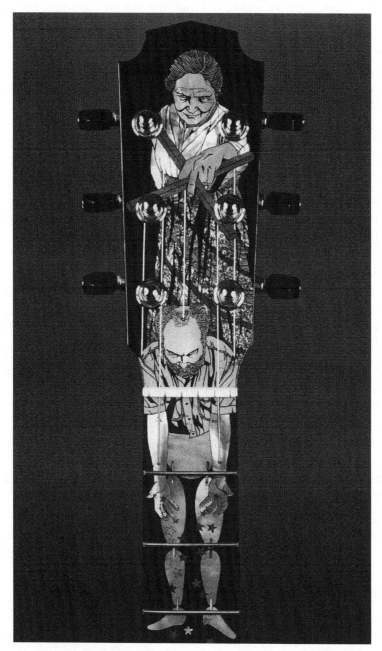

FIGURE 7.2. The Puppeteer. Guitar and inlay by William "Grit" Laskin CM, 1995.
Photograph by Brian Pickell.

world was politically divided into two realms: one, a lush forest ruled by the Queen of Trees, and the other, an arid wasteland ruled by the King of Deserts. The Queen's daughters, Rosewood, Mahogany, Spruce, and Ebony, spend their days tending their mother's garden, singing as they work, their voices "blend[ing] in beautiful harmony, sometimes join[ing] as one, in unison." Each princess takes care of one of "the first trees ever," the tree that eventually comes to bear her name.

Long envious of the Queen's trees, the King decides to invade her realm and rule it as his own, "never [thinking] to ask the Queen if she might share some of her trees." The four "Princess-trees" sense danger and reveal to the princesses that they are sentient beings, "able to see, hear, and talk, just like them." After Ebony's tree lifts her up to show her that the Queen's castle is on fire, the trees offer to protect the sisters from the King and his people. Each tree opens its trunk "like an owl spreading its wings," inviting its Princess to take refuge inside, where they bask in an "orange-brown glow of light."

When the sisters grow hungry and thirsty, the trees show them how to eat and drink by tilting their heads to receive drops of sap and "wiggling their toes in the earth" to find water. Months turn into years, and soon the princess become a "living part of the tree that saved them." As grand old trees, the sisters continue to take "pleasure in singing together as they did long ago." As time passes, the wind carries seeds from the four trees to distant lands, and they become trees that embody "the spirits of the first Princess-trees."

As Rosalie recalls, the legend explains why "in every guitar there is at least one piece of wood that comes from a tree-child of the first Princess-trees" and why the "best guitars in the world" are made with all four types of wood. Now, in the story's present, she discovers that the pieces of the guitar she is building automatically slide into position, sticking without glue, "as if the wooden parts *wanted* to be together." Soon Rosalie hears, faintly at first, and then with increasing clarity, a "group of voices":

> There was no mistaking it. The guitar was singing!
> Now she understood. In this guitar she had joined a part from each of the four true Princess-trees. Their spirits had passed through their seeds exactly as the legend described. Here, in this very guitar,

THE PRINCESS TREES
A Children's Fable by Grit Laskin

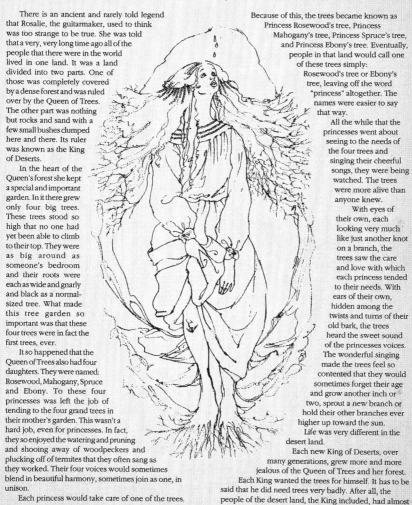

There is an ancient and rarely told legend that Rosalie, the guitarmaker, used to think was too strange to be true. She was told that a very, very long time ago all of the people that there were in the world lived in one land. It was a land divided into two parts. One of those was completely covered by a dense forest and was ruled over by the Queen of Trees. The other part was nothing but rocks and sand with a few small bushes clumped here and there. Its ruler was known as the King of Deserts.

In the heart of the Queen's forest she kept a special and important garden. In it there grew only four big trees. These trees stood so high that no one had yet been able to climb to their top. They were as big around as someone's bedroom and their roots were each as wide and gnarly and black as a normal-sized tree. What made this tree garden so important was that these four trees were in fact the first trees, ever.

It so happened that the Queen of Trees also had four daughters. They were named: Rosewood, Mahogany, Spruce and Ebony. To these four princesses was left the job of tending to the four grand trees in their mother's garden. This wasn't a hard job, even for princesses. In fact, they so enjoyed the watering and pruning and shooing away of woodpeckers and plucking off of termites that they often sang as they worked. Their four voices would sometimes blend in beautiful harmony, sometimes join as one, in unison.

Each princess would take care of one of the trees.

Because of this, the trees became known as Princess Rosewood's tree, Princess Mahogany's tree, Princess Spruce's tree, and Princess Ebony's tree. Eventually, people in that land would call one of these trees simply: Rosewood's tree or Ebony's tree, leaving off the word "princess" altogether. The names were easier to say that way.

All the while that the princesses went about seeing to the needs of the four trees and singing their cheerful songs, they were being watched. The trees were more alive than anyone knew.

With eyes of their own, each looking very much like just another knot on a branch, the trees saw the care and love with which each princess tended to their needs. With ears of their own, hidden among the twists and turns of their old bark, the trees heard the sweet sound of the princesses voices. The wonderful singing made the trees feel so contented that they would sometimes forget their age and grow another inch or two, sprout a new branch or hold their other branches ever higher up toward the sun.

Life was very different in the desert land.

Each new King of Deserts, over many generations, grew more and more jealous of the Queen of Trees and her forest. Each King wanted the trees for himself. It has to be said that he did need trees very badly. After all, the people of the desert land, the King included, had almost

46

FIGURE 7.3. A vision of symbiotic human and nonhuman materiality from the title page of "The Princess Trees" in Guitarmaker, 1992. Illustration by Janice Donato.

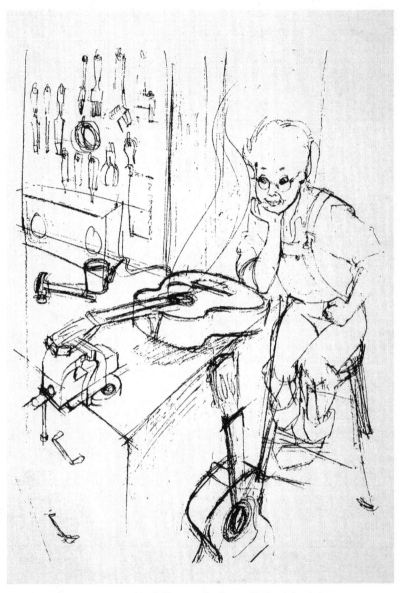

FIGURE 7.4. *Rosalie listens to the chorus of voices in her guitar.*

Illustration by Janice Donato.

they had been brought together for the first time since their days of harmonizing in the Queen's special garden.

"And to think," Rosalie said to herself, "it happened in my workshop . . ."

The primary subject of Laskin's origin myth, as I read it, is the "chorus of voices" embodied in the acoustic guitar.[31] The instrument's "voice" is not presumed to be the sole property of either the soundboard or the builder's touch. Rather, Rosalie discovers the parts of her guitar coming together as if magnetically attracted, a process she facilitates rather than controls. What cannot be "mistaken," and what the fable enjoins us to believe, is that the tonal qualities of the best guitars are produced by "spirits" or nonhuman agents who, dispersed by the forces of history, are reunited and live on in the present. As a field of desire and sentimentality, Rosalie's "workshop" is figured as a space of moral redemption.

That Laskin's scene of making has a history gives his narrative its political bite and bittersweet resolution. The epic battle it recounts — the conquest of the Queen of Trees by the King of Deserts — can be read as an allegory of European imperialism, in which people from lands of scarcity forcibly colonize feminized lands of abundance. Although the tale is critical of the King's violence, it also implicitly justifies the use of exotic tone woods, romanticizing the aesthetic legacy of imperialism and evoking nostalgia for the forests that our own political economy has helped to destroy.[32] In this way, the fable functions as a story of "anticonquest" that disavows the cruelty of empire but leaves the privileges of European hegemony intact.[33] Laskin's tale portrays luthiers as innocent heirs of colonialism, glossing over the ways they have benefited from the exploitation of resources from vulnerable habitats and communities around the globe.

Yet Laskin's story also troubles a central assumption of the capitalist world system within which guitar makers operate. Rather than characterizing trees as passive objects at the mercy of human agents, Laskin depicts a phantasmatic scene of gift exchange, consubstantiality, and survival. The princesses tend to their trees, and the trees shelter them; the princesses become their trees, and their trees become them. The otherwise terrifying prospect of being entombed inside a tree and turning into wood becomes, in this telling, spiritual communion and re-birth. If this is a children's story, it is a rare one in which princesses die, but as proud matriarchs whose legacy endures in forests and guitars. It is also a fairy tale with no prince, only a middle-aged woman presiding over a site of production in which a female experience of wonder and fortitude is materialized.

By installing feminine and nonhuman voices at the "origin" of a collective story of making, Laskin's fable disrupts lutherie's dominant origin myth. That story begins not with mercantile trade and colonial plunder but with the Renaissance and the transmission of a craft tradition through affective bonds between men and across generations of European ethnic groups. That narrative remains appealing to hand builders and industrial manufacturers alike. But its exclusive focus on individual genius and the patrilineal inheritance of skill reinforces prevailing distributions of power and disregards alternative constellations of value. In contrast, Laskin prompts us to realize that the problematic history of imperialism cannot be undone by ignoring it. Guitar makers, in his myth, are shamanistic intermediaries who orchestrate the sound of voices not otherwise heard in the hope of transforming our relationship to things and nonhuman materiality.[34]

Like the "What is your desire?" inlay on Laskin's bench the day of my visit, the Puppeteer and "The Princess Trees" visually and narratively elaborate upon the tone of the artisanal guitar. Directing our attention to the politics of animacy as an antidote to imperial rationality, these scenes convey a structure of feeling that orients artisans and their public toward the cultural logic of the gift, not the commodity. Understood as a gift, the vocality of trees both inspires and obligates them to create instruments that may themselves circulate as gifts despite periods of commodification. In the artisanal encounter, the voices that come together in the acoustic guitar have the uncanny quality of being both familiar and strange—at once echoes of human desire and signs of nonhuman agency—much as if they were the voice of a princess emerging from a mirror.[35]

To the extent that guitar makers can intervene in the market-driven maelstrom that endangers classic tone woods, they do so by drawing upon a countercultural sensibility that has been nurtured by the luthe-

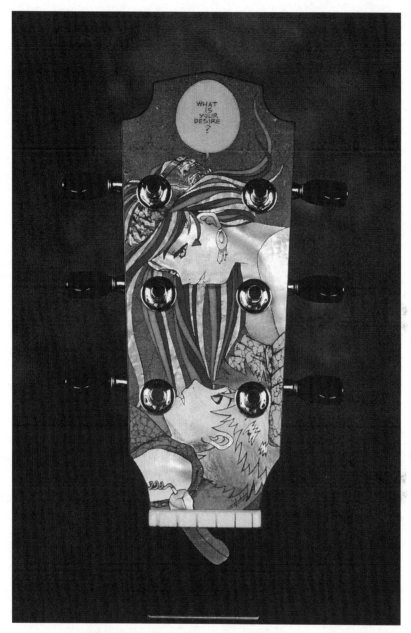

FIGURE 7.5. *What Is Your Desire? Guitar and inlay by William "Grit" Laskin CM, 2006.*

rie movement and its craft community for the last half-century. They persevere in the knowledge that although they cannot personally stop the devastation of ecosystems and the devaluation of manual labor, they enact craft practices that honor precious resources and employ marketing strategies that support sustainable consumption. Using only a small fraction of the world's rarest woods, luthiers are united by a commitment to forest stewardship unmatched by transnational construction, furniture, or paper and pulp industries. Unlike other end consumers, William Eaton argues, stringed-instrument makers value trees not for the profit they generate but for the history and intrinsic vitality they embody:

> Guitar making is closer than a lot of professions to the idea of, I'm working with wood that comes from a seed that comes from a tree that sprouted in the dirt and in that dirt is our history—the history that we share in that dirt. Trees are not only a symbol but a reality of how we exist on the planet. Without trees, without the exchange of oxygen that they put out, human beings don't exist. So we can take the layers of that relationship as deep as we want to—as deep as the roots: we are part of a symbiotic relationship. With a stringed instrument, there's the feature that it comes out of a seed from a tree and it grows, and now it has a *second life*. What creates the sound of a guitar, the magic of it, is intangible. There is something that we would call spirit, which comes from the word *breath*, so the breath of it is the life. So we sense a life to these instruments. The vibrational quality—which is the vibrating membrane, the top or the strings— suggests life. That's one of those qualities that everybody will experience in different ways. You'll have some that will look at it as truly spiritual, as having qualities of an almost ethereal nature—nirvana qualities. Then you'll have some that are very gutsy and emotional like the blues players or rock and roll that has to do with the beat of the heart, the simplicity of digging in there and hearing the emotional rawness of what that is about. So wherever you are on that spectrum, the guitar has a life of its own.

In academic circles, the perception of autonomous "life" in consumer goods is usually dismissed as an illusion spawned by capitalist ideology.[36] But the guitar makers I met while writing this book have taught me to revise that bit of received wisdom. Just as things may move in and out of commodity situations, producers and consumers may be more or less beguiled by the spectacle of the market. Those who work with their hands have long been in a position to recognize the dignity of human labor and qualitative differences in the tone of things. Knowing how the goods that populate our world are made, and having the skill to make some of them ourselves, confers an appreciation for the affective power of cultural artifacts and the raw materials that compose them. Far from mystifying social relations of production, embodied work with nonhuman matter exposes commodification for what it is: one system of value among others which, while formidable, has no monopoly on human desire.

North American lutherie came of age during a cataclysmic change in global capitalism. It augured a path forward for young men and women caught between blue- and white-collar worlds and the deepening precarity becoming endemic to both. While artisanal craft and its industrial counterpart are not panaceas for all postindustrial ills, they offer a glimpse of how alternative value systems can be realized in the midst of, and necessarily in interaction with, the hard realities of today's political economy. Although luthiers now face a grave threat to their professional autonomy, their insistence on the vitality of Pinocchio's body—on its capacity to mobilize gifted labor and elude capture by the market mechanisms arrayed against it—can give us reason for hope. Should Pinocchio's peregrinations come to an end, for the time being, at our doorstep, let us be attuned to the tone of things.

Epilogue

Toward the end of a two-day trip to Calgary, Alberta, I sit across from Judy Threet at the large workbench in the center of her shop. There is snow on the ground and rooftops, and the late afternoon sky is overcast. A fading light filters through the large windows of this former industrial space, now converted into studios for artists and artisans. Our conversation has turned philosophical, and she has brought out a pouch of tobacco and rolling papers in preparation for making herself a very thin cigarette. Over the course of my visit, I have come to anticipate these moments as the prelude to a Socratic dialogue in which Threet prompts me to think as much about my questions as about her answers.

THREET: It all goes back to what we keep dancing around and can't figure out: what is so important, what is so valuable about the human hand? It may be that we as a society are becoming more divorced from products of the human hand, so there's a nostalgia for it. But that just begs the question, because nostalgia presupposes that there was a good to it. So what is the good that's there? It's not just guitar makers. It's quilts, sweaters.[1]

DUDLEY: Do you have a theory?

THREET: This is all airy-fairy—and it certainly doesn't fit within the analytical tradition of philosophy—but it's conceivable that someone that's working with their hands, that is working that closely with the materials, is imparting some of themselves into what they're creating. Who knows? You don't say this to academics, but [*shooting me a warning look*] something like that could be going on. "There's more things in heaven and earth, Horatio, than are dreamt of in your philosophy!" [from *Hamlet*]. It may be that my intimately working with something actually infuses it with something it wouldn't otherwise have.

DUDLEY: Do you believe it does?

THREET [*pausing*]: Probably. But I wouldn't be able to tell you what the mechanism is.

DUDLEY: Is it something the player can recognize?

THREET [*pausing again*]: Well, if I think that it's there, I would have to think that it has some sort of discernible, experiential effect. I'm not sure that I would be willing to say that. I have no idea *why* hand stuff is valuable. I *believe* it's valuable—a lot of other people do too. So I'm just trying to think, why is it? Why do people seek that out? If you get two guitars that both sound good, would I prefer the handmade one? Let's do it this way—they sound the same, they're the same price, which would I pick? Even if I couldn't tell visually, I would choose the handmade one. Now, how's that for irrational?

DUDLEY: Why choose the handmade?

THREET: I don't know. [*pause*] Okay, here's why, in that case. It's a matter of respect. It's awe. It's "Holy crap! They sound the same; they're the same price!" Of course I would go with the handmade one, because that's the product of a person. That's something I value; not everyone would. It would be an interesting question for you to ask anybody else you talk to: if they sound the same, et cetera, which one do you want?

DUDLEY: Perhaps not quite in the same way, but I have asked this question.

THREET: What do they say?

DUDLEY: Usually it's a version of the Geppetto story. That wood-workers impart something of themselves into the wood; that guitars are their children going out into the world. [*She seems surprised that others have said this.*] Some even call it a spirit; that's what allows Pinocchio to get up and do his thing!

THREET: Dance, Pinocchio dance!

DUDLEY: And some say that the guitar rolling off the assembly line has no spirit in it until the player animates it. But if you buy it handmade, it's already got something.

THREET: That's just bull. I would want to make sure, if I were asking these people, that they had in mind two guitars that were visually and aurally indistinguishable.

DUDLEY: But isn't that impossible?

THREET: It's a *thought* experiment. I can't imagine any builder saying they'd always prefer the handmade guitar because it had a spirit. Maybe they're going to say some have a bad spirit and that's why they sound so lousy. Okay, I'll admit maybe the factory one won't have a spirit and you've got to put it in yourself. But to insist every handmade guitar has a spirit, but that some are odd or gimpy— maybe, but it's not anything I'd say.

DUDLEY: I'm not trying to put words in your mouth.

THREET: No, I'm thinking, would I say that, if hard pressed?

DUDLEY: Well, perhaps the builder who hasn't got their act together isn't making that thing happen.

THREET: Oh, true. Okay.

DUDLEY: So it's when you hit your stride and you're able to make this work—whoa, I think I've got it! Well, what is *that* about? It's sort of "Hey, it's talking back to me. It's got its own thing going on. It's not just me anymore—it's more than me."

THREET: It's a cooperative effort then. The wood tells you something, and you're actually listening to it as opposed to bullying your way through. That might be more what's being hinted at. And there's a certain point where people *do* start listening to their hands, start listening to their ears, to what these senses are telling them. And you try to make decisions based on the sensory input of the wood.

DUDLEY: That's really different than saying I'm putting something of myself into an inanimate object. Rather, there's something there that I'm responding to. This isn't an object anymore.

THREET: This is getting *really* philosophical. But listening *is* a giving enterprise. So if I am listening to the wood, in a sense I am giving to it. I am giving it my attention. It's some sort of homage that I'm paying to the wood. So it might just be differences in the way that you slice it. Whether you talk about a spirit that I build into it versus talking about a cooperative effort, where I'm communicating with the wood, it may boil down to the same thing, if you look at listening as a giving thing. [*Long pause as she rolls a cigarette and lights it.*] Deep down I'm more airy-fairy than I'm letting on. So here is what I believe. I have a suspicion that I would never be able to prove to anyone—if it allows of proof, it's like faith—that if I had a favorite rock that I carried everywhere with me, and I loved it and I rubbed it—a pet rock, I guess—and I bonded with it, eventually it would contain part of me. [*Her eyes grow misty.*] *That's* what I mean by dotty. See, I'm getting really emotional about this too. That, yes, it would have something to do with energy. Lord only knows what any of this stuff is, but the fact that I've cared so much about it, it's got *me* in it now.

DUDLEY: I don't think that sounds crazy.

THREET: Well, I do. It's totally loony. It's totally unprovable; I couldn't prove it. But that may be what some people are getting at when they say they are sending their children out into the world and this and that. I think that some people, myself included, think that part of them does [*pause with emotion*] go out.

On the last morning of the Healdsburg Guitar Festival, Ervin Somogyi and I sit in chairs sipping coffee and tea, respectively, outside his room at the L&M Motel in Healdsburg, California. This is where many first- and second-generation luthiers stay during the show, for old times' sake as well as the 1950s-style charm and modestly priced accommodations. Looking out at the single row of rooms around the motor court, we talk as we watch others packing their cars, pausing occasionally to give hugs and bid farewells. Somogyi is describing his guitar voicing class, a weeklong course he offers once a year for builders who already have some experience with lutherie. The key to effective teaching, he says, is to educate or "bring knowledge out" of his students, not instruct or try to "put it in."[2]

SOMOGYI: I've had student after student in my classes tell me at the end of them that my classes weren't at all what they expected. They expected me to show them mechanical methods: "Here, you do it like this, and this brace has got to be like that, and that's how you make a great guitar." And what I'm trying to do is to teach them how to think about how to make their *own* great guitars, which is totally unfamiliar to them. The educational system in this country has failed them, because it has not prepared anybody to depend on their own powers to do anything. They need to get tools, jigs, certificates, education, permission, permits, whatever, from other sources outside of themselves. A few schools operate differently, but most of them don't.

DUDLEY: There are so many barriers, institutional and otherwise, to that kind of experience. It leads me to ask an abstract sort of question. These are also lessons in living, right? How to live your life in a certain kind of way?

SOMOGYI: Putting it that way, that's my vantage point. Lutherie is not a useful skill but a way of life.

DUDLEY: It's not just about how to build a guitar.

SOMOGYI: Not for me. Making a *really* good guitar is different than making a guitar and making a living. It involves something more. You read [Rainer Maria] Rilke ever? [*I shake my head.*] Interesting fellow. I bring him up because there's a quote that comes to mind: he was describing how he had known this person for thirty years, and that person had never had a conversation with Rilke that involved his *whole* being. So we are describing things that touch my whole being, rather than my skill set or my area of credentialed expertise. You understand that.

DUDLEY: Yes, yet it also seems, after three years of talking with people [guitar makers], that there is a range of approaches, from the utilitarian and mechanical to maybe a middle group, where the guitar is a vehicle for a personal search for identity . . .

SOMOGYI: Well, I would be interested in asking you about this exact thing. What have you found in this network?

DUDLEY: Not everyone I talk to is able to articulate what's going on for them. But I get the sense from most builders that they are treating their materials and the guitars they make as a kind of relationship, where the instrument has a voice—that it speaks and can speak back to them.

SOMOGYI: Yeah, but is it an equal or a subordinate?

DUDLEY: Exactly, is the relationship intersubjective in a certain kind of way? Are you relating to another subject, and in that sense identifying your own beingness in that relationship? Versus it's an object on which you are working. I think that really comes out in one way or another for people who think about the guitar as an object. They are just doing something to it, and these are the steps by which they're doing that. They are not as comfortable with the idea of subordinating their own ego.

SOMOGYI: That's an interesting way to put it. Well, look, I'll bounce an idea off, which may or may not make any sense. There is truth to the proposition, as far as I'm concerned, that on this planet there are really only two fundamental stances you can take, which are to be *for* life or not. Does that make any sense to you?

DUDLEY: Yes.

SOMOGYI: Well, most people won't understand that.

DUDLEY: That the impulse to objectify is what leads to so many of the things that we deplore.

SOMOGYI: That's a concept that doesn't translate to a lot of people's brains. Literally. It's just an unintelligible sentence, if you were to write it out or put it in a fortune cookie or something.

DUDLEY: And when you're talking about a guitar—you know, those two different ways of treating the material, you can do it. It's not going to fight back.

SOMOGYI: Right. So the principal fork in the road, for people who think maybe like you and I do, is—before you pick up the first piece of wood—are you going to objectify it or not? That's a fundamental fork in the road upon which everything else is built, don't you think?

DUDLEY [*nodding*]: I'd like to start the book with the first part of the Pinocchio story where the wood says "ouch" when it's hit.

SOMOGYI: Oh yeah. Yeah.

DUDLEY: Do you hear it or not? Do you hear the "ouch" or not?

SOMOGYI: Some luthiers have that kind of relationship with their wood, although you really lose points in this culture if you cop to that.

DUDLEY: You mean admit it?

SOMOGYI: Yeah, it sounds weird.

Postscript

While this book was being prepared for publication, two policy developments both raised and dashed hopes in the lutherie world.

In March 2013, the Convention on International Trade in Endangered Species (CITES) approved a US recommendation that authorizes participating countries to issue "passports" for musical instruments containing protected species of wildlife. Designed to benefit musicians who frequently cross international borders, the resolution established a three-year "certificate of ownership" for individual instruments that are "hand-carried by the owner" and destined for personal use or exhibition. Expressly forbidden is the sale or transfer of the instrument (or "CITES specimen"), which must return to its "State of residence" before the certificate expires.[1]

The music industry greeted the CITES passport with measured relief. For musicians who own and travel with vintage instruments—and who can prove that the protected species these instruments contain were acquired prior to 1975 or before trade in those species was banned—the certificate reduces the cost and hassle of applying for a preconvention permit every time they travel. But the resolution offered no pathway to certification for artisanal instruments that contain preconvention wood for which no documentation exists. Nor does it reduce anxiety about enforcement action taken against the shipment of instruments for sale and service between luthiers and their customers.

In May 2013, the US Department of Agriculture (USDA) submitted a report to Congress on its implementation of the 2008 Lacey Act amendments. Unlike the CITES resolution, the USDA explicitly addressed the problem of artisanal guitars built with wood imported into the country before the amendments were enacted. As long as owners of such instruments carried them into the United States as "personal baggage," the report stated, no Lacey Act declaration was necessary.[2] Hastening to allay fears of governmental overreach, the USDA reiterated that the Department of Justice and US Fish and Wildlife Service did not consider "citizens traveling with their musical instruments [to be] an enforcement priority."

While the report played well to the press — prompting headlines that claimed the USDA had "eased the effect" of the Lacey Act on musical instruments and "okayed" them for travel—little had actually changed.[3] Instruments containing prohibited materials still require a CITES certificate, and those intended for sale must still be in compliance with Lacey's declaration requirements. Indeed, with regard to luthiers' "stockpiles of wood" that predate the 2008 amendments, the report confirmed that the law applies to *all* illegally harvested wood whenever "someone 'imports, exports, sells, receives, acquires, or purchases' such wood." Glossing over bureaucratic inertia, the USDA intimated that it was "currently examining this issue to determine if there are administrative steps that it might take to address [stakeholders'] concerns." In truth, however, the government only reinforced the legal limbo in which guitar makers now operate and deferred meaningful action to an indefinite future.

Acknowledgments

This project began with a hunt for a guitar. Not just any guitar, but one that would become a companion, a soul mate. I played cello as a child and have long remembered the reassurance I felt drawing the bow over its strings, my body resonating with its deep tone, a sensation that lasted even on the school bus, cello beside me on the seat, my arm flung over its shoulder. Much later in life I found myself in need of a similar kind of reassurance. The Twin Towers had been struck, and I was up for tenure at my university—a long, inscrutable process that made me feel judged and found wanting.

The dream was a simple one. It began with a haunting melody played fingerstyle on a steel-string acoustic guitar, yet as I strained to hear it, I would begin to wake and the music would fade, leaving me yearning for something I could not name. I had learned to play folk songs on guitar in high school but had not played in decades, and a natural-born musician I was not. But the dream persisted. So I embarked upon a quest that I now know many guitar lovers do. One guitar led to another, and I took lessons with anyone willing to teach a forty-something-year-old woman how to communicate with a six-string guitar. (Thank you, Geoff Bartley, Michael Corn, and Neal Fitzpatrick!)

My search led me to Acoustic Music in Guilford, Connecticut. Located in an unassuming house flecked with peeling paint, this boutique dealership was unlike any guitar store I had seen. No sooner did I set foot in the shop than a beautiful instrument appeared in my arms and others began to materialize in a semicircle around me, each one uniquely enticing. Orchestrating this sonic feast was Brian Wolfe, musician and guitar aficionado extraordinaire. Boyishly charming in his baseball cap and ponytail, he responded to my amazement (and performance anxiety) by playing a variety of guitars to demonstrate their tonal qualities and telling me stories about their makers.

Then it happened. Seated across from me, Brian picked up a guitar, deftly dropped the pitch of several strings, and played a fingerstyle tune. I was riveted: it was like the music in my dream but strangely unlike anything I had ever heard. Incredulous, I needed to know *what* he was doing.

So began my love affair with DADGAD tuning, Celtic instrumental guitar, and artisanal lutherie. Brian indulged me with several guitar lessons, showing me how to play "She Moved through the Fair" and "Black Waterside," and lent me CDs from his personal collection, introducing me to the music and guitarists associated with the British folk baroque and fingerstyle revolution. During those early visits, I got to know George Youngblood, the luthier with whom I eventually apprenticed. Between Brian's passion for fine guitars, mandolins, and other fretted instruments and George's encyclopedic knowledge of the American guitar and all things lutherie, I was drawn into a social world that spoke to my academic interest in forms of work that to greater or lesser extents contravene the cultural logic of capitalism. Without our many conversations and their willingness to let me hang out at the shop, this book would never have been written. They have my heartfelt admiration and respect.

I owe an incalculable debt to the one hundred fifty guitar makers, musicians, dealers, collectors, festival organizers, material suppliers, and lutherie school instructors who generously agreed to be interviewed for this research. Although I could not feature everyone's story, the perspective gleaned from these wide-ranging accounts informed my writing from beginning to end. The openness of spirit, sense of community, and

ACKNOWLEDGMENTS

dedication to craft that I experienced over four years of fieldwork made an indelible impression on me, and for it I am forever grateful. Special thanks go to Judy Threet and Linda Manzer, who went out of their way to make me feel welcome at lutherie events, often allowing me to sit at their exhibit tables to catch my breath between interviews and take in the scene from their point of view; to Dick Boak and Richard Hoover, who took me on fascinating and informative shop tours; to Jim Magill and Al Petteway, who invited me to attend the Swannanoa Gathering; and to Tim Olsen, Ervin Somogyi, and William Cumpiano, who responded to my persistent queries in good humor and took time out of their busy lives to comment on an early draft of the manuscript.

My thinking about the issues explored in these pages has benefited from invitations to present parts of this work at the Bard Graduate Center for Decorative Arts, Design History, and Material Culture and at several Yale forums, including the Material Culture Study Group, the Ethnography and Social Theory Colloquium, and Critical Encounters in American Studies. Catherine Whalen and Ned Cooke offered early guidance in the field of material culture studies, and my colleagues Jean-Christophe Agnew, Matthew Jacobson, and Joanne Meyerowitz provided valuable input at critical junctures.

I have been blessed with extraordinary graduate students, past and present. Their probing questions, keen insights, and insistence on political relevance have kept me on my toes, reminding me daily why cultural criticism matters. Carrie Lane, Andrea Becksvoort, Myra Jones-Taylor, Karilyn Crockett, Emily Coates, and Tisha Hooks have been sounding boards and voices of wisdom at various stages of this project. My renegade band of transdisciplinarians in the Ethnography and Oral History working group has offered constructive criticism, frequent reality checks, and ongoing inspiration with their own innovative scholarship. Hats off to Alison Kanosky, Chloe Taft, Ruthie Yow, Talya Zemach-Bersin, Sierra Bell, Andy Horowitz, Andrea Quintero, Dana Asbury, Rebecca Jacobs, Lauren Tilton, Chris Krameric, Karla Cornejo Villavicencio, Joey Plaster, and Jessica Varner. I am particularly grateful for the transcriptions provided by Talya Zemach-Bersin, Chloe Taft, Sierra Bell, and Alison Kanosky. Sierra Bell's timely assistance as the manuscript went to press saved the day.

At the University of Chicago Press, the manuscript was strengthened by comments provided by two anonymous readers and Ruth Goring's meticulous editing. It has been a special pleasure to work once again with Doug Mitchell. Doug saw my first two books through publication (oh so many years ago!) and brought the same mix of erudition and jazz drummer's tempo to my third. I have been lucky to be guided by such sure hands.

Over the years it took me to research and write this book, my twin nieces Annie and Emily Berman have catapulted through adolescence into their junior year in college. During that time, they gamely endured countless drafts of chapters read aloud, endeavored to update me on the latest indie music, and could always be counted on to join me in one more verse of "Desolation Row." For the guitar that brings such sweetness to my life, I thank Linda Manzer. And for being the human who had confidence in this project from the start, steadying me through its ups and downs, I am indebted to my wife, Maria Trumpler. She keeps me fed in body, mind, and spirit.

Notes

Prologue

1 George Youngblood and "Ed Putnam" (pseudonym), from a transcript of fieldwork recorded by the author, Guilford, CT, February 9, 2007.

Introduction

1 William Cumpiano, interview with the author, Northampton, MA, October 26, 2006.

2 Les Kerr, "Gallagher Guitar Takes Pride in Its Rich Past," *Tennessean News*, 2007, http://www.gallagherguitar.com/tennesseannews.html.

3 As "strong medicine," the guitar can also be considered an example of what Walter Benjamin called an "instrument of magic," an object central to sacred rituals which possesses an "aura of authenticity." "The Work of Art in the Age of Mechanical Reproduction," in *Illuminations* (New York: Harcourt Brace Jovanovich, 1968).

4 As Alice Kessler-Harris points out, well into the 1960s it was primarily white men who enjoyed the "right to work." *In Pursuit of Equity: Women, Men, and the Quest for Economic Citizenship in 20th-Century America* (Oxford: Oxford University Press, 2001), 10.

5 My characterization of Geppetto's dream as a story with a romantic plot builds on Lauren Berlant's analysis of the love plot as a form of fantasy that produces love as a lived experience. As she argues, romance narratives create the setting for fantasy, which "establish[es] dramas of love, sexuality, and reproduction as the dramas central to living" and "install[s] the institutions of intimacy (most explicitly the married couple and the intergenerational family) as the proper sites for providing the life plot in which a subject has 'a life' and a future." Berlant, *Desire/Love* (Brooklyn, NY: Punctum Books, 2012), 86. In lutherie, I argue, a variation of the love plot is deployed to bolster the legitimacy of a nondominant form of labor.

6 Rick Davis, quotation from a transcript of his presentation with Tim Brookes, "The Custom Guitar," at the Montreal Guitar Show, Montreal, Quebec, June 28, 2008. Event recorded by the author.

7 I do not use Pierre Bourdieu's theory of practice to theorize guitar makers' embodied labor as a "craft habitus" acquired over time as the result of habitual behavior. In my view, his analysis is insufficiently attentive to the aesthetic, affective, and ontological dimension of human interactions with material things. Bourdieu, *Outline of a Theory of Practice*, trans. Richard Nice (Cambridge: Cambridge University Press, 1977).

8 Guitar makers' intuitive interaction with wood is beautifully captured in two books about individual artisans that describe, from the author's point of view, the step-by-step process of building an acoustic guitar by hand. Acknowledging that builders are unable to articulate everything they do, these intimate portraits offer an almost cinematic documentary—blending first-person observation with conversational testimony—of how a guitar is made from beginning to end. This narrative structure is compelling because it allows us to feel that we "know" what is happening in the luthier's workshop in insofar as it finds expression in the satisfying resolution of stringing up and strumming a completed instrument. See Tim Brookes, *Guitar: An American Life* (New York: Grove Press, 2006) and Allen St. John, *Clapton's Guitar: Watching Wayne Henderson Build the Perfect Instrument* (New York: Free Press, 2006). I adopt a

different narrative strategy in this book. Because I am interested in the affective relationship between luthiers and their instruments, I disrupt and forestall a processual narrative about how great guitars are made in favor of dwelling on and in the "contact zone" between builders, wood, guitars, and myself. In this approach, I take my cue from Kathleen Stewart and her effort to track "ordinary affects" — "the varied, surging capacities to affect and be affected that give everyday life the quality of a continual motion of relations, scenes, contingencies, and emergences." Albeit with key stylistic and representational differences, I too have tried to register the textures and intensities of "complex and uncertain objects that fascinate because they literally hit us or exert a pull on us." Among other things, this has involved being attentive to the repetitive quality of guitar making and the recurrent scenes that luthiers inhabit and restage. Stewart, *Ordinary Affects* (Durham: Duke University Press, 2007), 1–2, 4–5.

9 As Sianne Ngai argues: "Tone is the dialectic of objective and subjective feeling that our aesthetic encounters inevitably produce." *Ugly Feelings* (Cambridge, MA: Harvard University Press, 2005), 30. To consider the tone of acoustic guitars as an aesthetic feeling is to ally myself with the affective turn in cultural studies, an approach associated with the philosophy of Gilles Deleuze and Félix Guattari as well as recent feminist and queer theory. This scholarship focuses on the relationship between contemporary transformations in global capitalism, shifting regimes of labor, and reconfigurations of the human body and its capacities. For an introduction to affect theory, see Patricia Ticineto Clough, introduction to *The Affective Turn: Theorizing the Social*, ed. Clough (Durham, NC: Duke University Press, 2007), 1–33; and Gregory J. Seigworth and Melissa Gregg, "An Inventory of Shimmers," in *The Affect Theory Reader*, ed. Gregg and Seigworth (Durham, NC: Duke University Press, 2010), 1–25.

10 *Structure of feeling* is the term Raymond Williams gave to a "social experience still in process," an affective register of felt phenomena that exceed the grasp of representation and cannot be articulated or semanticized. *Marxism and Literature* (New York: Oxford University Press, 1977), 132. As Ngai points out, Williams was not theorizing emotions per se, since emotions, unlike feelings, do have a cultural history (*Ugly Feelings*, 360).

11 Seigworth and Gregg, "Inventory of Shimmers," 1. "At its most anthropomorphic," they argue, *affect* consists of "those forces — visceral forces beneath, alongside, or generally *other than* conscious knowing, vital forces insisting beyond emotion — that can serve to drive us toward movement, toward thought and extension, that can likewise suspend us (as if in neutral) across a barely registering accretion of force-relations, or that can leave us overwhelmed by the world's apparent intractability."

12 Sara Ahmed makes a persuasive case for understanding relationships between people as well as between people and objects as "orientations" in space and time. In her analysis, objects "arrive" toward us as we "arrive" toward them, "creating an encounter" and a "bringing forth." *Queer Phenomenology: Orientations, Objects, Others* (Durham, NC: Duke University Press, 2006), 39.

13 Brian Massumi translates Deleuze and Guattari's concept of *affect* as the "ability to affect and be affected." "Notes on the Translation," in Gilles Deleuze and Félix Guattari, *A Thousand Plateaus: Capitalism and Schizophrenia*, trans. Massumi (Minneapolis: University of Minnesota Press, 1987), xvi. For Deleuze and Guattari, Massumi observes, neither affect nor affection is culturally elaborated as a "personal feeling"; rather, they are considered "prepersonal" intensities linked to bodily experience.

14 Mel Y. Chen, *Animacies: Biopolitics, Racial Mattering, and Queer Affect* (Durham, NC: Duke University Press, 2012), 55, 30. Chen develops the linguistic concept of an *animacy hierarchy* to analyze how "understandings of lifeliness, sentience, agency, ability, and mobility" are culturally organized and ranked, arguing that this conceptual structure is "also an ontology of affect," which is "precisely about which things can or cannot affect—or be affected by—which other things within a specific scheme of possible action" (29–30).

15 Elizabeth Povinelli uses the term *alternative social projects* to describe collective endeavors that run counter to the hegemonic tendencies of late liberalism by "attempt[ing] to capacitate an alternative set of human and posthuman worlds." They are "specific arrangements (*agencements*) that extend beyond simple human sociality or human beings" and depend on "a host of interlocking concepts, materials, and forces that include human and nonhuman agencies and organisms." Povinelli, *Economies of Abandonment: Social Belonging and Endurance in Late Liberalism* (Durham, NC: Duke University Press, 2011), 7.

16 Although wolf tones are more common in bowed instruments like the cello, guitars can exhibit similarly induced "dead spots" on the fretboard that produce rapidly decaying notes.

17 Jane Bennett, "Commodity Fetishism and Commodity Enchantment," *Theory and Event* 5, no. 1 (2001): 54. Bennett has been a forceful advocate for rethinking the classical Marxist understanding of *commodity fetishism*. In *The Enchantment of Modern Life: Attachments, Crossings, and Ethics* (Princeton, NJ: Princeton University Press, 2001), she rejects the notion that the "idolatry of consumption goods" and "blindness to the pain and suffering embedded in the commodity" constitute the only possible response to capitalist commodification and the animation of artifacts (113). And in *Vibrant Matter: A Political Ecology of Things* (Durham, NC: Duke University Press, 2010), she makes the compelling argument that anthropomorphism—and the "superstition, divinization of nature, [and] romanticism" attached to it—is a risk worth taking insofar as it serves to undermine anthropocentrism: "a chord is struck between person and thing, and I am no longer above or outside a nonhuman 'environment'" (120).

18 The concept of "socializing" the nonhuman comes from Bruno Latour's analysis of what happens in scientific laboratories between scientists and the nonhuman entities they observe, construct, and "discover" (*Pandora's Hope: Essays on the Realities of Science Studies* [Cambridge, MA: Harvard University Press, 1999], 259). Latour rejects the notion that such objects can be understood as either "natural" or "social." See *Politics of Nature: How to Bring the Sciences into Democracy* (Cambridge, MA: Harvard University Press, 2004).

19 William Eaton, interview with the author, Phoenix, AZ, October 16, 2008.

20 Michael Taussig, invoking Walter Benjamin's concept of the "mimetic faculty," has described the compulsion to "become the Other" as a form of imitation in which the imitator is endowed with the power of the imitated. In *Mimesis and Alterity: A Particular History of the Senses* (New York: Routledge, 1993), xviii–xix. Yet as Sara Ahmed observes, the perception of others as "strangers" orients us toward others as people that we already, in some sense, "know." The idea that "strangeness" originates in the other, she argues, is itself a form of "fetishism." *Strange Encounters: Embodied Others in Post-coloniality* (New York: Routledge, 2000). In the case of the exotic other as a maker

NOTES TO PAGES 9–11

or artisan, however, I understand the attraction to be driven by the desire to occupy an agential position within a site of production.

21 Eaton notes that Roberts "took on the pseudonym Juan Roberto because most of the world's famous guitar makers at that time were Spanish. William Eaton, "The Roberto-Venn School of Luthiery," *Guitarmaker*, no. 42 (Fall 2000): 35–43. For a more recent account of the school's history and mission, see Jason Kostal, "The Roberto-Venn Story," *Guitarmaker*, no. 61 (Fall 2007): 62–69.

22 As John F. Kasson observes, "The desire for unmediated contact with nature and occasions to test oneself against it constitutes an overriding element of American masculine identity." *Houdini, Tarzan, and the Perfect Man: The White Male Body and the Challenge of Modernity in America* (New York: Hill and Wang, 2001), 211. Needless to say, this desire can be shared and enacted by women as well.

23 The classic work on psychic aspects of dreams is Sigmund Freud, *The Interpretation of Dreams*, trans. James Strachey (orig. 1900; New York: Avon Books, 1980). I draw upon Wendy Brown's concept of "political dreamwork" (Brown, "American Nightmare: Neoliberalism, Neoconservatism, and De-democratization," *Political Theory* 34, no. 6 [2006]: 690).

24 On the fate of the European guild system in America, see W. J. Rorabaugh, *The Craft Apprentice: From Franklin to the Machine Age in America* (New York: Oxford University Press, 1986). And on racial exclusiveness in American craft unions, David Montgomery, *The Fall of the House of Labor: The Workplace, the State, and American Labor Activism, 1865–1925* (Cambridge: Cambridge University Press, 1987).

25 The countercultural celebration of Renaissance arts and crafts occurred in tandem with the revival of white ethnic identities in the wake of the civil rights movement. See Rachel Lee Rubin, *Well Met: Renaissance Faires and the American Counterculture* (New York: New York University Press, 2012), 80–110, and Matthew Jacobson, *Roots Too: White Ethnic Revival in Post–Civil Rights America* (Cambridge, MA: Harvard University Press, 2008).

26 In *Shop Class as Soulcraft: An Inquiry into the Value of Work*, Matthew Crawford argues that consumer society's efforts to suppress "our [masculine] nature as tool users" constitutes the primary source of men's contemporary discontent (New York: Penguin, 2009), 71.

27 Stewart Brand, introduction to the *Whole Earth Catalog*, 1969.

28 Jane Bennett points to the hubris of attributing creative agency only to humans and gods as part of her argument in favor of pursuing a "careful course of anthropomorphization" (*Vital Matters*, 120–22).

29 In two previous books, I analyze the impact of neoliberal policy shifts on unionized industrial workers and family farmers, respectively, in the 1980s and 1990s: *The End of the Line: Lost Jobs, New Lives, in Postindustrial America* (Chicago: University of Chicago Press, 1994), and *Debt and Dispossession: Farm Loss in America's Heartland* (Chicago: University of Chicago Press, 2000).

30 Judy Threet, from a transcript of the event recorded by the author, East Stroudsburg, PA, May 26, 2007. Threet's presentation was later published as an article, "The End of Our Golden Era?," *Guitarmaker*, no. 61 (Fall 2007): 50–60.

31 Davis Guggenheim's 2006 documentary film *An Inconvenient Truth* chronicles former vice president Al Gore's campaign to educate the world about the causes and consequences of global climate change.

32 As Mary Poovey points out, in today's world order "it is virtually impossible to imagine a definition of value that does not involve commodification" because finance capital has itself become a commodity, supplanting labor as the driving force of the global economy (412). Poovey, "For Everything Else, There's . . ." *Social Research* 68, no. 2 (Summer 2001): 397–426.

33 Writing with reference to women's contemporary crafting practices, Ann Cvetkovich argues that they are a "return to a different form of commodification or to different periods of commodification," which ultimately represent "another moment in a longstanding set of constituent tensions about the relationship between the premodern and the modern, women's culture and feminism, and handmade and industrial modes of production." For Cvetkovich, crafting is a "form of survival" that combats the enervating effects of the *political depression* caused by the intractable realities of today's socioeconomic order. Cvetkovich, *Depression: A Public Feeling* (Durham, NC: Duke University Press, 2012), 171–72, 155.

Chapter One

1 In *Producing Culture and Capital: Family Firms in Italy* (Princeton, NJ: Princeton University Press, 2002), Sylvia Yanagisako uses the term *origin narratives* to refer to the ways proprietors of Italian silk companies describe the founding of family-owned businesses. Despite individual differences, their stories shared an emphasis on visionary male founders and seamless patrilineal succession that overlooked women's economic contributions.

2 Charles Fox, interview with the author, Montreal, Quebec, July 8, 2007.

3 W. J. Rorabaugh, *The Craft Apprentice: From Franklin to the Machine Age in America* (New York: Oxford University Press, 1986).

4 On the cultural meaning of the frontier and westward expansion in the United States, see Henry Nash Smith, *Virgin Land: The American West as Symbol and Myth* (orig. 1950; Cambridge, MA: Harvard University Press, 1970).

5 Amy Kaplan shows how scholarly narratives of American exceptionalism rely on the notion of a "virgin land" to gloss over the imperial vision of geographical expansion and political domination that underwrote it. " 'Left Alone with America': The Absence of Empire in the Study of American Culture," in *Cultures of United States Imperialism*, ed. Amy Kaplan and Donald E. Pease (Durham, NC: Duke University Press, 1993), 3–21.

6 It was precisely luthiers' willingness to embrace "past" ways of operating in the "present" that gave their movement its countercultural appeal. In this sense, they opened themselves up to the cultural stigma and economic disadvantages of being associated with traditional societies and the politics of "tense" used to marginalize them. On the "tense of the other," see Elizabeth Povinelli, *Economies of Abandonment: Social Belonging and Endurance in Late Liberalism* (Durham, NC: Duke University Press, 2011).

7 On deindustrialization in the United States, see Barry Bluestone and Bennett Harrison's *The Deindustrialization of America: Plant Closings, Community Abandonment, and the Dismantling of Basic Industry* (New York: Basic Books, 1984) and *The Great U-Turn: Corporate Restructuring and the Polarizing of America* (New York: Basic Books, 1990).

8 Matthew Jacobson argues that Frederick Jackson Turner's 1893 "frontier thesis"— the idea that American democracy was forged in the experience of settling the land,

and that it was imperiled by the end of western expansion—became "impetus and rallying cry for the nation's late-century quest for overseas markets." *Barbarian Virtues: The United States Encounters Foreign Peoples at Home and Abroad, 1876–1917* (New York: Hill and Wang, 2000), 64–65. On current manifestations of empire, see David Harvey, *The New Imperialism* (Oxford: Oxford University Press, 2005).

9 The literature on rising inequality in America since the 1970s is vast. For an overview, see Steven Greenhouse, *The Big Squeeze: Tough Times for the American Worker* (New York: Alfred A. Knopf, 2008), and Timothy Noah, *The Great Divergence: America's Inequality Crisis and What We Can Do about It* (New York: Bloomsbury, 2012).

10 "On the one hand, information wants to be expensive," Stewart Brand said, "because it's so valuable. The right information in the right place just changes your life. On the other hand, information wants to be free, because the cost of getting it out is getting lower and lower all the time. So you have these two fighting against each other." "'Keep Designing': How the Information Economy Is Being Created and Shaped by the Hacker Ethic," *Whole Earth Review*, no. 46 (May 1985): 44–55.

11 Richard "R. E." Brune, interview with the author, Evanston, IL, August 9, 2009.

12 As Kevin and Moira Dawe observe, both the classical and the flamenco guitar have been important in Spanish culture since the medieval period. "Handmade in Spain: The Culture of Guitar Making," in *Guitar Cultures*, ed. Andy Bennett and Kevin Dawe (Oxford: Berg, 2001), 63–87.

13 Bruné's written account of this conversation employs slightly different language. "It'll be great, R E. We'll get everybody else to do all our research for us and get them locked in mortal combat with all the ivory-tower types while we skim off the best ideas and keep busy in our shops. Besides, we'll charge 'em money to belong." "In the Beginning," *American Lutherie*, no. 32 (Winter 1992): 25.

14 Fred Turner, *From Counterculture to Cyberculture: Stewart Brand, the Whole Earth Network, and the Rise of Digital Utopianism* (Chicago: University of Chicago Press, 2006), 5.

15 Tim Olsen, interview with the author, Santa Rosa, CA, August 19, 2007.

16 Deb Olsen recounts the guild's early history in "On the GAL's 40th Anniversary: How It All Began," *American Lutherie*, no. 111 (Fall 2012): 48–49.

17 The first issues of the *GAL Newsletter* were sent out in 1973. Consisting of legal-sized sheets of paper folded over and stapled at the center, the newsletter was a folksy amalgamation of member-contributed tips on instrument construction and tool use; reviews of books, issues, and events; reports on guild matters written by the president and editor; letters to the editor; and classified as well as member-sponsored ads. Starting in 1975, articles that addressed technical or instructional topics were published separately as a series of "data sheets," which were eventually reprinted and sold as bound sets. In 1984 publication of these materials ceased, and the quarterly journal *American Lutherie* appeared in 1985. Tim Olsen, foreword to *Lutherie Tools: Making Hand and Power Tools for Stringed Instrument Building*, ed. Tim Olsen and Cyndy Burton, GAL Resource Book (Tacoma, WA: Guild of American Luthiers, 1990).

18 Marshall Sahlins, *Stone Age Economics* (Chicago: Aldine, 1972).

19 When interviewed by Todd Brotherton in 1992, Olsen explained his objection to skill ratings as follows: "Initially this was because I was not about to do all the work to set up a system that would pronounce me inferior! . . . [But] this whole hierarchy thing is just a load of crap. That's why it was fun to mock it as a hippie teenager. From it

there drifts the foul stench of the arrogance and distrust that is an unfortunate part of our materialistic and competitive culture." Originally published in *American Lutherie*, no. 32, repr. in *The Big Red Book of American Lutherie* (Tacoma, WA: Guild of American Luthiers, 2004), 3:259.

20 Robert Hassan, *The Information Society* (Cambridge: Polity, 2008).

21 Information about the 1975 convention is drawn from two issues of the GAL *Newsletter*: 3, no. 1 (February 1975), and 3, no. 3 (May-June 1975).

22 Bon Henderson, "We Musta Been Nuts! A Nostalgic Look at the Guild's Early Years," *American Lutherie*, no. 32 (Winter 1992): 31.

23 Scott E. Antes, "Minutes: Guild Convention, 1975," *GAL Newsletter* 3, no. 3 (May-June 1975): 4.

24 The guild officially achieved this designation in 1983.

25 Italics in original. Bruné, "State of the Guild," *GAL Newsletter* 3, no. 1 (February 1975).

26 In *The Social Production of Indifference* (Chicago: University of Chicago Press, 1993), Michael Herzfeld applies the term *ethical alibi* to bureaucratic excuses for institutional failures. I use the term in a Goffmanesque sense to emphasize the moral cover that national museums gave middle-class youth who failed to pursue traditional careers. On the concept of "moral careers," see Erving Goffman, *Asylums* (New York: Anchor, 1961).

27 John Mello, interview with the author, Santa Rosa, CA, August 19, 2007.

28 Luthiers' understanding of distinction is consistent with Pierre Bourdieu's in *Distinction: A Social Critique of the Judgment of Taste*, trans. Richard Nice (Cambridge, MA: Harvard University Press, 1984), in the sense that both see it as a form of "cultural capital" associated with social status.

29 The "coolness" of guitars is also linked to the display of masculine heterosexuality that has historically been associated with playing guitars, banjos, and mandolins. As Jeffrey J. Noonan observes of the banjo, mandolin, and guitar movement in the United States between the 1880s and the 1930s, promotional advertising combined nostalgia for the "noble traits of the medieval court" with "the pursuit of a desirable woman by the musician/lover." *The Guitar in America: Victoria Era to Jazz Age* (Jackson: University Press of Mississippi, 2008), 100. By the 1960s, equation of the guitar with "coolness" also had a racial dimension, as white guitarists were keen to identify with the performance styles of black bluesmen. Fascination with "the sexual excess that African-American men were thought to embody," Steve Waksman argues, "found expression in rock's favored mode of phallocentric display, with the electric guitar as a privileged signifier of white male power and potency." *Instruments of Desire: The Electric Guitar and the Shaping of Musical Experience* (Cambridge, MA: Harvard University Press, 1999), 4–5.

30 The acoustic guitar can be said to magnetize what Lauren Berlant has termed an *intimate public*, a national sense of community that "flourishes as a porous, affective scene of identification among strangers that promises a certain experience of belonging and provides a complex of consolation, confirmation, discipline, and discussion about how to live as an x." *The Female Complaint: The Unfinished Business of Sentimentality in American Culture* (Durham, NC: Duke University Press, 2008), viii. However, rather than shoring up a feminine identity in relation to heteronormative experiences of romantic love, as it has in women's culture since the nineteenth century, I suggest that lutherie's intimate public arose in the 1970s to orient blue-

and white-collar men and women toward a nondominant masculinity grounded in a romantic conception of productive labor and sentimentalized experiences of work.

31 The acoustic guitar can be seen as a miniaturization of the cosmos as well the portal though which the infinite is imagined as a system of containment. As Susan Stewart writes, "Whereas we know the miniature as a special whole or as temporal parts, we know the gigantic only partially. . . . Consequently, both the miniature and the gigantic are metaphors of containment—the miniature as contained, the gigantic as container." *On Longing: Narratives of the Miniature, the Gigantic, the Souvenir, the Collection* (Durham. NC: Duke University Press, 1993), 71.

32 Michael Millard, interview with the author, Newfane, VT, September 28, 2006.

33 This argument is supported by research conducted by Christian G. Appy in *Working Class War: American Combat Soldiers and Vietnam* (Chapel Hill: University of North Carolina Press, 1993).

34 As music historian Elijah Wald points out, the lesser-known, least commercial black blues guitarists appealed primarily to white, not black, audiences. Yet as riveting as the repertoire of these musicians was to some whites, it was an acquired taste. Wald writes, "In the 60s, mainstream black blues buyers who stumbled across an LP reissue of [Robert Johnson's] work would have heard a guy who sounded like the old-fashioned countrified music their parents or grandparents might have liked. Meanwhile, young white fans were embracing the same recordings as the dark, mysterious, and fascinating roots of rock 'n' roll." *Escaping the Delta: Robert Johnson and the Invention of the Blues* (New York: Amistad, 2005), 220.

35 Bryan K. Carman argues that Walt Whitman embraced the "artisan republicanism" that came under attack with rapid industrialization during the nineteenth century, and that this vision of white male economic independence continues to inspire the figure of the "working-class hero" in the music of acoustic guitar troubadours. *A Race of Singers: Whitman's Working-Class Hero from Guthrie to Springsteen* (Chapel Hill: University of North Carolina Press), 2000.

36 A number of Gurian's early employees established themselves as independent builders—David Santo, David Rubio, Michael Millard, Thomas Humphrey, Jonathan Natelson, and William Cumpiano. Rick Davis, "The Pioneer: Michael Gurian's Life of Lutherie on the Third Planet from the Sun," *Fretboard Journal*, no. 5 (Spring 2007): 40–51.

37 On artisans' fight for independence in the nineteenth century see Sean Wilentz, *Chants Democratic: New York City and the Rise of the American Working Class, 1788–1850* (orig. 1984; New York: Oxford University Press, 2004), 102; David Montgomery, *Workers' Control in America* (Cambridge: Cambridge University Press, 1980), 13–15; and Rorabaugh, *Craft Apprentice*, 36–38, 42–48.

38 William R. Cumpiano and Jonathan D. Natelson, *Guitarmaking: Tradiation and Technology* (San Francisco: Chronicle Books, 1993.

39 Cumpiano described his publication ordeal for fellow luthiers in "The Story of Guitarmaking: Tradition and Technology," *American Lutherie*, 1989. The article is available on his website, accessed April 10, 2013, http://www.cumpiano.com/Home/Book/Bookhistory/bookhistory.html.

40 Frank Ford, interview with the author, Santa Rosa, CA, August 17, 2007.

41 These figures are taken from the text of the Martin Museum's exhibit "Acquisition and Diversification: 1970 to 1985."

42 Putting Gibson's production levels into perspective, Walter Carter observes that the company's single most popular acoustic model in the 1960s—the small, mahogany body LG-O—reached sales of 9,924 in 1964, a figure that was 50 percent higher than the total number of guitars produced by Martin that same year (6, 299). Carter, "Peak of Production," in *Gibson Guitars: 100 Years of an American Icon* (Nashville: Gibson Publishing, 1994), 233.

43 Under the Taft-Hartley Act, passed in 1947, individual states gained the authority to prohibit mandatory union membership. Twenty-two states, predominantly in the South and the western plains, passed laws that give employees the so-called right to work whether or not they join a union. Gibson had operated the Kalamazoo plant since 1917; Norlin decided to close it in 1983. A group of former employees eventually rented space in the plant to continue building guitars under the Heritage brand. Tom Mulhern, "The Long Decline," in *Gibson Guitars*, 260–61.

44 After a relatively brief attempt to recoup its fortunes by getting into the business of printing "stock certificates and other financial papers," Norlin merged with Pitney Bowes in 1993. Tom Mulhern, "The End of Norlin," in *Gibson Guitars*, 276–77.

45 Hugh Barker and Yuval Taylor argue that disco "came to challenge and undermine ideas of authenticity in contemporary rock music on every possible front." The critical variable in their analysis is how performers deal with the "gap between the person [they] think they are and the persona that others perceive." They conclude that "being yourself . . . simply can't be done." *Faking It: The Quest for Authenticity in Popular Music* (New York: W. W. Norton, 2007), 243–52. See also Richard A. Peterson, *Creating Country Music: Fabricating Authenticity* (Chicago: University of Chicago Press, 1999).

46 The charge that corporations had "turned their back on tradition" was a widespread refrain in the 1970s and 1980s, as well-known American companies were "milked" and dedicated workers were fired in a massive wave of plant closures. See Katherine Newman, *Falling from Grace: Downward Mobility in an Age of Affluence* (orig. 1988; Berkeley: University of California Press, 1999).

47 By the early 1970s, competition from Japan had effectively squeezed American guitar makers out of the low end of an increasingly global market for steel-string guitars. The two leading manufacturers of budget acoustics succumbed within five years of each other. Kay went bankrupt in 1969, and Harmony, which had set production records of almost 350,000 guitars a year in the mid-1960s, was out of business by 1974. Epiphone, Gibson's line of inexpensive acoustics, was moved to Japan in 1969, and C. F. Martin introduced Sigma, its low-priced line of Japanese-made acoustics, in 1970. Tom Mulheen, "The Quiet after Boom," in *Gibson Guitars*, 248.

48 Stephen Stills's willingness to pay top dollar for Martin Dreadnoughts is frequently credited (or blamed) for the rapid run up in the price they command. George Gruhn, "The Vintage Backlash," in *Gibson Guitars*, 267–69.

49 George Gruhn, interview with the author, Montreal, Quebec, June 27, 2008.

50 In Greek mythology, Pandora was made of clay by the god of artisans and drawn by curiosity to open a "box" or earthenware jar against Zeus's orders. Jennifer Neils, "The Girl in the Pithos: Hesiod's Elpis," in *Periklean Athens and Its Legacy: Problems and Perspectives*, ed. J. M. Barringer and J. M. Hurwit (Austin: University of Texas Press, 2005), 37–45.

51 Ren Ferguson, interview with the author, Guilford, CT, August 27, 2008.

52 Kay had been a leading supplier of inexpensive guitars to department stores since the

1930s, but competition from Japanese imports forced the company to close in 1968. Ferguson and his business partner Rob Ehlers purchased Kay's stock from C. Bruno and Sons, a musical instrument wholesaler.

53 Richard Sennett taps into this ahistorical discourse when he defines craftsmanship as "an enduring, basic human impulse . . . to do a job well for its own sake." This allows him to extend the term beyond "skilled manual labor" to include the work of computer programmers, doctors, artists, parents, and citizens. *The Craftsman* (New Haven, CT: Yale University Press, 2008), 9.

54 Existential thinking underwrote countercultural ideologies on both the left and the right during the 1960s. Doug Rossinow, *The Politics of Authenticity: Liberalism, Christianity, and the New Left in America* (New York, NY: Columbia University Press, 1998).

55 Dick Boak, "The Cage," *Stories*, accessed September 10, 2010, http://www.dickboak.com/dickboak_website/Stories.html.

56 Dick Boak, interview with the author, Nazareth, PA, October 19, 2006.

57 Jim Hatlo, "On the Beat," *Frets Magazine*, 1986.

58 Gila Eban was also elected to the 1987 board. "Lawsuit Settled," *American Lutherie*, no. 13 (Spring 1988): 59. Prior to the court's decision, Dick Boak, Duane Waterman, and others attempted to set up a "Colorado Guild," but after the settlement, this group disbanded.

59 Bruce Ross, letters to the editor, *Frets*, January 1987, 6.

60 That statement read as follows: "The goals of the association provide for but are not limited to: the establishment of a comprehensive database of resources, supplies and technical information; a means of providing multi-level education within the profession; assistance in marketing and promotion; health and insurance packages at group rates; a repair or service certification; an advertiser's marketplace; and the publication of informative newsletters and journals." *ASIA Newsletter*, no. 6 (March 1990): 2.

61 The board felt that this was a more "honest representation" of the "true intent of the association." "ASIA Business," *ASIA Newsletter*, no. 6 (March 1990): 17. As legal categories, both 501(c)(3) and 501(c)(6) designate nonprofit, tax-exempt organizations; the former includes religious, charitable, educational, scientific, and literary organizations, the latter, business leagues of various kinds.

62 The association did create a code of ethics for luthiers. Written by Grit Laskin, these guidelines emphasized information sharing, collegiality, and customer relations. "The ASIA Code of Ethics," *Guitarmaker*, no. 21 (September 1993): 22–23.

63 Bob Taylor, e-mail correspondence with the author, November 3, 2009. His talk was titled "CAD, CNC, and Acoustic Guitars."

64 Juszkiewicz's partners were David Barryman and Gary Zebrowski. Tom Mulheen, "Harvard Boys to the Rescue," in *Gibson Guitars*, 281.

65 Started by Stuart Mossman in 1965, the company had become an esteemed maker of Dreadnought guitars, which were popular with country and bluegrass flat-pickers. Mossman had bounced back from a fire that destroyed the factory's entire supply of Brazilian rosewood in 1976 to reach a production peak of 150 guitars a month in 1976. But the company never fully recovered from an incident in 1977, when a stock of 1,200 guitars stored in a warehouse in Nevada was damaged by the distributor's lack of temperature and humidity controls. By 1986, reeling from back-to-back recessions and ill health due to years of inhaling sawdust, lacquer fumes, and abalone

shell fragments, Mossman was ready to call it quits. He sold his business to Scott Baxendale, a former employee, who moved the company to Dallas in the late 1980s. Eric C. Shoaf, "Mossman Guitars: Triumph over Tragedy," *Vintage Guitar Magazine*, September 1997.

66 Stan Jay confirms that he urged Juszkiewicz to buy Flatiron Mandolins, personal correspondence with the author, March 14, 2013.

Chapter Two

1 The classic sociological studies on the importance of "weak" social ties for generating employment opportunities are Mark Granovetter, "The Strength of Weak Ties," *American Journal of Sociology* 78, no. 6 (1973): 1360–80, and *Getting a Job: A Study of Contacts and Careers* (Cambridge, MA: Harvard University Press, 1974).

2 Frank Ford, interview with the author, Santa Rosa, CA, August 17, 2007.

3 For more on Olson guitars and other luthiers in Minnesota, see Todd Lundborg, "Stars of the North," *Fretboard Journal*, no. 4 (Winter 2006): 82–99.

4 Joshua Gamson makes a persuasive case for understanding stardom as an interaction between the structured meaning of the cultural object and the constructive activities of the audience, in *Claims to Fame: Celebrity in Contemporary America* (Berkeley: University of California Press, 1994).

5 I draw upon Lauren Berlant's definition of an "object of desire" as "a cluster of promises we want someone or something to make to us and make possible for us." *Cruel Optimism* (Durham, NC: Duke University Press, 2011), 23.

6 Jeff Traugott, interview with author, Santa Rosa, CA, August 18, 2007.

7 Richard Johnston, "A Guitar Is Born: An Inside Look at the Making of a Steel String," *Acoustic Guitar*, June 1995.

8 Michael Herzfeld's ethnography of Greek artisans who preserve traditional crafts demonstrates the economic dangers of being perceived as marginal to modernity and global capitalism. *The Body Politic: Artisans and Artifice in the Global Hierarchy of Value* (Chicago: University of Chicago Press, 2003).

9 As Karen Hebert shows, "quality commodities" can have a paradoxical nature. Although upscale consumers prefer wild salmon, they expect it to conform to the aesthetic and technical norms set by the farmed-salmon industry. "In Pursuit of Singular Salmon: Paradoxes of Sustainability and the Quality Commodity," *Science and Culture* 19, no. 4 (2010): 553–81.

10 I refer to Erving Goffman's classic work on the dramaturgy of impression management, *The Presentation of Self in Everyday Life* (New York: Anchor Books, 1959).

11 In 2004 Traugott made Brazilian rosewood standard on all orders, effectively raising his base price by $7,000.

12 Jeff Traugott, from a transcript of the author's recording of the event, Montreal, Quebec, June 28, 2008.

13 James Olson, interview with the author, Circle Pines, Minnesota, July 25, 2009.

14 Irving Sloan's *Classical Guitar Construction* (New York: Dutton, 1966) is often mentioned as the first and only book aspiring guitar makers could find. Arthur Overholtzer's *Classic Guitar Making* (Chico, CA: Lawrence A. Brock, 1974) was a close second, although makers are quick to say that both books had their limitations and idiosyncrasies.

15 The term *manly flaws* comes from Elliott Liebow, who applied it to boasts about virile

sexual behavior on the part of unemployed African American men whose peer group validated their masculinity according to criteria other than mainstream economic success. *Tally's Corner: A Study of Negro Streetcorner Men* (orig. 1967; New York: Rowman and Littlefield, 2003).

16 Carrie M. Lane's ethnography of unemployment among men following the implosion of the dot-com industry in the 2000s is a case in point. As long as they adopted a "career management" ethos in which they took responsibility for their fate and actively sought pathways back into the market, they could count on the support of their heterosexual spouses. *A Company of One: Insecurity, Independence, and the New World of White-Collar Unemployment* (Ithaca, NY: Cornell University Press, 2011).

17 I am grateful to Chloe Taft and Aidan Grano for sharing their understanding of Reformed theology with me.

18 The term *commodity situation* is used by Arjun Appadurai to acknowledge that objects of exchange move into and out of different "social" situations over the course of their "life," only one of which may involve being commodified by market exchange. "Commodities and the Politics of Value," in *The Social Life of Things: Commodities in Cultural Perspective*, ed. Arjun Appadurai (Cambridge: Cambridge University Press, 1986), 3–63.

19 On singularization and diversion from market exchange as modes of decommodification see ibid. and Igor Kopytoff, "The Cultural Biography of Things: Commodification as a Process," also in *Social Life of Things*, 64–91. On singularization and qualification as emergent mechanisms of competition in the new "economy of qualities" that characterizes the postindustrial era, see Michael Callon, Cécile Méadel, and Vololona Rabeharisoa, "The Economy of Qualities," *Economy and Society* 31, no. 2 (May 2002): 194–217.

20 I make this point in *Debt and Dispossession: Farm Loss in America's Heartland* (Chicago: University of Chicago Press, 2000) when I describe the dynamics of the forced sale of farm equipment at foreclosure auctions during the farm crisis of the 1980s.

21 Clifford Geertz, "Deep Play: Notes on the Balinese Cockfight," in *The Interpretation of Cultures* (New York: Basic Books, 1973), 433.

22 As Geertz observes, the Balinese cockfight "provides a meta-social commentary upon the whole matter of assorting human beings into fixed hierarchical ranks and then organizing the major part of collective existence around that assortment." Or, as he puts it in his famous formulation: "[The cockfight] is a Balinese reading of Balinese experience; a story they tell themselves about themselves." Ibid., 448.

23 The Martin family settled in New York City upon arrival from Mark Neukirchen in 1833. In 1839 they came to Nazareth, where C. F. Martin built guitars in a barn north of town before moving into the North Street factory in 1859. Jim Washburn and Richard Johnston, *Martin Guitars: An Illustrated Celebration of America's Premier Guitarmaker* (Pleasantville, NY: Reader's Digest, 1997), 33, 40, 49. For a fascinating study of how C. F. Martin established and expanded his business during the first half of the nineteenth century, see Philip F. Gura, *C. F. Martin and His Guitars* (Chapel Hill: University of North Carolina Press, 2005).

24 Danny Brown, interview with the author, Nazareth, PA, October 19, 2006.

25 On corporate personhood and the legal history behind it, see Thom Hartmann, *Unequal Protection: How Corporations Became "People"—and How You Can Fight Back*, 2nd ed. (New York: Berrett-Koehler, 2010).

26 The strike brought production to a virtual standstill for eight months in 1977–78, as craftspeople accustomed to managing their own work schedules balked at the company's efforts to impose new restrictions on holiday and vacation time, among other things. Although workers eventually returned to the factory, mistrust of management lingered, especially among older workers who recalled the respect and autonomy accorded to them in earlier years. Martin company historians, however, dismiss the causes of the dispute as "trivial." Washburn and Johnston, *Martin Guitars*, 206.

27 According to Richard Johnston and Dick Boak, C. F. Martin was "almost solely responsible for getting his grandson a position of authority in the company after Frank's ouster," and when the company's stock was evaluated at his death auditors recommended liquidating the 153-year-old company. *Martin Guitars: A History* (Milwaukee, WI: Hal Leonard, 2008), 155–59. See also Washburn and Johnston, *Martin Guitars*, 213–14.

28 Susan Sontag, "Notes on 'Camp,'" in *Against Interpretation: And Other Essays* (orig. 1964; New York: Picador, 2001).

29 Martin's factory tour has been named by USA Today as the most popular of its kind in the United States. *Sound Board* 21 (July 2006): 6.

30 Johnston and Boak, *Martin Guitars*, 193.

31 Dick Boak, from a transcript of the Martin factory tour recorded by the author, Nazareth, PA, October 19, 2006.

32 George Gruhn uses the term *archetype* to describe these instruments. George Gruhn, interview with the author, Montreal, Quebec, June 27, 2008. The "orchestra model" is the OOO body size with a longer string length.

33 Washburn and Johnston, *Martin Guitars*, 122, see also 120–25. August Larson is credited with making the first guitar designed for the use of steel strings. His patent, dated July 12, 1904, expanded C. F. Martin's X-bracing pattern with additional laminated and hardwood reinforcement. Martin made some specially ordered flattop steel string guitars around this time but did not redesign the 2-17 for steel strings until 1922. Robert Carl Hartman, *Guitars and Mandolins in America: Featuring the Larsons' Creations* (Hoffman Estates, IL: Maurer, 1984).

34 Washburn and Johnston, *Martin Guitars*, 134.

35 Both instruments were made to the specifications of the artists' original instruments, but the inlay of Autry's name on the fretboard was optional. Johnston and Boak, *Martin Guitars*, 173–74.

36 Ibid., 176.

37 On Frank Martin's penchant for alcohol and women and the claim that the guitar company was used as a "cash cow," see Washburn and Johnston, *Martin Guitars*, 192, 203.

38 Whatever his personal failings may have been, Frank Martin acted in concert with others of his social class as he groped for a strategy to address the crisis of capital accumulation that engulfed the world's economies at the end of the 1960s. As David Harvey has argued, the precipitous decline—from 1965 to the mid-1970s—in the value of assets held by the wealthiest Americans forced them to devise new ways of accumulating capital and pursue new policies that would restore their economic power. "The capitalist world," Harvey observes, "stumbled towards neoliberalization as the answer [to the accumulation crisis] through a series of gyrations and

chaotic experiments that really only emerged as a new orthodoxy . . . in the 1990s." *A Brief History of Neoliberalism* (Oxford: Oxford University Press, 2007), 13–16.

39 In 1971, to reduce the number of instruments returned to the company for repair, Martin began using a large rosewood bridge plate to stabilize the top and bridge, effectively dampening the tone. Washburn and Johnston, *Martin Guitars*, 202.

40 Chris Martin is quoted in ibid., 215.

41 Johnston and Boak, *Martin Guitars*, 193.

42 The patriarchal bias of the "origin narratives" constructed for family firms is discussed by Sylvia Junko Yanagisako in *Producing Culture and Capital: Family Firms in Italy* (Princeton, NJ: Princeton University Press, 2002).

43 Dick Boak, from a transcript of the Martin factory tour recorded by the author, Nazareth, PA, October 19, 2006.

44 I thank Seth Moglen for discussing labor history in the Lehigh Valley with me. On the industrial employment of women in the textile industry in the United States and globally, see Jane L. Collins, *Threads: Gender, Labor, and Power* (Chicago: University of Chicago Press, 2003).

45 The classic account of the commodity was articulated by Karl Marx in "The Fetishism of the Commodity and Its Secret," in *Capital: A Critique of Political Economy*, trans. Ben Fowkes (orig. 1867; New York: Penguin Books, 1976), 1:163–77. In Marx's analysis, commodities appear to have a "life of their own" because the human labor that made them has been objectified as a factor of production. Marx used the term *fetishism* to describe the perception that commodities have power over their human creators—compelling them to work in order to acquire them. But the concept of fetishism that Marx used was a product of the colonial encounter in Africa, where it operated to impose Enlightenment rationality on what European traders considered "primitive" superstitions. As an analytical concept, it has long been biased against noncapitalist modes of relating to nonhuman nature. On the history of the fetish concept, see William Pietz, "The Problem of the Fetish, I," *Anthropology and Aesthetics*, no. 9 (Spring 1985): 5–17; "The Problem of the Fetish II: The Origin of the Fetish," *Anthropology and Aesthetics*, no. 13 (Spring 1987): 23–45; and "The Problem of the Fetish, III: Bosman's Guinea and the Enlightenment Theory of Fetishism," *Anthropology and Aesthetics*, no. 16 (Autumn 1988): 105–24.

Chapter Three

1 "Malescapes" was on exhibition at the Tria Gallery from January 8 to February 7, 2009. The featured artists were Daniel Anderson, Paul Hunter, ChungHwan Park, Antonio Puri, and Erick Sanchez.

2 Linda Manzer, from a transcript of the author's recording of the event, New York City, January 22, 2009.

3 Lewis Hyde, *The Gift* (orig. 1983; New York: Vintage, 2007), 59–60.

4 Hyde argues that artists have a dual capacity to both "disengage from the work and think of it as a commodity" in order to price it at fair market value and to "forget all that and serve [their] gifts on their own terms." Ibid., 360.

5 My formulation of the discourse of gifted labor owes much to John Frow's analysis of the cultural tension between the commodity form and the production of aesthetic goods. As he argues, a paradox in "the concept of the unique and self-determining person—precisely what most seems to resist the commodity form—lies at the basis

of values of singularity and originality that are central to the market in industrially produced aesthetic goods." *Time and Commodity Culture: Essays on Cultural Theory and Postmodernity* (New York: Oxford University Press, 1997), 144–47.

6 Marshall Berman, *The Politics of Authenticity: Radical Individualism and the Emergence of Modern Society* (orig. 1970; New York: Verso, 2009), 163–64.

7 Linda Manzer, interview with the author, Toronto, Ontario, October 30, 2006.

8 Gift exchange systems were seen in classic anthropological accounts as "primitive" precursors to "modern" market economies. The evolutionary model presumed that gift economies are incompatible with, and superseded by, market exchange. Not until feminist scholarship revealed the gendered aspects of gift-giving systems, and material culture studies recognized the impermanence of the commodity situation, have scholars begun to acknowledge the systemic interrelationships between gifts and commodities. On the classic view, see Bronislaw Malinowski, *Argonauts of the Western Pacific* (London: Routledge, 1932); Marcel Mauss, *The Gift: The Form and Reason for Exchange in Archaic Societies* (orig. 1950; London: Routledge, 1990); Marshall Sahlins, *Stone Age Economics* (London: Routledge, 1974).

9 Muriel Anderson, from a transcript of the author's recording of the event, Montreal, Quebec, July 3, 2009.

10 Linda Manzer, "The Making of the Metheny-Manzer Signature 6 Limited Edition Series," from a transcript of the author's recording of the event, Montreal, Quebec, July 3, 2009.

11 While roping the binding with surgical tubing involves use of a "modern" material, the method is still considered "traditional." It has been used by Spanish classical guitar makers since the eighteenth century and was used by the Martin Company up through the prewar period.

12 As Susan Terrio observes in her study of French chocolate makers, cultural authenticity is "not a pre-determined essence but an ongoing struggle whose meaning depends on the perceptions and practices of those who claim it." *Crafting the Culture and History of French Chocolate* (Berkeley: University of California Press, 2000), 15–17.

13 Artisanal guitar makers resemble studio furniture makers in their emphasis on the need for tactile and aural contact with tone wood. As Edward S. Cooke et al. observe of the early studio furniture movement in the 1940s and 1950s, the "essential aspect of craft" is not the rejection of machine tools per se but "reverence for wood as a primary material" and "maintenance of individual control over the process of fabrication from beginning to end, from the mind of the creator to the home of the consumer." *The Maker's Hand: American Studio Furniture, 1940–1990* (Boston: Museum of Fine Arts, 2003), 27–29.

14 David Pye describes this difference as one between the "workmanship of risk" and the "workmanship of certainty." As he writes, "An operative, applying the workmanship of certainty, cannot spoil the job. A workman using the workmanship of risk assisted by no matter what machine-tools and jigs, can do so at any minute. That is the essential difference. The risk is real." Pye defines "craftsmanship" as workmanship "using any kind of technique or apparatus in which the quality of the result is not predetermined, but depends on the judgment, dexterity and care which the maker exercises as he works." *The Nature and Art of Workmanship* (Cambridge: Cambridge University Press, 1968), 20–22.

15 Lewis Hyde puts the matter well: "A gift isn't fully realized until it is given away.

Those who will not acknowledge gratitude or who refuse to labor in its service neither free their gifts nor really come to possess them" (*Gift*, 63).

16 Four years after developing the design, she presented a detailed explanation of it at the 1989 Symposium of the Association of Stringed Instrument Artisans (ASIA) and in an interview published the same year by the *Experimental Musical Instruments* journal (EMI 4, no. 6). Manzer, "The Wedge: Invented in 1984—Now Standard on Manzer Guitars," accessed January 31, 2010, http://www.manzer.com/guitars/index.php?option=com_content&view=article&id=12&Itemid=15.

17 As Charles Lindholm writes, "There are two overlapping modes for characterizing any entity as authentic: genealogical or historical (origin) and identity or correspondence (content). Authentic objects, persons, and collectives are what they purport to be, their roots are known and verified, their essence and appearance are one." *Culture and Authenticity* (London: Wiley-Blackwell, 2007), 2.

18 On the distinction between design, workmanship, and craftsmanship, see Howard Risatti, *A Theory of Craft: Function and Aesthetic Expression* (Chapel Hill: University of North Carolina Press, 2007), 162–70. I concur with Risatti that artisanship (what he calls "craftsmanship") involves a combination of technical manual skill (workmanship) and abstract creative design. However, as I argue in this chapter, this dual capacity can be demonstrated only through the embodied enactment of a cultural repertoire.

19 As Richard Sennett observes, automation "depriv[es] people themselves from learning through repetition." *The Craftsman* (New Haven, CT: Yale University Press, 2009), 39–44.

20 Taylor's history with CNC is recounted by Michael John Simmons in *Taylor Guitars: Thirty Years of an American Classic* (Bergkirchen, Germany: PPVMEDIEN, 2003), 145, 148.

21 Ibid., 151, 153.

22 Bob Taylor, interview with the author, El Cajon, California, August 11, 2009.

23 Irving Sloan, *Classical Guitar Construction* (New York: Dutton, 1966).

24 Taylor's father was an enlisted man in the navy; his mother was a seamstress who worked at home. Ibid, 14.

25 Ibid., 55.

26 Taylor history is available on the company's website, "From the Beginning . . . ," accessed February 9, 2010, http://www.taylorguitars.com/history/essay.html.

27 The importance of Prince's guitar is recounted on Taylor's website, "Purple Reign," under "Timeline," accessed February 11, 2009, http://www.taylorguitars.com/history/timeline/year.asp?year=1984.

28 To the extent that industrial manufacturers are uninterested in the complex interdependencies that preoccupy artisanal makers, they employ a schematic vision that resonates with the broad-scale planning projects of imperial nation-states. See James C. Scott, *Seeing like a State: How Certain Schemes to Improve the Human Condition Have Failed* (New Haven, CT: Yale University Press, 1998).

29 My analysis of the dramaturgy of artisans' commercial transactions has benefited from Kaja Silverman's analysis of classic Hollywood cinema and the "discursive impotence" that characterizes viewers' exclusion from the site of filmic production. Silverman argues that the conventions of classic cinema allow the male viewer to enjoy "invisibility, omniscience, and discursive power" insofar as he disavows iden-

tification with the filmic spectacle of the female voice and body. *The Acoustic Mirror: The Female Voice in Psychoanalysis and Cinema* (Bloomington: Indiana University Press, 1988), 39, 99, 164. The theatricalization of the artisan's body, I suggest, can operate in a similar fashion to affirm the superiority of industrial production, but it can also offer the observer a point of identification with a body fantasized to be the unproblematic origin of individual agency and human making.

30 As literary critic Susan Stewart observes, souvenirs are acquired "to serve as traces of authentic experience," not solely for their intrinsic worth or usefulness: "the souvenir speaks to a context of origin through a language of longing, for it is not an object arising out of need or use value; it is an object arising out of the necessarily insatiable demands of nostalgia." *On Longing* (Durham, NC: Duke University Press, 1993), 135.

31 Richard Hoover, interview with author, Santa Cruz, CA, August 17, 2009.

32 Hoover studied with Bruce McGuire, a builder who had apprenticed with Arthur E. Overholtzer, author of *Classic Guitar Making* (Boulder: Brock, 1974).

33 Davis left the partnership eighteen months later; Ross and Hoover worked together for twelve years.

34 Michel de Certeau, *The Practice of Everyday Life* (Berkeley: University of California Press, 1988), 69, emphasis mine.

35 Nitrocellulose lacquer is applied in multiple coats, each of which is sanded flat to produce a final finish that is thin, durable, and repairable if necessary. In contrast to the time-consuming effort of lacquer, or "nitro" as it is sometimes called, some guitar makers have turned to fast-drying polyurethane finishes that do not require multiple coats or sanding. Purists tend to reject poly finishes as "glassy," sound-dampening, and difficult to repair.

36 Andy Mueller, interview with author, Newfane, VT, August 28, 2006.

37 Michael Millard, interview with the author, Newfane, VT, August 28, 2006.

38 By characterizing artisanal guitars as a "sentient subject in formation," I am drawing an explicit parallel between luthiers' relationship to the guitar and the process of subject formation as theorized by Judith Butler in *Giving an Account of Oneself* (New York: Fordham University Press, 2005).

39 My recognition of cross-species communication in lutherie and builders' intimate connection with wood is influenced by the posthumanism of Donna J. Haraway in work such as *When Species Meet* (Minneapolis: University of Minnesota Press, 2008) and the speculative realism and object-oriented ontology of work such as Ian Bogost's *Alien Phenomenology, or What It's Like to Be a Thing* (Minneapolis: University of Minnesota Press, 2012). What this scholarship has in common is an effort to decenter humans as the ultimate arbiters of what can be said to exist and have experiences.

40 *Hootenanny* aired on ABC from April 1963 to September 1964.

41 John Greven, interview with the author, Portland, OR, July 22, 2009.

42 Several builders recall being influenced by Betty Edwards's *Drawing on the Right Side of the Brain* (orig. 1979; New York: Tarcher/Penguin, 2012), a best-selling book that promised to help the artistically challenged access and express their right-brained, "creative self."

43 To the extent that the opposition associated with brain lateralization is culturally coded as one between masculine and feminine tendencies, recourse to neuroanatomical destiny is also used to mark and negotiate normative gender roles and pre-

dispositions. On postwar masculinity and its emphasis on self-mastery and control over the environment, see Susan Faludi, *Stiffed: The Betrayal of the American Man* (New York: Harper Perennial, 2000).

44 Heather Paxson makes the point that the development of a "trained palate" in artisanal cheese making involves the sensory apprehension of "perfection" as a "customary" rather than "platonic" form. That is, artisans are not aiming to produce a tone or a taste that can be standardized according to objective criteria, but rather to satisfy their customers' desire for novelty and variation within a spectrum of culturally recognized formal possibilities. *The Life of Cheese* (Berkeley: University of California Press, 2012), 156.

45 As Douglas Harper shows in his ethnographic portrait of Willie, a mechanic who runs a motor vehicle repair garage, the body's kinesthetic awareness of materials constitutes a form of knowledge in its own right. Difficult to attain because it cannot be conveyed in words, "working knowledge" "reduces the gap between the subject—the worker—and the object—the work." *Working Knowledge: Skill and Community in a Small Shop* (Chicago: The University of Chicago Press, 1987), 133.

46 Tim Brookes offers moving testimony to the limited life span of the artisanal guitar based on his experience of having one built for him by the (now) Portland-based luthier Rick Davis. *Guitar: An American Life* (New York: Grove, 2005), 196–97.

47 Diana Taylor opposes the concept of the "repertoire" to that of the "archive" in her analysis of cultural performances. While this distinction is a useful one, it does not account for the cultural product of ritualized knowledge such as lutherie, which also materializes its repertoire in an archive composed of craft objects. *The Archive and the Repertoire: Performing Cultural Memory in the Americas* (Durham, NC: Duke University Press, 2003), 20–21.

48 On the history of romantic science, see Richard Holmes, *The Age of Wonder: The Romantic Generation and the Discovery of Beauty and Terror of Science* (New York: Vintage, 2009).

Chapter Four

1 Alan Carruth, interview with the author, Newport, NH, June 18, 2007.

2 Alan Carruth, "Free Plate Tuning," in *Big Red Book of Lutherie* (Tacoma, WA: Guild of American Luthiers, 2004), 3:138–72. This three-part article originally appeared in *American Lutherie*, no. 28 (1991); no. 29 (1992); and no. 30 (1992).

3 The amplitudes Carruth illustrates are based on tests he conducted with a microphone one meter away from the soundboard. My account of this interview is augmented with information contained in Carruth's published article "The 'Corker' Guitar: A Sideport Experiment," *American Lutherie*, no. 94 (Summer 2008): 56–62.

4 Tim Olsen writes: "Our 'right way is a myth' slogan [is] something inflammatory that the young me wrote to try to keep people open to the idea that they really did have something valuable to share. It was meant to confront the lazy notion that there was an elite group of people somewhere that had everything properly figured out. As part of our magazine front matter, it has been revised now and then, but that phrase has always seemed to be right, so we keep using it. I'd say the past thirty-plus years have proven it out pretty well. I took a quick look at our back issues and saw that wording used in our volume 4, 1977. That's pretty much the very beginning." Personal communication, May 18, 2010. See also Tim Olsen, "The 'Right Way' Is a Myth," *American Lutherie*, no. 111 (Fall 2012): 59.

5 Carruth studied with Thomas Knatt in West Concord, MA, in 1973.

6 For a discussion of side ports, see Cyndy Burton, "There's a Hole in the Bucket," *American Lutherie*, no. 91 (Fall 2007): 6–7; John Monteleone, "Sideways," *American Lutherie*, no. 91 (Fall 2007): 8–10; Mike Doolin, "Herr Helmholtz' Tube," *American Lutherie*, no. 91 (Fall 2007): 11.

7 Carruth, "'Corker' Guitar."

8 The Catgut Acoustical Society was founded in 1963 by Carleen Hutchins, a former high school science teacher turned violinmaker. When Carruth met her, Hutchins was perfecting the use of free plate tuning in violinmaking, and Fred Dickens, an engineer at AT&T/Bell Labs who built classical guitars as an avocation, was extending this technique to research on the guitar. Paul R. Laird, "The Life and Work of Carleen Maley Hutchins," *Ars Musica Denver* 6, no. 1 (Fall 1993), http://www.catgutacoustical.org/people/cmh/index.htm.

9 Carruth's metaphor of navigating city streets resonates with Michel de Certeau's analysis of "walking in the city" as the creative experience of a placeless "space of enunciation." *The Practice of Everyday Life* (Berkeley: University of California Press, 1988), 98.

10 Mark Blanchard, from his typescript of the lecture which he shared with me. The talk was given in Santa Rosa, California, on August 19, 2007.

11 Ernst Chladni discovered his patterns in 1782 and published information about his technique in *Entdeckungen über die Theorie des Klanges* (Discoveries in the theory of sound, 1787).

12 Maria J. Trumpler, "Questioning Nature: Experimental Investigations of Animal Electricity in Germany, 1791–1810," PhD diss., Yale University, 1992.

13 In 1797 the German naturalist and explorer Alexander von Humbolt declared Chladni's experimental evidence of the physical properties of sound to be "the greatest discovery of the century"; quoted in ibid.

14 The only way to change a modal pattern, Blanchard discovered, is to alter the shape of the top. Thus he uses his initial Chladni patterns to select the best wood for the particular shape of the guitar under construction.

15 The effort to make the feminized nonhuman "speak," from a psychoanalytic perspective, could be said to enact a gendered scenario in which the guitar maker shores up a masculine identity by projecting feminine aspects of the self—including emotionality and voice—onto the craft object. In this analysis, the notion that wood has a voice of its own would be the result of fetishization. In *The Acoustic Mirror: The Female Voice in Psychoanalysis and Cinema* (Bloomington: Indiana University Press, 1988), Kaja Silverman identifies this scenario in classic Hollywood films. Insofar as luthiers attribute agency as well as voice to their wood, I suggest, they endeavor to disrupt this cultural script.

16 The work of Bruno Latour has greatly influenced my view of the lutherie workshop as a laboratory in which tone wood, as a nonhuman "actant," makes itself known to humans and petitions for entry into the collectivity. See Bruno Latour and Steven Woolgar, *Laboratory Life: The Construction of Scientific Facts* (orig. 1979; Princeton, NJ: Princeton University Press, 1986), and Bruno Latour, *Pandora's Hope: Essays on the Reality of Science Studies* (Cambridge, MA: Harvard University Press, 1999).

17 Deflection testing is a method used to gauge the stiffness of a soundboard by measuring and recording the movement caused by the application of weight. See

David C. Hurd, *Left-Brain Lutherie: Using Physics and Engineering Concepts for Building Guitar Family Instruments* (Westport, CT: Bold Strummer, 2004).

18 Sianne Ngai, *Ugly Feelings* (Cambridge, MA: Harvard University Press, 2005), 43. Italics in original.

19 As Ngai observes, the concept of tone is "ideally suited to the analysis of ideology, which, as the materially embodied representation of an *imaginary relationship* to a holistic complex of real conditions, clearly shares tone's virtual, diffused, but also immanent character" (ibid., 47).

20 On the romantic sense of wonder, see Richard Holmes, *The Age of Wonder: How the Romantic Generation Discovered the Beauty and Terror of Science* (New York: Random House, 2008).

21 As Jeff Dolven argues, "instruction [is] a representational problem with two aspects: the representation of knowledge, and of knowing; what the stuff being taught looks like, and what it looks like to learn it." *Scenes of Instruction in Renaissance Romance* (University of Chicago Press, 2007), 11.

22 Fred Carlson, interview with author, Santa Rosa, CA, August 19, 2007.

23 The Goddard professor was Dennis Murphy. For more on Carlson's life, see Tim Olsen, "Meet the Maker: Fred Carlson," *Big Red Book of Lutherie*, no. 5, 18–25, orig. pub. *American Lutherie*, no. 49, 1997.

24 Michael Herzfeld argues that analogical learning is the most important way apprentices acquire knowledge in an artisanal workshop. *The Body Impolitic: Artisans and Artifice in the Global Hierarchy of Value* (Chicago: University of Chicago Press, 2004), 105–7.

25 The first was Juan Roberto Guitar Works, which opened in Phoenix, AZ, in 1969.

26 An account of Fred Carlson's experience at Earthworks can be found in his article "A Tale of Two Schools," *American Lutherie*, no. 53 (Spring 1998): 27.

27 Fred Carlson's cooperative workshop was featured in an article in the *New York Times*. See David Duncan, "In Pursuit of Music in Vermont," May 19, 1985.

28 Tony Duggan-Smith, interview with the author, Montreal, Quebec, July 4, 2009.

29 Eric Nagler, "Biography," accessed June 24, 2013, http://www.ericnagler.com/.

30 Among the first cohort of luthiers to embark upon factory production were Augustino LoPrinzi in Plainsboro, NJ; Michael Gurian in Hinsdale, NH; Bob Taylor in Lemon Grove, CA; John and Don Gallagher in Wartrace, TN; and Stuart Mossman in Winfield, KS.

31 At the age of twenty in 1967, Larrivée served a year-long apprenticeship with the German-born Edgar Mönch in Toronto. It is through Mönch and Larrivée that Canadian builders trace their genealogy to Antonio Torres, the "father" of the modern classical guitar. Prior to moving to Toronto, Mönch had been conscripted into the German army and spent most of World War II in a British prisoner of war camp. While there, he learned guitar making from Marcello Barbero of Barcelona. Barbero had been a student of José Ramirez II, and the Ramirez "tree" goes back to Torres. Grit Laskin, interview with the author, Toronto, October 29, 2006, and Ken Donnell, "Lutherie Bloodlines," *Frets Magazine*, September 1985, 19.

32 Apprentices Michael Jones and George Gray also followed Larrivée to Vancouver. Michael Schreiner and David Wren remained in Toronto, both opening shops of their own.

33 Tony Duggan-Smith, "On Luthiery Apprenticeships," *Mel Bay's Guitar Sessions Online*

Magazine, April 2007, accessed June 28, 2009, http://www.guitarsessions.com/apr07/guitar_maker.asp.

34 The "habitual" modes of self-presentation that North American artisans must come to terms with are specific to entrepreneurial cultures in the United States and Canada. For an ethnographic study of artisanal self-fashioning in Japan that emphasizes the dynamic interplay between workplace identities and cultural conceptions of selfhood, see Dorinne Kondo, *Crafting Selves: Power, Gender, and Discourses of Identity in a Japanese Workplace* (Chicago: University of Chicago Press, 1990).

35 Roberto-Venn instructors also mentioned the enrollment of a few international or Asian students, but they were not considered to be "of color."

36 Joan Scott, "The Evidence of Experience," *Critical Inquiry* 17, no. 4 (Summer 1991): 780.

37 Ibid., 793.

38 Don Windham, interview with the author, Phoenix, AZ, August 15, 2008.

39 Jason Kostal, interview with the author, Phoenix, AZ, October 15, 2008.

40 On the contemporary conjuncture of neoliberal capitalism and preemptive war, see David Harvey, *The New Imperialism* (Oxford: Oxford University Press, 2005), and *The Enigma of Capital and the Crises of Capitalism* (Oxford: Oxford University Press, 2011).

41 Ethnographic work on the reproduction of class power is voluminous. Two studies that make explicit links between elite education and future success are Peter W. Cookson Jr. and Caroline Hodges Persell, *Preparing for Power: America's Elite Boarding Schools* (New York: Basic Books, 1987), and Karen Ho, *Liquidated: An Ethnography of Wall Street* (Durham, NC: Duke University Press, 2009).

42 As Carrie M. Lane demonstrates in her ethnography of unemployed high-tech workers, a neoliberal faith in self-reliance and individual "career management" is as much an economic necessity as an ideological commitment. *A Company of One: Insecurity, Independence, and the New World of White-Collar Unemployment* (Ithaca, NY: Cornell University Press, 2011).

43 "Making power visible," Marilyn Strathern argues, is the function of male initiation rites in Papua New Guinea. *The Gender of the Gift* (Berkeley: University of California Press, 1988), 103, 107.

44 Among the Gimi of Papua New Guinea, Strathern observes, flutes are "instruments of androgyny" that confer upon men the procreative power of women (ibid., 125–32). Anthropologists have long noted mythic beliefs that restrict women's access to a society's ceremonial objects, which often include musical instruments. In tribal societies marked by a strict division of labor by sex, these myths tell of how women made, or once owned, instruments such as sacred flutes or trumpets until men seized them by force and women were forbidden to see or touch them. Elaborate initiation rites accompany these myths, structuring boys' life passage into men as they are taught to play, and purified to receive, the instruments of the gods. See Ian Hogbin, *The Island of Menstruating Men: Religion in Wogeo, New Guinea* (Prospect Heights, IL: Waveland, 1970); Yolanda Murphy and Robert Murphy, *Women of the Forest* (New York: Columbia University Press, 1984).

45 Ervin Somogyi, interview with the author, Healdsburg, CA, August 18, 2009.

46 Among the Greek artisans studied by Michael Herzfeld, surreptitious imitation is the only way apprentices learn a craft, given the premium masters place on secrecy and the silent transmission of skills. Under social circumstances where apprentices

may become future competitors, masters rarely offer verbal instruction, hoping to inculcate in their charges individual initiative and discretion. To learn the skills of their trade, therefore, apprentices must remain silent, affect sullen boredom, and "steal with [their] eyes." In this way, Herzfeld observes, "playing dumb is the invisible mark of an intelligence that knows the arts of self-concealment." *Body Impolitic*, 105, 107.

47 Jason Kostal, interview with author, Santa Rosa, CA, August 15, 2009.

Chapter Five

1 Ervin Somogyi, from a transcript of the event recorded by the author, Montreal, Quebec, July 3, 2009.

2 Ervin Somogyi, *Making the Responsive Guitar* (Oakland, CA: Luthiers, 2009), chaps. 31–32.

3 The concept of "market makers" comes from Mitchell Y. Abolafia. The term is one that Wall Street's stock, bond, and futures traders use to describe themselves, expressing the sense that they individually create the market "by their own actions" as well as by "standardizing terms of trade, by enacting and enforcing rules of conduct, and by creating institutions to ensure that all traders' obligations are met." *Making Markets: Opportunism and Restraint on Wall Street* (Cambridge, MA: Harvard University Press, 1996), 6.

4 Michael Callon, Cécile Méadel, and Vololona Rabeharisoa, "The Economy of Qualities," *Economy and Society* 31, no. 2 (May 2002): 202, 204. A key aspect of qualification, Callon and his coauthors argue, is the ability to offer consumers a product that displays "singularity" — the quality of being tailor-made to what individual customers want and expect.

5 Arjun Appadurai, "Commodities and the Politics of Value," in *The Social Life of Things: Commodities in Cultural Perspective*, ed. A. Appadurai (Cambridge: Cambridge University Press, 1986), 50.

6 Clifford Geertz, "The Balinese Cockfight," in *The Interpretation of Cultures* (New York: Basic Books, 1973).

7 Appadurai, "Commodities and the Politics of Value," 21.

8 A video of Hecht performing with Somogyi's guitar and the double-capo machine is posted on Dream Guitar's website, at http://www.youtube.com/watch?v =7qoA7WYCyJg.

9 Bronislaw Malinowski, *Argonauts of the Western Pacific* (New York: E. P. Dutton, 1922).

10 A key concept in the Kula's gift-giving system is *keda*, which refers to the path that shells take from one island to another as well as to the route that men create through this ritual exchange toward wealth and renown. Keda, in essence, is the network of alliances that men establish to direct the flow of valuables and increase their influence and power. Shirley F. Campbell, "Kula in Vakuta: The Mechanics of Keda," in *The Kula: New Perspectives on Massim Exchange*, ed. Jerry W. Leach and Edmund R. Leach (Cambridge: Cambridge University Press, 1983), 203–4.

11 As Arjun Appadurai observes, "strategic skill [in all tournaments of value] is culturally measured by the success with which actors attempt diversions or subversions of culturally conventionalized paths of the flow of things." Appadurai, "Commodities and the Politics of Value," 21.

12 Jeff Doctorow, from a transcript of the event recorded by the author, Montreal, Quebec, July 3, 2009.

13 A number of high-profile guitar collectors have published books about their collections, and others like Doctorow often allow their instruments to be featured in coffee-table books about extraordinary guitars. See, for example, Akira Tsumura, *Guitars: The Tsumura Collection* (Tokyo: Kodansha International, 1987); Jonathan Kellerman, *With Strings Attached: The Art and Beauty of Vintage Guitars* (New York: Ballantine Books, 2008); and Robert Shaw, *Hand Made, Hand Played: The Art and Craft of Contemporary Guitars* (Asheville, NC: Lark Books, 2008). Shaw is not a major collector himself, but his book features a collection of noteworthy pieces made by prominent artisanal builders.

14 It remains unclear whether Scott Chinery's death was caused by the use of his own dietary supplements, but the company that his brother Bob Chinery inherited was soon embroiled in lawsuits stemming from ephedra-related strokes, heart attacks, and sudden deaths.

15 Scott Chiney is quoted in Ken Vose, *Blue Guitar* (San Francisco: Chronicle Books, 1998), 20.

16 The Blue Guitar Collection was exhibited at the Smithsonian from November 1997 to October 1998.

17 Kasha was a physical chemist at Florida State University who developed an avid interest in guitar acoustics. His ideas about soundboard design influenced the work of a number of hand builders, including Steve Klein, Richard Schneider, Max Krimmel, and Gila Eban. See Michael Kasha, Richard Schneider, and Kurt Rodamer, "The Reaction of a Research Scientist, a Master Luthier, and a Performing Artist in Developing a New Guitar," *Journal of Guitar Acoustics*, 1982, 127–30.

18 Before writing about Steve Klein, Paul Schmidt completed a book about John D'Angelico and James D'Aquisto. See Paul Schmidt, *Art That Sings: The Life and Times of Luthier Steve Klein* (Clifton, NJ: Doctorow Communications, 2003); and Paul Schmidt, *Acquired of the Angels: The Lives and Works of Master Guitar Makers John D'Angelico and James L. D'Aquisto* (Lanham, MD: Scarecrow, 1998).

19 As sociologist Howard Becker has written of art scenes in general, "the [art] world exists in the cooperating activity of those people, not as a structure or organization." Becker likewise treats aesthetic judgments as phenomena characteristic of collective activity: "the interaction of all the involved parties produces a shared sense of the worth of what they collectively produce." Howard S. Becker, *Art Worlds* (orig. 1982; Berkeley: University of California Press, 2008), 35, 39.

20 The festival enhanced the feeling of exclusivity by limiting the number of exhibitors, choosing a venue patronized by upscale consumers, and inviting performers such as Alex de Grassi and Sharon Isbin to star in headline concerts. Information about the event can be found in the festival program, *The Luthier's Art: A Showcase of Handcrafted Fretted Instruments* (San Anselmo, CA: String Letter, 1996).

21 "Holistic Music," *Economist* 31, no. 7988 (October 19, 1996): 88–90.

22 Michael Keller, interview with author, Rochester, Minnesota, May 27, 2010.

23 The key figure in going-to-Washington tales, Lauren Berlant argues, is the "infantile citizen." Faith in the nation is expected to be childlike in its innocence and trust, she observes, and politicians are expected to live up to this ideal if they are to realize the

nobility of democratic governance. *The Queen of America Goes to Washington City: Essays on Sex and Citizenship* (Durham, NC: Duke University Press, 1997), 20–28.

24 Judith Shklar, *American Citizenship: The Quest for Inclusion* (Cambridge, MA: Harvard University Press, 1991), 92–93.

25 As Alice Kessler-Harris argues, waged workers have long enjoyed a privileged social status vis-à-vis slaves, women engaged in unpaid domestic labor, and the unemployed. When New Deal legislation tied tangible public benefits such as unemployment insurance and social security to paid work, however, "employment emerged as a line demarcating different kinds of citizenship." *In Pursuit of Equity: Women, Men, and the Quest for Economic Citizenship in 20th-Century America* (Oxford: Oxford University Press, 2001), 4.

26 On the countercultural embrace of artisans at Renaissance festivals, see Rachel Lee Rubin, *Well Met Well Met: Renaissance Faires and the American Counterculture* (New York: New York University Press, 2012).

27 The rightward turn of American politics since 1980—a neoconservative agenda advocating "family values" in the private sphere and neoliberal values in the public sphere—has made the conduct of men and women in their domestic relationships a matter of greater national concern than equality of opportunity in the workplace. On the political relationship between neoliberalism and neoconservatism, see Wendy Brown, "American Nightmare: Neoliberalism, Neoconservatism, and De-democratization," *Political Theory* 34, no. 6 (2006): 690.

28 Beginning that year, the event was formally renamed the Healdsburg Guitar Show, instead of the Healdsburg Guitar *Makers* Show—a subtle shift in emphasis from makers to their instruments.

29 Michael Keller's work was featured in Simone Solondz, ed., *Custom Guitars: A Complete Guide to Handcrafted Guitars* (San Anselmo, CA: String Letter, 2000).

30 Harry Lowenstein, "Your Dream Guitar," in Zachary R. Fjestad, *Blue Book of Acoustic Guitars* (Minneapolis: Blue Book, 2005), http://www.kellerguitars.com/forums/index.php?showtopic=7; and Michael Keller, "Building the Dream Guitar," in the same volume, http://www.kellerguitars.com/forums/index.php?showtopic=16.

31 Julius Borges, interview with the author, Miami Beach, April 11, 2008.

32 Don Thompson uses this phrase to describe the promotional activities of Christie's and Sotheby's as well as art dealerships in *The $12 Million Stuffed Shark: The Curious Economics of Contemporary Art* (London: Palgrave Macmillan, 2008), 27.

33 "The Luthier's Art" echoes the title of a best-selling book on winemaking: Hugh Johnson and James Halliday, *The Vintner's Art: How Great Wines Are Made* (New York: Simon and Schuster, 1992).

34 Heather Paxson argues that American cheese makers use the concept of *terroir* to make the case that "the gustatory values that make artisanal cheeses good to eat are fundamentally rooted in craft practices that are themselves valuable." *The Life of Cheese* (Berkeley: University of California Press, 2012), 189. While luthiers do not explicitly use this term, they draw a similar analogy between the tonal qualities of geographically unique species of wood and the craft practices that bring out the distinctive "voice" of the wood.

35 Natalie Swango, interview with the author, Tacoma, Washington, June 13, 2008.

36 The origin of the MGS lies in another of Dupont's initiatives, the Montreal Musical Instrument Show (SIMM), which also runs during the Jazz Festival. Although he

made an effort to attract artisanal builders to this event in 2005 and 2006, its location in the center of a shopping mall and the presence of instrument manufacturers of all types was not conducive to the display of individually handmade acoustic guitars. Going back to the drawing board, Dupont decided to create a separate event for hand builders and asked for input from an advisory board of Canadian and American builders. The show that resulted is thus a blend of luthiers' desires and professional marketing savvy.

37 Jacques-Andre Dupont, interview with the author, Montreal, Quebec, December 18, 2009.

38 Dupont and his advisory board have adopted several approaches to soften or, at best, randomize the favoritism that "creating a star system" implies. One innovative initiative has been the creation of the Ste-Cat Guitar Collection, sponsored by SIMM and the Jazz Festival. Each year, at least two luthiers are selected "at random" from among participants in the Montreal Guitar Show and commissioned to build a guitar for this repository, which serves as a "bank" of instruments that are loaned out for one-year periods to young musicians who would otherwise be unable to afford a handmade guitar. Builders who contribute to this collection are free to make their guitars any way they wish, as long as they include the Ste-Cat logo, a cool cat figure named for Saint Catherine Street, where most of the Jazz Festival's performances are held. On display every year at the show, the Ste-Cat guitars can be seen as permanent market diversions—chosen by the impartial mechanism of chance—that circulate in a philanthropic realm, bringing hands-on as well as symbolic attention to individual makers and their craft.

39 In addition to his company's financial investment in the guitar show, Duppont has become an avid collector of and dealer in fine guitars, which he displays and sells on his website, GuitarJunky.ca. To invest in the artisanal guitar as a work of art is to place an economic value on its aesthetic qualities and the cultural accomplishment it represents.

40 Henry Lowenstein, interview with the author, Miami Beach, April 12, 2008.

41 William Leach, *Land of Desire: Merchants, Power, and the Rise of a New American Culture* (New York: Vintage Books, 1993), 79.

42 Darwinian language and logic is frequently used to characterize the operation of free-market capitalism, especially when the speaker is confronted with the intransigence of alternative moral economies. See Kathryn M. Dudley, *The End of the Line: Lost Jobs, New Lives in Postindustrial America* (Chicago: Chicago University Press, 1994).

43 Arjun Appadurai defines luxury goods as "incarnated signs" whose "principal use is rhetorical and social," in "Commodities and the Politics of Value," 38. The concept of "taste" as a mode of "distinction" in which class status is both signaled and reproduced is explored by Pierre Bourdieu in *Distinction: A Social Critique of the Judgment of Taste* (Cambridge, MA: Harvard University Press, 1984).

44 Henry Lowenstein, from a transcript of the author's recording of the public seminar "What It's Worth: Guitar Marketing 101," with Steve and Zach Fjestad and Denis Merrill, Newport in Miami Beach Guitar Festival, April 11–12, 2008.

45 The Met Guitars app was produced with the financial support of Jonathan Kellerman, a suspense writer and major guitar collector. Jason Kerr Dobney, *Met Guitars* (New York: Metropolitan Museum of Art, 2011), http://itunes.apple.com/us/app/met-guitars/id414964902.

46 In addition to the software application, visitors could purchase a jazz guitar CD and attend live concerts in the museum's auditorium, which featured jazz greats such as Steve Miller, John Hall, and Bucky Pizzarelli. For a description of the Met's Guitar Heroes concerts see http://blog.metmuseum.org/guitarheroes/related-events/.

47 This was the "Rawlins," one of four Stradivari guitars known to survive, on loan from the National Music Museum at the University of South Dakota, Vermillion. See Jayson Kerr Dobney, "Guitar Heroes: Legendary Craftsmen from Italy to New York," *Metropolitan Museum of Art Bulletin*, Winter 2011, 11.

48 For an analysis of the violence perpetrated by the "hegemony of the visual" over aurality, and black aural aesthetics in particular, see Fred Moten, *In the Break: The Aesthetics of the Black Radical Tradition* (Minneapolis: University of Minnesota Press, 2003), 171–231.

49 As Susan Stewart has observed of the miniature's promise of revealing a "secret life," "the state of arrested life that we see in the tableau . . . always bears the hesitation of a beginning, a hesitation that speaks the movement which is its contrary in the same way that the raised and hesitating baton speaks the bursting action that will result from its fall." *On Longing: Narratives of the Miniature, the Gigantic, the Souvenir, the Collection* (Durham, NC: Duke University Press, 1993), 54–55.

50 Jayson Kerr Dobney, "John D'Angelico," in *Met Guitars*, emphasis added.

51 Frederick Cohen, dir., *The New Yorker Special: Handcrafting a Guitar* (New York: Filmmakers Library, 1985).

52 The workbench was not D'Aquisto's own. It was part of a violin workshop in the museum's permanent collection. The clamps, guitar neck, guitar form, and violin template on display in the exhibit were on loan from New York collectors. Jayson Kerr Dobney, personal communication, July 24, 2013.

53 The "speaking subject" of a voice-over, Kaja Silverman argues, is "a symbolic figuration which always exceeds the individuals defined by it." Representing "transcendental vision, hearing, and speech," it offers viewers an "external" vantage point from which to observe the actors "inside" the film itself. *The Acoustic Mirror: The Female Voice in Psychoanalysis and Cinema* (Bloomington: Indiana University Press, 1988), 30.

54 The fact that D'Angelico and D'Aquisto both died at the age of fifty-nine, despite having been born thirty years apart, is often cited to suggest that a mystical bond existed between them. Jayson Kerr Dobney makes this point in "James D'Aquisto," in *Met Guitars*.

55 Jayson Kerr Dobney, "John Monteleone," in *Met Guitars*.

56 Jayson Kerr Dobney, from a transcript of the author's recording of the event, New York, March 26, 2011.

57 George Benson is pictured in the exhibit catalog with a D'Angelico New Yorker, but he is not among the musicians featured in Dobney's lecture. Dobney, "Guitar Heroes," 28.

58 James D'Aquisto, from a transcript of the author's recording of an excerpt of *New Yorker Special*, op. cit. The film clip is also available in Dobney, *Met Guitars*.

59 Mark Knopfler performed "Monteleone" live at the Hunting Club for the Prince's Trust Charity in London in 2009, on YouTube, http://www.youtube.com/watch?v=QxeSWKw3eto.

60 Mark Knopfler, from text that appears on his website, accessed April 9, 2012, http://

www.markknopfler.com/about/. He writes that there is a demand for his kind of songwriting because "people still want to hear crafted songs."

61 Annette B. Weiner, *Inalienable Possessions: The Paradox of Keeping While Giving* (Berkeley: University of California Press, 1992), 33.

Chapter Six

1 Rick Davis provides a vivid description of the docklands and New York City's guitar-making scene in the 1960s, in "The Pioneer: Michael Gurian's Life of Lutherie on the Third Planet from the Sun," *Fretboard Journal*, no. 5 (Spring 2007): 40–51.

2 Grit Laskin, "There Once Was a Time," *Guitarmaker* 40 (Winter 2000): 8–9.

3 Edgar Mönch was a welcome presence in the tight circle of German and Spanish immigrant builders who were members of the New York City Classical Guitar Society.

4 On the literary tropes employed by anthropologists and other explorers, see Mary Louise Pratt, *Imperial Eyes: Travel Writing and Transculturation* (London: Routledge, 1992).

5 Although the five-course double-strung guitar most likely originated in Spain in the late sixteenth century and became a popular folk instrument in that country, it became the instrument of choice among the Italian aristocracy through the 1630s. The Italian guitars that survive from this period are extensively adorned with ebony, ivory, and tortoiseshell in the form of detailed inlay, marquetry, and engraving. The rise of the Parisian school of luthiers in the 1640s, which came to prominence under the patronage of Louis XIV, introduced a somewhat plainer aesthetic, but tortoise-shell veneer and ebony and ivory appointments continued to be markers of quality and class. See Tom Evans and Mary Evans, *Guitars: From the Renaissance to Rock* (New York: Paddington, 1977), 24–39.

6 Between the Civil War and 1920, celluloid plastic made to resemble traditional materials came to replace the real thing—hence the "ivoroid" bindings, "pearloid" inlay, and faux tortoiseshell pick guards that grace factory instruments to this day. Martin continued to use ivory for guitar nuts and saddles well into the 1960s. The last recorded use of ivory on a Martin guitar was in 1980. Richard Johnston and Dick Boak, *Martin Guitars: A Technical Reference* (Milwaukee, WI: Hal Leonard, 2009), 40. See also George Gruhn and Walter Carter, "Endangered Woods: Immediate Action Requested," *Gruhn Guitars Newsletter*, no. 29 (March 2007): http://www.gruhn.com/newsletter/newsltr29.html.

7 The phrase *haunted by empire* has been used to examine the experience and legacy of interracial sexual liaisons during the colonial period. I build on this work to examine guitar makers' intimate relationship with exotic plant and animal materials. See Laura Ann Stoler, "Intimidations of Empire: Predicaments of the Tactile and Unseen," in *Haunted by Empire: Geographies of Intimacy in North American History*, ed. Stoler (Durham, NC: Duke University Press, 2006).

8 For press coverage of the 2009 Gibson raid, see in particular Heath E. Combs, "Details Come to Light on Gibson's Lacey Act Raid," *Furniture Today*, August 12, 2010, accessed May 10, 2011, http://www.furnituretoday.com/blog/The_Writer_s_Bureau/37515-Details_come_to_light_on_Gibson_s_Lacey_Act_Raid.php; J. R. Lind, "Federal Agent: Gibson Wood Investigation Likely to Result in Indictments," nashvillepost.com, December 29, 2010.

9 Gibson has participated in two certification programs, those of Rainforest Alliance and the Forest Stewardship Council. Chris Gill, "Log Jam," *Guitar Aficionado,* Spring 2010.

10 Madagascar has restricted the export of ebony and rosewood since 2000, but political unrest in that country has weakened the government's ability to combat illegal logging. Global Witness and the Environmental Investigation Agency, "Investigation into the Global Trade in Malagasy Precious Woods: Rosewood, Ebony, and Pallisander," October 2010, http://www.globalwitness.org/sites/default/files/library/mada_report_261010.pdf.

11 The categorical exceptions to Lacey's declaration requirement include common cultivars (except trees), scientific specimens, and plants that are to be planted or replanted. The full text of the 2008 amendments to the Lacey Act is available at the US Department of Agriculture's website: "Amendments to the Lacey Act from H.R. 2419, Sec. 8204," http://www.aphis.usda.gov/plant_health/lacey_act/downloads/background--redlinedLaceyamndmnt--forests--may08.pdf.

12 Robert S. Anderson, "The Lacey Act: America's Premier Weapon in the Fight Against Unlawful Wildlife Trafficking," *Public Land Law Review* (1995), http://www.animallaw.info/articles/arus16publlr27.htm; and Rebecca F. Wisch, "Overview of the Lacey Act (16 U.S.C. SS 3371–3378)," Animal Legal and Historical Center, Michigan State University College of Law, 2003, both accessed June 25, 2013, http://www.animallaw.info/articles/ovuslaceyact.htm.

13 Lacey's declaration requirement was phased in by the type of import as categorized in the Harmonized Tariff Schedule (HTS). As of April 2009, it became applicable to rough and sawn wood, and in April 2010, to pianos and acoustic stringed instruments. Department of Agriculture, "Implementation of Revised Lacey Act Provisions," *Federal Register* 73, no. 196 (October 8, 2008): 58,925–27: and "Implementation of Revised Lacey Act Provisions," *Federal Register* 74, no. 21 (February 3, 2009): 5,911–13, both available as PDFs at http://www.aphis.usda.gov/plant_health/lacey_act/index.shtml.

14 George Gruhn and Walter Carter, "Endangered Woods: Immediate Action Required," *Gruhn Guitars Newsletter,* no. 29 (March 2007).

15 Alex W. Grant, "Pernambuco and the CITES Appendix II Listing," http://www.grantviolins.com.au/newsdetail_6.php; and League of American Orchestras, "Pernambuco Update," accessed May 14, 2011, http://www.americanorchestras.org/advocacy_and_government/pernambuco_update.html.

16 The US Fish and Wildlife Service's Import/Re-export Plant (CITES) application form—section 12 of which is devoted to Brazilian rosewood guitars—can be found at http://www.fws.gov/forms/3-200-32.pdf (accessed June 3, 2011). The form indicates a fee of $75 and a wait of at least sixty days and possibly over ninety days. In an unpublished manuscript, "Customs Clearance on Shell, Other Natural Materials and Instruments Using These 'Wildlife' Products," (June 2010), Chuck Erikson claims that the processing time can take six months.

17 Associated Press, "Brazilian Police Arrest Gang That Exported Rare Wood to United States," October 8, 2007, accessed May 23, 2011, http://english.pravda.ru/world/99136-rare_wood-0.

18 John Thomas, "A Guitar Lover's Guide to the CITES Conservation Treaty," *Fretboard*

Journal, no. 11 (2008), accessed May 16, 2011, http://www.fretboardjournal.com /features/magazine/guitar-lover%E2%80%99s-guide-cites-conservation-treaty.

19 Evidently the government's abalone species detection "test" is not foolproof. In apparent reference to the same case, NAMM's James Goldberg says the dealer shipped a single guitar and paid a civil penalty of $250. See National Association of Music Merchants, "Lacey for Luthiers," webinar, June 25, 2010, accessed May 26, 2011, http://www.namm.org/news/articles/access-recording-namm-lacey-act-webinar -luthiers.

20 Ibid.

21 "Self-deportation" was a central plank of Republican Mitt Romney's 2012 presidential campaign. It has also been the guiding rationale behind an upsurge in anti-immigration measures proposed and adopted across the United States since 2010. See Ian Gordon and Tasneem Raja, "164 Anti-immigration Laws Passed since 2010? A Mojo Analysis," *Mother Jones*, March/April 2012, accessed June 30, 2013, http:// www.motherjones.com/politics/2012/03/anti-immigration-law-database.

22 Randal C. Archibold, "Arizona Enacts Stringent Law on Immigration," *New York Times*, April 23, 2010. "The [Arizona] law, which proponents and critics alike said was the broadest and strictest immigration measure in generations," writes Archibold, "would make the failure to carry immigration documents a crime and give the police broad power to detain anyone suspected of being in the country illegally."

23 Of particular concern to Schmidt Camacho are the ways in which random and sporadic enforcement of immigration law tears families and communities apart, undermining human dignity and vital networks of social support. Alicia Schmidt Camacho, "Hailing the Twelve Million: U.S. Immigration Policy, Deportation, and the Imaginary of Lawful Violence," *Social Text* 28, no. 4 (Winter 2010).

24 Chris Gill, "Log Jam," *Guitar Aficionado*, Spring 2010. My emphasis.

25 Michel Foucault, *The Birth of Biopolitics* (New York: Palgrave Macmillan, 2008), 259–60.

26 Jean-Claude Larrivée, interview with the author, Oxnard, CA, September 1, 2009.

27 Marc Greilsamer, "Chief, Cook, Bottle Washer: Jean Larrivée Favors the Hand-On Approach," *Fretboard Journal*, no. 10 (Summer 2008): 37–55.

28 Michael Gurian dealt directly with loggers to source the timber he processed at his sawmill in New Hampshire (Davis, "Pioneer"). Hart Huttig II, a classical and flamenco guitar maker in Miami, entered the wood business and became a key source of information and materials for young builders. Richard Bruné, "Huttig Obituary," Guild of American Luthiers (1992), accessed May 25, 2010, http://www.luth.org /memoriams/mem_hart-huttig.htm.

29 Information about Lewis and the Mediterranean Shop is provided by Sharon Scheurich, a friend and former student of Lewis and founder of the Vancouver Classical Guitar Society, on her blog, accessed August 11, 2010, http://canarybirdtenerife .blogspot.com/2009/03/vancouver-flashback-v.html.

30 Bill Lewis, *Catalogue for Musical Instrument Builders* (Vancouver: Lewis Luthiers' Supplies, 1974).

31 As Steven M. Gelber observes, the "kit boom" of the 1950s was "the ultimate victory of the assembly line," encouraging consumers to believe that craftwork involved "the superficial assembling of preformed pieces." *Hobbies: Leisure and the Culture of Work in America* (New York: Columbia University Press, 1999), 262.

32 Gulab Gidwani, "Ebony and Rosewood Revisited," presentation given at the Symposium of Stringed Instrument Artisans, East Stroudsburg, PA, on June 11, 2009. Quotations are from the transcript of the author's recording of the event.

33 Gulab Gidwani, personal communication, July 20, 2011.

34 Anna Lowenhaupt Tsing, *Friction: An Ethnography of Global Connection* (Princeton, NJ: Princeton University Press, 31), 68.

35 Ibid., 51, 31.

36 As Tsing writes, "A frontier is an edge of space and time. . . . Forests aren't just discovered at the edge; they are projects in making geographical and temporal experience. Frontiers make wildness, entangling visions and vines and violence; their wildness is both material and imaginative" (ibid., 28–29). For an ethnography of "forest wars" in the United States, see Jake Kosek, *Understories: The Political Life of Forests in Northern New Mexico* (Durham, NC: Duke University Press, 2006).

37 Following the "Nixon Shock" in August 1971, when the United States stopped converting dollars to gold at the fixed rate of $35, the price of gold fluctuated dramatically, reaching its highest values in the early 1980s. *The Privateer Market Letter*, 2001, http://www.the-privateer.com/gold2.html, cited in Tsing, *Friction*, 279n 11.

38 Erikson describes his mining days on his website, accessed August 10, 2011, http://www.dukeofpearl.com/.

39 Chuck Erikson, quoted in Margie Mirken, "Fruits de Mer," *Fretboard Journal*, no. 21 (2011): 84–93.

40 White and black abalone became candidates for protection in 1997 and 2001 — and were formally listed as endangered in 1999 and 2009, respectively. National Oceanic and Atmospheric Administration Fisheries, Office of Protected Resources, "White Abalone," http://www.nmfs.noaa.gov/pr/species/invertebrates/whiteabalone.htm, and "Black Abalone," http://www.nmfs.noaa.gov/pr/species/invertebrates/blackabalone.htm (both accessed June 20, 2013).

41 Chuck Erikson, interview with the author, Miami Beach, April 11, 2008.

42 As David Harvey would put it, the commodity chain is broken at the point where "the particularity of the commodity has to be converted into the universality of money." *The Enigma of Capital and the Crises of Capitalism* (Oxford: Oxford University Press, 2011), 106.

43 "The Duke of Earl" was a hit single of 1962, sung by the African American artist Gene Chandler. Chandler created a stage persona as the Duke of Earl, regularly appearing in a top hat, tuxedo, cape, and cane.

44 Abalam is made by laminating thin sections of abalone shell into flat sheets. Lamination distributes the figured pattern and color of the shell evenly over the surface of the sheet. Chuck Erikson, "Shell Veneer Ply (Laminated) Sheets," Duke of Pearl website, accessed July 25, 2013, http://www.dukeofpearl.com/.

45 Pakistan makes 80 percent of the world's soccer balls and together with India employs one-third of the world's underage workers. Sydney Schanberg, "Six Cents an Hour," *Life* 19, no. 7 (June 1996).

46 Naomi Klein highlights the underside of Nike's promotional strategy, which is based on the street culture of African American youth: "It is the cruelest irony of Nike's 'brands, not products' formula that the people who have done the most to infuse the swoosh with cutting-edge meaning are the very people most hurt by the

company's pumped-up prices and nonexistent manufacturing base." Naomi Klein, *No Logo* (orig. 2000; New York: Picador / St. Martin's, 2002), 365–79.

47 Greenpeace USA, "Our Vision," accessed July 20, 2013, http://www.greenpeace.org /usa/en/campaigns/forests/Our-vision/.

48 Environmental Investigation Agency, "Forest Governance," accessed July 20, 2013, http://www.eia-international.org/our-work/ecosystems-and-biodiversity/forest -loss/forest-governance.

49 Chuck Erikson, "CITES, Lacey Act, ESA, USFWS and Customs Regulation of Wood, Shell, Bone, Ivory, Fossil Ivory, and Finished Items (Such as Guitars) Which Contain Any of These or Other Wildlife or Plant Products," April 2011, unpublished manuscript distributed at the 2011 Symposium of the Association of Stringed Instrument Artisans. A slightly revised version of this piece was published on the Guild of American Luthiers' website, accessed July 25, 2013, http://www.luth.org/web _extras/CITES_Lacey-Act/cites_lacey-act.html.

50 Ibid.

51 "The agent we were dealing with," Erikson wrote, "indicated that Fish and Wildlife is well aware of [the guild] and ASIA, as well as suppliers such as Luthiers Mercantile and Stewart-MacDonald. Although non-committal about exactly what they intended to pursue with or through these entities, it's obvious they could very easily initiate investigations not only on the vendors but also on individual luthiers as named in customer files or membership lists." Ibid.

52 Chuck Erikson, from a transcript of the author's recording of the panel, Symposium of the Association of Stringed Instrument Artisans, East Stroudsburg, PA, June 11, 2011. For a published transcript of the first half of the presentation, see Nadine Nichols, "Special CITES/Lacey Edition," *Guitarmaker*, no. 78 (Winter 2011).

53 George Balady, from a transcript of the author's recording of the panel, Symposium of the Association of Stringed Instrument Artisans, East Stroudsburg, PA, June 11, 2011.

54 As John Frederick Walker observes of efforts to conserve African ivory, "In contrast with the overexploited environments that the European and North American public associates with its own countries (or at least parts of them), the 'animal Eden' that Africa conjures up inspires the desire to ensure that Africans don't follow the rape-of-the-land environmental despoilation policies that are now cause for regret in the first world." *Ivory's Ghosts: The White Gold of History and the Fate of Elephants* (New York: Grove, 2009), 188.

55 David Harvey defines the "new imperialism" as an unstable alliance of the expansionary logic of capital accumulation and the territorial logic of the nation-state. *The New Imperialism* (Oxford: Oxford University Press, 2005), 33.

56 The Forest Legality Alliance is a think tank in Washington, DC. It is led by the Environmental Investigation Agency and the World Resources Institute, and operates with taxpayer support from the US Agency for International Development (USAID).

57 Anne Middleton, from a transcript of the author's recording of the panel, Symposium of the Association of Stringed Instrument Artisans, East Stroudsburg, PA, June 11, 2011.

58 In Mary Douglas's classic formulation, pollution fears and taboos are the cornerstone of rituals that uphold a society's cosmology. They symbolically juxtapose order

with disorder, form with formlessness, and purity with the impure. "Pollution dangers strike," she argues, "when form has been attacked." *Purity and Danger* (New York: Routledge, 1966), 105.

59 Craig Hoover, Roger Sadowski, and others, from a transcript of the author's recording of the panel, Symposium of the Association of Stringed Instrument Artisans, East Stroudsburg, PA, June 11, 2011. For a published transcript, see Nadine Nichols, "CITES/Lacey Workshop Q&A Discussion," *Guitarmaker*, no. 79 (Spring 2012).

60 Gruhn, from transcript.

61 That NAMM was the negligent importer in this case is especially ironic, since only a year earlier NAMM had sponsored a webinar designed to inform hand builders about how to become compliant with the law. "Lacey for Luthiers."

62 Linda Manzer, interview with the author, East Stroudsburg, PA, June 11, 2011.

63 Middleton, transcript. For a published transcript, see Nadine Nichols, "CITES/Lacey Q&A Part 2," *Guitarmaker*, no. 82 (Winter 2012).

64 News reports did not reveal the names of Spanish guitar makers whose shops were raided. Tito Drago, "Environment-Spain: Record Seizure of Wood from Endangered Tropical Species," InterPress Service, October 13, 2004, accessed June 25, 2013, http://ipsnews2.wpengine.com/2004/10/environment-spain-record-seizure-of-wood-from-endangered-tropical-species/.

65 Michael Gurian and Craig Hoover, from a transcript of the author's recording of the panel, Symposium of the Association of Stringed Instrument Artisans, East Stroudsburg, PA, June 11, 2011.

66 Henry Lowenstein, from a transcript of the author's recording of the panel, Symposium of the Association of Stringed Instrument Artisans, East Stroudsburg, PA, June 11, 2011.

67 The desire to position American craft innovation as a rightful heir of the Renaissance finds current expression in a new book about C. F. Martin Sr. By the 1840s, says Peter Szego, the book's coeditor, the Martin guitar "deserves to be adjacent to a Stradivarius violin." Quoted in Larry Rohter, "Roll Over, Stradivarius," *New York Times*, October 14, 2013. See Robert Shaw and Peter Szego, eds., *Inventing the American Guitar: The Pre–Civil War Innovations of C. F. Martin and His Contemporaries* (Racine, WI: Hal Leonard, 2013).

68 I build on Elizabeth Povinelli's analysis of how settler nationalism relies on the concept of "governance of the prior" to manage the potential disruption of alternative social projects. By institutionalizing a "division of tense within the social fabric," nationalist ideology "bifurcate[s] the sources and grounds of social belonging" and "transform[s] the relationship between settler and Native/Indigenous from a mutual implication in the problem of prior occupation to a hierarchical relationship between two modes of prior occupation, one oriented toward the future the other to the past." *Economies of Abandonment: Social Belonging and Endurance in Late Liberalism* (Durham, NC: Duke University Press, 2011), 36.

69 Ibid, 76–77.

70 On the concept and prevalence of neoliberal exceptions, see Aihwa Ong, *Neoliberalism as Exception: Mutations in Citizenship and Sovereignty* (Durham, NC: Duke University Press, 2006).

Conclusion

1 Henry Juszkiewicz, "Gibson Guitar Corp. Responds to Federal Raid," Gibson.com, August 25, 2011, accessed September 10, 2011, http://www2.gibson.com/News -Lifestyle/News/en-us/gibson-0825–2011.aspx. Juszkiewicz elaborated upon his response in an editorial a month later. Juszkiewicz, "Repeal the Lacey Act? Hell No, Make It Stronger," *Huffington Post*, November 2, 2011, accessed March 15, 2012, http:// www.huffingtonpost.com/henry-juszkiewicz/gibson-guitars-lacey-act_b_1071770 .html.

2 Evidently a group of Australian tourists was touring the Gibson factory at the time of the 2011 raid. Newt Gingrich, "Out of Tune and Out of Touch," Gingrich Productions, September 7, 2011, accessed September 15, 2011, http://www.gingrich productions.com/2011/09/out-of-tune-and-out-of-touch/.

3 The RELIEF Act would also have established a federal database for illegal wood sources and a certification program for legal trade. Pete Kasperowicz, "Lawmakers Look to Ease Lacey Act Regulations after Gibson Guitar Raid," Floor Action (blog), The Hill, October 20, 2011, accessed June 27, 2013, http://thehill.com/blogs/floor -action/house/188831-guitar-heros-lawmakers-look-to-ease-rules-after-gibson -guitar-raid#ixzz2X0Sj3aHn.

4 Nashville musicians Roseann Cash, Vince Gill, and Big Kenny Alphin were among those endorsing the RELIEF Act (ibid.). Environmentalists' reaction is captured by Jake Schmidt in "House Committee Votes to Allow Illegal Loggers to Pillage World's Forests: Undercutting America's Workers and Increasing Global Warming," *Switchboard: Natural Resources Defense Council Staff Blog*, June 7, 2012, accessed July 1, 2013, http://switchboard.nrdc.org/blogs/jschmidt/house_committee_votes_to_allow .html.

5 Karen Koenig, "No RELIEF: Lacey Act Vote Cancelled," *Woodworking Network*, July 26, 2012, accessed July 1, 2013, http://www.woodworkingnetwork.com/news/wood working-industry-news/No-RELIEF-Lacey-Act-Vote-Cancelled-163855586.html #sthash.nT8tc2VS.dpbs.

6 As part of its settlement with the Justice Department, Gibson also agreed to establish a Lacey compliance program and relinquish $260,000 of confiscated wood. Pete Kasperowicz, "Gibson Guitar Agrees to Pay $300,000 Penalty to settle Lacey Act Violations," Floor Action (blog), The Hill, August 6, 2012, accessed June 27, 2013, http:// thehill.com/blogs/floor-action/house/242357-gibson-guitar-agrees-to-pay-300000 -to-settle-lacey-act-violations.

7 Henry Juszkiewicz, "Gibson Comments on Department of Justice Settlement," Gibson.com, August 6, 2012, http://www2.gibson.com/News-Lifestyle/Features/en -us/Gibson-Comments-on-Department-of-Justice-Settlemen.aspx; and Henry Juszkiewicz, "Gibson's Fight against Criminalizing Capitalism," *Wall Street Journal*, July 19, 2012, http://online.wsj.com/article/SB10001424052702303830204577448351409 946024.html, both accessed July 10, 2013.

8 David Harvey, *The New Imperialism* (Oxford: Oxford University Press, 2005).

9 The World Bank estimates that illegal logging causes annual losses of ten billion dollars in the global market and five billion in government revenue. "Word Bank: Weak Forest Governance Costs Us $15 Billion a Year," World Bank, news release 2007/86/SDN (September 16, 2006), accessed June 5, 2013, http://web.worldbank

.org/WBSITE/EXTERNAL/TOPICS/EXTARD/EXTFORESTS/0,,contentMDK:210557
16~menuPK:985797~pagePK:64020865~piPK:149114~theSitePK:985785,00.html.

10 Kathryn Marie Dudley, "Luthiers: The Latest Endangered Species," *New York Times*, October 25, 2011, accessed June 17, 2013, http://www.nytimes.com/2011/10/26/opinion/are-guitar-makers-an-endangered-species.html.

11 A number of large guitar companies now work with the Forest Stewardship Council to ensure, to the best of their ability, that the wood they buy has been legally harvested. The Musicwood campaign led by Greenpeace is a high-profile example of how major guitar manufacturers have joined forces with environmentalists to pressure timber corporations to adopt sustainable logging practices. However, Musicwood's showpiece effort to preserve the old-growth Sitka spruce forests managed by the Native Alaskan company SEAlaska was largely unsuccessful. That effort is chronicled the documentary film *Musicwood*, directed by Maxine Trump (2012).

12 In formulating the artisanal project as a "counterrationality" to neoliberalism, I build on Wendy Brown's analysis of the transformation of liberal democracy in America, in "Neoliberalism and the End of Liberal Democracy," *Theory and Event* 7, no. 1 (Fall 2003).

13 Alfredo Velazquez, interview with the author, Orlando, FL, November 10, 2011.

14 Luthiers' interaction with wood has much in common with the "scientific" process (lowercase *s*) defined by Bruno Latour as "the gaining of access, through experiments and calculations, to entities that at first do not have the same characteristics as humans do." The goal of this work, he argues, is to ensure that scientists "*do not make up*, with their own repertoires of actions, the new entities to which they have access. They want each new nonhuman to enrich their repertoire of actions, their ontology." *Pandora's Hope: Essays on the Reality of Science Studies* (Cambridge, MA: Harvard University Press, 1999), 259.

15 Brian Massumi identifies the phenomenon of "affective escape" as constitutive of the "autonomy of affect" as a material condition of existence, in *Parables for the Virtual: Movement, Affect, Sensation* (Durham, NC: Duke University Press, 2002), 35.

16 The uncanny feeling of apprehending aliveness in an "inanimate" object is similar to being "haunted" by incorporeal realities that are disavowed by the dominant culture. See Avery Gordon, *Ghostly Matters: Haunting and the Sociological Imagination* (Minneapolis: University of Minnesota Press, 1997).

17 Heather Paxson makes the compelling argument that artisanal cheese is an "unfinished commodity" because "it has not (yet?) been reduced to an apparent equivalence between intrinsic value and market value," in *The Life of Cheese* (Berkeley: University of California Press, 2012), 13. I am reluctant, however, to characterize this situation as "incomplete" commodification, as if the things in question were invariably oriented toward commodification. By pointing to makers' affective investment in the fate of their guitars, I wish to emphasize not the commodity status of the thing itself but the structural dimensions of the lutherie market that have allowed them to disrupt, if not subvert, the commodification process.

18 See Igor Kopytoff, "The Cultural Biography of Things," in *The Social Life of Things: Commodities in Cultural Perspective*, ed. Arjun Appadurai (Cambridge: Cambridge University Press, 1986), 64–91; and Arjun Appadurai, "Commodities and the Politics of Value," in *Social Life of Things*, 3–63.

19 Reflecting a point of view shared by scholars of materiality and the "new material-

ism," Peter Pels calls the notion that material goods have merely a "social life" a form of "animism" in which the "perception of the life of matter is only possible through the attribution of a derivative agency." "The Spirit of Matter: On Fetish, Rarity, Fact, and Fancy," in *Border Fetishisms: Material Objects in Unstable Places*, ed. Patricia Spyer (New York: Routledge, 1998), 94. As Bill Brown frames the broader issue, we must ask "less about the material effects of ideas and ideology than about the ideological and ideational effects of the material world and transformations of it." "Thing Theory," in *Things*, ed. Brown (Chicago: University of Chicago Press, 2004), 7.

20 Endorsing Jacques Rancière's "theory of democracy as disruption," Jane Bennett argues that "the locus of political responsibility is a human-nonhuman assemblage," and that "the political act consists in the exclamatory interjection of affective bodies as they enter a preexisting public, or, rather, as they reveal that they have been there all along as an unaccounted for part." *Vibrant Matter: A Political Ecology of Things* (Durham, NC: Duke University Press, 2010), 36–37, 105.

21 Collodi's novel is typically read as a coming-of-age story that captures a "universal" process of growing up and developing a moral conscience. As John Cech writes, "Pinocchio's journey takes him from that egocentric, undisciplined, inexperienced world of childhood into an adolescence or young adulthood that is self-sacrificing, responsible, knowing." "The Triumphant Transformation of 'Pinocchio,'" in *Triumphs of the Spirit in Children's Literature*, ed. Francelia Butler and Richard Rotert (Hamden, CT: Library Professional, 1986), 171–77. See also Ann Lawson Lucas, introduction to *The Adventures of Pinocchio*, trans. Ann Lawson Lukas (Oxford: Oxford University Press, 1996), vi–xlvi; Susan R. Gannon, "Pinocchio: The First Hundred Years," *Children's Literature Association Quarterly*, Winter 1981/1982, 1, 5–6; and for a feminist spin on the same theme, see Claudia Card, "Pinocchio," in *From Mouse to Mermaid: The Politics of Film, Gender, and Culture*, ed. Elizabeth Bell, Lynda Haas, and Laura Sells (Bloomington: University of Indiana Press, 1995), 62–71.

22 Grit Laskin, interview with the author, Toronto, October 29, 2006.

23 *Chatoyance*, as Judy Threet defines it, is "the reflective property of material." Luthiers use the term to indicate the "special pattern of reflection" that is apparent in shell or other material. Inlay artists often choose individual pieces with reflection patterns suggestive of the image they are designing. Judy Threet, "Inlay Design and Execution: A Conversation between Design and Materials," *Guitarmaker*, no. 55 (Spring 2006).

24 Jim Coyle, "Our True Heroes Are Appointed to the Order of Canada," thestar.com June 29, 2012, accessed July 25, 2013, http://www.thestar.com/news/gta/2012/06/29/our _true_heroes_are_appointed_to_the_order_of_canada.html.

25 Grit Laskin, "The Guitar as Canvas: From Tradition to New Directions in Inlay Art," presentation at Montreal Guitar Show, July 3, 2009.

26 Grit Laskin, personal statement, "Master Guitar Inlay, History and Design," Newport in Miami Beach Guitar Festival, April 12, 2008.

27 Grit Laskin, "The Puppeteer," in *A Guitarmaker's Canvas* (San Francisco: Backbeat Books, 2003), 100.

28 *Speculative realism* is the name given to a loosely organized philosophical movement that rejects the Kantian notion that our knowledge about the existence of things is solely dependent on human thought and perception. Speculative realists, argues Ian Bogost, speculate about "the logics by which things perceive and engage their

worlds," recognizing that "the problem of the being of things consists precisely in the ways those objects exceed what we know or ever can know about them." *Alien Phenomenology* (Minneapolis: University of Minnesota Press, 2012), 29–30. See also Quentin Meillassoux, *After Finitude: An Essay on the Necessity of Contingency*, trans. Ray Brassier (London: Continuum, 2008); and Graham Harmon, *Guerilla Metaphysics: Phenomenology and the Carpentry of Things* (Peru, IL: Open Court, 2005).

29 Visions of monstrosity and the grotesque are frequently used in folklore and popular culture—and were employed by Karl Marx himself—to represent the forces and effects of capitalism. David McNally, *Monsters of the Market: Zombies, Vampires and Global Capitalism* (Chicago: Haymarket Books, 2012).

30 Grit Laskin, "The Princess Trees: A Children's Fable," *Guitarmaker*, no. 17 (September 1992): 46–47, 50–51, 53–54.

31 Laskin's fable can be read as a "drama of discursive divestiture," Kaja Silverman's term for avant-garde film that works "to disclose a chorus of cultural voices in the text" and "install the female voice at the site of a very provisional point of origin." Scenarios such as these disrupt the heterosexist and antifeminist conventions of classic Hollywood cinema, she argues, by featuring male characters who are willing to "divest" themselves of the power and privilege culturally accorded to their sex. *The Acoustic Mirror: The Female Voice in Psychoanalysis and Cinema* (Bloomington: Indiana University Press, 1988), 211.

32 Renato Rosaldo developed the concept of "imperialist nostalgia" to describe the ideological project of imaginatively recuperating ways of life that have been destroyed by European colonialism. *Culture and Truth: The Remaking of Social Analysis* (Boston: Beacon, 1993), 68–90.

33 The narrative of "anticonquest," as Mary Louise Pratt argues, "'underwrites' colonial appropriation, even as it rejects the rhetoric, and probably the practice, of conquest and subjugation." *Imperial Eyes: Travel Writing and Transculturation* (New York: Routledge, 1992), 7, 52.

34 While the voices embodied in the artisanal guitar may ultimately criticize imperial history and its current manifestations, lutherie's scenes of making rarely lead to overt action on environmental or other political issues. Guitar making is thus a juxtapolitical cultural activity—Lauren Berlant's term for a mass-mediated nondominant community that "thrives in proximity to the political, occasionally crossing over in political alliance, even more occasionally doing some politics, but more often than not acting as a critical chorus that sees the expression of emotional response and conceptual recalibration as achievement enough." *The Female Complaint* (Durham, NC: Duke University Press, 2008), x.

35 The uncanny experience of the acoustic guitar's tone resembles Avery Gordon's analysis of haunting: the need to "talk to ghosts" as a "prerequisite for sensuous knowledge" and the task of "providing a hospitable memory for ghosts *out of a concern for justice.*" *Ghostly Matters*, 60 (emphasis in original).

36 The concept of *commodity fetishism* is typically used to reject any emotional connection or attribution of agency to objects of consumer culture. But as Peter Stallybrass argues, a distinction must be made between "fetishism" and "fetishism of commodities." The former is a product of European demonization of "primitive religions"; the latter is capitalism's defining logic: the reification of "immateriality" and market

values. "Marx's Coat," in *Border Fetishisms: Material Objects in Unstable Places*, ed. Patricia Spyer (New York: Routledge, 1998), 83–207.

Epilogue

1 Judy Threet, interview with the author, Calgary, Alberta, November 3, 2006.
2 Ervin Somogyi, interview with the author, Healdsburg, CA, August 18, 2009.

Postscript

1 United States Fish and Wildlife Service, "Interpretation and Implementation of the Convention: Cross-Border Movement of Musical Instruments," resolution proposed by the Unites States of America to the sixteenth meeting of the Conference of the Parties to the Convention on the International Trade in Endangered Species of Wild Flora and Fauna (CITES) in Bangkok, Thailand, March 3–15, 2013, accessed November 6, 2013, http://www.fws.gov/international/pdf/cop16-resolution-cross-border -movement-of-musical-instruments.pdf.
2 Animal and Plant Health Inspection Service (APHIS) and the US Department of Agriculture (USDA), "Report to Congress with Respect to Implementation of the 2008 Amendments to the Lacey Act," May 2013, accessed November 6, 2013, http:// iwpawood.org/associations/8276/files/Lacey%20Report%20to%20Congress%205 .30.13.pdf.
3 Wade Vonasek, "USDA Eases Effect of Lacey Act on Musical Instruments," *Woodworking Network*, June 13, 2013, http://www.woodworkingnetwork.com/wood-market -trends/woodworking-industry-news/production-woodworking-news/USDA -Eases-Effect-of-Lacey-Act-on-Musical-Instruments-211396991.html#sthash .LnkmshoL.dpbs; and Randy Lewis, "USDA Oks Musical Instruments for Travel under Lacey Act," *Los Angeles Times*, June 1, 2013, both accessed November 6, 2013, http://articles.latimes.com/2013/jun/01/entertainment/la-et-ms-lacey-act-musical -instruments-usda-report-amendment-20130531. The latter article goes so far as to say that the report has "in large part taken musical instruments out of the mix of problematic products made from endangered plants."

Index

Abalam, 266, 342n44
Ackerman, Will, 196
Acoustic Guitar (magazine), xiii, 16, 61,
  64–65, 67–71, 207, 213
acoustic music, 4, 27, 43–44, 110, 196
Acoustic Music (retail store), xi, 106, 311
acoustics, 1, 9, 148–53, 204
acoustic sound, 2, 5–6, 110, 123; archive
  of, 140, 145
Adventures of Pinocchio (Collodi), 1, 289
affect, 8; scholarship on, 314n9, 314n11,
  314n13, 346n15
Agnew, Jean-Christophe, 229–33
"A Guitar is Born" (Johnston), 64–68
Ahmed, Sara, 314n12, 315n20
alienation, 39, 52, 287
Allied Lutherie, 216
alternative social project. See counterculture
Amati, Andrea, 230
American Dream (guitar-making cooperative), 121–22
American Lutherie (GAL), 150, 318n17
Anderson, Muriel, 111
animacy, 9, 14, 287–89, 298, 315n14
Animal and Plant Health Inspection Service (APHIS), 269–70
anthropomorphism, 9, 315n17, 316n28
Appadurai, Arjun, 324n18, 334n11,
  337n43
apprenticeship, 3, 7, 13–14, 21, 26–28,
  167, 171–75, 189–91, 234, 332n24,
  332n31, 332n32, 333–34n46; impact
  on productivity, 187–88; unpaid, 109,
  171
Argonauts of the Western Pacific (Malinowski), 200
artisanship: authenticity of, 118; as cultural performance, 128, 144, 174, 244,
  328n18, 330n47; as economic independence, 40, 51; as embodied knowledge, 7–9, 41, 50–51, 58–60, 75, 134,
  145, 164–65, 173–75, 330n45, 332n20;
  as embodied labor, 4–5, 11, 16–18, 41,

58, 118, 128, 138,174, 301, 313n7; as
  personal service, 68; sensory aspects
  of, 140, 330n44; subjectivity of, 126–
  27, 153–56; theatricalization of, 328–
  29n29; transmission of, 147, 184–88;
  value of, 87, 108, 153, 205; as workmanship of risk, 327n14
Arts and Crafts movement, 13
Association of Stringed Instrument Artisans (ASIA), 16, 55–56, 127, 268; code
  of ethics, 322n62; goals, 322n60
auctions: as cultural rituals, 82; on eBay,
  71, 80–82
authenticity, 13–14, 16, 43, 52, 87, 104,
  113, 120, 134, 146, 327n12, 328n17; of
  the brand, 115, 118; collective stories of
  making and, 237; disco and, 321n45;
  golden era, 68; guitar as icon of, 192;
  nostalgia and, 329n30; politics of,
  35–36, 105, 109, 127, 147; of the self,
  128–29, 137–38, 181
Autry, Gene, 91–92

Baez, Joan, 94
Balady, George, 270–73
banjo conversions, 49–50, 139
Beall, Jerrold, 24–26, 28
Bechtel, Perry, 91–92
Becker, Howard, 335n19
Bennett, Jane, 315n17, 316n28, 347n20
Berkowitz, David, 269
Berlant, Lauren, 61, 209, 313n5, 319n30,
  323n5, 335–36n23, 348n34
Berman, Marshall, 105
Blackburn, Marsha, 283
Blanchard, Mark, 156–64
Blue Book of Acoustic Guitars, 214–15
bluegrass, 24, 48–50, 57, 139, 273
Blue Guitar Collection, 203
Boak, Dick, 52, 53–56, 83–104, 127
Bogost, Ian, 329n39, 347–48n28
Borges, Julius, 216–18
Bourdieu, Pierre, 313n7, 337n43
Bourgeois, Dana, 59

Bowden, George, 252
Brand, Stewart, 23, 25–26, 318n10
branding, 68–71, 96–97, 103, 195, 215, 218, 267; authentication, 115
Brazilian rosewood, 11, 94, 129, 197, 238, 242, 244–47, 250, 276–79, 285, 288
Brookes, Tim, 313n8, 330n46
Brown, Bill, 346–47n19
Brown, Danny, 84–87
Brown, Wendy, 316n23, 336n27, 346n12
Bruné, Richard (R. E.), 24–25, 28, 30–31, 33, 318n11
Butler, Judith, 329n38

camp aesthetic, 88–89, 93
Canadian Museum of Civilization, 290
Canadian Wildlife Service, 278
Carlson, Fred, 9, 85, 165–70, 204
Carlson, Steve, 57–58
Carman, Brian, 320n35
Carmel Music, 61
Carruth, Alan, 148–55, 157
Carson, Johnny, 63
Carter, Walter, 244–45, 321n42
Cash, Johnny, 93
Catgut Acoustical Society, 153, 331n8
celebrity endorsement, 94–95, 323n4; effect of, 62–64
chatoyance, 290, 347n23
Chen, Mel, 315n14
Chinery, Scott, 203
Chladni patterns (free plate tuning), 153, 156–64
Ciani, Raphael, 230
citizenship, 209, 211, 248, 335–36n23; economic, 336n25
Classical Guitar Construction (Sloan), 73, 120–21, 323n14
Classic Guitar Making (Overholtzer), 73, 323n14
Clapton, Eric, 90–91, 93, 96
Cockburn, Bruce, 170–71
Collings, Bill, 59
Collodi, Carlo, 1, 283, 347n21
commodification, xv, 17–19, 72, 103–4, 287, 298, 317n32; commodity situa-

tion, 224, 288–89, 301, 324n18; de-commodification, 82, 128, 200; modes of production and, 317n33; qualification and, 195, 334n4; recommodification, 82, 205; singularization and, 82, 159, 195; subversion of, 346n17; un-authorized, 264, 268, 273–75. See also fetishism
commodity chain, 238, 262, 268, 272
Computer Numerical Control (CNC) technology, 56–57, 59–60, 80, 98, 118–20, 124–28, 143, 146, 188–89; authenticity and, 120; Fadal, 59, 119
Convention on International Trade in Endangered Species (CITES), 242, 243–47, 268–69, 280; instrument passports, 308; preconvention certificates, 276, 278–80
Cooke, Edward, 327n13
coolness, 32–34, 45, 253, 319n29
Cooper, Jim, 283
corporations, 14, 18, 22, 42, 63, 87, 210, 257; body of, 89, 192; brand of, 51, 58, 96–97, 103; environmental issues and, 280, 286, 346n11; as family firms, 53, 97, 326n42; neoliberalism and, 60, 88, 95, 258; nonprofit, 29; personhood of, 86; transnational, 207, 250, 275; turning back on tradition, 46–47, 321n46
counterculture, 34, 38, 52; Renaissance festivals and, 13, 210, 336n26; white ethnic revival and, 316n25
craft ethic, 45, 47–48; survival of, 155; tradition, 17, 30, 58, 60, 317n33. See also artisanship: embodied knowledge
Crawford, Matthew, 316n26
Crosby, Stills, Nash, and Young, 47, 94
Cumpiano, William, 1–4, 37–42
Cvetkovich, Ann, 317n33
cybernetics, 25

Dadi, Marcel, 111
D'Angelico, 230, 233–34
D'Aquisto, James, 111, 203, 230–34
Davis, Rick, 313n6, 330n46, 339n1
Dawe, Kevin, 318n12
de Certeau, Michel, 331n9